The Male Body
in Ultra-Orthodox Jewish Theology

The Male Body in Ultra-Orthodox Jewish Theology

Yakir Englander

☛PICKWICK *Publications* • Eugene, Oregon

THE MALE BODY IN ULTRA-ORTHODOX JEWISH THEOLOGY

Copyright © 2021 Yakir Englander. All rights reserved. Except for brief quotations in critical publications or reviews, no part of this book may be reproduced in any manner without prior written permission from the publisher. Write: Permissions, Wipf and Stock Publishers, 199 W. 8th Ave., Suite 3, Eugene, OR 97401.

Pickwick Publications
An Imprint of Wipf and Stock Publishers
199 W. 8th Ave., Suite 3
Eugene, OR 97401

www.wipfandstock.com

PAPERBACK ISBN: 978-1-7252-8729-7
HARDCOVER ISBN: 978-1-7252-8730-3
EBOOK ISBN: 978-1-7252-8731-0

Cataloguing-in-Publication data:

Names: Englander, Yakir.

Title: The male body in ultra-orthodox Jewish theology / Yakir Englander.

Description: Eugene, OR: Pickwick Publications, 2021 | Includes bibliographical references and index.

Identifiers: ISBN 978-1-7252-8729-7 (paperback) | ISBN 978-1-7252-8730-3 (hardcover) | ISBN 978-1-7252-8731-0 (ebook)

Subjects: LCSH: Human body—Religious aspects—Judaism | Masculinity—Religious aspects—Judaism | Ultra-Orthodox Jews | Sex in rabbinical literature | Sex—Religious aspects—Judaism | Sex instruction—Religious aspects—Judaism

Classification: BM469.9 E54 2021 (print) | BM469.9 (ebook)

This book is dedicated to two souls who are my companions on life's journey: to my "godfather" Henry Ralph Carse ("Raphael"), theologian and peace-seeker, who shared with me the gifts of silence and of nature, and who accompanies my soul across the River Styx; and to my dearly beloved, Annika Laila Ecklund: "All that is mine, is yours."

Contents

Preface ix
Acknowledgments xi

Introduction: The Body Dilemma 1

PART I — *The Image of the "Real" Body: Challenge and Response*
1. *Musar* Teachings in the Second Half of the Twentieth Century 25
2. The Status of the Body in the Teachings of *Musar* 40
3. The *Musar* Movement's Responses to the "Problem" of the Body 73
4. The Body and Sexuality 98
5. The Teachings of Rabbi Avigdor Miller:
   An Encounter between *Musar* and Western Culture 128
6. The Other Voice: The Body and Sexuality According
   to the *"Nir'eh Likh'orah"* 156

PART II — *The Image of the "Ideal" Body: Wounded and Holy*
7. Ultra-Orthodox Lithuanian Hagiography 175
8. The Body of the *Godol* in Childhood and Youth 188
9. The Image of the Body of the Adult *Godol* 237

Summary 259

Bibliography 263
Index 275

Preface

ULTRA-ORTHODOX JEWISH COMMUNITIES, LIVING as they do in the midst of secular Western societies, pose fascinating sociological questions and theological challenges. These communities adamantly preserve their unique character, touching but not being touched by the norms of the surrounding majority culture. The critique leveled against the Ultra-Orthodox (known in Hebrew as *haredim (noun, plural)*, "those who fear God") in "normative" Jewish milieus is reflected in a number of books and articles disproportional to the actual size of the Ultra-Orthodox community itself—a fact that emphasizes its remarkable power to challenge the most sensitive elements in the lives and theology of the general Jewish population.

Both in the U.S.A. and in Israel, one of the primary Ultra-Orthodox groups, and the focus of my research, is the Lithuanian *haredim* (historically, this group lived mostly in Lithuania). Central to the theology of this group is the dilemma posed by the human body—especially the male body. With physical markers like their beards, side-locks, and distinctive clothing, *haredi (adjective)* men delineate boundaries between themselves and the Western secular society surrounding them, in which they are a minority. In their theology, the body is defined as a border between, on one hand, the divine image (*tselem 'elohim*) found among Jews (with emphasis on male Jews), and, on the other hand, the unreflective physicality associated with nature and the evil inclination (*yetser ha-ra'*).

The body is also, importantly, the *locus* where Lithuanian *haredi* Jews knowingly or unknowingly, design and structure the bulk of their ideologies and modes of thought. Employing a reading of boundaries inspired by Michel Foucault, I can determine that an examination of the image of the body and its characteristics in the context of the Lithuanian Ultra-Orthodox culture may thus provide new glimpses and understandings of human religious existence.

In this book, I examine the "problem" of the body and different attitudes towards it. I address the fact that the body took central place in *haredi* theology only after the Holocaust, replacing the mind. I assert that, for Ultra-Orthodox rabbis, the body constitutes a code and a category whereby they may broach sensitive and hitherto confusing ethical subjects, and define the ideal image of the male Jew. I focus on two rabbinical "solutions" offered for the rabbinical "problem" of the body. While these "solutions" contradict each other in many ways, still many Lithuanian rabbis and mentors employ both in their theologies. I will also examine two unique ethical Jewish voices endeavoring to radically change contemporary Ultra-Orthodox attitudes toward the body.

The book's second part addresses the ideal image of the Jewish male body, and the different ways leaders of the *haredi* community strive to train their bodies to conform to the Ultra-Orthodox understanding of perfection. Citing numerous stories where readers will find different and often coercive modes of shaping and training the body, I focus also on a unique ethical approach, which was deeply influenced before the Holocaust by the culture of the European Enlightenment. Rabbis in this approach endeavored to create an "honorable Jewish body," shaped by "honor codes" of the European aristocracy, translated into an Ultra-Orthodox idiom. I conclude this section about the image of the ideal Ultra-Orthodox male body, with historical/theological narratives emphasizing the emotional and somatic price often exacted from saintly rabbis who practiced a sustained and often violent subjugation of their bodies.

Acknowledgments

MY WORK ON THE subject of this book began when, as a young man, my personality and my body were formed and informed through an intimate discourse with the Jewish world of the yeshiva and Hasidic mysticism. Two figures from that period of my life still accompany me on my journey today, although both are no longer with us: Rabbi Moshe Yehoshua Hager, the Vizhnitz Admor (leader), and Rabbi Mordecahi Elefant, director (Rosh Yeshiva) of Yeshivas Itri.

Now, as this book's final passages are being penned, I want to thank all those dear ones who have been my companions during the years of this book's creation. The mentors of my doctoral thesis—of which this book is a natural outgrowth—surpassed in their support what any student might expect: Professor Avinoam Rosenak, whom I knew on my first day at the university to be my first choice as mentor of my doctoral thesis, and with whose help I grew academically day by day; and, Dr. Orit Kamir, who virtually adopted me as a son, nurturing me with kindness, and with stern words when needed. My deep gratitude goes to both of you, for our conversations, our reflections and writing together, and our collegial *havrutah*.

Through the years, I have enjoyed the refuge of several academic "homes." The first of these is the Hartman Institute in Jerusalem. The late Rabbi Professor David Hartman, of blessed memory, modeled the application of intimate critique of the Ultra-Orthodox Jewish world—a critical gaze informed by love. His son, Rabbi Dr. Donniel Hartman, continues to accompany me on my path, both as mentor and as friend.

My second home was The Hebrew University in Jerusalem. Thanks to Eli Lederhendler and Sidra DeKoven Ezrahi, Amalya Oliver and Louise Bethlehem, who encouraged me over the years, showering me with warmth and affection. Later, I had the privilege of teaching and learning at Northwestern University, at Harvard Divinity School and at Rutgers University, and more recently at the Academy for Jewish Religion. Thanks to Michael Jackson, Ann Broade, and Ora Horn Prouse, for their companionship, for their reading of my offerings, and for their help in so many ways.

My journey has given me the opportunity to sit at the feet of truly wise scholars. Professor Avi Sagi was and remains a spiritual father to me. For a decade, as I worked under his direction and at his side, Professor Sagi opened up to me a window into his rich interior world, and conferred on me not only critical research tools, but a deep love of learning for its own sake. The imprint of his inspiration is clearly visible on every page of this book. Professor Jonathan ("Yoni") Garb, with his unmatched sensitivity, provided me with a bridge spanning between the Ultra-Orthodox past and the present world of Western thought, while adding beautiful glimpses of Eastern thought as well.

Others who have been my companions include Yoske Achituv of blessed memory, Jean Vanier of blessed memory, Flouer Courttney, Rosa Gaya, Aharon-Oren Stern, Nir Stern, Meir and Tara Feldman, Sister Maureen Cusick, Sarah Thompson, and Bonnie Swencionis. All of them, through their physical presence and their strength of character, have taught me important chapters in ethics.

My heart overflows with love for my family. For my father, who has never ceased instilling in me a love of the way of Hasidism, and for my mother, a true *yiddish mama* and a woman of deep loving kindness; for my sisters and brothers, and my other family members, each of whom, in their own way, has made me who I am. Special thanks go to Faygili for reading these chapters with her characteristic sensitivity, and for Yechiel for being his inimitable self.

Friends are, for me, another family, a family of "the second innocence." I am grateful to Rita Lipkin, Natalie Bergner, Carol Long, Orit and Roni Freilich, Simcha and Menno De Leeuw, Shane Clark, Nadav Avruch, and my beloved intentional communities of Ellery and DTPT.

Years of academic study and writing have been interlaced with my work of peace activism. As Vice-President of the interfaith youth movement, Kids4Peace International, I encountered dear friends who found a direct path to my heart. It would be vain for me to try naming them all; I will mention only a few, with whom I wrestled day and night to put into practice the saying from the Mishnah, that "whoever raises up one human life, it is as if they have saved an entire world." My thanks to Rev. Josh Thomas, Rev. Brian Sullivan, Rev. Diane Nancekivell; and to Rula Saleh, Reeham Subhi, Zoubaida Salman, Rebecca and Naomi Sullum, Mohammad Joulany, Arwa Subhi Hussein, Saed Mashal, Samar Musarsa, Hussam Wattad, Steve Israeli, Jill Levenfeld, and Sari Oren of blessed memory.

I am grateful too for generous support from several sources along the way: the Hoffman Foundation for Leadership and the Presidential Scholarship—both of the Hebrew University; the Fulbright-Rabin Scholarship, and the Memorial Foundation Scholarship.

A number of colleagues participated in the years-long process or rendering the original Hebrew text into the English version of this book, and each of these deserves heartfelt thanks: Natalie Bergner, Sasha Weisse, and Elah Schild.

My thanks to Dr. Henry Ralph Carse, for rendering into English key Hebrew and Aramaic source texts, and for editing the entire volume. He translated, edited, polished, rewrote—and thus brought a breath of vitality and life to the manuscript; no written words can express my gratitude.

Introduction

The Body Dilemma

A. The Body as Focus

Rabbi Yaffen used to tell that he once saw Rabbi Kanievsky [as a young student in the house of study] sitting on his bench [toward evening], reflecting on the Scriptures, and beside him was the meal someone had brought him that morning. When Rabbi [Yaffen] asked Our Teacher [Kanievsky] why he had not eaten all day, the latter replied that he had indeed eaten, and having had his fill had recited the blessing after a meal. Rabbi Yaffen was astonished. "How can this be," he asked, "when your meal is still here, untouched, on the bench beside you?" Later, he found out that a lump of plaster had fallen from the ceiling of the house of study [onto the bench], and Our Teacher had eaten that, immersed all the while in his studies. Then, he had recited the blessing, under the impression that he had just eaten his breakfast, and not noticing anything amiss.[1]

THIS INTRIGUING TALE REFLECTS an entire spiritual culture. The young man, Ya'akov Yosef Kanievsky, devotes himself wholly to the sacred text,

---

1. Anonymous, *Hi Sichati, Vol. 1*, 326. Rabbi Yaakov Yisrael Kanievsky (1899–1985) has the honorific pseudonym of *The Steipler* – from the Ukranian city where he was born. At the age of eleven, the young Kanievsky was already at the Novardok Yeshiva, under Rabbi Horowitz—"the Grandfather of Novardok." He was drafted into the Soviet army, where he served for some time. He married Miriam, the sister of Rabbi Avraham Yeshayahu Karelitz, founded the Novadok Yeshiva in Pinsk, and then moved to Palestine. Rabbi Kanievsky headed two yeshivas in Israel. He is known especially for mentoring the community together with his brother-in-law, and then alone after Rabbi Karelitz's death. His later works include a Talmudic series *Kehillos Yaakov* and a collection of letters, edited in *Karyana D'Igarata*.

the very soul of the Jewish spiritual world in which one day he will gain renown as a leader known as "Our Teacher." A fascinating web of relationships is woven between the body of the holy youth and the sacred text he studies. Pride of place goes to the heavenly scripture, but earthly food also has a role to play: only if the body is nourished will the zealous scholar be capable of deepening his understanding of the text. A simple meal even takes on a religious meaning, since the youth must say a blessing before and after eating. This, then, is not a tale glorifying zealous self-harm, but rather a description of a unique ability both to nourish the body and simultaneously to be ignorant of doing so. One can surmise that the precocious young Kanievsky would have been delighted to have some sort of "feeding machine" attached to his body, so that he would need pay no further attention to mundane matters like meals.

The pious young man's "education" of his body thus allows him to practice total devotion to the sacred texts. In fact, what he does unconsciously consume, instead of his lunch, is a lump of plaster fallen from the study hall itself—the *beit midrash*, a physical space dedicated by the Jewish community to enshrine the efforts of those who in turn devote themselves to the community ideal of Torah study. The *beit midrash* is consumed, digested, incorporated into the body of the young saint: matter becomes spirit.

This tale from the Ultra-Orthodox Lithuanian tradition finds comparative echoes throughout Judaism, as well as in other religious contexts.[2] In a parallel Hasidic narrative, for example, we hear of two

---

2. Ultra-Orthodox Jews are also referred to—especially in Israel—by the Hebrew term *"haredi"* (plural—*haredim*)—that is "those who fear [God]." Ultra-Orthodox society can be defined, in various ways, as distinct from Orthodox Judaism in the USA or Religious Zionism in Israel. In Israel, the easiest distinction is between *haredim*, on one hand, and members of the Religious Zionist movement, on the other. The *haredim* do not serve in the army; they study in *yeshivas* (houses of study), where the curriculum is almost exclusively of religious character; and they vote for the political party of the Ashkenazi *haredim*—"*Agudat Yisra'el*." In the USA the distinction between Ultra-Orthodox and Orthodox Jews is much less apparent. Hasidic Ultra-Orthodox society is easy to identify since it is composed of several distinct Hasidic "schools," but Lithuanian Ultra-Orthodoxy is more difficult to define as many adherents dress in more modern ways, and, in the USA, are often working people, so the border between them and the general Orthodox community is more blurred. One way to distinguish them is by indicating the *yeshivas* linked with the Lithuanian Ultra-Orthodox world-view: students and alumni of these *yeshivas*, and their spouses and families, will all be considered Lithuanian Ultra-Orthodox, or—in the idiom of that community—"*yeshivesh*." It is important to point out that discussion of "defining features" of Ultra-Orthodox Jewish society is confined to outsiders; members of these communities themselves identify each other intuitively and effortlessly.

distinguished rabbis probing together the deepest secrets of human life, including a discussion about whether or not beef is a tasty dish. In yet another tale, two rabbis debate where their son and daughter—who have just now been married—should make their new home. In the end, they agree that the newlyweds should live with whichever of them can teach the young husband the most holy way of smoking his cigarettes.[3]

While these Hasidic and Lithuanian tales were all composed during approximately the same decades, the attitude toward the human body is, in each genre, quite distinct. In the Hasidic stories, it is the material pleasures of human life that take center stage: the savory meat and the act of smoking. The narrators see these physical contexts as occasions within which the sacred "takes place." In the Lithuanian Ultra-Orthodox accounts, by contrast, our young spiritual hero transcends the nourishing food, ingesting instead a lump of plaster from the ceiling of the study hall. The message he is communicating is this: while the laws of nature dictate that he must eat, in practice he will do all he can to ignore the lowly contingencies of his body.

Here it must be pointed out, that such Jewish hagiographical gems differ in essential ways, not only from each other, but also from religious systems (including Jewish ones) that harm the body through ascetical practices, and equally from various less explicitly religious "mindfulness" teachings that instruct practitioners to be wholly attentive to every bite while they eat. The attitude of Ultra-Orthodox Jewish hagiographies to the body is, in many ways, culturally unique.

It is no coincidence that it is Rabbi Kanievsky who is the hero of the Lithuanian tale we have cited. This is a man who grew up in the Lithuanian "world of Torah" on the eve of the Second World War and the Holocaust, in which this Jewish community, like many others, was all but annihilated. Later, Kanievsky became a leading light of the Ultra-Orthodox community of the city of Bnei Braq in the State of Israel, and many of the post-Holocaust generation in Israel met him in person. His son, Rabbi Chayim Kanievsky, is one of the great mentors of the same community to this day. The tale we have cited, then, has a deep cultural impact among contemporary Jews who have personal admiration for the Kanievsky family as quasi-miraculous models of the holy life, worthy of emulation.

The stated spiritual ideal of the Lithuanian Ultra-Orthodox community is ceaseless devotion to the study of Jewish sacred texts. On the

---

3. Englander, "Halakha as Praxis."

face of it, hagiographies that describe eating and other physical pursuits are a deviation from the act of learning so vaunted in this community. For this reason, the editor who compiled this collection of tales about the young Rabbi Kanievsky goes to some lengths to explain, and even apologize for, his choice of subject matter. In a preface to the book, the editor reminds his readers that most of us—ordinary members of the community—are not capable of sustained spiritual devotion to the ideal of Torah. Unlike exemplary saints like Kanievsky, we are beset by many distractions: food, drink, sexual relations with our spouses, and the need to be active members of our community. Attaining our spiritual ideal is not easy. It behooves us, then, to learn from the example of these ideal luminaries, to study the way they dedicate the physicality of their lives to the world of the spirit. As we follow in their footsteps, we too may one day "educate" our material bodies and bring them closer to the spiritual realm.

The Lithuanian Jewish Ultra-Orthodox discourse on the male body, after the Holocaust and until the end of the first decade of the twenty-first century, is the focus of this book.[4] This discourse was chosen because of its special status in Ultra-Orthodoxy: the body (especially the male body) is the axis around which this theology designs, knowingly or unknowingly, the bulk of its ideology and modes of thought. An examination of images of the body and its characteristics opens a window, then, to understanding the meaning of human existence for this community.[5]

There is an additional reason to focus on this discourse. Ultra-Orthodox Judaism is a unique minority group that aspires to live differently from "Western" (that is, secular and modern) majority norms. Because Ultra-Orthodox Jews are aware of the difficulties inherent in this aspiration, the principle of saying "no" to the majority, or to the "other," is one

---

4. The Lithuanian Ultra-Orthodox society is one of the two central Ashkenazi Ultra-Orthodox Jewish groups, the other being Hasidism. The term "Lithuanian" derives from the origins of this society in Lithuania. After the Holocaust and the destruction of the Jewish community of Lithuania, this group came to be characterized by its thought rather than by any national affiliation of its members.

5. For the concept of the body in traditional Jewish society, and changes it has undergone, cf. Biale, *Eros and the Jews*; Gluzman, *The Zionist Body*; Gilman, *The Jew's Body*; Presner, *Muscular Judaism*. For the image of the *Haredi* body, cf. Aran, "Fundamentalism and the Masculine body"; Hakak, "Haredi Male Bodies"; Aran, "Denial Does Not Make the Haredi Body Go Away"; El-Or, "The Length of the Slits and the Spread of Luxury"; El-Or, "Are They Like Their Grandmothers?"; Henkin, "Contemporary Tseni'ut."

of this society's main ideals. Members of this community achieve this by creating exclusive neighborhoods and by dressing in a unique way. Since their strict dietary regulations do not allow them to eat with "outsiders," and they practice strict segregation by gender, both outside and inside the community, they do not feel comfortable around "Western" people. As we will see later in detail, this wall of cultural separation is not impermeable to ideas from the outside. However, the Ultra-Orthodox ideal lifestyle is still an alternative to the ones we are more familiar with in Western society, and can serve as a critical lens through which to view our own way of life.

In every human society, the term "body" means more than the physical body; it includes value judgments, and other cultural beliefs. Ultra-Orthodox Lithuanian Jewish society views the body as one of the key, and most problematic, elements in human existence. In their theology, the fact that all human beings have a body is a mystery, and not taken for granted. Ultra-Orthodox Lithuanian thought tries to precisely define the scope and boundaries of the body, to identify all the potential difficulties it poses, and to suggest ways to deal with them. Moreover, because the body is an integral part of human existence, it is not solely a Jewish, Ultra-Orthodox, Lithuanian, or male problem. The "body dilemma" is recognized as universal and is subsequently associated with a variety of existential issues, both metaphysical and theological, as will become clear during the following chapters.

Before looking at specific texts, it is important to reiterate the observation that in this form of religious anthropological thought, a male gender bias is the default mode. Ultra-Orthodox teachings for yeshiva students concerning the body are primarily concerned with the male body; the female body as a "phenomenon" is entirely "other." Since this is the first book dedicated to the body in this community and theology, I have decided to focus only on the male body in order to understand what "body" means for this (male) community. Only in specific places (chapter 4) do I refer to images of the female body, in places where the "normative" body meets with the "other." In order not to hide or disguise the male bias in the original texts, I will intentionally retain the masculine forms found in the original Hebrew or Aramaic, rather than using gender-neutral English alternatives.

B. Research Method

The concept of the Ultra-Orthodox Lithuanian body, as I will present it, relies first and foremost on textual analysis. The works of the Lithuanian rabbis, in their two genres of *Musar*[6] and hagiography, are the main sources that I will analyze, explain, and interpret. In this community, as we have seen in the opening of this chapter, written texts enjoy a special status. The fundamental writings are primarily about striving for a worthy and ideal life, which is one of the cornerstones of this society. The role of philosophers, preachers, and poets who are members of the *Musar* leadership and editors of the hagiographical literature is to present to the community the right way of living. Their thought focuses not on present reality, but rather on the question of "what could be." Accordingly, in this context, I will focus primarily on the image of the "desired body," and will be discussing the *Musar* teachings directly rather than engaging in secondary socio-political discourse.

My choice to limit this study to the spirit and language of the relevant texts means that I examine the image of the "ideal body." However, this has wider importance for the study of reality itself. Since literary works are always written within a particular social setting, and since these *Musar* and hagiographical writings reflect (consciously and unconsciously) the choices of the Lithuanian rabbinic hegemony, the "ideal body" plays a role in shaping the reality of the community itself.

Attitudes to the body are never stagnant. Throughout the period here discussed there have been many developments in concepts and perceptions of "the desired body," but it still is at the heart of Ultra-Orthodox Lithuanian thought. The body is considered a "problem" with good reason. The literature deals almost entirely with the religious aspiration to a holy life, constantly drawing closer to the (Jewish male) ideal of the "worthy man." In this idealistic scenario, the body is cast in the role of anti-hero. Corporeal existence represents the starkest contrast to ideal (Jewish male) religious life. The body is the source of countless all-too human inclinations and shortcomings, and accordingly symbolizes everything that is spiritually deficient and incomplete. For the Lithuanian rabbis, as we shall see, the body is an existential platform upon which

---

6. The literal meaning of the Hebrew word *Musar* is "Ethics." In spite of the inherent affinities between the concepts "*Musar*" and "Ethics," I have decided to retain the Hebrew original, because in Lithuanian thought "*Musar*" implies both "Ethics" and "Morality."

Ultra-Orthodox Lithuanian Judaism problematizes a wide range of questions and multiple, sometimes contradictory meanings.

The French philosopher Maurice Merleau-Ponty, whose roots are in the phenomenological tradition, defines the body as an object like other objects, part of the world that cannot therefore be subject to the constant supervision of consciousness. The body has a knowledge of its own, arising from its inherent nature and from its dialogue with the world outside the human person.[7] The concept of the body in phenomenological research is, then, a danger to the ideal life of the *Musar* movement—which aims for the body to be controlled by the mind. The neuro-phenomenology of Merleau-Ponty, which investigated the relationship between the body and its surroundings, will provide us with an initial insight as well as a critical tool to examine the significance of the body for the Lithuanian rabbis. In other words, by looking at the body with phenomenological tools—which investigate the nature of the body as it is—I will contextualize the interpretations and assumptions of *Musar* rabbis about the body, as well as the areas where they identified bodily elements that are especially dangerous to humans, areas that Western culture often ignores.

There will be those who will challenge the ethics of applying hermeneutical and interpretive tools derived from Western culture and philosophical thought, to the study of non-Western religious texts originating from the Ultra-Orthodox Jewish world. It may be argued that the abyss between these two cultures is too deep to be bridged, and that measuring Ultra-Orthodox Jewish texts according to foreign standards is to do them injustice. I myself had this concern while writing this book, and I expressed my hesitations to an anonymous Lithuanian rabbi in an online conversation. His reply was interesting, and deserves to be cited in full. He first makes reference to Rabbi Karelitz (known as the "*Chazon Ish*") whom he admires for being "a completely simple and innocent person." Then he goes on:

> It never occurred to him [the "*Chazon Ish*"] to engage in intellectualizing or philosophy in any form, and he never tried to establish a theological system. All that he wrote in his *Musar* letters about his view of the world was, in my opinion, simply personal dialogue with others in the most simple and intuitive form. The purpose of this dialogue was just to express something

---

7. It is true that the mind too, like the body, has many layers, only a few of which an individual is conscious of. However, in this book I will focus on the bodily aspects of human experience, and will mention the mind only when necessary.

personal to the questioner, something with the simplest human meaning, and not to set up a philosophical methodology. In my opinion, the Torah is founded on the ability to contain contradictions and to move freely between opposite poles, without always trying to reconcile them or find some middle ground. On the contrary, the idea that we are obliged to settle everything in uniformity and coherence, and always strike a balance, is killing [the soul].[8]

According to this anonymous contemporary Ultra-Orthodox rabbi, reading religious texts through a critical-philosophical Western lens risks first and foremost mischaracterizing the essence of the texts themselves. Western philosophy, which this rabbi identifies as methodology [methodically], is a conciliatory way of thinking, advocating compromise because it does not tolerate contradictions, and therefore seeking solutions to any tension between opposing elements. In stark contrast, the dialogical approach characterizing the Lithuanian *Musar* literature draws its vitality from life itself, does not seek positional harmonization, and is able, therefore, to move freely between the extremes.

This critique of Western ways of thinking is important. I am convinced, however, that Western existential and phenomenological thought has the potential to understand concepts originating in the Ultra-Orthodox world, precisely because of the distance between these two conceptual worlds and the unfamiliarity of their respective languages. This unfamiliarity can lead to questions previously unasked within the Ultra-Orthodox literature, a possibility that can shed new light on the writers' ideas and choices. My hope is that Ultra-Orthodox readers will find in this book an invitation to reflect on their ethical decisions where their bodies are concerned. I also hope that Western readers, for their part, will learn more about the lives and beliefs of those who choose to live side by side with Western culture while still remaining essentially "other."

In the coming chapters I will write about the commonality between the *Musar* literature and the Lithuanian hagiographical literature—namely, their idealist characteristics—and the reasons for my choice to examine them together as the related objects of this study. Here, I would like to take a moment to look at the differences between them.

Musar literature, which features in the book's first section, is a contemplative/educational genre, emerging from life itself and from the challenges rabbis identify within their communities. The genre then shifts

---

8. Private email exchanges.

focus, to deal with the purely theoretical beliefs of the *Musar* leaders. After these two stages, the focus returns to the actual experiences of the students who learn the *Musar* texts and try to integrate the theory into their lives. The *Musar* genre serves, then, as a form of "safe space" within which Lithuanian rabbis may express the whisperings of their hearts and seek answers to their existential wonderments, while encouraging their students to do the same.

The hero in *Musar* literature is the ordinary yeshiva student, in dialogue with other yeshiva students who, like him, are grappling with the ethical challenges of their daily lives. The body of the religious Jewish male is a central element in *Musar*, but the images of the body emerging from this literature are mostly inconsistent, and contradict reality. The ethical questions and challenges described in *Musar* literature are, for their part, very real, since they come from life itself. Through these ethical dilemmas, the *Musar* literature tries to transform human bodies into their ideal form.

The genre of hagiography offers a contrast to the literature of *Musar*. While the latter tends to focus on the body of the average Ultra-Orthodox Lithuanian Jewish man, the hagiographical genre is concerned with the ideal image of the "righteous one"—the *tzadik*, or Jewish saint, and in particular the *tzadik*'s body. The tales of the "*gdolim*" (the "great ones," meaning the saints of the community) do not pretend to describe the average yeshiva student; rather they relate the various stages in the lives of those who were the leaders of the Ultra-Orthodox Lithuanian community, from their youth in the yeshiva until their death. I will examine how the editors of these stories teach the yeshiva students how the leaders of their community shaped a physical ideal, alternatively cultivating and neglecting their bodies to force them into a state of perfection.

C. Ultra-Orthodox Society: Cultural Isolation or Diffusion of Ideas?

Traditional research on Ultra-Orthodox Jewish society has always asserted that its views are the products of a struggle with the Jewish Enlightenment (*HaHaskala*) and Zionism, as well as with values identified as "modern."[9] Even if this assertion is accurate historically, it still contains biases that require examination.

---

9. It is not my intention in this book to discuss the definitions of "modern" and

Aviezer Ravitzky, for example, characterizes Ultra-Orthodox Jewish thought as endeavoring always to highlight whatever differentiates it from whatever it associates with the modern world. In Ravitzky's view, this highlighting allows Ultra-Orthodoxy to identify its enemies and protect itself from them.[10] This line of research, in other words, sees Ultra-Orthodoxy as adopting a negative self-definition, situating itself "over against" the secular "other." Ravitzky thus cites the famous dictum of the Ultra-Orthodox luminary, the *"Chatam Sofer"*—"New is forbidden by the Torah"—as the defining ethos of this society. The remarkable survival of the Ultra-Orthodox Jewish community into the twenty-first century, in spite of the terrible events of the Holocaust and the subsequent challenges of living in a secular public sphere, are seen as evidence of the uncompromising power of this "over against" stance.

Increasingly, scholars now point out that this stress on the power of inflexibility in the Ultra-Orthodox community is liable to distract us from appreciating the nuance of hues and the delicate brush-strokes on the canvas of Ultra-Orthodox thought. Close examination of Ultra-Orthodox ideas will reveal, in my opinion, how, in spite of the overt resistance to values perceived as modern or secular, there is simultaneously an introduction of some of these same value concepts into Ultra-Orthodox discourse and thinking, influencing them from within. For example, on the Ultra-Orthodox website *"Be-Hadrei Haredim"* there was a lively debate about who won and who lost in the struggle against holding gay pride events in Jerusalem. One of the most prevalent views was that the Ultra-Orthodox community lost this battle, even though the gay pride parade was cancelled, since the open debate inside the community ensured that every child and yeshiva student became aware of homosexuality, a phenomenon that, before this struggle, they had ostensibly not known existed.[11]

In the chapters to follow, I will develop the argument for such value influences through observations of the Lithuanian Ultra-Orthodox discourse concerning the body. I will also indicate how what Ultra-Orthodox

---

secular" (cf. Asad, *Formations of the Secular*). Rather, I am referring here to the way in which Ultra-Orthodox communities internalize values perceived as modern and secular into their internal discourses. For the resistance of Ultra-Orthodox society to the Jewish Enlightenment, cf. Katz, "Orthodoxy as a Response to Emancipation," 90–94.

10. Ravitzky, *Freedom Inscribed*, 167

11. See http://www.bhol.co.il/forums/topic.asp?topic_id=2080664&whichpage=&forum_id=771; http://havruta.org.il/archives/2225.

rabbis consider a Western-secular, and therefore faulty, discourse on the body has been internalized by a particular aspect of the Ultra-Orthodox world-view.

The influence of secular culture (or culture *perceived* as secular) on Ultra-Orthodox communities is nothing new. In Israel, a glance at the printed notices affixed to the walls of Ultra-Orthodox neighborhoods like *Mea She'arim* and *B'nei Braq* shows that the rabbis are aware of secular influences, and are opposed to them. Anyone familiar with the Ultra-Orthodox discourse also knows that the rabbis often adapt to them in some way, and endeavor to soften their impact by various means. Thus, for example, the blanket injunction against the purchase of cellular phones was adjusted to accommodate the creation of a "kosher" cellular phone network.[12] One expects a similar accommodation to the internet, eventually, although at the time of writing the Vizhnitz Rabbi is struggling to prevent its introduction into Ultra-Orthodox homes in the State of Israel.[13] Many other examples of adaptation could be cited, from the opening of vocational colleges for religious students to the discussion of changes in religious women's dress and career options.

Sensitive observation of Ultra-Orthodox society in general, and the Lithuanian context in particular, reveals a complex and multi-hued picture. This book takes as a given that the Ultra-Orthodox world is not simply "aloof from" or "over against" the surrounding society. Rather, Ultra-Orthodoxy engages in a searching intramural dialogue that is radically influenced by outside forces. It is not only true that some rabbis actually espouse secular values, portraying them as positive virtues for Ultra-Orthodox society. Even more significantly, these rabbis themselves often introduce these values into the Ultra-Orthodox discourse, without being prompted by debate in their own community. My aim in this work is identify external values subsumed into Ultra-Orthodox discourse, and the intense internal dialogue that accompanies this adoption.

It should not surprise us that Ultra-Orthodox thinkers will not openly declare that they are adopting secular values; we may in fact surmise that they themselves are generally unaware of this process. The values in question are translated into the Ultra-Orthodox idiom and linked with pre-existing Ultra-Orthodox norms, a cultural translation that makes it difficult even for an outside researcher to accurately recognize that these

12. http://www.bhol.co.il/news_read.asp?id=2404&cat_id=1.
13. cf. https://www.youtube.com/watch?v=yOWdoBf8gUg.

values are of foreign origin and therefore signal significant changes in Ultra-Orthodox tradition.

A number of characteristics help identify values that have entered Ultra-Orthodox thought from the outside. First, we may discern that the rabbis who adopt these values focus on issues that differ substantially from issues of concern to their contemporaries or their predecessors. Rather than exactly replicating the discourse of those who came before them, these rabbis are thus inspired to forge a new discourse, derived from the internalization of values from outside the Ultra-Orthodox sphere, while their peers might simply continue their predecessors' accepted line of teaching.

Evidence of outside influence can also be signaled by voices raised within the community in opposition to an innovative turn in the discourse. Rabbis who raise issues in a novel way may encounter strong resistance to values perceived as "foreign," or "Western-secular," and warnings against the dire consequences of such new thinking. Observation of the resistance that new thinking evokes can reveal that we are in the presence of external values that have been interiorized. This subject will become central in chapters 5 and 6.

D. The Theological Dilemmas of "Masculinity"

Throughout history, religious leaders and rabbis have created for themselves and for the entire (male) community different ideals of masculinity. Scholars now need to study the origins of these theological ideals, to learn how and why they were accepted. In this context, studies show that, in many cultures, masculine ideals have their origins in a denial of what the religious hegemony understood as femininity.[14] This analysis is getting a boost from psychological research, which emphasizes those early developmental stages when, as a baby, a man is very close to the women in his life. In Jewish Ultra-Orthodoxy, a young man achieves his independent self by rejecting the mother and other women in his life in favor of identifying only with his father and the world of men.[15] This example reminds us that scholars who explore the development of the masculine model in a given society must pay attention to the discourse

---

14. Brod, "A Case for Men's Studies," 16.
15. Segal, "Changing Men," 628.

about femininity, to examine each image and model against the background of the other.[16]

In some religious iconography, holy men are often portrayed with feminine features compared to the shape (or shapes) of the masculine in each specific culture.[17] Whether Jewish *tzadik*, Christian monk, or Sufi mystic—their features are rounded and delicate, their limbs and gestures follow soft lines. On the other hand, other depictions present holy men as rigid in both body and personality, as if forged by lives dedicated to uncompromising spiritual practices, designed to summon forth the divine spirit inherent within humanity. An uncompromising stance is considered a basic condition for imposing the spirit/mind upon the body. The heroism of the saints is not necessarily achieved by physical force, but through the mastery of their internal desires. In these traditions, religious masculinity is perceived as a symbol of religious willpower, and determination to implement the principles of faith in daily life.[18] But is that a desirable male image? Do religious men wish to adopt this particularly rigid masculinity, or do they prefer to adopt the image of a non-religious body? This question will be at the center of chapters 8 and 9.

One cannot imagine a contemporary study of Judaism without reference to the way masculinity is portrayed. Like other ethnic minorities, such as the Roma people, Jewish men were often perceived by the majority cultures in which they lived as lacking masculinity, as symbolic of perverted masculinity, or as unnaturally feminine or unhealthy. Daniel Boyarin has shown how the rabbis of the Talmud celebrated this uniquely Jewish masculinity as a choice made by Jewish men to shape their bodies as the (feminine) "other"—in contradistinction to Greek and Roman perceptions of masculinity. Just as today's queer culture has transformed the derogatory term into a symbol of empowerment, so Pharisee leaders in the Talmudic era voluntarily embraced the originally insulting body image assigned to them, making it a symbol of religious and national pride.[19] Following Boyarin, numerous studies have highlighted the relationship between concepts of masculinity in Judaism and the surrounding cultures of the Diaspora, including the role of these concepts in the struggle to protect Jewish identity against the threat of assimilation.

16. For more details, see chapter 4.
17. Kirkley, "Is It Manly to be Christian?"
18. Hansen, "In Search of God's Hand."
19. Boyarin, *Carnal Israel*.

In the late nineteenth century, the Jewish Enlightenment (*Ha-Haskalah*) and the Zionist movement began make inroads in European Jewish society. One of their main struggles was against the "unmanly" image of traditional Jewish men. *Haskalah* and Zionist thinkers abandoned the perception of the Jewish male body as the (feminine) "other," and strove to create a new Jewish male identity that could engage in active dialogue with European and (later) Arab Palestinian versions of masculinity.[20] Ultra-Orthodox Jewish society, however, particularly the anti-Zionist sects, continued to espouse the Diaspora image of the Jewish man.

Today, Ultra-Orthodox society is the only Jewish group in the State of Israel whose members do not serve in the I.D.F. Men in this society are often not the family's primary breadwinners, rarely engage in sport activities, and maintain their modest European dress code, covering their entire bodies even during the hot months of the Middle Eastern summer. All of this indicates how this Ultra-Orthodox group preserves the old Jewish image of masculinity and of the male body into the twenty-first century.

Recent research puts increasing focus on the images of the Ultra-Orthodox body in general and of men in particular.[21] In a pioneering article, Gideon Aran examines different aspects of how Ultra-Orthodox men dress, walk, and describe feelings toward their bodies.[22] Nurit Stadler dedicates her research to elements of fundamentalism and piety among yeshiva students, and how the students apply their devotion to God to the formation of their masculine identity.[23] Stadler and others suggest that the Ultra-Orthodox struggle against the evil inclination (*yetser ha-ra'*) conditions a masculine identity engaged in a constant inner conflict—a reality very different from the familiar extroverted Western male personality who focuses on the public sphere and on how he is perceived by society.[24] The Ultra-Orthodox man's internalized focus is consistent with the structure of the Ultra-Orthodox society in Israel, where the woman is often the main breadwinner, while the man dedicates his life to the "spiritual economy" of the next world. Yohai Hakak focuses on

20. For more details, see chapter 8.

21. In his important work, Caplan introduces the reader to the current academic map of the Ultra-Orthodox community. See Caplan, *The Internal Popular Discourse in Israeli Haredi Society*.

22. Aran, "Denial Does Not Make the Haredi Body Go Away."

23. Stadler, *Yeshiva Fundamentalism*.

24. Aran, "Fundamentalism and the Masculine Body."

how Ultra-Orthodox masculinity is formed and reflected in the order of study, the spatial design of facilities, and the eating and sleeping arrangements in the Lithuanian yeshivas.[25]

With all the welcome studies in this field, no researcher has yet closely examined the relevant Jewish Ultra-Orthodox theological and ethical writings, in order to bring to light the operative concept(s) of the ideal Jewish male body. It is this lack that the present book endeavors to address.

E. Critique of the Traditional Jewish Body and the Image of the Israeli Body

Most of the texts discussed in this book were written in the State of Israel. As already discussed above, the Ultra-Orthodox authors of the *Musar* literature and the hagiographies do not exist in a cultural vacuum, but rather interact with secular and otherwise non-Ultra-Orthodox Israeli concepts of the body. It is not surprising that the interaction between Ultra-Orthodox and secular Israeli images of the male body often takes the form of a "dialogue" that takes place *inside the mind of the Ultra-Orthodox writer*, not in actual engagement with secular Israelis.

In the second half of the nineteenth century and in the early decades of the twentieth, the Jewish Enlightenment and Zionism prompted many yeshiva students in Lithuania to abandon the traditional Jewish way of life. Much of their critique of the tradition revolved around the Diaspora Jew's relationship with the human body and with nature. Jewish secularists began to emphasize the role of *experience* as a feeling of life as it is, without religious-cultural agendas obscuring the direct sensation of being human in this world. In their view, a Jew may return to unity with self and nature only through acceptance of the experiences of the body and of this world ("the immanent"), without the constant need to appeal to spiritual authority beyond this world ("the transcendent").[26] Self-actualization is one of the terms most stressed and enhanced by the foundational Zionist thinker A. D. Gordon. At issue here is the coming together

---

25. Hakak, *Spirituality and Worldliness in Lithuanian Yeshivas*.

26. Shapira, *A.D. Gordon*, 94. I deliberately choose examples from A. D. Gordon, Bialik, Berdyczewski, and Rav Kook because all four grew up in religious Lithuanian families, and are familiar with this worldview. Their writing is also nearest to the traditions of Jewish religiosity, thus bringing their critique closer to that of the late Rabbi Avigdor Miller (see chapter 5).

"not only of all the spiritual and vital forces of the body's cells, but even of all the physical and chemical forces of each of the body's atoms."[27] To become truly supportive of the community, it is not necessary or helpful for individuals to deny their inner aspirations and feelings; rather, they must heed their inner desires and realize their private dreams, and thus find a way to benefit the collective.[28]

When they critique Jewish tradition, secular Jewish thinkers who grew up in the book-laden world of the yeshiva hold that an obsession with the written word is an obstacle to real experience:

> The book itself, when its importance is taken to an extreme, rebels against nature, flees from nature, and loses all understanding of nature.... And there is so much in life that precedes the book: life comes before the book, the world came before the book, the human being comes before the book, the soul comes before the book.[29]

> In every school, just as students are given times when they must study, so too they must not neglect life. So when their lesson is done, they should go forth from the world of lofty ideas into the world of life—to walk, to play and to amuse themselves. A child of Israel, however, who is born in the lap of the People of the Book, a people for whom Torah is life itself, this child abandons all the life of this world in order to be occupied with the world of Torah. A young man, from the age of twelve to the age of fourteen, sits and learns in the yeshiva, head bowed, without a break. All day long he "roars like a lion," toiling in his mind on works as mighty as the Temple of the deep Talmud.[30]

Another reason for this neglect of the experiential life is identified in the halakha, as it took form in rabbinic Ultra-Orthodox literature. Halakha is understood as separating one from personal desires, requiring that one sacrifice oneself to divinely ordained laws, and tearing one away from the ordinary flow of life. A fascinating example can seen in the writings of Rabbi Joseph Ber Soloveitchik who describes the image of the ideal "halakhic man":

---

27. Gordon, *Man and Nature*, 87.
28. Schweid, "Mutual Responsibility," 331–33.
29. Berdyczweski, *Collected Works Vol. 6*, 33–34.
30. Berdyczweski, *Collected Works Vol. 1*, 84

> When halakhic man looks to the western horizon and sees the fading rays of the setting sun or to the eastern horizon and sees the first light of dawn and the glowing rays of the rising sun, he knows that this sunset or sunrise imposes upon him anew obligations and commandments.[31]

Another assertion made about halakhic piety is that it makes any connection between human beings and the divine conditional *solely* on some level of halakhic and Talmudic aptitude; the divine will can only be apprehended by observing halakha and studying Talmud, and these ways are seen as contradicting human willfulness. This virtual equation of the divine with the halakha makes it practically impossible for any Jew to find the divine in nature itself or in the human condition. In stark contrast, the inclination of secular Judaism was to emphasize the importance of the human individual:

> Human beings and human commandments ... they are one and their name is one, and the Holy One had them in view at the hour of the creation of the world; they are the principle of principles, the foundation of all foundations, and they hold sway over everything that is.[32]

In his critical poem "City of Slaughter," Bialik chastises traditional Jewish society, contrasting its passive and pietistic conduct during the pogroms with the sheer Jewish courage of the Maccabees:

> Come, now, and I will bring thee to their lairs
> The privies, jakes and pigpens where the heirs
> Of Hasmoneans lay, with trembling knees,
> Concealed and cowering,—the sons of the Maccabees!
> The seeds of saints, the scions of the lions!
> Who, crammed by scores in all the sanctuaries of their shame,
> So sanctified My name!
> It was the flight of mice they fled,
> The scurrying of roaches was their flight;
> They died like dogs, and they were dead![33]

One of the first tasks undertaken by those who had left the world of the Lithuanian yeshiva was to bring the Jewish person back to a positive

---

31. Soloveitchik, *The Halakhic Man*, 20.
32. Berdyczweski, *Collected Works Vol. 1*, 27.
33. Efros, *Complete Poetic Works of Hayyim Nahman Bialik Vol. 1*, 134.

experience of his or her own body, and restoring a parallel perception of the natural world around us as part of our very life:

> The creativity that is inherent in human life is the creation of the human person herself/himself, a creative process constantly renewing itself by virtue of the unending renewal of nature.[34]

For secular Jewish thinkers, this creative process should have two important results for the Jew: a reunification with nature and, through this very reconnection, an increased ability to see the divine presence in places other than the sacred text or sacred law. Berdyczweski sums it up admirably:

> Return, return to Nature, O children of Israel! Kneel before her, and pray for compassion in place of the shame that has been heaped upon us for two thousand years. And if you should ask: What is her name, that we may know? I Am Who I Am! She answers you each evening, each morning, at all times and always.... Remember, there are not two authorities, world and humanity, God and humanity; no, for all is one, united and unique, and all is infinite and without end.[35]

Such critical insights are found not only in secular Zionism, but also in the teachings of Rabbi Abraham Isaac Kook, who recognized Diaspora Judaism's debased attitudes to the body and material existence in Diaspora Judaism, and set about changing them:[36]

> The physical exercise that is undertaken by the young people of Israel in the Land of Israel in order to strengthen their bodies and become powerful children of the new nation, also improves the spiritual strength of the highest *tzadikim*, whose work it is to bring about the union of the divine names.... This holy work lifts up the Shechinah ever higher and higher, as she is lifted up by holy worship and praises, as David the King of Israel said in the Book of Psalms... And

---

34. Gordon, *Man and Nature*, 54. For an understanding of the "Diaspora body" and the "Zionist body," cf. Gluzman, *The Zionist Body*, 67–95, 182–208.
35. Berdyczweski, *Collected Works Vol 7*, 28–29. cf. Schwartz, *Sefer Kdushat Israel*.
36. Achituv, *Mashavei Ruach*, 29–60.

let us not be surprised to find certain things lacking in the lives of those who strengthen their bodies and busy themselves with earthly things in the Land of Israel. For even the revelation of the Holy Spirit herself is in need of clarification and purification from admixtures of the unclean that is within her, until little by little she is purified, hallowed and clarified.[37]

Rabbi Kook compares the physical training of secular Zionists, and their efforts to develop their bodies, to the recitation of Psalms, traditionally seen as developing the strength of the soul. In his opinion, only when the body has been restored to full life can the *tzadikim* (Jewish saints) succeed in their required work of Torah and "union of divine names" (a reference to mystical accomplishments). Acknowledging that the body has been neglected in Judaism, he looks forward to a Jewish restoration of "well-formed bodies" and "strong muscles."[38]

Hasidic writings, too, join the extolling of the human body as a sacred and necessary tool for the worship of the divine. In Hasidic theology, God is to be found in every aspect of creation, and therefore the labor of Heaven is to be sought not only through mindful study and prayer, but also through the body. Indeed, the Hasidic movement's doctrines include corporeal components, like attention to worshipping the divine through dancing, eating, and even sniffing tobacco.[39]

In this context we must make reference to the Holocaust, during which the Ultra-Orthodox Lithuanian Jewish community was mortally wounded and its "World of Torah" almost totally destroyed. To rebuild it, this community was obliged to simultaneously embrace "seclusion during a monastic-ascetic act of concession over all material achievements"[40] and—at the same time—active reconstruction of the material and physical dimensions of human life wiped out by the war. To complicate matters, the near destruction of European Judaism during the war sowed

---

37. Kook, *'Orot*, 80.
38. Kook, *'Orot*.
39. Many studies have been written on this subject, including an entire book by Tsippi Kaufman (Kaufman, *In All ways Know Him*). Still, only certain aspects of physicality are condoned, and Hasidism—especially today—is far more conservative on sexuality than Lithuanian Ultra-Orthodox society; cf. Brown, "Kedusha"; Sagiv, "The Rectification of the Covenant." For contrasting Hasidic and Lithuanian attitudes to prayer and Torah study, cf. Nadler, *The Faith of the Mithnagdim*.
40. Schweid, *From Ruin to Salvation*, 234.

deep confusion among Zionist leadership in the Land of Israel, who now had doubts about how they should regard Holocaust survivors, whether religious or secular. Until the 1960s, the majority of Jewish Israeli citizens had not been born in Israel; they were European Jews who immigrated to Palestine before World War II, and consequently identified deeply with survivors of the tragedy of the Holocaust. On the other hand, Zionist leaders who saw themselves as *sabras* ("natives") in *Eretz Yisrael* continued to be critical toward the Jewish Diaspora, and the Ultra-Orthodox bore the brunt of this critique.[41]

Ultra-Orthodox communities in Israel and in the United States live as minorities within majority secular societies that have very different belief systems, especially in regards to the body. Secular thought, especially since the second half of the twentieth century, increasingly rejects the mind/body dichotomy, favoring a concept of physical activity as the center of human life, with very few boundaries imposed on modes of activity. From a secular standpoint, there is no real distinction between "body" and "spirit/soul"—both are subsumed in "person." Importantly, while the body could be seen by religion as "a silent physical object," this is impossible in secular thought, which sees a body-object as nothing but a corpse, devoid of dynamism. The living human body, on the other hand, is in a state of constant activity, both internally and in relation to other objects in the world. If the meaning of "subjectivity" is the spontaneous activity of mind and body holistically, then it is impossible to define the human person as a "subject" who can completely ignore physical being.

F. The Structure of This Book

In the following chapters I will provide a detailed description of the perception of the Ultra-Orthodox Lithuanian male body as it emerges from the *Musar* Literature and the Lithuanian hagiographies.

The first part of the book deals with different images of the body in the *Musar* literature: in chapter 1, a description of *Musar* and its role in Ultra-Orthodox society after the Holocaust; in chapter 2, focus on the body as "*the* problem" of human existence, and how this leads *Musar* movement rabbis to identify other existential life "problems" that the body symbolizes. I will explain the qualities of the body that have made

---

41. Weitz, *Aware but Helpless*, 75–80, 100–129. See also Englander, "Design of the Body."

the *Musar* rabbis so fearful of it, and how the disgust they feel toward the body actually helps them to deal with their fear. The third chapter describes two ways in which the *Musar* movement responds to the "body dilemma." While chapters 2 and 3 focus on problematic images of the *male* body and the way the *Musar* movement "resolves" them, the fourth chapter challenges these "solutions." I examine the attitude of the *Musar* movement toward male sexual spaces, and the inevitable encounter of the Ultra-Orthodox man with woman (and her body) after marriage. Chapters 5 and 6 address various critiques—raised by *Musar* teachers themselves within the movement—of the *Musar* attitude toward the body and its nature.

The second part of the book is dedicated to the hagiographies of Lithuanian saints (*gedolim*—"Great Ones") and the perception of their "ideal bodies." Chapter 7 analyzes the social/religious functions of this new genre in the Lithuanian community; chapter 8, how the body of the rabbis is described variously at different phases in their lives. Here, I will focus on one unique and important *Musar* method—the Slabodka movement. Slabodka was unique in acknowledging and striving to imitate the surrounding (non-Jewish) European culture, creating an image of the "ideal body" that is *sui generis*. Chapter 9 will study the limits of the mature rabbi's "ideal body," how the *gedolim* control their bodies, and which spaces are exempt from the saint's control. Finally, an appendix will provide brief biographical details of the Lithuanian rabbis who figure centrally in my narrative.

PART I

*The Image of the "Real" Body:
Challenge and Response*

CHAPTER I

Musar Teachings in the Second Half of the Twentieth Century

IN THE FIRST PART of this book, I will be exploring the different images of the Lithuanian Ultra-Orthodox male body as described in *Torat HaMusar*—the teachings of the *Musar* movement—after the Holocaust. Since this corpus has received very little scholarly attention and is virtually unknown to most readers, I will first describe the nature of this genre and its status in the Lithuanian community, in the hope that this will help readers follow my subsequent discussions.[1]

A. The Status and Role of the *Musar* Movement after the Holocaust

The main role of the *Musar* movement (*Tenu'at HaMusar*) is to teach the Jewish man[2] his mission in life, and to give him the necessary tools to fulfill it. There are many aspects to the inquiry into how to live a meaningful Jewish life. Crucial questions about the covenantal relationship between God and humans, the distinction between the private and public spheres, and right relationships between humans and nature, all set the

---

1. In 2017, the book *The Gedolim* was published. This is the first academic publication to focus on many of the leaders of the community during the twentieth century. See Brown and Leon, *The Gdolim*. For a general presentation of the history of the *Musar* movement with emphasis on its leaders see Ury, *The Musar Movement*; Goldberg, *The Fire within*; Brown, *The Lithuanian Musar Movement*.

2. I emphasize that although the writings of the *Musar* are for all the members of the community, in the end, they focus only on men, and not on women. See also chapter 4.

tone for any discussion of the status of the body in *Musar* theology. They reflect theological assumptions about human nature and human responsibilities that are at the foundation of the *Musar* movement, and are also important to help the male Jew fulfill his life's mission. Building on this theological basis, the founders of the *Musar* movement built a coherent method to enable their students to identify obstacles in their lives, and to resist the temptations of the evil inclination (*yetser ha-ra'*), which in their view poses these obstacles.

Before the *Musar* movement, traditional Lithuanian Judaism found its spiritual focus in the study of Talmudic logic and debate. The Lithuanian yeshiva system asserted that if Jewish men invested all their energy in understanding the Talmud, the sacred text itself would forge a parallel internal transformation in the student's life. It was considered a unique characteristic of the Talmud, that hidden in its very letters is a force that can render the student's soul more sensitive, while simultaneously defending him from *yetser ha-ra'*. As Rabbi Chaim from Volozhin wrote:

> It is truth that any man (*sic*) who steadfastly studies Torah [i.e. Talmud] for its own sake . . . has no need of work or trouble during the time spent studying these awesome books. . . . For the Holy Torah[3] will itself clothe the student's face with the fear of the Lord, in a very short time and without any effort.[4]

Such emphasis on speculative study of the Talmudic text led naturally to a focus on the student's intellectual abilities. If in other methods[5] the development of mental prowess was considered only one thread in the overall weave of the human person, here in the traditional yeshiva system the student's effort was almost exclusively given to speculative learning. Strict devotion to the sacred text was simultaneously an act of voluntary alienation from what is not text, especially the body and embodied life in the world.[6]

It is not surprising to find the early teachers of the new Lithuanian *Musar* movement shifting their focus from the text of Talmud to the

---

3. "Torah" here, as is often the case in rabbinic sources, refers to the Talmud, as the ultimate study of Torah.

4. Volozhin, *Nefesh Ha-Hayim*: section 4, chapter 9. See also: Stampfer, *Lithuanian Yeshivas*, 84–96, 274–79.

5. A good example is Hasidism. This movement saw the study of Torah as an important value, but as one value among many. The method of Talmud study used in the Hasidic schools also differed from that of the Lithuanian yeshiva system.

6. Katz, *Out of the Ghetto*, 24–32.

actualities of human life. This shift, however, was considered to be a challenging innovation and vigorously opposed by many yeshiva leaders,[7] many of whom prohibited the teachings of *Tenu'at HaMusar* among their students, and sometimes even publicly denounced the movement.[8]

Rabbi Israel Salanter, the originator of the *Musar* movement, pointed out that it is a mistake to think that speculation on the minutiae of every aspect of the Talmud can provide a defense against the evil inclination. It was essential, he thought, to move the focus of attention from the intellect to the human psyche in its innermost processes, both conscious and unconscious. It was Rabbi Salanter's conviction that classical Jewish ethical texts from the Bible, as well as the *aggadah*[9] and moral aphorisms—rather than the Talmud—provided the ideal place for the religious Jewish individual to encounter the ethical teachings and lifestyles of the nation's great sages. Jewish men in particular, in Slanter's opinion, are obligated to pursue a deeper reading of these sources, and to look for opportunities to apply them in their daily lives.[10]

As years passed, the *Musar* teachings were implemented as central aspects of the Lithuanian yeshiva agenda, particularly in those yeshivas established by students of Rabbi Salanter, of which Telshe, Mir, Novardok and Slabodka are examples. Rabbi Doron Gold describes the process in these words:

> The study of *Musar* and the rubric of the "*seder Musar*"[11] have gained such prevalence in yeshiva halls [i.e., in the yeshiva way of life] that they have become an organic aspect of the institution,

---

7. On the traditional conception of the yeshivas see Wozner, *Legal Thinking*.

8. On the historical challenges and struggles before the *Musar* literature became part of the recognized yeshiva sphere see, Katz, *Pulmus HaMusar*; Tikochinski, *Torah Scholarship*. Today, the yeshiva community tries to hide the history of resisting the inclusion of *Musar* literature and thought into canonical yeshiva studies. For example, Rabbi Lifkowitz writes, "All the other rabbis and yeshiva directors were inspired to follow Rabbi Israel Slanter's example." (Gold, *Hachzek BaMusar*, 11). In his book, Rabbi Gold decided to open this chapter on the Lithuanian history by speaking openly about the resistance of the traditional yeshivas against the *Musar* ones. Moreover, he asks in the name of his students, "Why must they study *Musar* when so many rabbis in the past were against the *Musar* movement?" (Gold, *Hachzek BaMusar*, 49).

9. Aggadah are non-legalistic texts in the classical rabbinical literature, such as in the Talmud and Midrash.

10. Salanter, *'Or Yisra'el*, 294. See also, Goldberg, *Israel Salanter*, 114–30; Stone, *A Responsible Life*, 73–76.

11. The daily yeshiva schedule is divided into portions, each of which is called a *seder*.

and one cannot imagine a yeshiva without a *seder Musar*. Rabbi Nosson Meir Wachtfogel of blessed memory described how Rabbi Elchonon Wasserman of blessed memory spoke to the "Hafetz Chaim"[12] in praise of a newly opened yeshiva. The "Hafetz Chaim" asked him: "Do they study *Musar* there?" When he replied in the negative, the "Hafetz Chaim" said: "Well then, that yeshiva is not worth a pinch of tobacco."[13]

During the 1890s, a significant disagreement arose among the leaders of the second and third generations of the *Musar* movement, leading to a schism between two main streams. One of these was the Slabodka method, the brainchild of Rabbi Nosson Tzvi Finkel (1849–1927), known as *"Der Alter fun Slabodka"* ("The Grandfather of Slabodka"); the second was the Novardok method, established by Rabbi Yosef Yozel Horwitz (1850–1919), known as *"Der Alter of Novardok."* ("The Grandfather of Novardok").[14] The heart of their contention concerned human nature and its implications for how humans should live their lives. The school of Novardok continued Rabbi Salanter's basically pessimistic view of human nature. For the "Grandfather from Novardok," human beings incline fundamentally to sinfulness, given the constant pressure of a powerful urge to transgress divine laws. The role of Jewish ethics (i.e. the *Musar* teachings) is, then, to foster an existential approach to instinctual elements in human nature, first by deconstructing a person's sinful instincts, and then and then by rebuilding a new person worthy of standing in the presence of God.[15]

The "Grandfather of Slabodka," on the other hand, was more optimistic, viewing the human being as created in the very image of God and exalted by nature. The role of ethics, for the Slabodka method, is to enhance the positive aspects of humanity and to nurture human faith in moral goodness. The Slabodka philosophy endeavored to emulate the European "honor system" and to create a Jewish yeshiva student who sees himself as equal in honor to secular Europeans.[16]

---

12. "Hafetz Chaim" is the honorific pseudonym of Rabbi Israel Meir from Radin.

13. Gold, *Hachzek BaMusar,* 59. On the structure of the yeshiva, see, Stampfer, *Lithuanian Yeshivas.*

14. It should be noted that there have been other *Musar* methods. One example is that of Kelm, which was founded by Rabbi Simcha Zissel Ziv Broida. His honorific pseudonym is the "Grandfather of Kelm."

15. Ben-Artzi, *Novardok*; Goldberg, *Israel Salanter,* 129–53.

16. Goldberg, *Israel Salanter,* 154–78; Brown, "Human Greatness and Human

Despite these differences, however, the two prominent *Musar* methods shared much common ground, especially in their agreement on the ability of humanity to reach its destination by dedicating itself to the *Musar* way of life. Unlike other approaches in Lithuanian theology that we shall meet later, the Slabodka and Novardok methods were both unwavering in their conviction, that when a man walks the right path, he should not worry about his inner scruples. Rather, he should rely on his conscience, without fearing that it has been corrupted by the evil inclination.

The active teaching years of the two "Grandfathers" (of Slabodka and Novardok) marked the golden age of the Lithuanian *Musar* movement. Their students established numerous *Musar* yeshivas, whose influence extended beyond their walls and across the whole Lithuanian Jewish community. Even yeshivas that historically opposed the *Musar* movement, refusing to include *Musar* writings in their curriculum, could not for long ignore the existence of the movement; they were required to explain their opposition, and found themselves in a defensive position.

After the death of the "Grandfathers," and especially after the Holocaust, which led to the destruction of both the Lithuanian Jewish communities and the world of the yeshivas, the *Musar* movement lost much of its power.[17] This appears to be due in part to the strong desire of the Lithuanian hegemony to revitalize the community, and especially the yeshiva institutions, after the catastrophe. They decided to do this by reverting to the traditional yeshiva texts of the Talmud and the Responsa literature,[18] thus requiring that yeshiva students spend most of their time re-engaging with the Talmud, rather than exploring other writings, including those of *Musar*:

> In this generation, after the destruction of [Jewish society] in Europe, when the centers of the Torah were destroyed and the world became desolate . . . , the supreme mission imposed upon the Jewish communities in Israel and in the USA was to rebuild

---

Diminution," 244–45; Katz, *Tenu'at HaMusar,* Vol. 3, 97. In chapter 8, I will explore the thought of Slabodka in detail.

17. Tikochinski, "Land of Israel," 235–36. It is important to note that the "Grandfather of Slabodka" immigrated to Palestine in 1924. Therefore, the center of the method shifted from Lithuania to the land of Israel. The transition to Palestine before the Holocaust strengthened the status of Slabodka in Palestine and later in the State of Israel, compared to other *Musar* movements. See Tikochinski, "Land of Israel."

18. The Responsa literature focuses on Jewish law and how the rabbis made decisions through reading the Talmud and its interpretations.

[Jewish life] from the ruins ..., without becoming distracted by anything marginal or external.[19]

In chapter 8, I will explain in detail how The *Musar* methods of both Novardok and Slabodka were closely connected to the general European culture that preceded the events of the Holocaust and were virtually extinguished after World War II. Subsequent cultural changes in European society in general, and in Jewish society in particular, dictated a need for the creation of new *Musar* literature. Reflecting on the horror of war and the debasing of human behavior during the Holocaust, the *Musar* movement was forced to reexamine its faith in humanity and in the ability of people to trust each other. In addition, one of the main leaders of the Lithuanian community in Israel after the Holocaust was Rabbi Karelitz (known as the "*Chazon Ish*"), who openly opposed the *Musar* movement.[20] It is only natural, then, that it was harder for the *Musar* teachers to regain their hegemonic status, at least in the yeshivas of Israel. From that time and until the present day, as we shall see, the *Musar* movement has had to continually reconsider its basic assumptions and to exercise caution in promulgating its beliefs and methods.

Today, in a typical Lithuanian yeshiva, personal reflection on the *Musar* literature is introduced for half an hour at the end of each day of study, when the students are already exhausted after many hours of Talmud.[21] In addition, once a week, the *Musar* leader of the yeshiva (known

---

19. Kotler, *Kuntres Keter-HaTorah*, 31–32. See also Finkelman, "An Ideology for American Yeshiva Students."

20. Brown, *The Hazon Ish*; Kaplan, "Hazon Ish"; Englander, "The Conception of the Human Being." Rabbi Avraham Yeshaya Karelitz (1878–1953) is known by the honorific pseudonym *Chazon Ish* (the title of his most famous work). Upon his arrival in Palestine, he became a luminary of the post-Holocaust community, and until his death was regarded as the most prominent leader of Lithuanian Ultra-Orthodoxy world-wide. He is known for his writings on the Talmud and Maimonides, for his modest life-style, and for his strict and clear ideology. According to Ultra-Orthodox lore, it was Rabbi Karelitz who convinced the first Prime Minister of Israel, David Ben-Gurion, to release yeshiva students (there were only a few hundred at that time) from military service. In addition to *Chazon Ish* his famous series on the halakhic writings of Maimonides. He is known also for his book on faith *Emunah U'Bitachon*.

21. In a eulogy for Rabbi Shmuel Rozovsky (one of the heads of the Ponevezh yeshiva), a student said that Rabbi Shmuel Rozovsky spoke to him about the Talmud during the *Musar* portion of the day (*Seder Musar*), and when he saw Rabbi Yechezkel Levenstein (the *Musar* leader in the Ponevezh yeshiva) he ran and hid: http://www.shtaygen.co.il/?CategoryID=851&ArticleID=5686). Another example of the tension between *Musar* and Talmudic studies appears in the description of Rabbi Lefkowitz,

in Hebrew as the *Mashgiach*, whose main role is to facilitate the ethical and spiritual growth of the students) teaches a session on various aspects of *Musar*. Then, on Shabbat, one of the heads of the yeshiva (appointed to his position because of his knowledge of Talmud, not of *Musar*) gives a short lecture, partly on the weekly portion of the Torah and partly on a *Musar* subject. On most occasions the style of these lectures is very logical, in the mold of Lithuanian Talmudic study, and the speaker will employ a *Musar* text in order to prove the logic of his Talmudic argument rather than the other way around.

A session of the kind just described, devoted to *Musar* studies, is referred to as "*Seder Musar.*" Generally, a text chosen for a *Seder Musar* will be drawn from classical medieval *Musar* sources, not the later Lithuanian *Musar* movement. *Chovot HaLevavot* (*Duties of the Heart*, written in 1080), and *Mesillat Yesharim* (*Path of the Upright*, written in 1740) are the most popular texts. In an effort to restore the reputation of *Musar* in the eyes of their students, teachers who present a *Seder Musar* may choose to quote with admiration a passage of *Musar* literature composed by leaders of the community already well known for their Talmudic scholarship.[22]

Today, very few yeshiva students are familiar with the writings of the originators of the *Musar* movement. Almost no remnant can be found of the unique *Musar* spiritual gatherings (*Va'ad Ha-Musari*), which were intimate meetings of the *Musar* rabbi with a select few of his elite students and a regular feature in the *Musar* yeshivas in Europe before the Holocaust. After a long day of Talmud sessions, many contemporary yeshiva students opt out of the daily *Seder Musar*, preferring to use this short period to rest, chat, or have a smoke, before joining in the evening prayer and then returning to Talmud study. Rabbi Gold has described the negative attitude towards the *Musar* teachings in contemporary yeshiva life:

---

at the transition time between Talmudic studies and the half-hour dedicated to *Musar* studies: "In the Lithuanian Slabodka yeshiva, the *Musar* instructor, when it was time to close the Talmud and turn to study of *Musar*, would signal the transition by rapping with his knuckles on the table. Often, he would raise his hand, ready to give the signal, and pause. 'The students are so deeply engrossed in Talmud,' he thought, 'how can I disturb them?' He would raise his hand again . . . and again, until finally he would force himself to rap out the signal to turn to *Musar* study." (Lefkowitz, *Darkei Chaim*, Vol. 1, 152–53).

22. Gold, *Hachzek BaMusar*, 14.

> It is a now simply a fact that in our yeshivas we treat *Musar* teachings with indifference; its teachings, thought, and discourse attract no attention or interest. No one has even considered how dangerous this indifference is, not only during the years students spend at the yeshiva, but for the rest of their lives as well! . . . One may find Jewish scholars who are ignorant of Mishna tractates like *Teharot and Kodshim* ["Purity" and "Sacrifices"—portions of the Jewish law rarely studied in yeshivas], but a scholar who knows nothing of Jewish ethics and the foundations of the Torah is nothing but *'am ha'aretz*![23] What kind of wisdom does such a scholar have?[24]

One of the fundamental principles of the *Musar* teachings is the natural relationship between theoretical study and the concrete actuality of human life. Yeshiva students may find themselves studying Talmudic texts as a purely theoretical exercise, cut off from their daily lives, and often even from the practice of Jewish law. *Musar*, however, may emphatically *not* be studied as a theoretical text, divorced from the existential contingencies of life. From its beginning, the goal of *Musar* teachings has always been to introduce wisdom into the everyday life of students.[25] Today, *Musar* is encountered by most yeshiva students *en passant*, as they study a Talmudic page, without any basic sense that the study of *Musar* must lead to concrete action.

In summary, there is no question that the status of the *Musar* movement suffered greatly after the Holocaust. Nevertheless, the *Musar* genre is still the literature that all Lithuanian men will go to when they have existential questions in their lives, and when they want a Jewish view on ethics.

Most of the pre-Holocaust leaders of "The World of *Musar*" (*'Olam HaMusar*) died between the 1950s and the 1980s, among them Rabbi Eliyahu Dessler (Ponevezh Yeshiva), Rabbi Yechezkel Levenstein (Mir and Ponevezh Yeshivas), Rabbi Eliyahu Lopian (Knesset Chizkiyahu Yeshiva), and others. By the eighties, Judaism had lost a generation of students who had received the *Musar* teachings as young adults in Lithuania before the Holocaust, and who had survived to transfer the aura of

---

23. "Earth-folk"—a Talmudic reference to people lacking in cultural knowledge, often described as untrustworthy or even savage.

24. Gold, *Hachzek BaMusar*, 46.

25. In some *Musar* yeshivas in Lithuania, there was a designated time, called *Bursa*, to connect theoretical studies to life itself.

the European yeshivas to Israel and the USA—people like Rabbi Shlomo Wolbe (Be'er Yaakov Yeshiva), Rabbi Chaim Friedlander (Ponevezh Yeshiva), Rabbi Sholom Mordechai Schwadron—known as the "Maggid of Jerusalem"—(Hebron yeshiva), and others.

The students of these teachers, in their turn, are currently in positions of leadership in the Lithuanian "World of *Musar*." While they continue to grapple with the classical *Musar* questions regarding human nature and the role of human agents in the world, it is easy to see the significant differences between the current generation of leaders and their teachers. The most obvious of these differences concerns the role of the body. Before the Holocaust, as a result of European influence, the *Musar* movement emphasized the human psyche; questions concerning the body were secondary. Today, due to Western society's increasing interest in the body in the second half of the twentieth century, the *Musar* movement has gradually started focusing on the role of the body as well.

In his scholarly works, Jonathan Garb identifies a new blossoming of the *Musar* teachings in the yeshiva sphere in the first decade of the twenty-first century.[26] The main goal of the Lithuanian community—that is, the rebuilding of "The World of Torah" in Israel and the United States—has been achieved, and immediate fears that Ultra-Orthodox society will not survive have been allayed. It can be assumed, then, that this new and calmer reality encourages the leaders to feel more confidence, and relax their previous demand for focus on the knowledge of the Talmud; now, they are more free to allow their students more time for self-examination through *Musar* teachings.

In addition, we must consider that in recent decades, Jewish Ultra-Orthodox society is grappling with new temptations and seductions, (both real and imagined), especially in light of the increased availability of interactive media and virtual realities, from which yeshiva students are not exempt. Young Jewish men are now exposed to Western culture at a more rapid pace, requiring that their rabbis resolve more existential questions arising from daily life in modern times, so that finally *Musar* teachers must now respond to these challenges with new and contemporary *Musar* teachings.

---

26. Garb, "Towards the Study of the Spiritual-Mystical Renaissance in the Contemporary Ashkenazi Haredi World in Israel." It is important to mention the influence of the Kabbalah and Hasidic theologies on Lithuanian thought. See Garb, *The Chosen Will Become Herds*, 21–36.

B. The Status of the *Musar* Text

Despite substantial changes in the status of *Musar* leaders after the Holocaust, they clearly remain part of the Lithuanian Ultra-Orthodox hegemony, and thus benefit from its "cultural capital" (in Pierre Bourdieu's sense) and from their ability to influence the opinions of community members.[27] When members of the community, including Talmudic yeshiva leaders, wonder, for example, about the proper relationship of a Jewish man to his body, they will undoubtedly turn to *Musar* teachings.[28]

Current *Musar* writings can be divided into two subgenres, each unique in its style and purpose. In the first category, I include transcriptions of oral ethical teachings, delivered in weekly yeshiva lectures by *Musar* rabbis and written down by their students. These are devoted mostly to clarifications of the meaning of the daily Torah portions, of holidays in the Jewish calendar, and of other events, like *yahrzeit*.[29] In the majority of these, the rabbis do not try to construct a well-organized philosophical or ethical system through their oral teachings.

The second category of current *Musar* writings comprises more systematic theological and ethical works. These books, which are rare, aspire to present clear Jewish theological answers to *Musar* challenges and ethical questions concerning the nature of human beings and their role in life.

Recent decades have brought numerous new *Musar* writings, distinctly different in content and style. *Alei Sure*, written by Rabbi Shlomo Wolbe, has become one of the foundational works of contemporary *Musar*. In this unique book, one can find, for the first time, a dialogue on sensitive subjects like sexuality.[30] While traditional *Musar* writers imme-

27. Robbins, *The Work of Pierre Bourdieu*.

28. One popular exception, written by Rabbi Chaim Shmuelevitz—*Sichot Musar* (Shmuelevitz, *Sichot Musar*)—uses primarily Talmudic and Midrash sources including Maimonides. My assumption is that the success of his book is because of its simple and colorful writings and its reliance on Jewish sources known and loved in yeshiva discourse. It seems that his book should not be considered part of the *Musar* genre. Rabbi Shmuelevitz did not serve as a *Musar* leader, but as head of a yeshiva. His book uses lectures that he gave in his final years in the yeshiva, and anyone advanced in *Musar* teachings can feel that the Shmuelevitz does not speak in the language and tone of *Musar*, but rather in the Talmudic style. Rabbi Chaim Leib Shmuelevitz (1902–1979) was head of the Mir Yeshiva in Poland, in Shanghai, and later in Jerusalem).

29. Memorial Day. The myths surrounding the personalities of the *Musar* leaders will be explored in detail in the second part of the book.

30. See more in chapter 4. Rabbi Shlomo Wolbe (1914–2005) was born in Berlin

diately condemn questions about sexuality as forms of heretical thinking, Rabbi Wolbe asks his readers to suspend judgement and, rather than adopting a hostile stance, to listen carefully to the needs and challenges arising from students' sexual identity and experience.[31] The very fact that Jewish adolescents and young adults are asking questions and raising concerns about sexuality is a sign of honesty and courage for Rabbi Wolbe. His book explicitly integrates Jewish theology with (Western) psychological ideas, clearly endeavoring to build a bridge—to use the old image—"between Jerusalem and Athens."

In his introduction to 'Alei Shur, Rabbi Wolbe forestalls negative reviews of his work in the Ultra-Orthodox community, pointing out that none of his ideas are new, and that he is simply translating ideas of the founders of the *Musar* movement into a more contemporary idiom. Standing on the shoulders of previous generations of *Musar* rabbis is a frequent claim for Lithuanian Ultra-Orthodox leaders interested in bringing innovation to the community.[32] Innovative writings are often said to reflect teachings previously taught orally by respected and credible leaders of the community who have since passed away, leaving to younger rabbis the role of committing those oral teachings to writing.[33]

Especially in the State of Israel, genres not found previously in the Lithuanian *Musar* writings have been published in recent decades, authored by rabbis not considered part of the main rabbinic hegemony, who are nevertheless gaining strength within the community. Rabbi Benjamin Hecht's *Shut Libnei Ha-Neurim* (Q&A for adolescents), for example, has the style and structure of traditional Responsa, although the questions are not from interlocutors, but are composed by the author himself. Hecht's book, characterized by open discussion of the personal

---

and studied at Berlin University. He joined the Mir Yeshiva in Poland, and was a student of Rabbi Yeruchom Levovitz. Rabbi Wolbe founded the Be'er Yaakov Yeshiva in Israel, and was one of the prominent Musar leaders in the second part of the twentieth century.

31. Wolbe, *Alei Shur* 1. Rabbi Wolbe's unique perspective is influenced by his engagement with Kabbalah and Hasidic literature. See Garb, "Towards the Study of the Spiritual-Mystical Renaissance in the Contemporary Ashkenazi Haredi World in Israel."

32. Recently, there has been much more courageous literature willing to speak openly about the challenges of the community. One example is the book by Rabbi Gold (2011). Although Gold does not offer new solutions, he openly writes about the challenges of yeshiva students.

33. Wolbe, *Alei Shur* 1, 8.

difficulties of male yeshiva students during their adolescent years, has not been censored by the Ultra-Orthodox hegemony, probably due to the author's wise decision to design his book to resemble a traditional work of *halakha*.³⁴

A further new precedent in the *Musar* genre, this one dealing directly with the body, as its title indicates, is Rabbi Eldad Naker's, *Kol Atzmotai Tomarna: Sfat Ha-Guf KaHalakha* (My Bones Will Speak: The Proper/Halakhic Body Language).³⁵ The great discomfort occasioned by the publication of this work is reflected already in the book's *haskamah*.³⁶ In the case of Rabbi Naker's work, the authors of the *haskamah*—who represent Hasidic as well as Lithuanian hegemonies—display obvious reluctance to sanction a book specifically about the human body, claiming instead that it deals with the relationship between body and soul (or mind), highlighting Rabbi Naker's insights on religious intelligence.³⁷

For his part, Rabbi Naker highlights in his preface the importance of bodily knowledge and the need to learn how to control the body, since the latter influences not only our physical actions, but also our mind and emotions. He goes on to study the physical behavior of famous Jewish sages following traditional Jewish texts. Going further, and citing non-Jewish scientific sources including the practice of Oriental medicine, Rabbi Naker aims to prove that the sages' behavior is valid from a non-Ultra-Orthodox point of view.³⁸ *Kol Atzmotai Tomarna* carefully balances descriptive passages about various parts of the body with practical recommendations concerning, for example, correct sitting posture, how to tilt the head, or how to move different limbs. Several chapters deal with the details of why Ultra-Orthodox men keep their heads covered; others present the correct manner of sleeping, or the right way to relate to communication technologies, or to film and other forms of media.³⁹

---

34. Hecht, *Shut Libnei Ha-Neurim*.

35. Naker, *Kol Atzmotai Tomarna*.

36. (Literally: "agreement")—the equivalent of an *imprimatur* in the Jewish context. Ordinarily, an Ultra-Orthodox Lithuanian book will open with a *haskamah*, including letters from the leaders of the Lithuanian community who vouch for the religious propriety—*kashrut*—of the book in question.

37. Naker, *Kol Atzmotai Tomarna*, 5.

38. Naker, *Kol Atzmotai Tomarna*, 13–24.

39. On proper dress, see chapter 35–39. On the right attitude to media, see chapters 44–48. On sleeping, see chapters 50–51.

A major section of Rabbi's Naker's work addresses the body language of leading Lithuanian rabbis, with portraits of that serve to exemplify and substantiate the author's claims. Only one subject excluded: sexuality; there is no discussion of sexual desire or fulfillment, nor any mention of the relevant bodily organs. It may be assumed that this significant exclusion allowed the Ultra-Orthodox rabbinical hegemony to bestow its *imprimatur* of *kashrut*, despite the book's innovative views.

Considering the special social/religious context of Israel today, with the diffusion of Eastern philosophies and other alternative world-views into the heart of Israeli society, the publication of Rabbi Naker's work is a prime indication of the increasing influence of general Israeli views and mores on Ultra-Orthodox Jewish communities.

In 2008, the first examples of *Musar* composed by Lithuanian Ultra-Orthodox rabbis appeared in the blogosphere. While the rabbis failed to prevent the advent of computers in Ultra-Orthodox homes, they have been largely successful in delaying the spread of the Internet in the *Haredi* (Ultra-Orthodox) private sphere. Nevertheless, Ultra-Orthodox content sites and forums do exist, with growing numbers of followers: the best known are *Kikar Ha-Shabat* ("The Shabbat Square"), *Haredim* ("Ultra-Orthodox") and *Shtaygen* (a Yiddish word expressing deep Talmudic learning). In addition to these, there are some Ultra-Orthodox forum sites, the most famous being *BeHadrei Haredim* ("In the Rooms of Haredim"—a Hebrew pun),[40] with discussion of topics ranging from the daily news to Ultra-Orthodox secret swingers.

Internet contexts like these are constantly growing and gaining new audiences.[41] The Lithuanian hegemony has more than once voiced their disapproval of these sites, and as a result some of them have gone

---

40. Literally: "In the Rooms (*hadarim*) of the Ultra-Orthodox (*haredim*)"—a word-play on the familiar term *behadrei hadarim* ("in the rooms of rooms"), meaning the secret things hidden in the inner rooms of the house. The site's moniker hints at the fact that the Internet is allowing hidden feelings to be made known.

41. The rabbinic hegemony understands that the Internet must be used for work, especially by women, who are the main breadwinner of the community. They separate between the work place, where Internet is allowed, and the private sphere, at home, where it is forbidden. Another challenge for the rabbis is the use of the Internet on the mobile phone, which has recently become possible in Israel. The Lithuanian community arranged cheap mobile packages for its members, without Internet access. The Hasidic community is even stricter in its "war" against any Internet usage, on computers or phones.

inactive. Most of them, however, persist, and have slowly become part of normative Ultra-Orthodox media.

Recently, two personal blogs have been launched by bloggers claiming that in their "real" lives they are rabbis in the Lithuanian yeshiva world, although for obvious reasons they prefer to remain anonymous. These blogs are creating an utterly new form of rabbinical discourse. Like the authors of more normative Lithuanian writings, these blogs address traditional Talmudic and halakhic subjects. However, here there is a uniquely bold and open dialogue between the authors of the blogs and readers who respond to them. The intrinsically safe and anonymous nature of the blogosphere admits the possibility of a new kind of relationship between rabbis and students, and most especially between rabbis and women respondents—an important topic to which we will return in a later chapter.

An important element in classical *Musar* tradition is the reverential attitude of *Musar* leaders toward classical Jewish sources. As the renowned psychoanalyst Julia Kristeva writes: "*any text is constructed as a mosaic of quotations*; any *text is the absorption* and transformation of another."[42] In the Lithuanian *Musar* tradition, as part of the wider Jewish tradition, citing quotes and traditional sources are part of the process of writing.

Moreover, Lithuanian Ultra-Orthodox composition is intertextual, in the meaning of this term applied by the Talmud scholar Daniel Boyarin to the Midrashic text:

> The first is that the text is always made up as of conscious and unconscious citation of earlier discourse. The second is that texts may be dialogical in nature—contesting their own assertions as an essential part of the structure of their discourse, again conscious and unconscious, which both constrain and allow the production (not creation) of new texts within the culture....[43]

Any Jewish source—whether from the Bible, Talmud, Midrash, Kabbalah, or Halakha—upon entering the traditional Lithuanian *Musar* canon, is promptly raised to the level of "truth," and does not require further justification. This is true even in cases when these canonical texts disagree with each other. The classical Jewish axiom "*'elu v'elu divrei 'elohim hayim*" ("both these and those are equally words of the living God")

---

42. Kristeva, *Kristeva Reader*, 37.
43. Boyarin, *Intertextuality and the Reading of Midrash*, 12.

shapes the traditional Jewish mind, enabling it to hold together several contradictory texts, seeing them all as part of one divine truth.

Quoting from a classical source without discussing other texts that undermine it is further grounded in the concept of *"yeridat ha-dorot"* ("the decline of the generations"), reflecting a conviction that each generation of teachers is inferior to its predecessor.[44] Accordingly, the current generation should never challenge classical sources already within the Jewish canon. Embracing a total reliance on the Jewish past, *Musar* teachings do not read texts in the light of critical, historical, or scholarly interpretations. The art of writing in the *Musar* movement can be understood as a mosaic, combining texts and text-fragments from different periods and schools, not necessarily related or compatible, without considering the text's cultural background, conditions, or original audience. This absence of any critical criteria helps scholars to identify the ideology of each *Musar* writer, since every cited classical source reflects this particular author's ideological collage.[45]

Lithuanian Ultra-Orthodox *Musar* compositions appeal to readers with previous cultural knowledge, especially those who are familiar with the quoted classical Jewish texts. More importantly, they appeal to those who know the names of the *Musar* authors and identify them as religious/cultural icons, and therefore have no need to justify their positions or challenge their claims. Quotations from prior *Musar* rabbis in contemporary *Musar* writings constitute, above all, the current author's moral manifesto, allowing him to harness the prestige of the historical *Musar* rabbis to his own ideological purposes. *Musar* writers are not overly concerned about the "real" or "original" meaning of their citations. Knowing this, therefore, whether I am reading older or more contemporary *Musar* texts, I avoid trying to force a "reasonable" but artificial distinction between arguments brought forward by the *Musar* writer on his own behalf, and arguments he cites in the name of others. The most creative and fruitful way to read any *Musar* text is to experience it as a unique, original, and independent unit, belonging on some deep level to the mind of the writer.

---

44. In chapter 5, I will introduce the *Musar* method of Rabbi Miller, who disagrees with this perspective.

45. Boyarin, *Intertextuality and the Reading of Midrash*, 23–24.

CHAPTER 2

The Status of the Body in the Teachings of *Musar*

MUSAR TEACHINGS PRIMARILY ADDRESS existential questions that Ultra-Orthodox men must deal with, including the appropriate relationship men should have with their bodies. As we will see in this chapter, *Musar* rabbis all share common assumptions about human nature—assumptions that reveal not only these teachers' image of the body, but also the *Musar* movement's more general perspective on the human condition.

Not only do different body images appear in the Lithuanian *Musar* genre, but changes have been taking place in these images from the 1980s to the present. On one hand are those rabbis who claim that we should resist the bodily dimensions of our human selves. On the other hand are those who, against the majority, insist on establishing a different and more positive relationship with our physical nature. *Musar* teachers from the 1950s to the 1970s spoke mainly about the imaginary-ideal body and how their students should shape it. From the 1980s onward, a growing number have accepted the reality that we are embodied beings. It is fascinating to find that in recent decades, widely seen by the Ultra-Orthodox as an era of ethical decadence, a growing number of voices inside the *Musar* movement are calling for more openness and tolerance in relation to the body.[1] These voices recognize the *real body*, not the imaginary one, as part of who we are, and try to find new ways to involve the body in the Jewish religious way of life. According to these new views, the body is not

---

1. As Rabbi Meir Tzvi Bergman, for example, described the current generation: "Our own generation is a sad example, with its darkness that covers the land and its stormy winds wildly buffeting us from every direction, until we must cling with all our might to every page of the holy Torah, our beleaguered vessel, to save ourselves from the waves that would overwhelm us. For the sea around us is more and more furious and storm-tossed." (Gold, *Hachzek BaMusar*, 14).

only inextricably part of our human identity, but also needs to be part of our dialogue with God.

A. Framing the Problem of the Body

Historically, many schools of Jewish thought have ascribed negative qualities to the human body (passion, weakness, and illness are only few examples), while attributing to the soul everything perceived as noble and spiritual. According to this dualistic-hierarchical approach, to have a body is in effect a disorder that separates humans from their quiddity and self-realization.[2] It is not surprising, then, to find the "problem" of the body surfacing already in the writings of Rabbi Israel Salanter, the founder of the *Musar* movement, and also in the writings of his disciples in the period before the Holocaust. However, there is no doubt that it was only after the Holocaust that the body became a prominent subject in *Musar*, as evidenced by a dramatic increase in the volume of writings on the subject in the second half of the twentieth century.

Until the Holocaust, *Musar* endeavored to understand the conscious and unconscious aspects of the human *soul*—i.e., imagination, passion, will, and mind. The body was regarded as secondary, being nothing but a locus where the unconscious psyche becomes tangible and speaks to us.[3] After the Holocaust, the focus shifts to the body itself, in its own right, as a specific subject of *Musar* investigation. This shift is not unique to the *Musar* movement; it is paralleled by changing attitudes toward the body in Western society from the 1900s and into the twenty-first century.

Before looking at specific *Musar* texts, it is important to reiterate the observation that in this form of religious anthropological thought, a male gender bias is the default mode. *Musar* teachings for yeshiva students concerning the body are primarily concerned with the *male body*; the female body as a "phenomenon" is entirely "other."

Discussion about the role of the body appears in Lithuanian writings in the context of the frequently recurring question: What makes human beings unique? The relevant texts use here the Hebrew term *'adam*, which may mean "human" but is most commonly understood as "man." For *Musar* thinkers, it is of utmost importance to see "man" (*'adam*) as

---

2. Gilman, *The Jew's Body*. Louise Jacobs has pointed out that "Western civilization has a Greek mind, a Roman body, and a Jewish soul" (Strandberg, *Greek Mind, Jewish Soul*, 111).

3. Ross, *Moral Philosophy*; Garb, *Shamanic Trance in Modern Kaballah*.

special and different from all other objects in the world. *Torat HaMusar* offers one clear formula that unites the various opinions, i.e., *man ['adam] differs from other objects because of his ability to reflect upon himself, his choices, and his life.* "Reflection" in this context means to pause amidst the natural rhythm of life and take time to consider human consciousness and existence. In the words of the *Musar*:

> The ability of man ['adam] to develop conscious thought is an expression not only of his superiority to other creatures, but also of his essence, for "to be human ['adam] is to think." . . . The more man ['adam] develops his cognitive ability, then, the stronger his essential identity as "man" [ke-'adam] becomes. . . . Whoever lives and acts without reflective thought . . . is in principle no different from animals, that may be trained to perform all sorts of complex actions, . . . none of which derive from conscious thought, but are merely reactions to various stimuli.[4]

> Man ['adam] is neither a single passage of the Talmud [sugiah] nor even a full volume [masechet]. No!—rather he is "the entire Torah" [torah sh'lemah]! Man, then, must study diligently to know himself. . . . The Sages [hazal][5] tell us that when a man dies, three angels come to him and say, "Stand, and tell us your name." He replies: "As Heaven and Earth are my witness, I do not remember my name." Then one of the angels beats him with a heavy iron chain breaking his bones. . . . We understand from this that the angels' question is not literally about the dead person's name; here, "name" denotes a man's essence [mahut ha-'adam]. The angels are asking him, "What is your essence?" Whoever lives eighty years without knowing who he is—deserves to be beaten. . . . A man's deepest aspect is the essential quality of his being [midotav]. Often, a man has such an erroneous grasp of his own essence, that he can never truly know himself.[6]

From these citations, we can learn some of the fundamental elements and priorities of the *Musar* movement. *Musar* teachers are concerned about

---

4. Friedlander, *Siftey Chaim*, Vol. 2, 85–86. See also Friedlander, *Siftey Chaim*, Vol. 1, 411. The fact that citations are incomplete arises from the nature of Lithuanian writings, which differ greatly from Western academic norms in that they wander from one subject to another.

5. *Hazal* is a Hebrew acronym for: "*hakhameinu zikhronam liv'rakha*"—meaning: "our Sages, may their memory be blessed!"

6. Gold, *Hachzek BaMusar,* 75–77.

the connection between man and nature mostly because humans are *natural beings*, a condition regarded as a burden rather than a blessing. The *Musar* movement is not like some other spiritual traditions, which endeavor to bring humans back to nature and identify reflective thought as a form of alienation from nature. For *Musar* teachers, "human nature" inspires a kind of terror; they would prefer to widen the gap between "man" and nature. They also identify self-reflection, which is uniquely human, as an expression of the image of God in humans. Although nature, too, is certainly the creation of God, the most visible imprint of the divine is found in man. Our role, then, is to explore what is unique to the human condition—and for the *Musar* movement this means the ability to reflect on life by alienating ourselves from nature, even going against some parts of ourselves, in order to find our true meaning in life.

The *Musar* rabbis are aware that one of the unique elements in Orthodox Jewish tradition, compared to other religions and to other movements in contemporary Jewish life, is the emphasis on halakha (Jewish law). In this tradition, *actions* take precedence over feelings and even beliefs, as Orthodox Jews express their faith by performing religious acts and ceremonies, following specific halakhic guidelines. Traditional Jewish literature has focused primarily on the proper specific religious act of the Jewish person, while neglecting mental/psychological reflection.[7] By contrast, the *Musar* teachers invest great effort in a constant state of self-reflection, which they see as the most crucial element in religious life. Rabbi Friedlander writes:

> Even good deeds done habitually, rather than as reflective actions, cause him [the Jew] to live like an animal. A man who rises in the morning, for example, and washes his hands according to the halakha, reciting the morning blessing and the relevant prayers, all out of unreflecting habit—his actions are hardly different from those of a monkey.[8]

Rabbi Gold expresses his critique even more harshly:

> To the extent that a man lives without *Musar* and without self-examination, he is worse than the animals. For an animal's

---

7. For a phenomenological enquiry into the meaning of halakhic actions, see Englander, "The Halakhic Body."

8. Friedlander, *Siftey Chaim*, Vol. 2, 85–86. Rabbi Chaim Friedlander (1923–1986) served as a *Musar* leader in Azata and Ponevezh Yeshivas. He is known for his dedication to the kabalistic teachings of Moshe Chaim Luzzatto (1707–1746) and edited many of his books.

instincts preserve its existence, while a man's instincts destroy him.⁹

According to Gold, those who live without self-examination and self-reflection, even if they care deeply about the details of the Jewish law, do not fulfill their religious obligation. When a man performs the morning blessings automatically, without reflecting on their meaning, it is as if he does not bless at all. The essence of self-reflection is to initiate a conscious thought, separate and different from the natural stream of unconscious impressions and reactions of life. Self-reflection is to suspend the natural flow of our inner cogitations, and to encourage deeper consideration of our mental structure, our actions, and human existence in general.¹⁰

Jewish theologians have always debated the need for *kavanah* (intention) while observing Jewish law. However, with the exception of Jewish mysticism, Jewish theology generally accepts the opinion that for the requirement of *kavanah* to be met, it is enough for one to be aware of performing a Jewish *halakha* and not merely acting from personal volition. The *Musar* literature, on the other hand, uses the principle of *kavanah* in Jewish law as an occasion to practice the meaning of self-reflection, in order to educate the *Musar* person as a reflective being.

Self-reflection requires a pause in the flow of life, and therefore a "disconnect" between the reflective self and the world in which that self exists. For some existential philosophers, such separation from the spontaneous context of life leads to an alienation of human experience from the world, and hence to a profound anxiety:

> The mark of the new consciousness is the discovery that the individual faces the world and existence as a subject faces an object. Human beings are neither part of the world nor of society; they are different from them, observe them, draw a distinction between themselves and the surrounding, and this distinction is itself the experience of alienation. The experience of separation evokes anxiety and leaves us without support.¹¹

However, what may be a philosophical problem in existential literature is seen as a distinct advantage in most of the *Musar* sources, that decry

---

9. Gold, *Hachzek BaMusar*, 121.

10. There is no question that, throughout history, Jewish voices have advocated the necessity of *kavanah* (see, Englander, "The Halakhic Body.") However, these voices do not appear in the writings of the Lithuanian yeshivas before the *Musar* movement.

11. Sagi, *Albert Camus*, 18.

similarities between man and the world, while extolling the differences.[12] For *Musar* thinkers, alienation from nature is positive proof that a man is indeed different from all worldly objects, and aspiring to achieve the true purpose of human life.

Going further, *Musar* describes man, as a self-reflective being, as unique in both the natural and the supernatural worlds. Angels, like animals, lack the capacity for reflection.[13] Since they are so close to the divine, they exist in total devotion, which by definition entails identification with the other through abolition of the self. For angels, free will is demolished before the divine Presence they serve and with whom they desire to be united, leaving no room for a separate existence. No self-reflection, then, can exist among the angels, whose actions are outside the realm of *Musar*.[14]

There is, however, an additional consideration. No man is capable of uninterrupted reflection, and everyone lives a portion of life without reflective thought, in an immediate and concrete fashion. As Rabbi Friedlander puts it: "Most bodily functions, like sight, hearing, and gestures of the hands and legs, happen mechanically."[15] *Musar* teachers acknowledge that life entails concrete, unmediated, and essential particularity, which, as we shall see, must be attributed to the fact that man is an "embodied being."

In recent decades, *Musar* teachers have blamed the current generation for slowly losing the ability to practice self-reflection. In their opinion, the social media revolution has given us the ability to communicate with other people at any moment in life, without the need to share physical space. As a result, we are almost never alone, even for a short period of time. In the current reality, social interaction invades all spheres of life, including moments when in the past we could be alone. More than that: according to the *Musar* teachers, never in history have so many people experienced such deep loneliness, although we are almost never

---

12. A unique exception is Rabbi Wolbe, who does identify alienation between man and nature as problematic. See Wolbe, *Alei Shur 1*, 12–13.

13. Rabbi Yechiel Michel Epstein (1884–1908) wrote that "the angels worship their Creator and are not subject to the evil inclination [*yetser ha-ra'*]; therefore angels do not deserve a reward for their service." (*Aruch HaShulchan*, Orach Chayim, 1:1; note that "service" and "worship" are the same word in Hebrew).

14. Povarsky, *Musar Ve-Daat*, Vol. 1, 198–99. On the meaning of the term devotion in Judaism see, Afterman, *Devequt*.

15. Friedlander, *Siftey Chaim*, Vol. 2, 87.

alone. Paradoxically, this loneliness is related to the loss of our ability to be alone: we are now unaccustomed to listening to our inner selves and reflecting on our lives.[16]

B. The Challenges in Reflective and Unreflective Modes of Existence, and the Choice of the *Musar* Rabbis

According to the *Musar* teachings, both reflective and non-reflective ways of life raise challenges, temptations and dangers, each of which *Musar* students must learn to face and grapple with. But to lead a life without reflection is to leave the gates of the fortress open to the enemy, allowing the evil inclination to take over a man's soul, even as he diligently observes the Jewish law:

> The evil inclination [*yetser ha-ra'*] became active when [the people of] Israel were calm and relaxed, when they were "happily eating and drinking, and strolling about the marketplace."[17] At that moment, the evil inclination found an opening whereby it could invade their hearts. Eating, drinking, enjoying oneself, and strolling about . . . are all permitted actions [according to the halakha]); however, they are still points of weakness.[18]

These words of Rabbi Mordechai Kukis faithfully reflect the spirit of the *Musar* movement in relation to halakha: it is not enough to follow halakhic obligations in order to guard against the evil inclination. Whenever a person is not vigilant, surrendering to the flow of life, the evil inclination threatens to conquer him, no matter how perfectly he may fulfill halakhic requirements.[19] Physical pleasure, writes Kukis, is not dangerous *per se*; rather, pleasure is a signal that an individual is simply enjoying life's vicissitudes, and has stopped being reflective about choices and actions.

The life of contemplation and reflection on human existence, especially reflection on the religious life, is also not without danger, as it may

---

16. See the quotation in the name of Rabbi Avraham Isaac Barzel (Gold, *Hachzek BaMusar*, 18).

17. Yalkut Shimoni, *Neviim*, portion 526.

18. Kukis, *Siach Mordechai*, Vol. 2, 228. See also his explanation of the sin of King David and Bathsheba in the same chapter.

19. See also Rabbi Shmuelevitz's interpretation of the role of Amalek, identified in the Torah as the worst of Israel's enemies. According to Shmuelevitz, this nation was uniquely dangerous since it endeavored to tempt the people of Israel to abandon their duty to reflect on the meaning of their lives. See Shmuelevitz, *Sichot Musar*, 104–5.

lead to heretical thoughts.[20] It is for this reason, historically, that religious devotion has been perceived as contrary to reflection, since the activity of contemplation encourages freedom and an openness to possibilities that are often denied and prohibited by religious institutions. In the words of Avi Sagi:

> A relationship with God that passes through the act of contemplation becomes a problematic relationship, since it opens the possibility that humans will, by their own reflective activity, conflate the will of God with their own personal desires.[21]

Yet another peril lurks in the life of contemplation. While the act of reflection is somewhat contrary to life itself, as we have seen, interrupting the natural flow and spontaneity of human existence, it is also true that pausing to reflect may actually enhance the experience of physical sensations. This can be problematic in the *Musar* tradition, certainly when it comes to sexual desire. Pausing to reflect on the source or nature of a sexual stimulus will hardly help in suppressing a sexual feeling; on the contrary, reflection often intensifies sensations, urging one more forcefully toward an ecstatic sexual experience.[22] As Michel Foucault has shown in his research on sexuality,[23] the prohibition of sexual discourse is an integral part of that discourse.[24] Sexual desire will always find avenues to circumvent explicit prohibitions, via implicit paths into the margins of reflection, and into taboo. Reflection, then, may strum exactly the same strings as the repressed discourse, increasing a desire considered negative and forbidden by *Musar*.[25]

Despite concerns about the dangers inherent in both reflective and non-reflective life, the *Musar* movement unequivocally prefers contemplation as the proper Jewish way of life, believing that man's uniqueness shines forth only when he ponders and reflects on his actions. As Rabbi Elyah Lopian states clearly: "the essence of the study of *Musar* is contemplation."[26] For *Musar* teachers, to pause in the midst of life's flow,

---

20. Friedlander, *Siftey Chaim*, Vol. 2, 88.
21. Sagi, 'Elu va-Elu', 208.
22. Dessler, "Minut Shelo Lishma," 6.
23. See chapter 4.
24. Foucault, *The History of Sexuality*, 1–50.
25. Dessler, "Minut Shelo Lishma," 7.
26. Lopian, *Lev Eliyahu* Vol. 2, 155. See also Friedlander, *Siftey Chaim*, Vol. 1, 86. Rabbi Eliyahu Lopian (1876–1970) served as head of the *Etz Chaim* Yeshiva in

and to observe oneself, is to renounce the evil inclination and take a first step toward achieving the knowledge of what is proper and good.[27]

To this end, *Musar* teachers require, each day, that yeshiva students actually stop their study of Talmud to spend some time reflecting on their lives: "The best and strongest medicine that one may propose against the evil inclination, . . . is that a man pause every day for at least one hour, and empty himself of all his other [mundane] thoughts."[28] The ideal goal of *Musar* is a state of existence where actions occur only after an act of contemplation. A good example is found in Rabbi Friedlander's commentary on the opening passage of a renowned work by Rabbi Moshe Isserles (1520–72). Isserles opens his classical halakhic masterpiece with the words from Psalm 16:8: *shiviti 'adonai lenegdi tamid* ("I keep the LORD always before me")—and adds, "This [way of living] is a great principle of Torah."[29] Rabbi Friedlander quotes Isserles, and then comments:

> The whole purpose of the divine commandments [*ha-mitzvot*] is to give every [Jewish] man the opportunity to be fully aware, that every detail of every halakhic action, and even every one of his voluntary movements—has meaning. . . . Certainly, then, a man should think long and hard about each of his actions. . . . Not only during the action itself, but even before he begins, he should consider, and plan each movement in advance, that all may be done in a way that is most fitting and good, and most pleasing to Him [God].[30]

It is fascinating to note similarities and the differences between *Musar* teachings and other spiritual movements. In the practice of mindfulness, for example, as in other forms of meditation, practitioners learn to pause their daily life in order to "reflect"—i.e., to allow the stream of thoughts to subside, to become closer to nature, and *to simply be*, as nature is, without willful striving. In the *Musar* teachings, on the other hand, "reflection"

London. Later, he became the *Musar* leader of *Knesses Chizkiyahu* Yeshiva in Kfar Hasidim (Israel).

27. Wolbe, *Sichot*, 22–23.
28. Friedlander, *Siftey Chaim, Vol. 1*, 88.
29. *Shulchan Aruch*, Orach Chayim 1:1.
30. Friedlander, *Siftey Chaim, Vol. 1*, 405–6. Friedlander deeply believes in this way of living and claims that the distinction between a person who is under the category of Righteous and one who doesn't under this category depend only on this element of life. In his opinion, the righteous is one who lives almost in complete reflection of his life.

has the opposite intention: not to allow a person to become part of nature, but rather to strengthen his ethical willpower to overcome his nature.[31]

C. The Body as Symbol of an Unreflective Life, and as an Obstacle

The Sleeping Body

Musar teachers are fully aware of the fact that no one is able to live in a state of constant self-reflection. They see a causal link between this inability and the fact that humans are "embodied beings": "For this is the power of the materiality of the human body—that it is filled with desire and hurries to act in everything without prior reflection."[32] Whether a person is awake or asleep, the body at times performs various actions without reflection. When we sleep, we are not completely unaware of events occurring around us, and we may respond quickly and awaken if something threatens us, but these liminal states of alertness are entirely somatic, and do not include any conscious reflection.

This is also true of our dream, which may be described as subliminal mental activities that are, by nature, not amenable to reflection, until after the dream is over. Rabbi Friedlander stresses this inability to be reflective: "In sleep, the bond which unites the soul and the body is loosened, ... and then, in the absence of the soul's light that purifies it, the body is itself more vulnerable [to the evil inclination]."[33] Sleep is perceived in *Musar* literature as a dangerous time, since during sleep the body acts automatically, while the soul—which during the day oversees the actions of the body—is not entirely present. Moreover, dreaming frees those parts of the self that are kept at bay during waking life. A prime example is the occurrence of nocturnal emission, which has been causing generations of rabbis to lose sleep. According to *Musar* teachings, when a man is asleep, the mental element that ordinarily governs his body loses control, and the body surrenders to the "imaginary realm" of sheer physiology. *Musar* emphasizes the urgent need to constantly control the body through

---

31. See for example the writings of Sharon Salzberg and Thích Nhất Hạnh as only two of many examples.
32. Chasman, *Or Yahel*, Vol. 3, 121
33. Friedlander, *Siftey Chaim*, Vol. 1, 413.

contemplation and mental reflection, and these are seen as the only realms within us where we bear the divine image of God.

There are opposing views about sleep in the *Musar* movement, and especially about passions and desires aroused during sleep. Some argue that sexual fantasies (identified with the evil inclination) do not appear during the ordinary number of sleeping hours required for health, but only when someone chooses to sleep longer than necessary. This kind of assertion is based on an assumption that we can maintain a clear division between "good" and "problematic" parts of our lives, and that we can control the evil inclination, even when the natural course of life requires us to forego reflection. The boundary between good and evil may be safeguarded during slumber, for example, if we carefully regulate our hours of sleep.[34] A related approach argues, that if we train our mind and body with constant self-reflection during our waking hours, this will have an influence beyond wakefulness, and give us full control of our mind even during sleep.[35]

These different approaches share the common belief that during sleep the person ceases to exist as a full human being, i.e., as a creature endowed naturally with the divine image and the unique ability to reflect. In the traditional morning prayer of *Modeh 'Ani*, for example, a Jew thanks God for restoring the soul that during the night has left the body to abide in the presence of the divine. Time spent in sleep is clearly not considered part of natural *human* life. This has important implications for traditional Ultra-Orthodox Jewish theology, with its emphasis on living a full life of Torah. Classical Ultra-Orthodox sources, as well as modern *Musar* teachings, speak about the need to engage in sacred study continuously, taking as few breaks as possible. Naturally, sleep is a problem in this context, since during sleep Jewish men do not study Talmud. To identify sleep as a time when the full human self does not exist, allows the rabbis to claim that a Jewish man can learn for his entire life without pause. While awake, he studies the Jewish texts with all his might; when he sleeps, he ceases to exist as a fully human person. When he awakens, after having slept only for the correct amount of time needed to renew his strength, it is as if this new day and the day before were connected continuously.[36]

---

34. Lefkowitz, *Marbe Yeshiva Marbe Chohma*, 87.
35. Schwartz, *Gadlut HaAdam*, 104–13.
36. Lefkowitz, *Ol-Torah*, 10.

An unusual opinion about sleep can be found in the work of Rabbi Eliyahu Dessler, who was influenced by psychoanalytic methods of his time.[37] Dessler claims that what we call the "self" actually does not exist in the conscious realm, but is mostly unconscious. The "self" that is familiar to us during our waking hours is actually only a fragment of the hidden and repressed "real self," that can find free expression only during sleep. Dessler does not claim that it is wrong to reflect during the day, since in the act of contemplation Jewish men try to guide their humanity—which is a combination of the image of God and their own physicality—in the best way they can. However, for Dessler, dreams are gifts that can teach humans about their own mental and spiritual state, and help identify what they need to work on as part of their *Musar* journey.[38]

While they grapple differently with the problem of sleep and especially its attendant sexual fantasies, the various *Musar* teachers share the view that in sleep a man is not fully present as a human being. They also believe that repose is no more than a necessary time to regain strength for the sacred studies of the morrow, when the human soul will return from its nocturnal visit to divine realms, and that the same hidden spiritual energy of the Torah that motivates the Jewish scholar during the day, protects him also during sleep from the evil inclination and sexual fantasies. Sleeping only the correct number of hours is a constant struggle for the rabbis; they seek to give their body rest at the exact moment this is needed, and not an instant earlier. In a biography of Rabbi Avrohom Yeshaya Karelitz, for example, we read:

> For many years he slept two and a half hours a day. He would fall asleep after midnight on the study-table, exhausted from his efforts in studying Torah. Or, he would go to his bed only after receiving the last of the visitors who came to consult him in their search for God. He slept in his clothes, without a pillow under his head, but lying across the bed with his head leaning up against the wall.[39]

---

37. Rabbi Eliyahu Eliezer Dessler (1892–1953) served as a rabbi in England. Later he was ordained as the *Musar* leader of Ponevezh Yeshivain Bnei-Brak. More information about Rabbi Dessler see, Rosenblum, *Rav Dessler*.

38. Dessler, *Michtav me-Eliyahu Vol.* 5, 347 See also there page 127. In the same direction writes Rabbi Moshe Shapira in his unique voice and way of thinking. See Shapira, *Afikey Maim*, 172–77, 212–16.

39. Levi, *Mashal HaAvot al 48 Kinyanei HaTorah, Vol. 1*, 305.

It is very rare that one will find in the Lithuanian *Musar* literature descriptions that are more common in Hasidic hagiographies—namely, stories of rabbis who continue their studies during sleep. Unlike *Musar* tradition, Hasidic theology has created an ontological gap between the spiritual master and the community of his followers, with the former being exempt from the laws of nature and convention that govern the latter. The *Musar* movement, by contrast, teaches that there are no ontological gaps between laity and rabbis; all must abide by the same natural laws. *Musar* rabbis need to sleep like everyone else. A unique exception to this is found in a story about Rabbi Aaron Ha-Cohen, the head of the Hebron Yeshiva:

> Once I went to the home of Rabbi Aaron, and I suggested to him a new idea that had occurred to me while studying [a passage of Talmud]. We discussed the sacred text together for a while, and when we had finished, Rabbi Aaron asked me: "And did you have any new ideas [on the sacred text] while you were asleep?" He seemed surprised when I said, "No." Then, as if he were talking to himself, he said: "God's Torah is a teaching for [all of] life. A man must be so immersed in the study of Torah, that even while he is sleeping, his heart and mind will be absorbed in learning Torah." Then he shared with me a wonderful new insight that had come to his mind during sleep.[40]

The story about Rabbi Karelitz cited above, like tales of many other *Musar* teachers, shows us that the ideal spiritual scholar needs very little sleep.[41] However, in recent decades a growing number of voices from contemporary *Musar* leaders now critique this idealized image. The Lithuanian Ultra-Orthodox model of the "sleepless Jew," they say, is impractical and even dangerous.[42] Sleep deprivation can lead to chronic fatigue, lack of concentration on Talmud study during the day, and a diminishing of the reflective life of *Musar*. In a state of fatigue, Rabbi Gold explains, the natural gap between the waking state and sleep is narrowed. Consequently, a person's unconscious aspects assert themselves, the ability to lead a life of

---

40. Levi, *Mashal HaAvot al 48 Kinyanei HaTorah*, Vol. 1, 306.

41. I will speak on that subjects in more details in chapter 8.

42. There are still some opinions in the *Musar* tradition that encourage yeshiva students to reduce sleeping hours. See Levi, *Mashal HaAvot al 48 Kinyanei HaTorah*, Vol. 1, 301.

contemplation falters, and the evil inclination finds an easy path to exert its influence.[43]

The Body Knows

Not only during sleep, but also during much of our waking hours, our lives are saturated with unconsciousness. Most of our actions, both voluntary and spontaneous, are in fact undertaken without any reflection. We raise a glass of wine to make a toast, turn to the right or to the left, bring the fork to our mouth, pick up our children from school, swerve to avoid an oncoming truck, and even make fateful decisions about our future—all unthinkingly.

Western psychology and philosophy at the beginning of the twentieth century was divided into two opposing schools concerning the meaning of our actions: intellectualism and empiricism. Intellectualism identifies even spontaneous movement as the result of a prior mental decision, an expression of "mental movement" preceding physical movement (the raised physical hand only followed the "mental hand").[44] By contrast, empiricism claimed that physical movement is a circumstantial chain of nerve stimulation and motor muscle mechanics, all transmuted by the brain into a coherent action. In this approach, human knowledge is not by definition a part of physical movement.[45] Rabbi Friedlender meditates on this question and writes:

> Most physical functions, such as sight and hearing, but also many gestures of the hands and legs, occur mechanically. Walking down a staircase, for example, is a complex action, since the foot must measure the height of each step, making adjustments as you go down, or you will find it hard to descend, or even stumble and fall. It sometimes happens that you mistakenly think the stairs have ended, and so you step out as if onto a level floor, and you take a tumble. All this complex activity is performed by the feet on their own, without the participation of the conscious mind. This why we can walk along beside our

---

43. Gold, *Bnei Chail Vol. 1*, 160–65, 312–16; Lefkowitz, *Darkei Chaim*, Vol. 1, 246–47.

44. Such an attitude one can find also in the *Musar* teachings. See Grosbord, "Shilton HaSehel."

45. Merleau-Ponty, *The Phenomenology of Perception*, 84–100.

friend, talking with him all the while, usually without any need to monitor where each foot falls.[46]

Rabbi Friedlander emphasizes here the sheer physicality inherent in human movement. The relationship we have with the world is first of all instinctive and intuitive; only then is it reflexive. Moreover, the human body has the ability to acquire specialized knowledge based on habit, which allows it to move easily and to perform complex tasks simultaneously without the need to reflect on them.

A deeper look at Friedlander's thought will show that neither the intellectualist nor the empiricist approach can be fully consistent with or explanatory of his description of the human body. When Friedlander writes that "most physical functions . . . occur mechanically," he contradicts intellectualism with its assertion that thought activates the body.[47] But he also departs from empiricism, when he says that a person may be fully aware of descending a staircase, yet nevertheless the body is responsible for the action itself, through some kind of inner somatic and independent knowledge that is not reflective. The threefold relationship between the free choice to descend the stairs, the reflection on this decision, and the instinctual knowledge of the body—is never spelled out clearly by Rabbi Friedlander.

Neither intellectualism nor empiricism can account for an essential element of Friedlander's perspective, an element that we have already identified as characteristic of the *Musar* movement as a whole: a deep and pervasive fear of the human body. Intellectualists would argue that the body should not pose a threat to *Musar*, since the intellectualist "self" is entirely unidentified with the body. Empiricists, for their part, would say that the body, although lacking the unique glamor of the mind, is still nothing more than a tool for life, amenable to our conscious control, and thus hardly threatening to *Musar* teachings. In order to understand Friedlander's perspectives on the body's nature, and the visceral aversion to the body found in his *Musar* model, we must turn, rather, to the phenomenology of Maurice Merleau-Ponty. Striking resemblances between the thinking of this French philosopher and of Rabbi Friedlander may, in my opinion, shed light on the problematic and vexing role of the body in the rabbinical system of *Musar*.

---

46. Friedlander, *Siftey Chaim*, Vol. 2, 87.

47. On Merleau-Ponty's phenomenological critique see, Merleau-Ponty, *The Phenomenology of Perception*, 88–89, 233–77.

Merleau-Ponty, writing in the second half of the twentieth century, developed a theory that the human body has intrinsic knowledge unknown to our conscious selves. The body does not wait for a command from the mind to move; rather, *the body moves*. If we needed to control every movement (in the spirit of intellectualism), all movement would be unnatural, sloppy, disjointed, and hesitant. For example, if someone chooses to move an arm in space, the arm basically moves itself. If someone picks up an apple from the table, she does not give an order to her hand; rather, *she/her hand takes the apple*. Most importantly for Merleau-Ponty: bodily organs "know" how to move because, while they are part of the "self," *they are also part of the world outside the "self."*

This description of human existence contains two assertions relevant to our discussion. First, the human person is indeed different from all other objects in the world because of the capability of self-reflection. However, and equally important, each human "self" is also to some extent part of the surrounding world, never completely separate from it. The second assertion is that the mind never completely controls the body, and therefore any attempt to subject physical movements (even conscious movements) to the human mind will fail. Merleau-Ponty shows that the act of reflection itself relies entirely upon the body, since reflection is based on data gathered from interaction with the world, and on the accumulation of physical experiences mediated by the body. Intellectual realization is not exempt: it too is conditioned by the sum total of physical information that plays a part in forming our mental consciousness.

Rabbi Friedlander perceives the body as a threat, not only because it stands in contrast to the act of spiritual reflection, but also because it carries unique knowledge, selected and accumulated without the supervision of our conscious awareness. This is one source of the moral danger that *Musar* writers recognize in physical existence. In a similar vein, Merleau-Ponty teaches in his phenomenological work that human decisions are based on semi-automatic bodily knowledge. If this is true, then what else does the body "know"? What other reflective instances can be attributed to the body? If we admit that there is some sort of bodily effect on our consciousness, how can we determine exactly the extent of this effect? Questions like these reflect these the fears lurking behind the idealistic aspirations of the *Musar* movement, and they come into clearer focus through Merleau-Ponty's phenomenological work. *Musar* teachers cannot adhere to a simple ethical ideal of the human body; eventually they must pay closer attention to those physical realms of action that evade the conscious control of the reflective mind. Although Merleau-Ponty is not known to the *Musar* rabbis, his insights are not at all strange to them. They are deeply disturbed by the burgeoning of physical knowledge, as we shall see.

The body carries within itself its own knowledge. This has led many *Musar* teachers to identify this knowledge with the evil inclination (*yetser ha-ra'*) of Jewish tradition. Such an identification would brand the body as a potential obstacle to any innocent attempt to perform a *mitzvah*—a good deed prescribed by divine law. In this context, heeding the body acquires a religious meaning: the body reveals its nefarious motives to those who devote themselves to careful listening. Thus, in the words of Rabbi Yechezkel Levenstein:

> In *Avot de Rabbi Nathan*[48] a midrash interprets how the evil inclination governs a man ['*adam*]. When he goes to fulfill a good deed, all his limbs resist his progress. But [when he goes] to commit a sin, all his limbs rush to hurry him on his way. In this way, any one of us can know, if an action that we intend to do for the sake of Heaven, is really for the sake of Heaven. For if we feel any kind of physical urge toward an action, then clearly it is not for the sake of Heaven. And if, when beginning an action, we feel no resistance from our body's desires, then this is already a sign that our intention is not entirely for the sake of Heaven.[49]

Levenstein's insight here is fascinating, since he identifies the body as the only litmus test for the right service of God. Human consciousness, he says, cannot in itself be trusted; it is subjective, biased and influenced by the evil inclination. In fact, it is *only the body* that is the locus of ethical awareness—not the mind or the disembodied conscience. The body alone has a truly "objective" knowledge, not conditioned by religious/cultural dictates of moral approval or disapproval. In this system of innate knowledge—or "body ethics"—the body defines truth, since a human being can know that an action is right, *only when the body transmits a strong negative signal of resistance to that action*. In other words, in a sort of ethical *via negativa*, if our own desire urges us toward an action, and we receive no sign of resistance from the body, then we are surely on the pathway to sin, and we should refrain.

---

48. Jewish Aggadic work, 700–900 CE.

49. Levenstein, *MeMizrach Shemesh: Bamidbar*, 43. Rabbi Yechezkel Levenstein (1895–1974) was the *Musar* leader of many yeshivas, including Mir and Ponovezh.

Ken Wilber, a contemporary writer whose focus is on the spiritual life, emphasizes the artificial choice humans make to create boundaries in their lives, in order to forge a clear distinction between good and evil, between what is safe and what is dangerous. Society, by creating boundaries, aspires to "progress," but this will fail:

> For in seeking to accentuate the positive and eliminate the negative, we have forgotten entirely that the positive is defined only in terms of the negative. The opposites might indeed be as different as night and day, but the essential point is that without night we would not even be able to recognize something called day. To destroy the negative is, at the same time, to destroy all possibility of enjoying the positive. Thus, the more we succeed in this adventure of progress, the more we actually fail, and hence the more acute becomes our sense of total frustration.[50]

Any society striving to maintain such an artificial distinction between good and evil preserves its boundaries by gradually pushing out elements that were once part of the "pure" and the "good." This is inevitable as more and more elements that were once identified as good fail to live up to the demands of the society within that boundary.

Levenstein's theology bears out Wilber's theory. The *Musar* movement begins by identifying some elements in a Jew's life as "good" and others as "bad." Levenstein pursues the inevitable logic of this boundary, gradually forcing more and more mental activities outside the definition of "good." Eventually, he reaches an impasse where the category of "good" becomes empty, and all he has left to work with is the human body, which he identifies as completely evil. Reflective thought, once identified positively with the divine image in every human being, can no more be relied upon now than any other thought. A Jew seeking the right path is now reduced to relying only on the body, and only because—as the incarnation of the evil inclination—it can be counted upon to resist an action that is virtuous.[51]

The body and its "knowledge" force the *Musar* movement into uncharted ethical territory. In contrast to the negative approach of Friedlander and Levenstein, Rabbi Wolbe recognizes the virtues of bodily desire and tries to characterize the unreflective way of the body in a positive light, as a set of instincts that are responsible for the continuation

---

50. Wilber, *No Boundaries*, 27.
51. Wilber, *No Boundaries*, 27.

of the human species. Still, we are left with a profound question, since Wolbe stresses that there is no true understanding of the "Why" of life within the unconscious forces that preserve it:

> Bodily forces are blind. . . . The lust for life compels us to take care of our health, and every danger activates all of our survival instincts, to keep the ember of life burning. Our sexual desire urges us to build a home and have children. . . . All of these forces, then, are excellent guardians for us humans. But why do they guard us? They do not know, for they are blind.[52]

D. The Angel and the Pig: Making Spiritual Sense of the Body

Musar writers express their aversion for, and fear and rejection of, the human body in harsh literary images, often accompanied with lists of guidelines for proper physical conduct. Readers of these works discover that the body does not represent only itself, but stands for all that is reprehensible about an unreflective human existence. Rabbi Yehuda Leib Chasman expresses this vividly:

> Wherever a man turns, whether to the most holy place or the most abominable, the angel and the pig are there, tightly bound to each other, yoked together inseparably. If a man goes to offer a holy sacrifice requiring pure, worthy and sinless thoughts, still he knows that the part of him formed of the "dust of the earth"[53] is always present. It is urgent that a man take utmost care, so easy is it for him to exchange the service ['*avodah*] of the Holy One, Blessed be He, with the worship ['*avodah*] of his own body, wanting what the body wants, thus defiling the pure and materializing the spiritual.[54]

The Gordian knot binding the human soul to the body is a central dilemma of classical dualism; here, Chasman employs the more Jewish images of angel and pig. The pig symbolizes impurity and evil in Jewish tradition, and the angel purity of mind and absolute good. Here, they are "yoked together inseparably."

---

52. Wolbe, *Alei Shur* 1, 143.
53. Gen 2:7.
54. Chasman, *Or Yahel*, Vol. 3, 87.

Chasman simultaneously separates and connects man from and to his body. While *Musar* teachings do not identify a man entirely as a "bodily being," still, in his personal experience, body and soul are inextricably related. The pious Jew is condemned to live forever, as Rabbi Levinstein implied, in the shadow of the fear that his good deeds are inspired by a blind and improper physical desire. However, despite his negative view of bodily motives, Chasman does not take Levinstein's extreme position that any expression of physical desire necessarily proves that a man is in the grip of the evil inclination. For Levinstein, and many like him, the human body is simply not capable of spiritual greatness. Rabbi Dov Povarsky, speaking of the holy season of Rosh Hashanah (the Jewish New Year), puts it this way:

> Let us define our situation more precisely: certainly, we approach Rosh Hashanah with our body! With this simple, corporal body of ours, we [make as if] to draw near to the holy day! But our Sages [*Chazal*][55] have already told us: "When Moses ascended to the Heights, [to receive the Torah], the ministering angels said before the Holy One, 'Blessed is He: Master of the Universe, what is someone born of a woman doing among us?' God said to them: 'He has come to receive the Torah.' They said before Him: 'The coveted and treasured [Torah] that was stored by You 974 generations before the world was created, and You intend to give that to flesh and blood?'"[56] The Grandfather,[57] of blessed memory, explained this as follows: the angels were asserting, that the fact that Moses comes to receive the Torah is of itself [*gufa'*] a sin, for here a man born of woman, a man with a body [*guf*][58], approaches to touch the Torah! Let us now imagine with what kind of "body" Moses approached [to receive the Torah]! His is a body of which scripture says: "He (Moses) ascended on high [into Heaven]," and, He "neither ate bread [nor drank water]."[59] And yet, for all that, the ministering angels assert that [even with such an exalted body as Moses had] it is impossible to approach the Torah! How then can we, with our [very

---

55. An acronym for Hebrew "Hakhameinu Zikhronam Lib'rakha"—Our Sages, may their memory be blessed

56. *Talmud Bavli*, Shabbat 88b.

57. Rabbi Salanter, the founder of the *Musar* movement

58. 'The Grandfather' plays on words here, relating the Aramaic term *gufa'* (meaning "of itself") to its Hebrew cognate *guf* (meaning "body"). The clear implication is: "the body [*guf*] is of itself [*gufa'*] sinful!"

59. Deut. 9:9.

ordinary] bodies, dare to approach the [Torah observance] of Rosh Hashanah, and to recite *Malkhuyot*?[60]|[61]

In this fascinating passage, when the angels call Moses "flesh and blood," this is a derogatory reference to aspects of the body so base that they do not even possess "feeling." In addition, Moses is twice called "born of a woman"; this too is derogatory, since in this Jewish Ultra-Orthodox tradition, woman is not identified with Torah study. The fundamental problem, for Povarsky, is not physical desire *per se*, but rather the very fact that every Jew is not only himself a "bodily being," but also the offspring of another body (his mother's), that is not by nature sheltered under the wings of the Torah.

This point is essential for understanding Povarsky's argument. Moses is not hindered by his physical desires or needs, for scripture tells us not only that he "neither ate bread [nor drank water], but that he was able to 'ascend [bodily] on high' (i.e. into Heaven)."[62] And yet, even his exalted devotion to holiness cannot erase the fact that Moses is a "bodily being"; therefore it should be impossible—say the angels—for him to approach and receive the Torah. In fact, Povarsky strongly implies that the very desire to approach the holy is, for an "embodied being," sinful—a confounding assertion for yeshiva students who devote their lives to approaching the holy through Talmud and *Musar* studies! Povarsky's citation of Rabbi Salanter ("The Grandfather") is carefully crafted to include, as we have noted, the Hebrew/Aramaic word-play: to approach Torah with a body (*guf*) is of itself sinful (*zeh gufa chet*), consciously or unconsciously, Provarsky makes it clear that for a "bodily being" to desire to touch the holy is intrinsically sinful.

The pious Jew is now caught in a trap. He cannot free himself from the sin he carries in his body, for he is by nature an "embodied being." On the other hand, as an Ultra-Orthodox man he cannot release himself from his fervent desire to touch the holy Torah, through his required Talmud studies. His forbidden desire for sanctity is itself an occasion of constant guilt.[63]

---

60. *Malkhuyot* means literally "Sovereignties"—a portion of the special prayers for the Rosh Hashanah service.

61. Povarsky, *Musar Ve-Daat: Yemei HaRachmim VeHadin*, 42–43. Rabbi Dovid Povarsky (1902–1999) was head of the Ponevezh Yeshiva in Bnei-Brak.

62. Deut. 30:12.

63. The connection between the body and sin appear many times in the *Musar* literature. See for example, "but sin belongs only to the body" (Weintraub, *HaChodesh*

The midrash about the angels arguing that the Torah should not be given to someone "born of a woman" is quoted by Povarsky from the Babylonian Talmud. It is fascinating to note that he omits what follows in that same passage—i.e., the convincing response of Moses himself. Having heard the angels' assertions, Moses addresses God:

> [Moses] said before Him: Master of the Universe, the Torah that You are giving me, what is written in it? [God said to him]: "Remember the Shabbat day to sanctify it." [Moses asked the angels]: Do you engage in any labor from which you would need to rest? . . . What else is written in it? "You shall not murder, you shall not commit adultery, you shall not steal." Moses asked the angels: Is there envy among you, or is there an Evil inclination among you? Immediately they conceded to the Holy One, Blessed be He.[64]

The message of this midrash is unequivocal: the Torah was given specifically to humankind and not to angels, because only human beings, who are "embodied beings," can perform the commandments of the Torah in practice. Embedded in the human body, limited and defective as it is, an advantage over the angels is hidden: the body, in other words, does not make humans as inferior as one might think.

The Talmud does not intend to imply that angels are incapable of obeying divine commands. Angels, in fact, never commit murder, adultery, or theft. But this is because they lack the evil inclination that would prompt them to do so, not because they are virtuous. The good behavior of an angel simply "happens"—it is not the result of reflection and choice. Only humans, who experience the temptation of a desire to sin, are also able to consciously choose an act of reflection and a meaningful decision to do good, or to do evil.

Knowing Povarsky's stated bias ("the body is of itself sinful!") we are now not surprised that he chooses to omit from his teaching the answer Moses gives to the angels' assertions. The full midrash teaches, that "embodied beings"—in fact *only they!*—may "ascend on high" to receive the Torah. Only men, by their very nature as "bodily beings," have the ability to resist evil and live according to *Musar* teachings. Povarsky, however, by

---

HaShvii, 85).

64. *Talmud Bavli*, Shabbat 89a.

the pedantic device of dismissing the reply of Moses, contrives to imply that a man's physical nature must forever be a source of shame.[65]

***

So far we have focused on how the *Musar* movement perceives the body as a kind of "secret agent" (with hidden knowledge and disguised desires) engaged in constant subterfuge against the reflective way of life. The pious Jew must first neutralize his body's active natural opposition to observing the sacred Jewish law, and then train the body to become a passive conductor of holiness.[66] The body, paradoxically, is the condition for fulfilling the divine commandments of the halakha, through a struggle to remove the resistance that the body itself presents. In this context, it is interesting to examine a particularly bold ethical approach that is absent from *Musar* literature but sometimes appears in Hasidic teachings. Rabbi Abraham Chaim from Zlotchov wrote:[67]

> Rabbi Dov Baer[68] explained this passage from the Talmud: "I [the LORD] created the evil inclination, and I created Torah as its antidote (*tavlin*—literally: 'herb')."[69] Apparently, this analogy is out of place, since when we spice our meat with an herb

---

65. Rabbi Dov Zochowski also quotes the midrash on the challenge of the angels and the answer of Moses, and his interpretation is the opposite of Povarsky's explanation. For Zochowski, the reply of Moses emphasizes the responsibility of humans to choose how they will lead their lives, exactly because they have a body, unlike the angels. See Zochowski *"Gadlut HaAdam."* It is important to note that Povarsky himself, elsewhere in his writings, does cite the answer of Moses to the angels. See Povarsky, *Musar Ve-Daat*, Vol. 1, 198–99.

66. Lopian, *Lev Eliyahu Vol. 1*, 24.

67. Rabbi Abraham Chaim from Zlotchov was a Hasidic master who died in 1848. Among his disciples we find Rabbi Yechiel Michel of Zlotchov and Rabbi Shmelke of Nikolsburg, both representing the third generation of the Hasidic movement.

68. Referring to the Rabbi of Mezeritch whose honorific pseudonym is "The Magid of Mezeritch."

69. The Hebrew *tavlin* means "herb." This may be a "spice" (usually applied to savor meat), or—as here—it may denote a substance for healing, since herbs (*tavlinim*) were used in both contexts. The full citation from Talmud Bavli, Kidushin 30b reads: "So too the Holy One, Blessed be He, said to Israel: 'My children, I created the evil inclination, which is the wound, and I [also] created Torah as its antidote [*tavlin*]. If you are engaged in Torah study, you will not be given over into the hand of the evil inclination.'"

> (*tavlin*), the meat is the essential element, not the herb.⁷⁰ The *Magid* (i.e. Rabbi Baer) explained that this is the truth of the matter. The Torah is indeed the *tavlin* (the herb acting as "spice" or "antidote"), and the essential reality of life is indeed the evil inclination. Man, then, must serve [God] with a burning energy (*hitlahavut*)⁷¹ that may be drawn forth with effort from the evil inclination.⁷² The Torah, for its part, is our guide and mentor in this endeavor; in that sense it is more like an "herb" or "spice" (*tavlin*).⁷³

This bold text identifies the vital power hidden within the evil inclination as the source and essence of divine worship and service. This raw energy is the "meat of life"—an essential force that may be harnessed by human spiritual endeavor. The Torah has an ancillary role in this drama: as a source of guidance and inspiration it is likened to the *tavlin*: both a healthy "antidote" for the wounds of spiritual struggle, and a tasty "herb" to make this "meat" more palatable. Similarly, Rabbi Nachman of Bratslav writes:

> If the evil inclination persists in a man,⁷⁴ this is actually a spiritual advantage, for then he will be able to serve the Blessed One precisely by means of the evil inclination itself. That is, he can apply all the inclination's warmth and fiery energy to the service of the God, praying and beseeching earnestly and, as it were, with his heart on fire. If, however, a man has no trace of the evil inclination in him, then his worship can never really be whole.⁷⁵

We have seen that Rabbi Dov Baer regards the inclination whispering in the human heart as one of the pillars of religiosity. Rabbi Lopian's essay, entitled "Herbs and Compresses in the Torah," focuses on the identical Talmudic midrash, but explains that there are two types of evil inclination: "natural" and "spiritual." In order to deal with the "natural evil

---

70. In other words, we would expect the Torah to be the essential, but here it is human life itself is the essence of existence and the Torah is only a "spice" that helps humans make their way through their lives with virtue.

71. This word can mean "enthusiasm" but contains the element of fire and flame associated with energy and zeal.

72. In Jewish mysticism, the passion we need to live our lives fully (equivalent to psychology's "Eros") derives from the evil inclination.

73. *Orach LeChaim*, 25.

74. The assumption is that some rabbis succeed in repressing their evil inclination.

75. Nachman of Bratslav, *Likutei Moharan Tanina*, chapter 49. For a further discussion about the role of the evil inclination, see Sagi, *Albert Camus*.

inclination," including physical needs like hunger and thirst, it is enough to apply only one herb. Rabbi Lopian means by this that a man should carefully monitor his needs, allowing the body the exact amount of sustenance necessary, but no more. On the other hand, the "spiritual evil inclination" is "most unnatural, evil and fierce of countenance." It is not possible for a man to grapple with such a force alone; this requires the grace of God. In other words, according to Lopian, we should not allow these kinds of inclinations to find expression; if, moreover, we are spared this kind of temptation, we must credit not our own virtue, but rather the grace of God.[76] Lopian's approach resembles Baer's in giving spiritual meaning to the (natural) evil inclination. By contrast, however, the majority of *Musar* writers are not willing to risk explicitly encouraging the faithful to harness the burning energy of their physical desires for the service of God.

E. Loathing and Lies: The Ongoing Struggle with the Body

As we have seen, *Musar* writers experience feelings of disgust for the body, which they reduce to its rawest material dimensions:

> Proteins, chromosomes . . . this is what we are made of. Substances that flow in the same form and manner in the veins of a rat; even a cow is composed of finer stuff than we are. The world at large [i.e., non-Jewish society] sees [these material elements] more or less as the sum of man: a big rat. So, what? We weigh more? A rat that weighs more is more nauseating. It is told of the philosopher Diogenes, that this thought so shocked him that for a long time he was too disgusted to touch his own body![77]

Julia Kristeva directs our attention to the abject feelings experienced by human beings in relation to different sites on their bodies, and to how these feelings share in the design and definition of the body's boundaries.[78] The unity of the body, and its separateness from the outside (that which is not the body) is threatened around sites that we perceive as

---

76. Lopian, *Lev Eliyahu Vol.* 1, 23–26.

77. Friedman, *Shtaygen*, 56–57. Rabbi Yaacov Friedman represents the more conservative position against the body. This is an important issue, considering the popularity of his books.

78. Kristeva, *Powers of Horror*.

"fluid," including, for example, portals of the digestive tract (mouth and rectum).[79] Persons are highly motivated, then, to define and fix boundaries between "self" and "world." Mary Douglas—like Kristeva—sees "cultures" as systems of efforts to provide various responses to the human fear of "leakage" of the "self" through escape/expansion of the body into space perceived as "non-self."

Douglas focuses on cultural laws, especially laws of "purity" (*taharah*) in the biblical Book of Leviticus, that prohibit a menstruating woman, for example, from entering the boundaries of the Israelite community during her period. Kristeva points more broadly to cultural attitudes to substances produced and then shed/excreted by the body, like fingernails, dry skin, and feces—i.e., "self" that eventually becomes "other."[80] Revulsion to such substances excites the urge to immediately get rid of them, removing them from both the eye and the (reflective) mind, and to restore more "stable" bodily boundaries.

We have seen that the human body evokes a similar revulsion in the *Musar* man. There is, however, an important distinction. Douglas and Kristeva share a Western cultural assumption that the human "self" includes *both* the mental/spiritual realm and the physical/somatic. They describe religious taboos and prohibitions as setting boundaries between this two-fold "self" and the outside world ("the other"). The assumptions of the Jewish *Musar* are very different. For the man of *Musar*, the Western distinction between "self" and "world" is barely meaningful, since he is engaged in defending an entirely internal boundary, striving to protect the soul (which only is the "self") from transgression by the body (exiled from the boundaries of the "self" and quintessentially "other"). *Musar* standards establish the boundary between the soul and the body through a sharp distinction between "reflective" and "non-reflective" existence. The reflective mind, on one hand, is the unique sign of the divine image in man; on the other hand, all other objects in the world—*including the non-reflective body*—and are not essentially human.

The following observations from Rabbi Yehezkel Chasman's essay entitled "Reflections on the Condemnation of Sinfulness" are relevant here:

---

79. Douglas, *Purity and Danger*.

80. In Jewish mysticism, for example, a Jewish man or woman must wash the hands after cutting the nails or hair, because of *"tum'ah"* (a state of "impurity"—helpfully described by Douglas as the transgression of a sacred boundary). Clipped fingernails must also be buried in the ground, as if they were corpses.

> Let us consider what the Sages have said, including [wise men] who did not know of the Torah [i.e. gentiles]. After considering [this matter], they declared—as Rabbi Moshe Ben Maimon [Maimonides], of blessed memory, tells us: "The sense of touch is abominable to us." If a man ['adam] were to imagine, even for a moment, the naked bestial acts [of sexuality], just as they are, without the spirit of human desire or the force of longing, would anyone endowed with the divine image be capable of ever performing them? Will a man not observe in his own flesh exactly how he despises [these actions,] the moment his desire abates? As the scripture says: "When you have eaten your fill [of honey] you will loath the honeycomb!"[81] . . . The truth is that all of a man's wishes and desires spring from the source of his deep-rooted natural urge to want and to covet. The careful observer will see, that these have no foundation and no place in a man's [reflective] mind; they are all illusions, intended to lead men [bnei 'adam] astray.[82]

Chasman espouses the approach of Maimonides (who quotes from the gentile sage Aristotle)[83] adopting a negative view of the sense of touch in general. This attitude, however, is controversial in the history of Jewish thought,[84] since for many rabbis the "sense of touch" is a euphemism for sexual desire, perceived as the origin of man's disgrace, usually without any explicit explanation in the sources.[85] Chasman is more broadly critical of all the senses, arguing that whenever we experience any kind of physical desire, the boundary between attraction and disgust may become blurred, resulting in a powerful sense of confusion. This, for Chasman, is evidence that all these physical experiences are fundamentally a kind of aberration and the work of the evil inclination. All bodily desires, he concludes, are disgraceful both to man and to the image of God inherent in him.

Chasman invites his readers to actively observe, first-hand, their own physical experiences, including the structure of their desires, after

81. Prov 27:7.

82. Chasman, *Or Yahel*, Vol. 1, 15. The same claim appears also about the lust for food, see, Chasman, *Or Yahel*, Vol. 3, 6 –7.

83. Aristotle, *Nicomachean Ethics*, Book 3, chapter X.

84. Other Jewish voices disagree with this opinion. See for example the *Ramban* (Rabbi Moses ben Nahman or Nahmanides, 1194–1270) in his *Iggeret ha-Kodesh* (The Holy Epistle). See also, Maharal of Prague (Rabbi Judah Loew ben Bezalel) in *Be'er Hagolah*, chapter 5.

85. See for example, Iserlish, *Mechir Iiain*, 88.

establishing a certain "distance" from the experience, as a condition for observation. It terms of *Musar* norms, this invitation entails considerable moral risk, for readers are asked to re-experience (or at least summon a clear memory of) something shameful. This is what is implied by quoting the proverb about "loathing the honeycomb." The moral of the proverb is that a man should despise himself for continuing to eat from the honeycomb when his belly is already full. However, in this form of *Musar*, a Jewish man must learn through his own experience what "loathing the honeycomb" means, by revisiting his sexuality, for example, *as part of his sacred studies*. The feelings of nausea and disgust that follow the arousal and satisfaction of physical desire are crucial and necessary steps before a man of *Musar* may enter the sphere of deep reflection on himself and his actions. Under these conditions, he can reflect on the desire that prompted the action, and on the nausea that followed it, and grasp an essential connection between the sense of release and the experience of disgust. Clearly, Chasman believes that such reflection can only reveal, that passion *per se* has "no foundation and no place in man's [reflective] mind," and that desires are merely "deceptions," designed to seduce a man away from the right path:

> The essence of lust is this: the power of desire holds sway only until a man achieves what he wants so badly. . . . After, when he has gained the object of his desire, he is like a little child in bed at night, delighting in the shadowy playthings cast by his candle upon the wall. But only bring the candle nearer [to the shadow], and the child's [playthings] are all gone; they have no substance, and are founded only in the imagination.[86]

Chasman highlights the *impermanence* of desire, assuming that his *Musar* readers will recognize a reference here to the temporality of the human body in general. The body and all its desires are perceived as threatening, because they symbolize the transience of human life. The knowledge that human beings spend their lives moving toward their death, prompts *Musar* teachers to seek immortality in the areas of human life they identify with the soul/mind; their fear of death prompts them to condemn the body and anything associated with it. As Friedlander puts it:

> The Sages identify this world as a world of lies, not only because we can speak falsehood here, but because the true essence of this world—the material world of bodies—is impermanent and

---

86. Chasman, *Or Yahel*, Vol. 1, 75.

transient, like an article of clothing. . . . A world that is only transitory cannot be an eternal reality or a world of truth; the values of this transient world are not true reality.[87]

The fact that Friedlander relegates the human body to the (transient) material world is probably not coincidental, and is consistent with the description of Chasman. To see our passing physical life in this world as inferior to the spiritual, reflects the *Musar's* prevailing cultural tendency to view the body as a threatening element, precisely because of the temporality it imposes on us. Temporality is a "lie" compared to the eternity that characterizes the World to Come, a world of "truth."[88] So falsehood is anchored in the physical. This serves *Musar* teachers like Chasman as a central argument for avoiding, to the best of one's ability, any physical experiences: the transience of physical pleasure is perfect proof of the "lie" it entails.[89] Further, since merely remembering a pleasure is rarely sufficient for satisfying a desire, humans strive to re-experience satisfaction again and again. Rabbi Dov Yaffe highlights this when he interprets the words of Rabbi Chaim Luzzatto, who wrote:

> Pleasure in [eating] food is the most tangible, the most directly felt; and yet, is anything more swiftly lost and gone? For its duration is only the length of our throat; once the morsel is past that point and on its way down to the intestines, all remembrance of its taste is lost and forgotten, as if it had never been.[90]

Rabbi Yaffe, in response, remarks:

> Who would be fool enough to exchange spiritual pleasures—which are real and eternal—for imaginary and momentary delights, which only deprive us of the enjoyment of spiritual pleasure.[91]

In other words, the satisfaction of desire is nothing but a fleeting and futile exercise in any case, since after a short time the stimulus is repeated,

---

87. Friedlander, *Siftey Chaim*, Vol. 1, 46.

88. This identification of temporality as negative is itself an interpretative choice. A contrasting view is found, for example in a midrash where temporality and death are positive elements of life. See *Bereshit Rabba* 9:10.

89. See for example Kanievsky, *Chayey Olam*, 10–11.

90. *Mesillat Yesharim*, the chapter entitled 'Perishut.' *Mesillat Yesharim*—written by Rabbi Moshe Chaim Luzzatto (1707–46)—is a foundational work of Jewish ethics (*Musar*) from before the *Musar* movement.

91. *Yaffe, LeOvdeh*, 48. See also *Chadash, Netivot*, Vol. 3, 196.

ad nauseam. The constant repetition of desire attests to the insight that its root cause (the existential issue of human insatiability) is not clearly understood. As Rabbi Shmuelevitz writes: "When a man dies, he will not have satisfied even half of his desires, and all his life he will have suffered grief and sorrow for what he feels he has missed out on."[92]

A more moderate position is to draw attention to the eternal tension between physical and spiritual desires, and to emphasize the value of eternal pleasure (in the World to Come) over the momentary pleasure of satisfying the desires of the physical body (in this life). Two quotations suffice to illustrate this approach:

> In order to attain this [spiritual] level, to merit the "crown of Torah,"[93] the hardship of toiling in Torah is in fact necessary. If, therefore, Rabbi Akiva had accepted payment [for teaching Torah], thus improving his material situation, then he would have forgone [the merit] of the difficult labor of Torah; consequently, he would never have been able to reach the exalted level [of spirituality] he in fact attained.[94]

> The *Maharitz Dushinsky*[95] would always say, that to merit the "acquisition of Torah"[96] a man (*'adam*) must sanctify himself [by refraining even from that] which is permitted to him [by the Torah].[97] [He must] distance himself from all of this world's delights and delicacies, and to be satisfied with only bread, salt, and water, all in moderation, . . . living a life of asceticism and abstinence even from this world's permitted pleasures, and making do with as little as possible.[98]

---

92. Shmuelevitz, "ShTihiyu Amelim BaTorah," 13.

93. The Mishnah and other classical Jewish texts make reference to divine crowns that may be acquired by human beings—one of these is the "Crown of Torah." See "There are three crowns: the crown of Torah, the crown of priesthood and the crown of kingship—but the crown of good name mounts above them" *Mishna Avot* 4:13. Translation is from Tropper, *Wisdom*, 267.

94. Levi, *Mashal HaAvot al 48 Kinyanei HaTorah Vol 2*, 36. This quotation is cited in the name of Rabbi Reuben Yossef Gershonowitz.

95. The pseudonym of Rabbi Yosef Tzvi Dushinsky (1867–1948).

96. The Mishnah's sixth tractate—*Avot*—is also commonly called "The Acquisition of Torah." Here, the term refers to the ability of a Jew to gain the "crown of Torah," one of the three "honorable crowns" in Jewish tradition.

97. See *Talmud Bavli*, Yevamot 20a.

98. Levi, *Mashal HaAvot al 48 Kinyanei HaTorah Vol 2*, 51.

Whether moderate or extreme, *Musar* teachings in general hold that material and physical pleasures hinder a man's spiritual development, distracting him from the pathway to real fulfilment. By contrast, Wilber claims, as we have seen above, that it is impossible to set up clear boundaries between objects and feelings, and by extension between "matter" and "spirit":

> Boundaries are pure illusions—they pretend to separate what is not in fact separable. . . . Our words, symbols, signs, thoughts, and ideas are merely maps of reality, not reality itself, because "the map is not the territory."[99]

It is not surprising, then, to learn that many *Musar* students complain that their efforts to curtail their physical pleasure also affect their spiritual fulfillment, and that they do not derive pleasure from learning Talmud, or that it does not match their enjoyment of the body. *Musar* teachers, predictably, respond that these students must have failed to completely give up all physical pleasures, as a precondition for attaining spiritual delight.

The repeated assertions of *Musar* rabbis, connecting the body with the evil inclination and with "lies," often prompt their students to become estranged from the world around them, and to doubt the reality of material objects, considering that "all the possessions of this world are external to us, and should not be part of our existence at all."[100] These students must internalize—to an extreme degree—the insight that their existence in this world is secondary and temporal, nothing more than a means to prepare themselves for the World to Come. This internalization has certain implications for how *Musar* teachers interpret traditional Jewish traditional concepts. For example, in the general Jewish tradition, "nature" refers to our present life, while "miracle" refers to the World to Come. *Musar* teachings the reverse: "nature" (where a man feels he most belongs) is the World To Come, where, as Rabbi Levenstein puts it: "life is entirely 'natural,' while this [material] world is entirely a 'miracle,' since

---

99. Wilber, *No boundaries*, 26–27.

100. Dessler, *Michtav me-Eliyahu* Vol. 1, 284. See also in page 197. According to Dessler, the main problem today is that humans are unaware of this, and therefore the evil inclination (for which he uses the synonym *ha-sitra 'achra'*—the "Other Side") rules their lives: "In our generation it is even worse, since people are not even aware of the existence of two sovereignties [i.e. this world and the next]. They feel [the power of] only one, namely the sovereignty of the evil inclination—only that and nothing else." (Dessler, *Michtav me-Eliyahu* Vol. 1, 239).

we understand 'miracle' as the opposite of 'nature!'"[101] For Levenstein, and for *Musar*, the very existence of this transient world most of us experience daily is "unnatural" and therefore "miraculous"; the World to Come is, on the other hand, entirely "natural" and "real."

The *Musar* community treats this world as a passageway to the next:[102] "Everything that this world entails is nothing but a corridor leading to the World to Come, not a real world in its own right."[103] *Musar* teachers consider it essential to avoid confounding the characteristics of the two worlds, especially since material claims to "reality" clamor so loudly for the attention of our senses, threatening the credibility of *Musar*'s highly skeptical religious view of this world. The *Musar* movement recognizes that the human soul has always been trapped within the narrow boundaries of the human body, impermanent and lustful as it is. In light of this, the exhortation of *Musar*, to forsake all desires and transcend the senses, seems nothing less than a clarion call to the miraculous. For the desire to bring the phantom life of this world closer to the real life of the World to Come is itself an attempt to defy nature and challenge its laws, through a miracle of human spirituality.

The absolute division between good and evil, however, must sometimes summon the human body into the essence of the work of *Musar*:

> For in order to transform the body, with all its characteristics, knowledge alone will never suffice; hard work and diligent labor are essential. With hard work the body may even draw close and cleave to the divine, but without it . . . [a man's] body remains unchanged, "evil from his youth" (Genesis 8:21).[104]

This quote from Rabbi Lefkowitz offers fascinating insights. The verse he cites from Genesis speaks of the "inclination" (*yetser*)—a term developed in Jewish theology as the "evil inclination"—applied here to the human body that requires a radical transformation. But, most importantly, for Lefkowitz, reflective thought as ordained by *Musar* can never be enough in order to lead a full life of *Musar*. Only hard work involving the body

---

101. Levenstein, *Or Yechezkel—Irah UMusar*, 251.

102. This voice is not unique to the *Musar* movement but is heard in many Jewish schools of thought.

103. Dessler, *Michtav me-Eliyahu* Vol. 1, 20.

104. Lefkowitz, *Ol-Torah*, 8; Kotler, *Mishnat Rabbi Aharon Kotler*, Vol. 1, 24–26. Rabbi Michel Yehuda Lefkowitz (1913–2011) was head of the Ponevezh Yeshiva in Bnei-Brak (Israel) and a board member of Degel HaTorah—the political party of the community.

itself can lead to a positive change away from the immaturity of "evil" and toward spiritual growth.[105]

Musar voices like this one are unique examples of an understanding, that by trying to manufacture set boundaries between "right" and "wrong," between soul and body, we will only end with borders that become blurry, making inevitable a return to the spiritual validity the human body. However, as this chapter has shown, predominant strains in *Musar* literature clearly identify the worldly stumbling blocks that prevent a Jew from devoting himself to the sacred task of studying Talmud: nature; women, family, and sexuality in general; the need to satisfy physical needs (food, shelter, etc.); and *especially the imagination* that causes him to yearn for things not essential to his fundamental existence. All these distract the Jewish man (*'adam*) from his role as a "reflective being." In addition, many teachers in the *Musar* movement express intense aversion to, even disgust for their own bodies; this is repeatedly highlighted in *Musar* texts. A model for a radically different "ideal body" is presented, but can never be realized, since—as the *Musar* movement claims—man is always bound to his body, eternally in disgrace, and may never simply separate his body from himself. Thus, the existential gap widens between the ideal and the real, between spiritual aspiration and the disappointment of daily realties; what ensues is a profound experience of alienation between the *Musar* man and his body.

---

105. While neuroscience is clearly beyond the scope of this study, it is important to note that radical progress in brain research deepens our understanding of the essential role that the body plays in all human cognition, especially the processing of emotional experiences, including both intense pleasure and severe trauma. For a good example of the prolific literature on the subject, see Van der Kolk, *The Body Keeps the Score*.

CHAPTER 3

The *Musar* Movement's Responses to the "Problem" of the Body

IN THE PREVIOUS CHAPTER, I explored the approaches to the body of prominent *Musar* leaders; I will now focus on the two main perspectives on the "problem" of the body within the broader *Musar* movement. The first approach, which I call the "new self," identifies the body with the *yetzer hara'* (the evil inclination) and demands that *Musar* men dedicate themselves to a persistent struggle against the body. This struggle is intended to reconstruct the "self" as a pure spirit, liberated from the body and its evil impulses. The second approach, which I call the "protected body," views the body as part of a general problem of human existence: the impossibility of constant self-reflection. According to this view, instead of fighting against the body, the *Musar* movement should create physical safe zones, where men can live naturally with their bodies. In these spaces, *Musar* men may live their lives without much self-reflection, since there, the body cannot harm them.

These two solutions do have some common ground. Their representatives agree that the body is a source of danger, dominated by instinctual drives that must be overcome. The point of tension lies in the extent to which they *identify the body with the self*. While the first approach tries to change the way humans self-identify with the body, the second accepts this identification and tries to focus on creating safe zones. Viewing the body not as fundamentally evil but as a meaningful part of life, the second approach has become more popular since the 1980s. This shift in popularity has led both perspectives to become more adamant in their views, and more polarized in their opposition to each other.

A. The First Response:
The "New Self" as a Disembodied Self

Rabbi Friedman tries to drive a wedge between the *Musar* student and his body by removing the body from the domain of the self:

> If you see your body as a "horse," your life will change utterly. You must internalize, and root within yourself the understanding, that you and your body are two forces, two entirely separate beings!!! The moment of this blessed distinction is a moment of new birth. Has someone hurt you? They hurt the "horse!" Has your *Musar* mentor publicly humiliated you for being late, for contempt of learning, for the materiality that takes control of every good part of you? It is the "horse" that he castigates! You are tired? Hungry? Miss home? Depressed? [This is] the "horse." . . . If your "horse" is having a life crisis, is slandered in the yeshiva, or is unsuccessful at *shiduchim* [matchmaking—i.e., finding a spouse], understand that it is your "horse" that is being called ugly, idiotic and uncouth. . . . You must take the reins of this maligned, crude and ugly creature. . . . Exert your control! Make it clear who is the king, and who is the subject![1]

Friedman knows that a yeshiva student, in his personal life, experiences his body as a central part of himself, connected to every aspect of life. The problem of the body concerns both externals, such as sexual attraction, and internal experiences, such as depression. To overcome this, the rabbi emphasizes that his students must actively dissociate from their bodies, regarding them as servants, utterly distinct from their true identity. Friedman uses the language of alienation to describe the self and the body as completely separate beings or forces. Only through this separation is the *Musar* disciple reborn as a "disembodied self." In this way, the body plays a paradoxical role, since it must first *exist* to be denied, and for the true self to be freed from its corporeal bondage.

Friedman's perspective on the body is among the most extreme. He implores his students to see all physical sensations and feelings—hunger and fatigue, longing and depression—as entirely disconnected from themselves. Our feelings and sensations, even the most intimate, are actually not "ours" at all. The body becomes a satellite sensory center of the self; in other words, our feelings and sensations belong to a physical space external to ourselves! This fundamental rupture between self and body

---

1. Friedman, *Shtaygen*, 57–58.

naturally leads to a profound experience of alienation both from oneself and from the world—an alienation that is the explicit goal of the "new self" response in the *Musar* movement.

The "new self" approach is based on a particular theology of the fall, according to which the "ideal self," before original sin, did not include the physical body. Adam, the first human being, treated the body simply as an external object, an auxiliary tool to be used much as we now use our clothing.[2] After the fall, as punishment for original sin, Adam (and all subsequent humanity) began to experience their bodies and its desires as integral aspects of the self, as we see in the words of Rabbi Chaim Friedlander:

> He [i.e. Adam, representing all humanity after the fall] identifies the "I" ['*ani* in Hebrew] with the body, not the soul. . . . In his imagination he can envision the soul as another entity, not "myself." I live with my body. What the body enjoys, I enjoy; and if I am in pain, then my body is tormented.[3]

In this interpretation, although Adam was created with a body, it cannot be said that God created anything imperfect. The experience of body as integral to self, rather than as a divinely created "tool," is not God's work but a result of humanity's original sin. Every Jewish man, born after the fall, must devote his life to resolving this primal existential problem: the experience of embodiment. A lifelong struggle against every physical and erotic dimension of life is the only possible response.

This approach establishes a crucial distinction. The "body" before the fall is ideal/imaginary. The "body" after the fall is also imagined, but now is wrongly identified as a real being (a "self"). This distinction enables the *Musar* rabbis to reject the body that is familiar to us, and to demand that men of *Musar* re-create an ideal body, guided only by conscious choice.

The objection to the actuality of the physical body appears, for example, in Friedlander's praise for a famous Jewish sage:

> Let us consider the *Vilna Ga'on* [the honorific title of Rabbi Eliyahu ben Shlomo Zalman, 1720-97] while he was eating. Can

---

2. Friedlander, *Siftey Chaim*, Vol. 1, 70–72. This line of interpretation is taken also by Rabbi Shmuel see (Auerbach, *Ohel Rachel*, 65). It is surprising to find that Rabbi Hutner follows the same reasoning as well, although he does not come to the same conclusions. See Hutner, *Pachad Itzchak: Sukkot*, 236.

3. Friedlander, *Siftey Chaim*, Vol. 1, 76.

> you imagine that he would take the kind of pleasure from his meals that we take from ours? It is inconceivable to even think such a thing.[4]

Going beyond "before the fall/after the fall," Friedlander here makes a further distinction: between earlier (superior) and later (inferior) generations. He refuses to believe that the former masters of his community comported themselves physically in any way as his inferior contemporaries do. He then describes proper physical conduct, guided by unceasing reflection:

> Whatever path the righteous may choose, and wherever they may stand, always and in everything they must engage in an "act" [ma'aseh: meaning an act of self-reflection]. The angels have no need of this, [since] they inhabit their own world; for the righteous, however, everything must include a [reflective] act.[5]

> Like Abraham, peace be upon him, at all times [the man of Musar] should go about with contemplation, giving thought to the oversight of his actions. As long as he is still in this world [not the world to come], he must reflect at all times on his actions, whether they are good or evil.[6]

The separation between "self" and "body" enables the rabbis to minimize the guilt occasioned by sin, without losing one's spiritual virtues. Physicality is identified with an existence deprived of reflection; the body is liable to punishment, but no longer comprises any substantial part of the self. As Rabbi Yisrael Eliyahu Weintraub says, "Sin belongs only to the body."[7]

This alienation from human embodiment and feelings has serious phenomenological, psychological and ethical implications. The self, as we know it, is fragmented, with each and every bodily action scrutinized suspiciously by the "real self," until it is nearly impossible to discern which aspects of life belong to the "real self" and which to the body. How could anyone create a clear, stable distinction between the two? *Who in fact is the self?* Who makes decisions and interacts with the world? Who

4. Friedlander, *Siftey Chaim*, Vol. 1, 229.
5. Friedlander, *Siftey Chaim*, Vol. 1, 198.
6. Friedlander, *Siftey Chaim*, Vol. 1, 199.
7. Weintraub, *HaChodesh HaShvii*, 85.

has the ability to sin if the one who commits the sin is not the self, but a foreign entity or force that evades any intelligible definition? Who, then, is held responsible for committing a crime, and who deserves praise for good deeds?[8]

Such fundamental questions become unanswerable, if not meaningless, with the rejection of the body found in this branch of *Musar* literature. What is clear is that this approach can avoid a substantive engagement with issues of guilt and responsibility. The man of *Musar* cannot be punished for his actions, and he can be praised only for choosing to live according to this model of bodily alienation, nothing else.

***

We must now look more closely at the design and direction of the "new self." This vision demands of men in the *Musar* tradition a life of extreme (even unnatural) authenticity, resulting in the existential isolation of the student, even within his own community. The Ultra-Orthodox neighborhood and public sphere, the yeshiva and its constituent society, and formative life experiences (such as unavoidable failures during matchmaking) are all seen as outside the "true self." Emotions too, like sadness and loneliness, belong, according to Rabbi Friedman, to the "horse" on which the "self" should ride. Not a single familiar mental or physical aspect of the student's inner or outer life is part of the "real" self; rather, these are all of the body, and must be treated with skepticism and mistrust. The student is left with a vague and ill-defined conception of "self" and he is beset by perpetual self-doubt.

This crisis of identity can only be resolved by the *Musar* hegemony, who alone can define the boundary between true self and bodily deception, and upon whom the student is totally dependent.[9] This dependence cements the power of the *Musar* authorities: they are perceived as knowing the students better than the students can know themselves. The *Musar* mentor is understood to be an indispensable *pastor*, whose guidance alone can give the student's life meaning: "With your real 'self' he [the *Musar* Teacher] establishes a covenant of friendship; it is he who assists you in steering your 'horse.'"[10]

8. Kukis, *Siach Mordechai*, Vol. 1, 60.
9. Levenstein, *Or Yechezkel*, Vol. 1, 49.
10. Friedman, *Shtaygen*, 57.

The concept of pastor is taken from Christian theology. The term means "shepherd"; in ancient Christian lore, the pastor guides the souls of believers, symbolized by sheep.[11] In the Roman Catholic tradition, the term specifically denotes the "priest who has the cure of souls (*cura animarum*), that is, who is bound in virtue of his office to promote the spiritual welfare of the faithful by preaching, administering the sacraments, and exercising certain powers of external government."[12] The Catholic Church clearly defines the pastors' duties: "They must preach and take care of the religious instruction of the faithful, especially of the young, supply their spiritual needs by the administration of the sacraments, ... watch over the moral conduct of their parishioners, and remove, as far as possible, all hindrances to their salvation."[13] The *Musar* movement adapted the role of pastor to define the work of the rabbi who guides his students to self-knowledge and to the capacity to distinguish true piety from illusory feelings.

Requiring a "new self" to solve the challenges of the outside world demonstrates how *Musar* rabbis, representing the Lithuanian Ultra-Orthodox Jewish social structure, are able to reshape not only their students' spirituality, but also their biological conception of the human body. In the words of Bourdieu: "The analysis of objective structures is inseparable from the analysis of the genesis, within biological individuals, of the mental structures which are to some extent the product of the incorporation of social structures."[14]

The process of alienation from the body and identification only with the "new self" signals a profound change in those who follow this path of *Musar*, as Rabbi Friedlander describes, quoting Maimonides' interpretation of the classical Jewish text of the *Mishna*:

> One of the pious was asked: "What was the happiest day of your life?" He answered: "Once I was traveling on a ship, and my berth was among the lowliest of the passengers.... While I was lying in my berth, one of the ship's company got up to urinate.

---

11. See Eph 4:11; John 10:11. On the pastor's roles in Christian tradition, see *Constitution and Canons of the Episcopal Church*, 18–63; *The Book of Common Prayer*, 510, 855–56.

12. See *The Catholic Encyclopedia*, s.v. "pastor," http://www.newadvent.org/cathen/11537b.htm.

13. *The Catholic Encyclopedia*, s.v. "pastor," http://www.newadvent.org/cathen/11537b.htm.

14. Bourdieu, *In Other Words*, 14.

> So demeaned and base did I appear to him, that he exposed himself and urinated on me. By heaven, his act did not disturb me, nor was I aroused to any reaction. I rejoiced with great joy that I had reached the point where I was not upset at all by the degrading conduct of that base person, and was able to pay him no attention whatsoever."[15]

Relying on Maimonides, Friedlander presents the *Musar* ideal as going beyond the preservation of the human body or of human honor. That mainstream society views the pious as despicable is understood as an ultimate proof that Jewish idealism does not comply with social conventions. Likewise, yeshiva students are expected to eschew conformity and to uproot themselves from their familiar cultural sphere. Once the *Musar* movement was established in Israel, the model of the "new self" distinguished itself from the mainstream Ultra-Orthodox community, which was seen as the realm of the evil inclination, outside the boundaries of the yeshiva. *Musar* rabbis in Israel direct their teachings to yeshiva students who grew up in Ultra-Orthodox neighborhoods, or in Ultra-Orthodox cities such as Bnei B'raq, Beitar and Modi'in Illit.

Young yeshiva students are expected to create a new worldview based on shaming themselves, according to a particular Ultra-Orthodox understanding of shame.[16] The yeshiva student, by choosing shame voluntarily, uproots himself from the entire social game of pursuing honor and avoiding shame, and declares himself outside of his former society. In the exiled social territory of the *Musar* movement, there is a kind of ethical inversion, whereby the despised and the humiliated are praised as noble and glorious figures.[17]

As noted above, *Musar* leaders recognize that identifying as a self without a body is unfamiliar to their students, so they employ "performative utterances" to create this "new self." Performative utterances not only describe but also create a demonstrably different reality; they acquire creative power through repetition within the social sphere. For example,

---

15. Maimonides' interpretation of *Mishna Avot*, 4:4 (our translation).

16. There are some connections between this *Musar* method and the pre-Holocaust method of Novardok. Surprisingly, there are no self-identifications between these rabbis and Novardok.

17. One can see the similarity between this *Musar* method and the early Christian movement. The "shame" of the persecuted Christians was also seen as a proof of their faith in Christ. The shamed person, brought to trial by "them," entered the "us" group, i.e., believers who resemble Jesus, shamed at the time of his crucifixion. See Elliott, "Disgraced Yet Graced," 170–72.

when a Jewish man says to a woman: "With this ring, you are consecrated to me according to the Torah of Moses and Israel"—these words not only describe this holy union (*kiddushin*), but also constitute an act that creates the reality of marriage.

Through new performative utterances, the man of *Musar* first of all distinguishes himself from his former society and its culture. He also acclimates his body and mind to new customs, distinct from those of the mainstream Ultra-Orthodox community. A clear example is Maimonides' pious man on the ship, who describes himself in a manner that would be disgraceful in ordinary terms, but is seen by the *Musar* spiritual elite as worthy of high praise. Likewise, the yeshiva student is encouraged to "disgrace" his ordinary, sensory, embodied self in order to gain a new understanding of disembodied selfhood.

The attempt to reshape the self invites an exploration of the question of nature versus nurture.[18] The *Musar* effort is not limited solely to the creation of a different social sphere for the yeshiva students, but intervenes in the so-called natural sphere, as well. Judith Butler's work will be instructive here. In *Gender Trouble*, Butler sets out to undermine the common distinction between "nature"—signifying the permanent, nonhistorical dimension of human existence, and "nurture"—or that which depends on influences of society and culture, and changes over time.[19] Butler relies on anthropological and philosophical research to assert that it is impossible to describe the physical body as a purely natural product, without recognizing how cultural discourse and practices surrounding the physical body contribute to its creation and status. Her claims are based in part on the work of Clifford Geertz, who writes: "There is, there can be, no backstage where we can go to catch a glimpse of Mascou's actors as "real persons" lounging about in streets clothes, disengaged from their profession. . . . This circumstance makes the drawing of a line between what is natural, universal, and constant in man and what is conventional, local and variable extraordinary difficult."[20] Both the concept of "nature" and the claim that something is "natural," says Butler, are themselves the products of a particular social discourse, used as an ideological tool. A dominant ideology attempts to anchor certain "existing order" values, while at the same time establishing the illusion that these

---

18. "Nature" describes the physical reality of humans, and "nurture" describes human cultural creation (social norms, law, art, etc.).

19. Butler, *Gender Trouble*, 163–80.

20. Geertz, *The Interpretation of Cultures*, 40.

values are "natural," that is, devoid of ideology and therefore "fixed" and not subject to cultural disagreement.

Geertz perceives the biological sphere, including our most basic physical experiences, which supposedly precede all conditioning, as "natural." Butler, however, reveals how even biology is mediated by the dominant culture, while performative utterances shape human society, constructing identity (including gender and sexual identity) according to a predetermined social "prescription." Society's demand for the daily repetition of myriad familiar acts demonstrates that "nature" is second-order to cultural expectations, and that the existence of a "real and primary self" is a fiction used to serve dominant ideology.[21]

Similar assumptions can be found in Lithuanian *Musar* thought. Through re-education, practice, and adoption of performance "errors" contrary to the prevailing social order, the student experiences the self in a different way than before entering the yeshiva. The role of the mentor/pastor in the *Musar* hegemony is to remind the yeshiva student that even the most basic and familiar experiences are wrongly perceived as "natural" and "essential" qualities of life, while in reality they are unnatural results of original sin. These qualities are fluid rather than permanent, and can be changed, but only through a persistent struggle.

The disciple of *Musar* must identify solely with the "new self" and reject everything else: his body, society, culture, and any experience incompatible with the demands of the *Musar* rabbinical hegemony. The journey to piety has a goal but not an end. Even "rebirth" does not guarantee anything, since as long as the man of *Musar* lives in this world, he is forced to struggle against the body, and against both Western and Ultra-Orthodox societies that try to "seduce" him to return to his evil ways.[22] As we shall see later, only the luminary leader of the Musar community—the *Godol*—will attain complete realization of the primordial *Musar* nature, and become free from the sinful inclination of the body.

---

21. For example, in order for a "female" to become a "woman," society requires that she adhere to a defined set of proscriptions from the moment of birth, including dress codes, speech patterns, etc. If these are "social" rather than "natural," it is possible to challenge normative expectations and to expand and even play with gender expressions typically perceived as fixed.

22. Povarsky, *Musar Ve-Daat*, Vol. 1, 348. For a softer version of this claim see, Weinberg, *48 Ways to Wisdom*, 69.

***

Creating a "new self" means experiencing life as an existential struggle, in constant opposition to the forces of Nature, society, and the body. As Rabbi Baruch Dov Povarsk put it: "What is the greatest battle? . . . The battle against the [evil] inclination and its warriors! For even a man's own virtues can become soldiers of the [evil] inclination."[23] Similarly, Rabbi Rosenstein admonishes: "Sometimes we forget, that we are soldiers on the battlefront—and more!"[24] This military metaphor is common in the *Musar* movement, especially in the State of Israel, where *Musar* rabbis keep their Israeli Jewish students out of the Israeli Defense Forces (IDF) by comparing them to soldiers enlisted in a spiritual war to defend Jewish *Musar* values.

The question of military service is part of a broader discussion of Ultra-Orthodox versus secular Israeli masculinity. Western history, as we have seen, is marked by the recurring tension between religious and secular models of masculinity.[25] In Israel, Ultra-Orthodox yeshiva men are the only male Jewish citizens in Israel who do not serve in the IDF; this supports an old exilic perception, that Ultra-Orthodox masculinity tends toward femininity. It is no surprise, then, to find the rabbis' persistent attempts to offset this image by emphasizing the ongoing difficulty and danger of the struggle against the evil urge:

> This war [against the evil inclination] is eternal! Really, it goes on forever, without a break, and with no opportunity for distraction. A man may not rest, not even for a fraction of a second, from this struggle against the inclination, or say to himself, "All is well!" [*Shalom alai nafshi*][26]

> One may, by one forbidden glance, lose everything [all moral achievements], and when a single impure thought enters the mind, it is possible, Heaven forbid, to be thrown into the depths of hell.[27]

23. Povarsky, *Musar Ve-Daat*, Vol. 1, 212.
24. Rosenstein, *"Mihtav LeBein Hazmanim,"* 73.
25. Kirkley, "Is It Manly to Be Christian?"
26. Chasman, *Or Yahel*, Vol. 3, 4. See also Kukis, *Siach Mordechai*, Vol. 2, 19–20. *Shalom alai nafshi*—literally "my soul is at peace within me"—a phrase applied in classical Jewish texts to Jews who avoid getting involved in a crisis of the Jewish community; i.e., "It is none of my concern!"
27. Rosenstein, *"Mihtav LeBein Hazmanim,"* 74

In fact, *Musar* rabbis argue that if a man lives comfortably and without struggle, this is proof that the evil inclination holds him captive:

> The road to the World to Come is thorny from the outset, and this is itself the test whereby a man may know if he is heading in the right [*Musar*] direction. If he encounters thorns and obstacles, then he is walking on the right path; but if everything is smooth, conforming to his natural desires rather than contradicting them, then he has gone astray.[28]

A sense of guilt arising from error, however, should not be seen as proof of spiritual failure; rather, it is the *Musar* student's first step on the right path to the World to Come. In the words of Rabbi Chaim Ephraim Zeichik:

> One should learn from this, that the more [the People of] Israel ascend, and the higher the spiritual level they attain, the more acutely will they feel and recognize their sinfulness and their unwitting errors committed carelessly; their eyes shall be enlightened, and they will recognize their guilt.
>
> When a man's spirit is weak, he does not feel guilt for his actions, nor blame himself. This is because he cannot see his transgressions, since darkness covers his eyes; his soul is blind, so he is not fearful or anxious about sinning. But once he has improved his behavior, then indeed both his fear of God and his love of God increase; and then he feels the coarseness of his heart, even in matters that are seemingly insignificant. When the light in a man's soul begins to shine, then indeed he begins to see his sinfulness. . . . And even if a man's wrong deeds evade his own perception, in God's light all sins are illuminated.[29]

The *Musar* movement seeks to establish a cultural sphere based on guilt but immune to shame. Scholars distinguish between "honor cultures" and "guilt cultures."[30] In the first, shame and guilt are intertwined, and both are considered negative, dishonorable qualities. Failure to acquire honor, based on external, social judgments of the individual in the public sphere, can lead to both shame and guilt. In "guilt culture," on the other hand, the gaze of the "other" is internalized or transposed into a relation-

---

28. Levenstein, *Kovetz Inyanim*, 31.

29. Zeichik, *Or Chadash*, 90.

30. For research on "guilt cultures" see, Delumeav, *Sin and Fear*. For details on honor cultures see later here, chapter 8.

ship between the human individual and a divine agent who scrutinizes all actions and thoughts, both public and private. "Guilt culture" is not organized around shame (which is solely a public and social phenomenon), but only around guilt, which permeates all spheres of life, private as well as public.

We have seen how Rabbi Friedlander requires that his yeshiva students withdraw from the economy of honor, even Ultra-Orthodox honor. Going a step further, Rabbi Zeichik emphasizes the place of guilt, rather than honor, as a proper attitude for disciples of *Musar*. To clarify the meaning of guilt culture in this specific Jewish context, we first turn to Rabbi Moshe Isserles, in his notes to Rabbi Yosef Karo's masterpiece, the *Shulchan Aruch*. Rabbi Isserles opens with a citation from Psalm 16:8—"I have set the LORD before me constantly," which he calls "a great principle of Torah [*klal gadol be-torah*], and a virtue of all those who walk before God." Then he goes on to say:

> The manner of a man's [*ha'adam*] sitting and walking and all his behavior when he is alone in his house, is by no means the same as his sitting and walking and behavior when he is in the presence a great king. . . . Even so, when a man ['*adam*] is aware, with all his heart, that the King of Kings, the Holy One Blessed Be He, whose glory fills the whole earth, is standing over him, watching all his actions, . . . at that moment he will be touched by awe and submission, and by a holy fear of the Blessed Name [of God], and will always have a sense of [reverent] shame before Him. Such a man, then, can never be shamed by anyone else who mocks him for his worship of the Blessed Name [of God].[31]

The transition to guilt culture can occur only when honor culture, with its dependence on the public sphere, has been left behind. For this transition to be complete, the Jewish *Musar* student must maintain a reflective existence, and consider that God constantly observes humanity. While Rabbi Isserles maintains that the righteous who live always under the gaze of the divine feel reverent shame for their failings, Rabbi Zeichik takes this a step further. For him, God's penetrating watchfulness (the reflexive gaze), guarantees human guilt, not human righteousness. Moral imperfection is inherent to humanity, and therefore irredeemable, at least when compared to God's perfection. The choice of living a reflective life imposes on us a *blessed* guilt-ridden life, for it enables us to make moral choices *in spite of* our flawed moral nature.

31. *Shulchan Aruch*, Orach Chaim 1.1.

When we have clarified the transition from shame to guilt, we can more easily understand how the *Musar* movement utilizes guilt for its own agenda. In modern Western societies, guilt is perceived as fundamentally psychological—an emotional reaction to life's circumstances, when a particular event might leave a person feeling responsible for moral failure. If guilt moves beyond specific events and actions to encompass the entire personality, then something is essentially wrong with that personality, requiring psychological treatment. In Rabbi Zeichik's alternate conception of guilt, however, a man is not "innocent until proven guilty"; rather, guilt is embedded in man's ontological structure and fundamental to a reflective life. Such a consciousness of guilt will be enhanced in a culture where a man has an ongoing moral duty inseparable from his basic humanity.

In other words, guilt reflects the gap between the real and the ideal, between the limited actuality and the infinite possibility that is now defined as man's task and destiny. The awareness of guilt is the responsibility of every man, as he scrutinizes his every choice, always recognizing alternatives that could have brought him closer to his infinite potential.[32] We are forever unable to fulfill our *Musar* ideal, because, as Rabbi Levenstein puts it: "sin is a reality that is not nullified."[33] For those who take upon themselves this assumption, sinfulness is a constant presence, and guilt is a way of life.

For Zeichik, guilt signifies high spiritual attainment; it is a sign of detachment from the daily sphere of existence, perceived by *Musar* as a physical and therefore unreflective space. Only when the *Musar* man honestly observes his existential situation, does he understand that he is composed of a physical dimension (the body) and a spiritual dimension (the image of God). It is this very coexistence of sacred and impure that inspires a sense of guilt and a desire for moral perfection. This is a predicament that the *Musar* disciple himself can never transcend without the guidance of a *Musar* master, who alone is free of the guilt of physical existence.

The *Musar* master appears, to the ordinary eye, to be divorced from all pleasures and all physicality,[34] practicing an asceticism that is seen as a necessary condition for the "true" study of Judaism:

---

32. Tennen, *Karl Jaspers*, 90–92.
33. Levenstein, *Or Yechezkel—Irah UMusar*, 49.
34. Gifter, *Pirkey Torah*, 135.

> Who deserves to attain the cream of Torah? They say it is precisely that man who vomits out and distances from his body the whole substance of this world, the whole substance of physicality. For as long as his portion is with material things, he will lack any grasp of Torah.[35]

Most *Musar* writers distinguish between abstaining from physical pleasure, as an appropriate way to treat the body, and intentional injury to the body, which they do not encourage. They teach students to do the minimum to maintain a healthy existence, but to eschew all luxury. For example, Rabbi Friedman writes about the eating habits of his teacher Rabbi Gershon Liebman:

> It is not accurate to say that he detested food; Rabbi Gershon ate. But his way of eating always reminded me of a *man pouring fuel into his engine* [italics mine].... There was no connection between his act of eating and his soul, his true self. Rabbi Gershon's body always stood to one side, alongside his burning spiritual world. His body was always being dragged along, smoldering, behind his great spirit, and he would occasionally toss his body something material, so it could carry on.[36]

Luxurious consumption implies that the person gives value to the body and to physical life—which would be a betrayal of the "real" self.[37] Other writers take a more harsh approach, encouraging fasts and even virtual torture, like placing food and drink in front of a student but preventing him from touching them, or[38] swallowing food without chewing, with the intention of giving the body basic sustenance while avoiding the pleasure of eating.[39] In the words of Rabbi Chasman: "The body understands

---

35. Lefkowitz, *Darkei Chaim*, Vol. 1, 383.

36. Friedman, *Nafshi Yazaa Bedabro*, 319.

For other examples, see Lefkowitz, *Darkei Chaim*, Vol. 2, 98. Of the Radin Rabbi it is said that once he mentioned that a certain food was tasty, and immediately he refused to eat it ever again, claiming that "this had clearly taught him that he harbored some kind of connection with materiality." (Levi, *Mashal HaAvot al 48 Kinyanei HaTorah Vol 2*, 15). In recent years, one hears voices inside the *Musar* movement critiquing the refusal to enjoy tasty food. Rabbi Hecht, for example, claims that it is not the taste that matters, but the reason a person decides to eat (Hecht, *Shut Libnei Ha-Neurim*, 269–71).

37. Wolbe, *Alei Shur 1*, 59–60.

38. Citing Rabbi Raphael Eliyahu Eliezer Mishkovsky. See *Chizuk* 6 (2006), 282.

39. Yaffe, *LeOvdeh*, 102–3, 185. A unique and indirect critique of this attitude can be found in a biography of Rabbi Moshe Feinstein: "Someone once told Rabbi Moshe

only the language of the carrot and the stick [literally: the whip and the manger]."⁴⁰

These efforts do not guarantee complete separation from the body. A man can strive for disengagement, but is never able to achieve the desired change through his own powers; ultimately he is at the mercy of Heaven. However, the divine grace may be obtained through the very relinquishing of every bodily experience. In this case, as a result of the desired divine transformation, the "new self" no longer has a familiar physical aspect, for "the nature of the body will change, until it becomes itself in some way equal in characteristics and nature to the soul."⁴¹ Thus the *Musar* master is "re-created," as if his actual body becomes an ideal-imagined body, obeying only the will of the reflective human mind. The "new self" exists in utter devotion to the divine, and "the self enters into a marriage covenant with the page of *Gemara* [Talmud]."⁴²

Many *Musar* writers clearly state that the attempt to become a purely spiritual being is rarely complete: "our physical aspect understands only a simple language—the language of force. . . . The body derives no benefit whatsoever from things of the intellect . . . and we can earn eternal life only by putting to death all desires and wishes."⁴³

However, on a deeper level, *Musar* masters must affirm the positive value of physicality. The unceasing effort of physical discipline, and the coercive subordination of the body to the will of the spirit, are themselves what shatter the spiritual foundation the *Musar* rabbis are trying to build. In striving to regulate or eliminate physical pleasure, Michel Foucault reminds us, the subject is overcome by the very substance he or she tries to eradicate, leaving the temptation of bodily pleasure even stronger than it had been at first. *Musar* writers are well aware, that attempted repression backfires, giving greater power to the body and sensuality. Chasman, for example, spells out the essential sensuality of devotion:

---

about a famous tzadik (righteous master) of the last century who would swallow scalding food without chewing it, in order not to derive any pleasure from the delights of this world. Rabbi Moshe replied that he could not believe that such a great *tzadik* would do anything so injurious to his health." (Finkelman and Sherman, *Reb Moshe*, 78).

40. Chasman, *Or Yahel*, Vol. 3, 114–16.
41. Povarsky, *Musar Ve-Daat*, Vol. 1, 105.
42. Friedman, *Shtaygen*, 43. See also Wolbe, *Alei Shur 1*, 59–60.
43. Levenstein, *Or Yechezkel—Irah UMusar*, 223.

> We should know, that if the study of Torah is the essence of devotion [*dvekut*] for the Holy One Blessed Be He, if the real meaning of learning Torah is—as it were—to embrace and kiss the Holy Name [of God] Blessed Be He, then it follows that the real meaning of *bitul torah* [neglect of Torah] is a personal insult directed at Torah. . . . The Holy *Shekhinah* [the "Indwelling Presence"—a feminine revelation of the divine] stands here before us, and we ignore her! . . . The ultimate end of devotion [*dvekut*] is [to embrace the divine], mouth to mouth. . . . [As it is written]: "Let him kiss me with the kisses of his mouth!" (Song of Songs 1:2).[44]

Spiritual perfection, paradoxically, is often described in terms of physical pleasure and sexual arousal. Rabbi Chasman exhorts his students to a spiritual experience through sexual images, such as an embrace and a kiss, "mouth to mouth." He uses the name of a feminine revelation of the divine (*Shekhinah*) and likens the divine to a woman waiting for her lover to come and caress her.[45] Similarly, a unique aspect of the Hasidic tradition, especially the early generations, as Gershom Scholem and David Bial have shown, is the use of sexual metaphors to describe the devotion of the Hasid to God and the *Shekhinah*. While the Kabbalah had attributed such ecstatic devotion only to exalted Jewish saints (*tzadikim*), the Hasidic movement broadened the experience to include any devout person.[46] So also in Lithuanian *Musar* thought, where the passion and ecstasy of total devotion to God and the *Shekhinah* is no longer only the prerogative of distinguished scholars, but is open to every yeshiva student who earnestly strives for it.

B. The Second Response: The "Protected Body" and the Role of the Yeshiva

We have been describing a response to the "problem" of the body characterized by an attempt to place the body beyond the limits of the self, and create (or re-establish) a disembodied self. This response takes as its premise that the primordial, ideal self did not include a body, and that before the fall, Adam and Eve saw their bodies as "external objects" much as we might view a suit of clothes. Especially since the end of the

---

44. Chasman, *Or Yahel*, Vol. 1, 43–45.
45. Scholem, *Explications and Implications*, 257–309.
46. Biale, *Eros and the Jews*, 121–48; Scholem, *Explications and Implications*, 33.

twentieth century, however, many *Musar* teachers have refused to subscribe to the idea that there is a wide gap between the ideal and the actual self, or that the body with which we are familiar is essentially different from the pre-fall body, or that the original sin described in Genesis could alter the nature of the body.[47] These teachers hold that, even before the fall, human beings sometimes lived impulsively and without reflection. Consequently, also today, a man's thoughts, words and actions will always express the intertwining of material and spiritual dimensions.[48]

For this second response, human nature entails constant tension between reflective and unreflective aspects of life; this duality is foundational to the *Musar* movement's study of humankind. God created Adam (the primordial human being) with the capacity to be unreflective; *Musar*, then, should not endeavor to change this. Indeed, this approach—which I call the "protected body"—balances self-reflection with being immersed in unmediated life, and is certainly strongly opposed to harming the body in an effort to transform it.[49] Asceticism can damage a man's soul and, thus, his ability to study Talmud:

> A yeshiva student asked about another student who practiced all kinds of self-deprivations, such as sleeping on a plank, etc. Rabbi Lefkowitz replied, "Try hard to prevent him from doing these things, because they can lead to psychological problems." And that is, in fact, what actually happened—may the All-Merciful protect us![50]

The "protected body" approach is also different from the first response in another striking way: there, the pastoral role of the spiritual mentor was absolutely essential, but here there is emphasis on the *Musar* movement's trust in the individual's own feelings. Rabbi Sarna writes:

> As for the personal "work of heart": in this matter every man is unique, standing solitary and alone in his own existence. No one in the world can presume to delve into the personal depths of anyone else; only that man himself can know his heart.... For it

---

47. Rabbi Sarna, for example, in an essay on the evil inclination, explains the changing existential human condition before and after the fall, and never even mentions the body as a cause of this change, or of original sin itself. See Sarna, *Daliyot Yehezkel 2*, 179–81.

48. Wolbe, *Alei Shur 1*, 138. See also, Dessler, *Michtav me-Eliyahu Vol. 1*, 305; Povarsky, *Musar Ve-Daat*, Vol. 1, 198.

49. Wolbe, *Igraot*, 64, 66.

50. Lefkowitz, *Darkei Chaim, Vol. 2*. See also, Hershkovitz, *Sheifot*, 11–12.

is only the "I" of a man who can see and understand that same "I" in its intimate essence.[51]

Musar teachers like these accept that the body is integral to the self. They believe that coercion cannot change the body's nature and that, inescapably, a man must live part of his life without conscious reflection. The solution they offer is the construction of the yeshiva, as a religiously protected physical space. In the yeshiva context, a Jewish man of *Musar* is free to live with his body in an unreflective state, while retaining his spiritual integrity. Here he may conduct himself, for most of the day, without constant self-surveillance and constant monitoring of his body, his thoughts and his desires.

Of course, teachers and students of the "new self" approach described earlier also work in yeshivas, and there is virtually no visible difference between their yeshiva contexts and those of the "protected body" school. However, the role of the yeshiva itself is different. Those who follow the "new self" principle focus on the student, and on his relationship with the spiritual hegemony, in the person of the pastor who directs his path. On the other hand, for *Musar* teachers of the "protected body" method, the yeshiva itself must provide a unique atmosphere with special qualities. It must become a communal "body" that encloses and shelters the bodies and souls of the students, protecting them from a non-reflective life.

The "protected body" system minimizes forbidden stimulations in the physical environment of the yeshiva, so students are not required to monitor themselves beyond the basic requirements of *halakha* (Jewish law).[52] The yeshiva is isolated from the surrounding public sphere, students do not encounter women, technological distractions are limited, and even visual stimulants like bright colors are typically avoided. Only sacred texts are found in the yeshiva; other books, even holy works

---

51. Sarna, *Daliyot Yehezkel 2*, 55. Rabbi Yechezkel Sarna (1890–1969) was a disciple of Rabbi Finkel ("The Grandfather of Slabodka") and served as head of the Hebron/Slabodka Yeshiva in Jerusalem. He is known for being the mentor of many of the current leaders of the community.

52. In general, a yeshiva student is not allowed, during his studies, to touch any body parts that are covered by his clothing; long sleeves and pant-legs provide such protection to most of his body. If he inadvertently does touch these parts, the student must go and "purify" himself by washing his hands. The subject of purity (*taharah*), which has a central place in Hasidic yeshivas, is almost totally ignored in Lithuanian ones. See Hakak, *Spirituality and Worldliness in Lithuanian Yeshivas*.

engaging in dialogue with the outside world, are absent or at least kept out of sight.

Within this isolated system, yeshiva students are able to move and speak freely, without restraint. Familiar examples of their behavior include much vigorous arm-waving, speaking loudly, pacing energetically while studying, and generally milling about. The actual content of the yeshiva discourse is also practically uncensored, and it is permitted to quarrel and argue with every point of opinion, even if it is raised by an older and more esteemed yeshiva member. Ethical works by *Musar* teachers of the "protected body" school are full of testimonies to the uninhibited comportment of "worthy" yeshiva students:

> At Grodno [a town in Belarus], there was a certain student, a lion among his peers, who, when he would wag his finger at his opponents in the yeshiva, would often strike his thumb violently on the floor.... And this same student, in the heat of Torah study, would boil with anger when a colleague would stray from the path of logic. For such occasions he reserved the Russian expression *foyer!* ("stupid peasant" in Russian)—as an insult to hurl at his opponent. While arguing with the great teacher Rabbi Shimon[53] this student jumped to his feet and shouted *foyer!* in the teacher's face.[54]

This story is found in a book of *Musar*, intended, in the author's own words, to guide the reader on "the road to excellence." Here, the ideal student is described as one who pays no attention to his own behavior, either physically or in terms of his speech. His entire being, free from all reflection, is devoted to a passionate study of the Talmud. Although self-reflection is the essence of *Musar*, these *Musar*, these students want to be utterly free of it, if it stands in the way of Torah study. Here, the *Musar* rabbis focus on structuring the yeshiva to be free from stimulation, rather than on the personal development of the *Musar* student as a reflective being, which was the original goal of the movement as envisioned by Rabbi Salanter. It is not surprising, then, if we hear in these writings the voices of yeshiva students who do not understand why they should be connected, personally, to the *Musar* movement, as this description by Rabbi Doron Gold shows:

---

53. 1860–1939.

54. Friedman, *Shtaygen*, 211. See also, *Chizuk* 4 (173–74); Sofer, *Raboteinu Shebedarom*, 347; Bergman, *Orchot Chasideha*, 292.

> A well-known spiritual [*Musar*] director related that one of his most outstanding yeshiva students asked him why he should be required to stop in the middle of his [Talmudic] studies, when he was completely absorbed in studying that *sugiah* [Talmud portion] just in order to learn *Musar*. "I can understand," the student claimed, "that the study of *Musar* might be greatly needed in times of spiritual distress when either devotion or Torah study are in question. But when yeshiva life is going smoothly, is it not better for me to learn another page of *Gemara* [Talmud]?"[55]

In the Hasidic tradition, Jewish devotion to God is usually expressed in prayer, singing, and the forging of a strong relationship between the hasid and his Rebbe (spiritual mentor). By contrast, Lithuanian devotion is directed primarily toward the sacred text of the Talmud itself. Rabbi Chaim of Volozhin explicitly states that the Jewish axiom "*torah lishmah*" (literally: "Torah for its own sake") is not to be interpreted (as it usually is in Hasidism) to mean that we should study Torah "for the sake of heaven." Rather, says Rabbi Chaim, *torah lishmah* means precisely that: we study Torah "for the sake of the Torah text itself."[56]

The Hebrew term *lishmah* (literally "for the name of . . .") denotes the deeply ethical idea "for the sake of . . ." The concept of *torah lishmah* therefore encapsulates the question of *why a devout Jew reveres Torah*. In the particular religious culture of Lithuanian Ultra Orthodoxy, "Torah piety"(*torah lishmah*) is defined as fundamental devotion and adherence to the text of the Talmud.[57] To study Talmud "exempts" yeshiva students from ethical questions about their actions, since according to traditional yeshiva theology, the Talmudic text contains and reveals the very words of God. Yeshiva students can focus themselves entirely on the abstract Talmudic text, without relating it to the daily challenges of real life, since the text itself safeguards them from sin. Study in fact buffers the student

---

55. Gold, *Hachzek BaMusar,* 45.

56. To identify "devotion" with the unreflective life is not accepted by all *Musar* teachers. See for example, Lefkowitz, *Darkei Chaim, Vol. 2,* 328.

57. Of course, the text of Talmud and the text of Torah (the Jewish Bible) are distinct, and from different periods of Jewish history. However, for Ultra-Orthodox Jews in general, the Talmud has in essential ways "replaced" the Bible as the foundational religious document. In our rabbinical sources, the Hebrew word *torah* often really means "Talmud."

from every other experience: "So it is with one who loves the Torah . . . when he learns, he feels nothing but the learning."[58]

It is not surprising then, to find descriptions of a yeshiva student in the midst of a romantic relationship but still immersed entirely in Talmud:

> "He led me into the 'house of wine' (*beit ha-yain*)" (Song of Songs 2:4). . . . If a man loves wine, it is enough for him to be in the "house of wine," and to smell its fragrance, and he will become intoxicated and remain there. Even so, everyone should become intoxicated with Talmud [*torah*], and remain [long hours] in the study hall (*beit midrash*—literally "house of study").[59]

This midrash on the Song of Songs employs a common mystical metaphor for immersion in divine love: intoxication with wine. In this Jewish context, however, the student loses the sobriety of self-reflection, not to seek divine union, but to remain at his studies in the "house of study"— an obvious play on the biblical "house of wine." The yeshiva scholar finds ecstasy only in Talmud.

Immersed body and soul in Talmud study, the yeshiva student need not fear the evil inclination; he has laid down his shield of self-reflection, but the sacred text itself will protect him. For this protection to be effective, however, it is crucial that the yeshiva student *not relate* the Talmudic subject he is examining to his personal life or feelings. This is especially true when he is studying sensitive real-life issues like sexuality. Yeshiva adolescents must explore Talmud texts on female virginity, seduction, and even rape, without having any personal reaction. They are expected to be immunized from sexual arousal even while reading explicit physical descriptions of women from the Talmudic texts. When asked whether it is appropriate for teens to study texts related to sexuality, Rabbi Lefkowitz replied:

> We are capable of having in-depth discussion of how to understand a text [with sexual content], without thinking even for a moment that the subject is a woman, as if it were in no way different from [studying] a text about laws for Sabbath observance.[60]

---

58. Friedlander, *Siftey Chaim*, Vol. 1, 415. See also, Wolbe, *Igraot*, 11.

59. Cited in the name of Rabbi Shmuel Rozovsky. See the website *Shtaygen*: http://www.shtaygen.co.il/?CategoryID=851&ArticleID=5686

60. Lefkowitz, *Darkei Chaim*, Vol. 1, 245.

When asked about young men studying portions on virginity in the Talmud tractate *Ketubot,* Rabbi Avrohom Yeshaya Karelitz replied: "The Torah can cause no harm!"[61] As long as the Talmud is studied within the yeshiva context, there can be no detriment to yeshiva students.

In the "protected body" mode, Musar teachers do not strive to create a "new self"; they do, however, sterilize *Musar,* distancing it from its original (ethical) meaning. Yeshiva students are here not encouraged to explore existential and concrete life questions, rather, they are given an alternative space, protected from life, where they must endeavor to erase forbidden emotional and physical stimuli. A modicum of spontaneity is encouraged—as long as it conforms to Jewish law—but this is far from true freedom.

Through the "protected body" approach, *Musar* literature loses its connection to real life in the community at large. Teachers in this system are fully aware that they are creating an alternative to Ultra-Orthodox Jewish life outside the yeshiva; in fact, this is their primary aim. Rabbi Wolbe states:

> A yeshiva is not a place only for obtaining knowledge, but rather a place for living a full life in accordance with the Torah. In the yeshiva, students learn to live as much as they learn to learn! . . . What then is a yeshiva? A place for the nurturing of the most ideal society: a society that exists to fulfill the purposes of heaven. Know this, that when you enter the yeshiva walls, you must become a builder of a community that is unequaled in this world.[62]

In the yeshiva, a student finds a "new family," and becomes an entirely unique kind of Jewish person. His reflections turn constantly to matters of Talmud, until he finally loses all connection with his interests and concerns prior to yeshiva life:

> What does it mean, then, to become a "member of a yeshiva" [*ben yeshiva*]? One becomes exactly what the phrase implies: a "son [*ben*] of the yeshiva." Just as we know that *ben torah* refers to someone who has become a "son of the Torah"—here too, a "son of the yeshiva" becomes a man (*'adam*) entirely different from all others; in fact, a "new man."[63]

---

61. *Darkei Chaim, Vol. 1,* 245.

62. Wolbe, *Alei Shur 1,* 31, 33.

63. Povarsky, *Musar Ve-Daat, Vol. 1,* 255. This passage plays on the idiomatic use of the Hebrew construct case for *ben*—which can mean "belonging to" or "member

Importantly, although the "protected body" of the yeshiva is far from what I described above as the "new self," still there is a similarity: here is the making of a "new Jewish person"—but through isolation rather than transcendence.

The process of such radical separation from the public sphere of normal Jewish life impacts not only *Musar* literature but also, increasingly, the cultural structures of Ultra-Orthodox society. Yeshiva students in pre-Holocaust Lithuania, for example, would often eat their meals with Jewish host-families in the city where they studied; after the Holocaust, yeshiva buildings are equipped with dining halls and even dormitories, further isolating students from the surrounding Ultra-Orthodox community.[64] In Israel, a growing sector of the rabbinic hegemony now encourages the building of yeshivas entirely outside the urban context of Haredi society, further removing students from external temptations. The *Musar* rabbis have even criticized students who refuse to distance themselves from home and to devote most of their time to the yeshiva.[65]

In this way, yeshivas are becoming "total institutions" in Erving Goffman's sense: institutions in which a large number of similar people are isolated from general society and live together for an extended period of time, following a shared, closed, and formally structured lifestyle.[66] And *Musar* teachers explicitly advocate for such radical alternatives to ordinary Jewish life:

> Whoever has put the Torah at the center of his life has no interest in wasting even a single night on pastimes like sleeping, eating or chatting with others. Whoever has reached this level of spiritual achievement surely will win the crown of the Torah.[67]

The same teachers also insist that it is impossible to bridge the divide between the yeshiva and the "outside world" and that anyone who attempts to do so is incapable of adhering to the Torah:

> Many mistakenly imagine that they can have it both ways: on the one hand to study all day and be admired as a "son of the

---

of" as well as—literally—"son of" or "child of."

64. Lefkowitz, *Darkei Chaim*, Vol. 2, 156. On the structure of the Lithuanian yeshivas before the Holocaust see, Stampfer, *Lithuanian Yeshivas*, 265–66.

65. Lefkowitz, *Darkei Chaim*, Vol. 2, 153–54.

66. Goffman, *Asylums*, xii. See also, Finkelman, "An Ideology for American Yeshiva Students."

67. Cohen, "Keter Torah," 74.

Torah" and, on the other hand, to live a life of pleasure in this world, fulfilling all the heart's desires. They are wrong. They do not know that the very foundation of spiritual possessions in this life is the distancing of oneself from the world.[68]

It is important to note that, as was the case with the "new self" model, the primary struggle of the "protected body" yeshiva model is not with the secular (and non-Jewish) world, but with mainstream Ultra-Orthodox Jewish culture outside the yeshiva. As Rabbi Kanievsky puts it, "In the past, someone who did not study in a yeshiva could still be a God-fearing and 'kosher' Jew, but today this is impossible."[69] *Torat HaMusar* now offers the yeshiva student the alternative of living exclusively within an environment that is as "sterile" as possible, cleared of all forbidden physical stimulations. Here, the student can be "free" in his own body, while the rabbinic hegemony can be "free" of real life's influences and undesirable consequences.

The isolated yeshiva world strives to distinguish itself from general Ultra-Orthodox Jewish society, precisely in the same way that Ultra-Orthodox Judaism strives to distance itself from the outside, secular, and non-Jewish world. In both cases, we see an embedded and zealous minority struggling for its identity against a more dominant culture seen as "other." Rabbi Schwardon, for example, states:

> [Rabbi Shalom] exhorted his listeners: "Let us despise the street, ... let us ridicule them mightily, with all our strength...." Rabbi Shalom taught the yeshiva students of this generation to despise the street, to make fun of it. He raised everyone up to his understanding that everything outside is vanity of vanities.[70]

"Everything outside" is not only vanity—it is threatening. Just as a Jew would only venture out of the medieval ghetto with trepidation, so Haredi yeshiva students think twice before venturing onto "the street"—even of a Jewish town. Yet venture out they must. Shielded from life in the all-male yeshiva, Jewish men could never marry or start a family; the real-life Jewish community would wither away, and the yeshiva with it.

Students are exempted from self-reflection within the yeshiva walls; outside, however, they are required to maintain a constantly reflective

---

68. Lefkowitz, *Darkei Chaim*, Vol. 2, 323.
69. Vaanunu, *Torah Me-shulchan Rabotenu*, 232.
70. Anonymous, *Kol Chozev*, 318.

state, as they encounter the "other" (Jewish Ultra-Orthodox) society. Rabbi Friedlander writes:

> When a man leaves the accustomed pathway of his life [in the yeshiva] and takes to the open road, he becomes vulnerable to physical and spiritual dangers, and in order to earn the divine protection, he will need to be strong and to remember that at every step God is with him, carefully watching his actions.[71]

Neither the "new self" nor the "protected body" approach can fully respond to the "problem" of the body and of physicality in Jewish religious terms. The "safety" of the yeshiva is illusory, and to wave one's arms and shout at a teacher is a symbolic freedom at best. Spontaneity is not the same as an open discourse engaging the body and the soul equally. Neither can either approach adequately address the ethical questions posed by sexual fantasies and physical/emotional urges naturally experienced by yeshiva students.

The effort to define the boundaries of a religious "safe space," where the body can comport itself "freely," raises a new series of challenges, and, as will be seen in the next chapter, these challenges also find expression in the writings of the *Musar* teachers.

---

71. Friedlander, *Siftey Chaim*, Vol. 1, 769.

CHAPTER 4

The Body and Sexuality

IN THE PREVIOUS CHAPTERS, I have described the *Musar* understanding of the Lithuanian Ultra-Orthodox male body. I have also analyzed the "problem" of the body as a symbol of a life devoid of reflection, and discussed the two "solutions" offered by the *Musar* movement, both of which are well known to anyone participating in a yeshiva lifestyle. Yeshivas are conceived as asexual places, designed to suppress and deny natural sexual instincts by blocking external stimuli. However, sexual desires arise spontaneously, and humans are not capable of fully controlling them. In fact, the effort to suppress our desire often becomes part of the desire itself, since our sexuality is a constituent of both our conscious and unconscious selves.

As we have seen, most *Musar* rabbis identify human sexuality only as an aspect of the body, ignoring the deep connections between sexuality and the whole self. Even a progressive *Musar* teacher like Rabbi Shlomo Wolbe devotes only one chapter of his major *Musar* work to sexuality.[1] And yet, while discussions on sexuality are rare in *Musar* literature, any research on the images of the male body in this tradition would be incomplete without an in-depth examination of this complex subject.

Michel Foucault suggests, that in modern Western society, human beings are now chiefly defined by their sexuality,[2] but that this was not the situation in the past. Before the seventeenth century, sexual acts and preferences were obviously part of individual lives in general, but

---

1. Wolbe, *Alei Shur 1*, 59–62. This is the same opinion voiced by Rabbi Yoel Schwartz in his discussion of sexuality. See Schwartz, *Binyan Adei-Ad*, 74; Lefkowitz, *Darkei Chaim, Vol. 1*, 379.

2. Foucault, *The History of Sexuality*, 15–50.

contributed much less than they do today to the establishment of self-identity. In Foucault's reading of history, for example, the now-familiar term *homosexuality* is a modern invention. Also, far from connoting merely the preference of individuals who choose sexual relations with members of the same gender, homosexuality is a defining identity indicator for these individuals. They feel that they belong primarily to a social group of people who are homosexual, no less than others may feel that their primary identity is defined by their religion, their artistic vocation, or their political convictions. The same is true, of course, for heterosexual individuals as well.[3]

Sexuality plays a subtle but crucial role in defining the identity of today's yeshiva students. Since they do not live in a vacuum, entirely disconnected from Western culture, they are influenced, and even largely defined by the rabbinic prohibition against the "outside" norm of premarital sex. Unlike Catholic and Buddhist monks, who spend their entire lives in a monastic context, an Ultra-Orthodox yeshiva student normally leaves the yeshiva between the ages of nineteen and twenty-five, when he is expected to marry. Now, living conjugally with his wife, he is required by his Jewish society to submit his body to intimacy with a female body. In the yeshiva, he had never experienced any connection with a woman—a being deeply associated in *Musar* teachings with the (dangerous) "other." Moreover, once married and "exiled" from the protected space of the yeshiva, the *Musar* man must also encounter other women in "the street"—meaning the Ultra-Orthodox public domain. The problematic of a Lithuanian Haredi man's sexuality is revealed and exacerbated once he marries and sexual encounter with his wife becomes part of his daily life, especially now that he is no longer aboard the "ark" of the yeshiva.[4]

In this chapter, I will focus on two main elements of *Musar* sexuality: autarchic sexuality and the conjugal life of yeshiva students after marriage.

A. Autarchic Male Sexuality

Masturbation is a vital test case for the clash between contradicting traditional Jewish-halakhic and Western-modern concepts of the body. In

---

3. Halperin, *One Hundred Years of Homosexuality*.
4. Hakak, "Haredi Male Bodies."

Western culture,[5] at least since the mid-twentieth century, masturbation is perceived as a normal phenomenon and part of a healthy lifestyle.[6] This reflects a view of physicality and sexuality as constituents of a personal project of self-realization, whereby individuals learn to know their body, to give themselves pleasure, and to explore their preferred sexuality.

Psychological literature places particular emphasis on masturbation during adolescence as part of sexual awakening and as a fantasy experience that is beneficial before engaging in sexuality with others. Studies show that men and women who practice masturbation are in closer touch with their sexuality as an important aspect of their lives.[7] Psychology views the ban on masturbation as one of the factors leading to adolescent guilt feelings detrimental to healthy sexual development and self-esteem.[8] This subject, then, is a classic instance of liberal Western culture setting limits on societal interference, arguing that regulating such a private practice is not a prerogative of the broader society.[9]

Masturbation, of course, is not an innovation of modernity but an integral element of human sexuality. Accordingly, Judaism has had a sustained discourse on the practice.[10] However, while energetic and public rabbinic dialogue characterizes other halakhic issues, there are very few records in Jewish history of such exchanges on the subject of masturbation. Concealment has ruled this discourse, preserving a clear distinction between the public sphere of books and halakhic rulings, and the private sphere, where the halakhic expert and the questioner conversed directly. However, what remained hidden in halakhic discourse was revealed in other literary genres. Kabbalah (Jewish mysticism) and Hasidism both expound on the gravity of masturbation, probably to compensate for the secrecy of halakhic literature on the matter.[11]

---

5. On Western views of masturbation, see Coontz, *Marriage, A History*, 150, 189. On Judaism's attitudes, see Pachter, *Shemirat ha-Brit*.

6. Regnerus, *Forbidden Fruit*, 20, 58, 114–18; Neuman, "Masturbation, Madness, and the Modern Concepts of Childhood and Adolescence," 3–5.

7. Simon, *Postmodern Sexualities*, 65–68, 83, 119–20.

8. Greenberg and Archambault, "Masturbation, Self-Esteem, and Other Variables"; Lo Presto and Sherman 1985.

9. Dobbins, *Teaching Your Children the Truth about Sex*. The modern person's quest for individual privacy touches on autarchic sexuality and the desire to create a sexual space detached from the public arena.

10. Hundert, *Jews in Poland and Lithuania in the Eighteenth Century*, 131–35; Ahituv, "*Tsni'ut* between Myth and Ethos." Biale, *Eros and the Jews*, 75–79, 107–10, 137.

11. See Pachter, *Shemirat ha-Brit*, 244–74.

In contrast to modern Western attitudes, traditional Jewish halakha views masturbation as a forbidden act with very serious consequences:

> Anyone who wastes his seed[12] is liable to the death penalty, as it is written, "... and the thing which he did displeased the Lord; so he slew him also" (Genesis 38:10). Rabbi Yitzhak and Rabbi Ami said, "It is as if he were a murderer, as it is written, "... [they are] slaying the children in the valleys under the clefts of the rocks" (Isaiah 57:5). Do not read *shohatei* [slaying] but *sohatei* [wringing out].[13]

Another halakhic source spells out the same idea: "He who wastes his seed, and he who speaks falsehood—it is as if he were a murderer."[14] Since, in Judaism, idolatry is worse than murder, the sages further highlight the gravity of the sin of masturbation when they state—in the continuation of the same Talmud passage quoted above—"Rabbi Assi said: 'It is as if he were an idolater.'" The authoritative *Shulhan Arukh* subsequently sums up the matter when it rules: "'It is forbidden [for a man] to waste his seed, and this sin is graver than any other mentioned in the Torah.'"[15]

The *Musar* movement, from the outset, has rarely addressed this challenge directly; when rabbis do offer an opinion, they struggle to remove the sting of condemnation. The minimal extant discussion of masturbation originates with rabbis who are not prominent leaders of the community. They confine themselves to brief references to the halakhic sources, and often refer the readers to the Kabbalistic discourse, which perceives masturbation as threatening and dangerous.[16]

---

12. In biblical Hebrew, male masturbation is described graphically as *lehotsi' zera' levetalah* ("to expel seed in vain," or "to waste seed"), with "seed" meaning semen, and "in vain" meaning outside the context of marital intercourse.

13. Talmud Bavli, *Niddah* 13a. This Talmudic "correction" of the biblical text understands "wringing out" ("expelling") as a euphemism for masturbation, and equates it with "slaying" in terms of guilt; the two words are also orthographically alike in Hebrew. Note that *responsa* literature has relied on these halakhic sources for its rulings. See, for instance, *Responsa Maharil*, #4; *Responsa Havat Ya'ir*, #31; *Tsits Eliezer*, Part 9, #51; *Seridei Esh*, Part 1, #162; *Responsa Beth She'arim*, #50; *Responsa Rav Pe'alim*, Part 3, *Even ha-Ezer*, #2 ; *Responsa Piskei Uzi'el*, vol. 4, *Hoshen Mishpat*, #46.

14. *Kalla Rabbati* 2:4–5.

15. *Shulhan Arukh, Even ha-Ezer*, #23 (1).

16. Ochana, *Kocha Shel Torah Lishmah*. We must remember that, unlike some Hasidim, most Lithuanian students do not study Kabbalah, which they see as a mysterious genre, expounding heavenly truths that they do not know how to approach. In

Three *Musar* works voice important opinions on the subject: *Tiferet Bachurim* ("The Glory of Youths");[17] *Kedushat Bnei-Yisrael* ("The Holiness of the Sons of Israel"); and *Kedoshim Tihiu* ("You Shall Be Holy"). In the first of these, published by a popular yeshiva press (*Bnei Torah*), and enjoying the *imprimatur* of major rabbis, the author quotes Kabbalistic sources against masturbation. However, he closes his book on a conciliatory note, with a personal exhortation to yeshiva students not to grieve when they fall into this sin.[18] A similar spirit emerges from *Kedushat Bnei-Yisrael*, which is published entirely on the Lithuanian website *Shtaygen*.[19]

Of the three works mentioned, *Kedoshim Tihiu*, a pamphlet published anonymously in the early 1980s with the *imprimatur* of Rabbi Nissim Karelitz, takes the most rigid approach.[20] It opens with traditional sources forbidding touching the genitals, or thinking of Torah in "impure" places such as the toilet.[21] To counter sexual thoughts, the author advises yeshiva students to cool the body, by leaving the legs uncovered during sleep, for example. They should never stay in bed when they feel sexual arousal, even if this occurs in the dead of night. If the stimulus continues, the author counsels students to avoid going back to bed; instead, they are to stand up, remaining thus until they fall asleep in that position.[22] They are not to wipe the genitals after showering and not to bathe them for several weeks, if necessary, to avoid temptation.[23]

The ultimate remedy, however, is matrimony, and the author urges yeshiva students to marry at the age of eighteen so that they may thereafter discharge their sexual need with permission.[24] At the end of the book, the author cites a whole collection of warnings from various Jewish

---

modern Western writings on spirituality, many contemporary rabbis choose colorful, gentle, and uplifting quotes from the Kabbalah; in Lithuanian *Musar*, on the other hand, Kabbalistic citations are often harsh and terrifying.

17. Anonymous, *Tiferet Bachurim*. This book had an earlier (1992) version titled *Kuntres Ohel Kedoshim*.

18. Anonymous, *Tiferet Bachurim*, 106–8.

19. A Yiddish term meaning to study deeply and intensely. http://www.shtaygen.net/sprim/kdusht_bny_israel.pdf. Ratzabi, *Kdushat Bnei-Israel*.

20. Anonymous, *Kedoshim Tihiu*.

21. Anonymous, *Kedoshim Tihiu*, 13–14.

22. Anonymous, *Kedoshim Tihiu*, 19–21, 43.

23. Anonymous, *Kedoshim Tihiu*, 62.

24. Anonymous, *Kedoshim Tihiu*, 42.

sources, detailing the metaphysical damage caused in Heaven by an autoerotic act, and including descriptions of the divine punishment awaiting the masturbator. For example, the author asks young men to imagine the pain of passing a kidney stone, and suggests that this is mild compared to the punishments decreed for anyone who "expels his seed in vain."[25]

Among prominent named *Musar* leaders, most, as we have said, avoid this subject. A unique exception is Rabbi Eliyahu Dessler. He cites one of the Kabbalistic masters—Rabbi Isaac Luria, known as *Ha'ARI*—who claims that a yeshiva student can, by even one act of masturbation, lose all the holiness he has accumulated through his Talmud studies.[26]

The threatening discourse on masturbation, however, is almost imperceptible with in the wide spectrum of Lithuanian literature. The *Musar* hegemony counsels yeshiva students not to raise the subject, or "even to [dwell in] regret about it,"[27] since regret over "wasted seed" is a preoccupation with sexuality, and "it may be that this [regret] itself is the doing of the evil inclination, to cause a man to have [sexual] thoughts."[28] Rabbi Michel Yehuda Lefkowitz instructs a father not to tell his son that masturbation is a sin, but only that it harms the body and should therefore be avoided;[29] he also forbids *Musar* teachers from speaking to their students about it.[30] It is Rabbi Yaakov Yisrael Kanievsky's claim, that nocturnal emissions result from thoughts about sexuality while the individual is awake, and that an emission might be traceable to a sensual thought from weeks in the past. In his view, yeshiva students cannot be held responsible for controlling their bodies; he even quotes one of the masters of the Hasidic tradition as "poking fun at people who have regrets about nocturnal emissions."[31] All of these examples confirm that, according to the rabbinical hegemony, the way to prevent sexual stimulation is not by zealous preventative measures, but by a total devotion to Torah study.[32]

---

25. Anonymous, *Kedoshim Tihiu*, 53.
26. Lopian, *Lev Eliyahu Vol. 3*, 27–28.
27. Lefkowitz, *Imrei Da'at*, 105.
28. Lefkowitz, *Imrei Da'at*, 105.
29. Lefkowitz, *Darkei Chaim, Vol. 1*, 37, 58.
30. Lefkowitz, *Darkei Chaim, Vol. 1*, 46.
31. Kanievsky, *Kovetz Igrot*, 180–81.
32. Lefkowitz, *Darkei Chaim, Vol. 1*, 106, 182–83.

Rabbi Chaim Friedlander views the sin of masturbation not as a "failure" but as a "fall," with "failure" denoting an existential evil state, while "falling" is a natural part of human growth. Even the righteous must, on occasion, fall: "For a righteous man falls seven times, and rises" (Prov 24:16). This being so, "We must, like the righteous, get up and renew our strength, trusting in God, who extends His aid to everyone seeking to be pure."[33]

One can find an even more moderate approach in a letter sent by Rabbi Yitzchok Hutner to a yeshiva student who complained about his "falls" in the area of sexuality. The young man's letter is not available to us, but it can be inferred from Rabbi Hutner's response that the student wrote of his failings in the area of sensuality, and complained that he could not reach the level of Torah scholars who were free of any sexual thought. Due to the unique insights in Rabbi Hutner's long reply, I consider it appropriate to quote here significant portions:

> It is a serious failing of ours, that when we dwell on the perfections of our sages (*gedoleinu*), we are actually only looking at their ultimate attainments. We tell of their perfect ways, but at the same time skip over the internal struggles that raged in their souls. So you get the impression that the sages of Israel (*gedolei Yisrael*) came forth from the hand of God with their stature and character fully formed.
>
> As a result, any young man with spirit, aspiration and zeal, upon finding within himself stumbling blocks, failings, and weaknesses, may regard himself as not "planted in the house of the Lord" (Psalm 1). For such a youth imagines that to be "planted in the house of the Lord," means precisely to sit with a tranquil soul in "green pastures beside still waters" (Ibid) enjoying the good inclination (*yetser ha-tov*), even as the saints sit and enjoy the radiance of the divine Presence (*ha-shekhinah*), with their crowns upon their heads, in the Garden of Eden, never troubled, on the other hand, by the evil inclination (*yetser ha-ra'*).
>
> But know this, dear friend: your soul is rooted, not in the tranquility of the good inclination but precisely in the war waged with the evil inclination. And your precious and heartfelt letter bears witness a hundredfold that you are indeed a faithful warrior in the army of the good inclination.

---

33. Anonymous, *Kedoshim Tihiu*, 89.

In English they have a saying: "Lose a battle and win the war!" Certainly, you have stumbled, and will stumble again, and in more than one engagement you will fall captive. But I promise you, that after having lost every battle you will yet finish this war with the victory wreath upon your brow!

The wisest of men [i.e. King Solomon] says, "For a righteous man falls seven times, and yet rises" (Proverbs 24:16). Fools may think that this means, that even though the righteous man may fall seven times, each time he is able to stand up again. The wise, however, know well the true meaning: the righteous man's very ability to "stand up" derives essentially from his "seven falls." If your letter had told me only of your good deeds and the divine commands [*mitzvot*] you fulfilled, I would have said, "That was a good letter." But now that your letter tells me of your falls and failings, and the obstacles [you encounter], I can say, "This is a *very* good letter you have sent me!" Please, do not imagine the sages and their good inclination as being one and the same. Rather, portray in your mind's eye the greatness of the sages of all time [*gadlutam shel gedolei 'olam*] in terms of a terrible war against all kinds of impulses and humiliations and failings. So, whenever you feel the storm of the evil inclination in your breast, know that in this you are like the great sages themselves, much more than when you are resting in the perfect tranquility you so desire. For it is at those very junctures where you feel the most failings, that you stand most ready to become a vessel for the excellence of heavenly glory.[34]

Rabbi Hutner's approach here upends the image of the worthy yeshiva student prevailing in *Musar* writings in general. There, the young man aspiring to virtue must compare himself to ideal models entirely free of sin. For Hutner, this tendency toward moral idealization in the literature is not only mistaken, but also sets up a false pedagogical equivalence between Jewish ideals and the sinless life. In reality, Hutner asserts, the ideal human being—the *tzadik*, or Jewish saint—is to be recognized precisely by his constant struggle with his own sinfulness. Wrestling day and night with his desires and flaws, the *tzadik* more often than not fails to

---

34. *Hutner, Pachad Itzchak: Igrot*, 228. Rabbi Yitzchok Hutner (1906–1980) was born in Poland. He had roots in both Hasidic and Lithuanian traditions, and studied in the Slabodka Yeshiva, first in Lithuania and later in Palestine. Rabbi Hutner was one of the prominent post-Holocaust leaders of the community in the U.S.A., where he served as head of the *Chaim Berlin* Yeshiva. His honorific pseudonym was *Pachad Yitzchok*—from the title of his well-known series of books on *Musar*.

overcome them. But the very fact that he engages in this spiritual combat, the very fact that he strives to forge a new life—it is this that defines the Jewish spiritual hero. Moral mentoring of the yeshiva student must not, then, be reduced to measuring him against unapproachable models. Rather, the pedagogical thrust must be focused on grappling with reality, and a deep desire for change.

Over the past fifty years, many *Musar* teachers have emancipated yeshiva students from guilt and self-flagellation, directing them instead to devote themselves to Talmud study. Responding to a student, Rabbi Kanievsky writes: "The only counsel for a young [i.e. unmarried] man [who wants to] avoid [sexual desires], is to engage himself in the study of Torah for the sake of Heaven. . . . But you should not harbor hope that in a day or two you can be saved from this deep-rooted sin."[35] In another letter, Kanievsky parts company from rabbis who cite threatening discourses from the *Zohar* and other Kabbalistic mystical texts. Instead, he chooses positive Kabbalah passages to empower unmarried students and simultaneously comfort them:

> The holy books [i.e. classical Kabbalistic works], were intended to stop the sinner, and therefore describe in great detail how, by this sin [of masturbation], our deeds may be abducted, Heaven forbid.[36] These works, however, give short shrift to explaining how, while a man may fail many times, still, on other occasions he triumphs and overcomes his lust. And then, in that very moment when he masters the passion burning within him, he draws forth the light of sanctity, in himself and in the whole cosmos [*ha-'olamot*] in a most holy way. . . . And the supreme holiness of such a man is indescribable.[37]

Kanievsky is a fascinating example of how Ultra-Orthodox rabbis may express opposition to previous traditions that they identify as depressive. Kanievsky seemingly accepts the Kabbalah's stand against masturbation, but at the same time he emphasizes the spiritual courage of a pious young man, and the positive meaning of every moment of his life when he does not masturbate. These positive elements are not even mentioned in the mystical Kabbalah texts that Rabbi Kanievsky responds

---

35. Anonymous, *Kedoshim Tihiu*, 152–53. See also, Hecht, *Shut Libnei Ha-Neurim*, 91–95.

36. This passage implies that through the sin of masturbation, evil powers divert the power of good deeds to their sinister realm.

37. Anonymous, *Kedoshim Tihiu*, 154.

too, but he highlights them nonetheless. Some other prominent *Musar* rabbis take a much harder line, inveighing harshly against autarchic male sexuality. However, even those rabbis unequivocally reject the idea of self-punishment, whether monetarily or by multiple visits to the *mikvah*.[38]

Rabbi Shlomo Wolbe, who is among the moderate *Musar* voices in his approach to masturbation, offers a fascinating new proposal. His view is that male sexuality is not a constitutive element within masculine identity, and that its primary purpose is not to satisfy a man's needs. Rather, a man's sexuality is only given to him as a means to satisfy a woman, within the framework of marriage:

> The evil inclination [*yetser ha-ra'*—i.e., sexual desire] was created [in a man] for the sake of his wife.... What, then, is the *evil* in this inclination? It is when a man embezzles the *kodashim*,[39] awakening the [sexual] instinct (created for his wife's sake) for his own personal pleasure, God forbid! For this inclination, by its very nature and purpose, does not belong to us [men], nor for our pleasure was it given to us. When we use this instinct, that was entirely created for our "other" [i.e. our wife], with a selfish and egotistical intention—then it becomes an "evil inclination."[40]

Kodashim—as objects dedicated to the Temple—are not a man's private property, even if the objects remain in his home and under his protection. Lay people must safeguard these priestly objects, and anyone who uses them to satisfy personal needs "embezzles" their sanctity.

Rabbi Wolbe's *Musar* view of men's sexuality as held in "sacred trust" for their female companions, is not only unique, but does not correspond with either of the solutions to the "problem" of the body outlined earlier.[41] Proponents of both the "new self" and the "protected body" teach that the body as a whole—including its sexuality—is *not part of the self*, and is only experienced as such because of original sin, when humans partook of the Tree of Knowledge of Good and Evil. Wolbe, by contrast, sees male sexuality as a "sacred" gift, entrusted to men by God in order that they in turn may give it to women. It is easy to see how Wolbe is

---

38. A bath used for the purpose of ritual cleansing through immersion. See Lefkowitz, *Darkei Chaim*, Vol. 1, 404–6.

39. This biblical term means "holy things" and refers to sacrificial animals or anything dedicated in former days to the Temple, and therefore belonging to God.

40. Wolbe, *BeTzel HaChohma*, 75.

41. See chapter 3.

tending closer to the views of modern society, which sees sexual identity as a constitutive component of the self.[42]

Wolbe's teaching of sexuality does not judge yeshiva students harshly for masturbation, but responds in a sensitive and understanding way. In one passage, he opens with a quote from the Talmud: "If this wretched [evil inclination] troubles you [*paga' bekha*], then drag it into the study hall [i.e. go and study Torah]."[43] Then, Wolbe goes on:

> It is clear that every son of Torah [i.e. yeshiva student] must fearlessly combat the evil inclination, repelling its advances as best he can. If, however, after all this struggle, he has still not managed to push it back, and it continues to torment him [*metzik lo 'od*]—let him not become at all spiritually despondent. Do not ever despair, or become sad, but rather continue all the more in your study [of Torah], with joy and with vitality, and there will come a time, with God's help, when you will be victorious![44]

Moreover, Wolbe writes that "every healthy young man sometimes feels lustful," explaining that this is because of the important role that sexuality will play after marriage.[45] In one of his letters, he cites the *Vilna Ga'on*[46] as saying that the warnings in the Kabbalah and Zohar concerning those who "waste their seed in vain" do not apply to anyone engaged in learning Torah.[47] In another letter, he relies on a similar oral tradition attributed to the *Chazon Ish* (Rabbi Karelitz). My assumption is that he mentions these august authorities precisely because he is aware of how radical his opinion is, compared to other senior *Musar* rabbis.[48]

Whether liberal or conservative, Lithuanian *Musar* literature, as we have pointed out, rarely addresses the subject of masturbation. When it does, the grave nature of the act is emphasized, but *Musar* distances itself from the characteristic Kabbalistic and Hasidic exhortations to self-flagellation and self-loathing. In my opinion, the *Musar* hegemony has no interest in dealing directly with sexual desire, because Lithuanian *Musar* theory, which is concerned with existential questions about the

42. Foucault, *The History of Sexuality*, 17, 27.
43. *Talmud Bavli*, Kiddushin 30:b.
44. Wolbe, *Igraot*, 11.
45. Wolbe, *Igraot*, 11.
46. Rabbi Elijah ben Solomon Zalman (1720–97).
47. Wolbe, *Igraot*, 22.
48. Wolbe, *Igraot*, 25.

uniqueness of man and the observation of his desires and actions, lacks the necessary tools to adequately address this issue. Encouraging reflective activity as a means to achieving a moral life, while simultaneously demanding a stark prohibition of sexual urges, can only lead to a diametric opposition in values, since there is a fear that reflecting on sexual desire may actually intensify it. *Musar* rabbis, then, avoid confronting the "evil inclination" of sexuality directly, and seek different ways to thwart it more obliquely. They achieve this end by diverting the student's attention away from his sexual experiences and back to the study of Talmud, a pursuit that becomes thus, paradoxically, almost the opposite of reflection. We have seen in chapter 3 how Lithuanian *Musar* teachings preach deep reflection in all other aspects of human activity. Here, however, we see that Talmud study itself is the exception, and becomes like a solitary island of unreflective practice surrounded by a sea of self-examination. This delicate and contradictory balancing act at the core of *Musar* theory allows crucial subjects such as masturbation to be pushed into a non-reflective corner, never to be examined.

Not only masturbation, but suggestive thoughts about the opposite sex are thoroughly suppressed in the same way. *Musar* rabbis strive not only to prevent yeshiva students from encountering women, but also to curtail any reflection on the meaning of women in their lives. Rabbi Michel Yehuda Lefkowitz even forbade married men from hosting evening Talmud study for unmarried yeshiva students, because of the possibility that the visiting students might encounter the host's wife.[49]

Yeshiva students wear clothing no less modest than that of girls in the community. They avoid shorts, short-sleeved shirts, and anything colorful. They usually wear a white shirt and dark pants, and do not leave the yeshiva without a top garment, including a dark suit and hat. Lithuanian yeshiva students avoid nakedness or partial nudity, even in the dormitory with their bunk mates; even sandals in the heat of summer are rejected, lest their feet be exposed to view.

Musar literature elaborates on the reasons for this strict modesty of dress, and sexuality plays a significant role in this reasoning. The rabbinical hegemony assumes that a man's attire will identify him as Ultra-Orthodox, even outside the yeshiva walls, and that being visible in this way will prevent him from sinning, for example, by going into a cinema

---

49. Lefkowitz, *Darkei Chaim*, Vol. 1, 89.

to watch a movie.⁵⁰ The principle of visibility and its role in preserving and enforcing social norms has been discussed in many studies. Michel Foucault shows how society imprints its ideology and laws on the body. Prisoners' uniforms, for example, are not only markers informing outsiders of a person's affiliation with a detention center; they also remind the prisoner of her/his place in society, and of the rules that derive from this status. The same applies in hospitals to both patients' gowns and nurses' "scrubs," and, of course, to police and military uniforms.⁵¹

The layers of clothing worn by yeshiva students are also intended to help them "forget" their sexual organs by keeping them out of sight. The idea here is that the very act of seeing creates an identification between a man and his body. Thus, concealing the body reduces the encounter between the self and those physical limbs and organs that the Lithuanian Ultra-Orthodox society would prefer to ignore. There are, in fact, laws that enforce this separation. For example, there is a strict halakhic prohibition against contact between the "pure" body parts (those that are not covered, like the face and hands), and the "impure." The latter must always be covered, and include not only the genitals, but also the chest, back, legs, feet, and (for some) the hair as well. Contact with these must be mediated by a garment, so that the cloth separates the touching hand—which is identified with the self—from the skin of "impure" body parts. Whenever it is absolutely necessary for a yeshiva student to touch his private parts, he is instructed to wash his hands immediately after contact.⁵² The enforced invisibility of certain parts of the body eventually habituates the yeshiva student to an organization of his self-image without reference to those parts, resulting in alienation between the experience of the individual's "self" and the experience of the (mostly covered) body.

A strict dress code also reflects the view that yeshiva students are tasked with representing "the honor of Torah" and must dress accordingly.⁵³ In the State of Israel in particular, this honor discourse is given a unique edge, as some *Musar* rabbis there compare yeshiva students' attire

---

50. Aran, "Denial Does Not Make the Haredi Body Go Away"; The world of "virtual reality" is especially terrifying to the Ultra-Orthodox community, precisely because there even the most rigidly modest clothing cannot shield the student from temptation.

51. Foucault, *Discipline and Punish*, 217; Milles, *Discourse*, 33–52.

52. Aran, "Denial Does Not Make the Haredi Body Go Away," 106.

53. Schwartz, *Sefer Kdushat Israel*, 35–37.

to military uniforms. This comparison is symptomatic of the tensions within different Israeli Jewish communities around the fact that yeshiva students are exempted from service in the Israel Defense Forces.[54] For example, descriptions of encounters between Israeli military figures and leaders of the Ultra-Orthodox community highlight the honorable role of yeshiva students as "soldiers of Torah":

> At one of the meetings between the [I.D.F.] military commanders and the rabbinic leaders of the Ultra-Orthodox community [*gedolei ha-dor*], Rabbi Yisra'el [Gustman] rose to speak. He began to describe the appearance of a great army in the most picturesque terms, including the deployment of troops and the array of regiments for battle, as well as the challenges they must face. Then he gave more details, saying: "Do you know who this army is [that I have just described]? It is the [host of] yeshiva students, in the yeshivas of Hebron, ... of Ponevezh, of Mir. ... And do you know where they store their mortars and their missiles? In the bookcases of those yeshivas ...." *And I have been told by eyewitnesses, that the then Defense Minister himself, Mr. [Yitzhak] Rabin, a military man to his core, ... was so impressed by this powerful description [of yeshiva life], that he rose from his seat, and saluted [Rabbi Gustman], the Commander in Chief of the forces of Torah.*[55]

For *Musar* teachers, combat with an external foe can be likened to the struggle with the enemy within, the evil inclination, especially in the arena of sexual impulses. However, while the Israeli army confronts finite and recognizable enemies, yeshiva students grapple with an internal assailant, whose strength is never exhausted and who never declares a cease-fire. Moreover, Lithuanian society espouses the belief that the establishment and continuing survival of the beleaguered State of Israel is literally miraculous, and that the way to convince God to perform miracles and save the Jewish people is through the power of Torah study:

> Immediately after the Six-Day War, Rabbi Sarna travelled to Rachel's Tomb and there met Ben-Gurion [the first Israeli Prime Minister]. Ben-Gurion knew Rabbi Sarna, and asked him: "Well, Rabbi Sarna, what do you say about our victory?" Without blinking an eye, Rabbi Sarna retorted: "*Your* victory?! Had

---

54. Stadler, *Yeshiva Fundamentalism*, 96–116; Aran, "Denial Does Not Make the Haredi Body Go Away."

55. Friedman, *Shtaygen*, 39.

it not been for the yeshiva students standing at their stations [studying Torah], twenty-four hours a day, you would have been lost."[56]

This image of yeshiva students as fighters is enhanced by the Lithuanian dress code, perceived as one of the essential weapons in the struggle against temptation. The soldiers of the army of God will spend their entire lives on the front lines. Since they must be constantly vigilant against seduction, they are never allowed to remove their uniforms, as secular soldiers can do, for example, when at home, on leave from their army units.[57] It is not surprising, therefore, to find that when a yeshiva student ventures into "enemy territory" by leaving the study hall for the street, he is compelled by his teachers to armor himself all the more, by means of his distinctive dress.[58]

In recent years, awareness of the issue of homosexuality has increased in the rabbinic hegemony, along with the fear of sexual tension between young men and their fellow students in the yeshiva.[59] Rabbi Yehuda Lefkowitz has written in the name of Rabbi Yechezkel Levenstein, that sexual desire is directed not only toward women but also toward men, and therefore, in his opinion, the dictates of modesty should be observed between men, just as between men and women.[60] In a few cases, he even requires that youths who study together in *chavruta*[61] be separated (sometimes by sending one of the boys to another yeshiva) if there is concern that the intimacy of shared study is excessive, or that homoerotic desire is emerging between the two students.[62] In addition, Rabbi Lefkowitz forbade adult yeshiva students (bachelors in their late twenties) from studying alongside younger students, for fear of sexual tension.[63] Concerning this issue, he wrote explicitly:

56. Wolbe, *Avnei Shlomo*, 95.
57. Turner, "Social Body."
58. On clothing as defending see, Barnard, *Fashion as Communication*, 51–53.
59. Friedlander, *Siftey Chaim*, Vol. 2, 46.
60. Lefkowitz, *Darkei Chaim*, Vol. 1, 401.
61. The traditional yeshiva way of study is in *havruta*, meaning two students learning together intensely for several hours each day.
62. Lefkowitz, *Darkei Chaim*, Vol. 2, 46–47, 321, 400–404; Lefkowitz, *Darkei Chaim*, Vol. 1, 402–3.
63. Lefkowitz, *Darkei Chaim*, Vol. 2, 69.

Sometimes, due to their personalities, two young men may become too attached to and too dependent upon each other. Such close fraternity is not at all desirable, and if we think [carefully] about such behavior, [we see] that to separate [the boys] is "for the sake of heaven" [i.e., the best option]. And do not allow your heart to grieve over this [decision].[64]

B. The Female Body as a *Musar* "Problem"

From our discussion thus far, it should be obvious that the apparently generic references in *Torat HaMusar* discourse to "body" and "person" (*guf* and *'adam* in Hebrew) are in fact intended to mean only the body and person of the Jewish *man*. Women are entirely excluded, along with any effort to provide Jewish women with a pathway to a reflective life. *Musar* literature here continues the long tradition of Jewish writings that ignore women and are addressed only to men.[65] In Ultra-Orthodoxy, the habitual social chasm between the genders is so deep, that *Musar* teachings addressed to yeshiva students do not even need to explain why women are automatically excluded from the discourse. We have already noted that women and children are all exempted from the formal Jewish obligation to study Torah. However, the rabbis make it clear that *male children* are in a privileged category, even at a tender age, as compared to women and girls. For example, while young children of both sexes may, like women, read and study Torah (including biblical stories), Rabbi Aharon Kotler explains that there is an essential difference between boys and girls in this regard:

> True, both [boys and girls] are exempted from the command [*'ainam metzuvim*] to study Torah. However, a male child is inherently under the category of being commanded. His tender physical age poses a [temporary] impediment to fulfilling this command; his soul, however, is fully and actually capable of holiness. ... This is not the case with a [girl or] woman, who is never obligated to study Torah [no matter what her age]; the command simply does not apply to her [*lo' mefikda klal*]. As a woman, she is excluded [*mufka'at*] from the sanctity of the mitzvah inherent in Torah study. If she does study Torah, then, this

---

64. *Darkei Chaim*, Vol. 2, 321.

65. On the status of women in Haredi society cf. Blumen, "Crisis-crossing Boundaries"; Feder, *Mizvah Girls'*.

can never be understood as fulfilling [the scriptural passage] that says "If it were not for [the observance of] my covenant day and the night, then [it would be as if] that the statutes of heaven and earth had never been established" (Jeremiah 33:25).[66] The woman's [sacred] work is in [supporting the study of] her [male] children.[67]

It is clear from Rabbi Kotler's remarks that there is no debate in the male yeshiva sphere about whether women are exempt from the obligation of learning Torah, and therefore not qualified for this type of holiness, and excluded from the benefits of those who are obligated to study. These writings do try to explain why "human" and "body" refer only to the Lithuanian *man*, not the woman, but they do so only when the precise boundary of the "we" male group becomes blurred, as it does in marriage.

An example of this "blurring" is encountered when Jewish women acquire expertise in sacred learning. Since the axis of male yeshiva studies has been fixed by the rabbinical hegemony on a set number of tractates from the Babylonian Talmud, there remain many genres of sacred texts that remain outside this basic yeshiva canon. These genres include the entire Jewish Bible (*Tanach*), classical moral texts, Hasidic works, Jewish historical sources, and even a large number of halakhic compositions. In the course of time, Jewish women have appropriated these cultural treasures to themselves, with the result that the male hegemony feels its authority challenged. As one rabbi remarks dolefully:

> I am ashamed to tell you that I have myself encountered situations where the young man [upon meeting a potential spouse] has said [of the woman]: "This is not what I was looking for! She

---

66. In the Ultra-Orthodox interpretation of the biblical verse from the prophet Jeremiah, pious Jews are daily responsible for "observing the covenant" through their commitment to study Torah. If, then, there is one moment when no (male) Jew is somewhere studying Torah, then the world would be instantly destroyed. In an essay entitled "Torah and Mitzvah Called to Her," Rabbi Sarna explains, that Jewish men center their lives around being "God's slaves" unequivocally commanded to study Torah constantly. Women are not subject to this command and are not "slaves," but study Torah voluntarily. Therefore, they do not share the existential intensity of men's life experience. See Sarna, *Daliyot Yehezkel 1*, 411–12.

67. Kotler, *Mishnat Rabbi Aharon Kotler, Vol. 1*, 12. Rabbi Aharon Kotler (1891–1962) became one of the prominent leaders of the community in the U.S.A. and founded *Beth Midrash Govoha* (BMG, also called the Lakewood Yeshiva) in Lakewood, New Jersey. This is one of the two largest Lithuanian Ultra-Orthodox yeshivas in the world, together with the Mir Yeshiva in Jerusalem.

is a much better [student] than I am; she is more pious than I am. I could never handle [being married] to someone like her!⁶⁸

Every few years, the debate about whether or not women should delve into non-Talmudic Jewish studies re-emerges:

> These days, we teach women [*ha-banot*] an abundance of study material, even including sacred texts.... We should remember, however, that we have no interest in [i.e. we cannot approve of] this multiplicity of studies [for women], even if [they do include] sacred subjects.⁶⁹

These criticisms are oblique. More direct rebukes appear in some rare cases, especially when women claim that their Jewish knowledge bestows on them authority to make decisions in the community, or even at home: "First, [a woman] feels that she has already studied Torah, and has already gained understanding [*kvar mevinah*]; then she begins relying on her own personal insight [*ha-havanah ha-'ishit shelah*]."⁷⁰

We have noted that yeshiva students live among the larger Ultra-Orthodox population, and are thus exposed to constant stimuli, whether in their parents' home or in public places, but most especially when dating.⁷¹ For a young Jewish man, marriage is a kind of exile from the yeshiva; it is a critical initiation to "the street," as well as a first intimate encounter with a member of the other sex. Conjugal relations entail sexuality, but also—and no less importantly—the rounds of daily life with the other gender. The married couple shares conversations, family meals, the challenges of raising children, and every night they sleep next to each other. All of these experiences are, first and foremost, *physical*; they can profoundly shake the *Musar* perception of the body, especially since women in this tradition are certainly not raised with the same concept of "body" that the men are taught.⁷²

Men who continue their studies after their marriage do so not in a yeshiva, but rather in a *kolel*—a study framework that is closer to home and therefore to feminine realities.⁷³ The end of the yeshiva chapter is,

68. Stern, *Bait u-Menucha*, 59.
69. Friedlander, *Darkei HaChaim Vol. 1*, 439.
70. Stern, *Bait u-Menucha*, 59.
71. Stadler, *Yeshiva Fundamentalism*, 119–20.
72. There is almost no scholarly research on Ultra-Orthodox sexuality. For first academic works see, Brown, "Kedusha."
73. El-Or, "Visibility and Possibilities." It is important to note that the critical

for these men, an irreversible loss, and may occasion bouts of anxiety and denial. For example, this tale of Rabbi Reuven Yoself Gershonowitz's wedding day focuses on the rabbi's pursuit of study until the last possible moment, when he had to tear himself away from the Talmud text and its sacred protective sphere:

> The *Matmid*[74] he was called by the young students, who admired his constancy in study. Even on his wedding day [*be-yom chuppato*], the *Matmid* stood in his usual place in the yeshiva study hall, learning as diligently as always. No one could discern any change in his behavior. An hour before the time of the wedding ceremony [*ha-chuppah*] he closed the Talmud volume, saying that now it was time to make the journey to [the city of] Ramat Ha-Sharon, because in an hour's time—as he said—"a wedding will be taking place there."[75]

This vignette highlights the transformative—and traumatic—moment when the "best student," the symbol of constant piety, is uprooted from his place of safety, and is transplanted to the new and unfamiliar soil of sharing life with a woman. The *Matmid* chooses words that reveal a deep dissociation: not "*his* wedding," but "*a* wedding will be taking place." For a yeshiva man, marriage is simply an unavoidable event, since the law Jewish life does not offer a monastic option.

The *habitus* of the yeshiva provides the Jewish man with a refuge from the reality, sometimes fantastical and sometimes horrifying, of the encounter between the sexes. When the *habitus* is broken, and the chasm between the imagined and the real is revealed through marriage, the resultant shock may trigger the surfacing of other contradictions long concealed.[76] Thus Rabbi Stern teaches:

> As long as a young man is within the yeshiva, living a common way of life in the yeshiva day and night, this in itself strengthens him in Torah study and in piety. The situation is very different

---

attitude toward marriage adopted by the *Musar* movement (and a handful of other Jewish ideologies) is the exception rather than the rule in Judaism, which generally regards the married state positively, as the only sanctioned path to spiritual and physical fulfillment; cf. Biale, *Eros and the Jews*.

74. The honorific *Matmid* ("Diligent One") denotes someone who studies the Talmud constantly.

75. Anonymous, *Hi Sichati*, Vol. 1, 811.

76. Robbins, *The Work of Pierre Bourdieu*, 112.

for an *avrech*[77] who has started a family; even if he continues his path in the world of the *kolel*, and in study of Torah ... he is still liable to fall by the wayside.[78]

Thus, leaving the yeshiva and its protected space is perceived by the *Musar* teachers as a threat to the spiritual progress of Jewish men.

We must remember that my research here focuses only on the study of the texts upon which the discourse the Lithuanian hegemony is formed. We do not know whether these texts represent a sociological reality, or only describe the *Musar* ideal, while ignoring the surrounding actualities; for that, further study is needed. Conversations I initiated with Lithuanian yeshiva students frequently indicated a gap between the texts and what is said during living encounters between students and rabbis. Even if this (unrecorded) oral debate surrounding marriage and sexual relations is fundamentally different from the texts we are citing, it will be necessary to examine how and why the discrepancy occurs; this however is not the purpose of this book. In the pages that follow, I focus on what is written in the works of the *Musar* leaders, exposing the image of the sexual body that emerges from them; the encounter between the written theory and the lived praxis must be deferred for future research.

Writings intended for men on matters of sexuality are not popular.[79] Special preparation for grooms usually takes the form of private conversations, considered "oral teachings." Nevertheless, the way *Musar* writers critique the way of life of Lithuanian men after they are married, can teach us about significant changes in the Ultra-Orthodox sphere, especially around the transition into married life. *Musar* literature, as I argue, finds it difficult to explain to yeshiva students the Jewish role of sexuality in the framework of *Musar*. The writings therefore strive in various ways to prevent sexuality, or, alternatively, to transform it into an idealized surrogate with a spiritual and symbolic character, having little in common with sexuality in its realistic sense. The literature therefore focuses on preparing the yeshiva student for encounter with sexuality in two distinct areas: the home (private space) and "the street" (public space).

77. "*Avrech*" is a term used to designate a yeshiva student after he has been married.
78. Stern, *Bait u-Menucha*, 42.
79. Only in the past few years can one can see more writings on this subject. See for example, Lorincz, *Binat HaMidot*. In the Lithuanian community in the USA there are, recently, more books of marriage guidance. See for example, *Kuntres Sehel Tov*.

C. Encounters with Sexuality at Home

According to Rabbi Chaim Friedlander, who quotes a letter from Rabbi Yaakov Israel Kanievsky, male sexuality is an instrument given to a man in order to pleasure his wife. We have seen a similar sentiment in Wolbe's writings. Wolbe, however, claimed that a man's sexuality *does not* essentially belong to him; Kanievsky holds that it *does* belong to him, and that he shares it with his wife *as an act of charity*. For Kanievsky, when a man makes love to his wife he gives her his sexuality as a gift, and this is a voluntary act of grace:

> When a man draws [his wife] close, and intimately embraces her, and does other such things, all for the sake of Heaven and out of compassion, so that she will not be hurt or unhappy, then this will not in any way entail a weakening of his piety or cause him to fall into lust. On the contrary, this brings him into holiness, and thus he will fulfill the positive divine command [*mitzvat 'asseh*] written in the Torah: "Walk in His ways" (Deuteronomy 30:16), and "Just as He is compassionate [*rahum*], so too should you be compassionate" (Talmud Shabbat 133:b).[80]

Friedlander does not attribute any positive *Musar* significance to the sexual act itself; on the contrary, he accepts the assumption that a man's sexual activity in general "weakens his piety and causes him to fall into lust."[81] However, sexual intimacy in marriage can also be an act of compassionate grace toward the other—the man's wife; God, in this case, ensures that the *Musar* man does not fall from his spiritual level.[82] For Rabbi Kanievsky, a husband's empathic intimacy with his wife measures up to the compassion of the merciful God—a remarkable comparison between male sexuality and divine mercy. As God sometimes is persuaded to act according to his mercy and not only his justice, here too, the *Musar* man takes a "divinely modeled risk," acting against his *Musar* instinct of piety and its judgments.[83]

---

80. Friedlander, *Kuntres LeChatanim Bnei-Torah*. The source of these words is the letter of Rabbi Kanievsky. See Kanievsky, *Kovetz Igrot,* Letter A.

81. In Lithuanian literature there is no discussion of the appropriate attitude toward the pleasure experienced by a man during the sexual act.

82. See also the words of Rabbi Yosef Shalom Elyashiv about the responsibility of the husband to be sensitive to the emotional pain of his wife (Lorincz, *Binat HaMidot,* 3).

83. In this letter, Rabbi Kanievsky explains that intimate touch is naturally required in order to fulfill the divine command (*mizvah*) for a man to have a full sexual

There is a strong tone of condescension and male superiority even in the invitations to compassion in the above sources; in fact, Lithuanian *Musar* in general holds a dismissive and condescending attitude toward women and women's sexuality. In general, a *Musar* man is encouraged, in his daily married life, to treat his wife with love, warmth and respect, but often with condescension too, not as an equal adult, but more as a parent treats a young dependent child. For example, Rabbi Lefkowitz writes: "I have heard it told of Rabbi Shlomo Heiman, that whenever he heard the rumblings of a thunderstorm occurring in the middle of a class he was teaching, he would immediately stop the lesson and set out for his home, since [he knew that] his wife had a terrible fear of these loud sounds."[84]

Rabbi Shlomo Wolbe published one book of guidance for future husbands, and another for future wives. In both works he speaks openly of the challenges facing both men and women, and of the need for integration of the totally polarized male and female ways of living in the world. Wolbe's words teach us about the fears of yeshiva students facing their upcoming marriage:

> There are those who approach their own wedding day with a feeling that they should have some misgivings about [experiencing] full union with a woman, as if this must entail some spiritual harm either to their studies or their purity.... [The yeshiva student] has been raised and educated to do his utmost to resist his [sexual] inclination, to refrain from having too many conversations with women, and perhaps even to become accustomed to seeing both his own urges and women themselves as impure. Now that he is entering into marriage, he is required to draw close to himself what he has, for years, been accustomed to reject and keep at a distance. Still, the Torah says, "For this reason a man will leave his father and his mother and cleave to his wife, and they become one flesh" (Genesis 2:24). "They become one flesh . . ."—this is the physical bond that is more [sacred] even than devotion, for they become truly "*one*." If, then, the Torah itself has commanded this, then of course it is possible and even necessary, and natural as well.[85]

---

relationship with his wife. Therefore, intimate touch is part of the Jewish law itself (Kanievsky, *Kovetz Igrot*, Letter A).

84. Lorincz, *Binat HaMidot*, 23. On the right attitude of a husband to his wife according to Rabbi Avraham Yeshaya Karelitz see, Brown, *The Hazon Ish*, 823–26.

85. Wolbe, *Kuntres*, 13–14.

Rabbi Wolbe's position differs from the one reviewed above in that he does not refrain from addressing the physical sexuality of the young grooms directly and without embellishment. In spite of his conciliatory and realistic approach, however, he still finds it difficult to attribute positive meaning to conjugal sexuality, beyond saying that it is explicitly commanded in the Torah. His inability to find intrinsic value in marital sexual relations stands in contrast to his positive perspective regarding other elements of married life:

> The boarding school atmosphere in which the yeshiva student has lived for many years is detrimental to his spiritual development in many ways. There he becomes accustomed to a life that is totally divorced from reality. . . . All around him he sees only people with a single ambition, and cannot imagine that there could be virtuous folk [*b'nei 'adam k'sherim*] with different aspirations. . . . Finally, he sees around him only men, and grows up in a "masculine" world.[86]

> The man whose only aspiration is to study Torah is liable to so strongly prefer intellectual effort over emotion, that his emotional capacity becomes stunted . . . . After all, for [sacred] work emotion is also needed, whether for prayer, or for the fulfillment of divine commands regarding our fellow human beings [*mitzvot ben 'adam lehavero*], whether for practicing ethics [*Musar*] or for spiritual growth. The loss of emotion is a great danger to man's spirituality; a relationship of intimacy with his wife saves the husband from this inner danger.[87]

D. Encounter with Sexuality in the Public Sphere

As we have seen, to leave the protected space of the yeshiva, whether before or after marriage, exposes the devout student to challenges that may endanger his spiritual wholeness, and so the rabbis try to insulate their students from "the street." Here is how Rabbi Yechezkel Levenstein recalls the *Kelm* yeshiva, where he studied in the years preceding the Holocaust:

> An example of piety can be seen in a tale about the yeshiva [*beit talmud*] of *Kelm*. There, the study hall [*beit midrash*] had windows that looked out onto the street, and so these windows

86. Wolbe, *Kuntres*, 14.
87. Wolbe, *Kuntres*, 17.

were curtained. Once, the "Grandfather of Kelm,"[88] entering the study hall, observed a student parting the curtains to look out. The Grandfather scolded him, saying, "How are you not afraid to look [outside], when you may see something there that will harm you?"[89]

I submit that, since the beginning of the twenty-first century, the Lithuanian rabbinic hegemony in the State of Israel has adopted a new attitude toward the public sphere, and that there is now a concerted effort to restructure "the street" in the image of the yeshiva—as a space devoid of the female gender.[90] This effort is reflected above all in the discourse concerning *tzni'ut* (modesty), or, more precisely, in the (male) ethicists' complaints about women's lack of *tzni'ut*. This discourse, which is only in its early stages, is characterized by the active support that even women in leadership roles give to the arguments of the male hegemony:

> Miriam Kanievsky, the wife [*rebbitzin*] of Rabbi Yaakov Yisrael Kanievsky of blessed memory, used to say that in order to receive the gift of bearing sons who will become [Torah] sages, women must ensure that their sleeves cover the entire length of their arms. Once, when she [the *rebbitzin*] came home from the synagogue, she said that she had not been able to pray with full intention [*bekhavanah*], because of distractions. What had happened? The sleeves of one of the women praying there were not long enough, and this made it impossible for her to worship attentively [*lekhaven*]. This story speaks for itself. And it is not for nothing that a woman like this [i.e. the *rebbitzin*] was granted [the honor of becoming the mother of] sons who were great in Israel.[91]

Another example can be found in Rabbi Shmuel Auerbach's obituary for his wife:

> She would watch over me with the greatest of care while I walked with her in the street, or took a bus ride with her. The whole way, all of her senses and all of her thoughts [were on the alert], whether we were on foot or in a vehicle. Taking great effort, she

---

88. The honorific pseudonym of Rabbi Simcha Zissel Ziv Broida.
89. Levenstein, *Or Yechezkel—Irah UMusar*, 91.
90. El-Or, "Visibility and Possibilities."
91. *Keter* 36 (2007), 2 (in Hebrew). *Keter* is a bi-weekly publication. There are no article names, so in notes I will simply designate the issue and page number for references.

stood guard constantly over me. "Do not look this way, or that way," [she would say] "for there is promiscuity [*peritzut*] there." Once, when I told her that I would go out [alone,] and would avert my eyes lest I see [anything unseemly], she was angry with me. "Why would anyone walk into the fire? And why would you [knowingly] cast yourself into 'flames'? I will conceal [and protect] you!"[92]

It is important to note that these stories are written by men, and intended for male yeshiva students, not for women—although women often read them as well. Moreover, a complex image of the role of the Ultra-Orthodox woman emerges from these tales. On the one hand, she is (in the opinion of male authors) a tempting sexual object, and therefore a part of the sexual "problem" (for men). On the other hand, a pious woman is not in danger of being molested in the streets, so she may also play the alternative (and perhaps ironic?) role of safeguarding her man's sexual purity, like Rabbi Auerbach's wife, who became his "moral bodyguard."

In recent writings of this kind, men complain that today's Ultra-Orthodox women seem unaware of their own lack of modesty (*tzni'ut*):

> Dear *avrech*![93] The time has come to drive the physical and moral "angel of death" from our encampment! You will probably make excuses, like: "This is not my concern; I entrust this matter to my wife." To this we must give the painful reply: many women lack any feeling for what may be harmful, and therefore they pay no attention to the details of *tzni'ut*. Thus, even women of importance err and wear skirts that are tailored narrow and straight—an abomination to the Lord. Respected women in the community . . . are setting fire to the House of Israel. . . . Transparent stockings; short skirts—and all this forbidden and impure apparel comes strutting out of the homes of women who have been educated in the very best Haredi schools. Terrible! . . . Time for you [the Jewish man] to take this matter in hand.[94]

This text makes it clear that women are unaware that they are neglecting *tzni'ut*. What is more, these are not "secular" women, or even Ultra-Orthodox women who have been corrupted by secularism. On the contrary:

---

92. Auerbach, *Ohel Rachel*, 6.

93. The term *'avrech* refers to a married Jewish man who continues to study Talmud all day and does not work.

94. *Keter* 25 (2007): 2 (in Hebrew).

these are "respected women," some of them graduates of Ultra-Orthodox seminars.[95] By definition, their clothing conforms to all the basic and standard halakhic guidelines of *tzni'ut*. For all that, the rabbinical hegemony claims that this halakhic *tzni'ut* is insufficient, and that men still feel tempted. As a result, during the last decade, an increasingly prevalent ethical literature on women's modesty has emerged, a literature addressed expressly to Ultra-Orthodox men, as the ones responsible for ensuring that their wives and daughters dress with utmost modesty in public.

The tract we have just cited—entitled "*Keter: A Collection of Articles to Strengthen Tzni'ut*"—is important in this context. Here, for the first time, a bi-weekly publication is devoted to an entirely male discussion of modesty requirements for women.[96] The editors of *Keter* see husbands as the appointed guardians of the conscience and modesty of their wives. A few weeks after the *Keter* passage quoted above, Rabbi David Cohen wrote as follows:

> '*Avrechim* ask, "Why are you addressing the '*avrechim* [about modesty]? Why not address the women—the 'daughters of Israel'?" But it is evident that even respectable women, who studied in seminars with the loftiest values, after their marriage see these values fall by the wayside, deteriorating into an attraction to "the street" (*harehov*, meaning public places) and to fashion.[97]

Married Torah students are, then, exhorted to assert their moral authority over their wives. That this causes the husbands no little discomfort is largely due to the prevailing power dynamic between the sexes in the home. With rare candor, one of the '*avrechim* writes in *Keter* that the real reason yeshiva students do not speak to their wives about immodesty, is that a husband's authority is limited, and the wife makes most of the substantial domestic decisions for the family. In the passage above, Rabbi Cohen strongly implies that it is now the responsibility of

---

95. The author does not specify if by "respected women" he means the wives of rabbis or Ultra-Orthodox women in general. Presumably this intentional ambivalence allows him to criticize rabbi's wives without being explicit. The word "respected" (*mekhubedet*, literally: "honored") resonates with the passage in Psalm 45:14 stating that "all the honor of the king's daughter is within," which is often cited to justify excluding women from the public sphere.

96. What is unique about *Keter* is that it creates a link between mainstream Musar literature and the media. *Keter* is addressed exclusively to men, in a style reminiscent of Musar literature. For this reason I have chosen to cite *Keter* here, rather than daily newspapers like, for example, *Yated Ne'eman*.

97. *Keter* 29 (2007), 1 (in Hebrew).

the Jewish husband to regain control of defining the moral structures and practices of the home.[98]

The discourse of *Keter* and similar platforms is for Jewish men only; in it, various rabbis (and other men) engage in a frank but exclusively male conversation on their private thoughts and feelings regarding modesty in the public sphere. Rabbi Reuven Karelinstein writes:

> Some '*avrechim*—and more than one or two!—have come to me with tears in their eyes, pleading with me: "Rabbi Reuven, since you often speak in public, please ask the women—yes, the Haredi women!—not to cause us to sin! . . . Ask them to take utmost care [for] we simply are not able to bear it!"[99]
> We are not concerned here [just] with [a man] glimpsing any revealed part [of a woman's body]. More to the point, [a man] might be tempted to impure thoughts; and he will be tempted to these thoughts by her way of walking and by her movements, even if she is completely covered. For even women who go about with perfect modesty wearing loosely fitting garments may, by their gait and by their way of moving their limbs, arouse impure thoughts.[100]

These sources do not impute to Jewish women (who are of course wearing modest attire in the street) any improper or seductive intentions. Rather, in these writings, it is the very presence of the female gender in the Lithuanian Ultra-Orthodox street that constitutes temptation for the pious Jewish male. Relying on Rabbi Shlomo Yitzchaki,[101] Rabbi Chaim Friedlander expresses this bluntly when he writes: "to merely see [a woman], without having any [sexual] thought, this is enough to require atonement."[102]

What is the rationale for this radical shift toward stricter definition of female modesty codes in the public space, and why is it occurring now? The answer, in my opinion, is the rising strength of the yeshiva system within the overall Lithuanian society, especially in the State of

---

98. *Keter* 24 (2007), 2 (in Hebrew). See also, *Keter* 22 (2007), 1 (in Hebrew).

99. *Keter* 22 (2007), 2.

100. *Keter* 29 (2007), 3.

101. A famous Jewish commentator from the Middle Ages generally known by the acronym Rashi.

102. Friedlander, *Darkei HaChaim Vol. 1*, 433. We should point out that, of course, in a case like this, the religious obligation for making atonement for this "transgression" falls, not on the man, but on the woman.

Israel. The majority of Haredi Jewish men under the age of fifty have studied in closed yeshiva contexts and have passed through the acculturation process of strict yeshiva ethics. This vastly enhances the power of the Lithuanian hegemonic *gedolei hador*[103]—i.e., the yeshiva masters and *Musar* teachers, who control access to the "cultural capital" of this society, and can effect the changes that encourage the entire Haredi population to model itself increasingly on the yeshiva ethos.

These *Musar* teachers, then, are now endeavoring to apply to the entire Ultra-Orthodox population at large, that same solution to the "problem" of the human body that they have successfully established within the yeshiva walls. As we have seen, the realm of the yeshiva is devoid of any trace of the female gender; and "feminine" is identified exclusively with "carnal" (and "forbidden"). Now these same attitudes are being extended into the community outside the yeshiva. It should not be surprising, then, that women in the community are increasingly perceived as sexual temptations, solely on the basis of their gender, even if they dress completely according to halakha.

In the communities in question, in spite of the immense power of the rabbis to redefine the rules of the public sphere, they still know that they cannot entirely prevent women from entering that arena. Because of the rabbinic authorities' decision that Jewish men should spend their entire lives, ideally, in Torah study, Ultra-Orthodox women are increasingly becoming the primary breadwinners, and must work outside the home. The solution to this dilemma (for the *Musar* hegemony) is to pressure women in the public sphere to conceal their gender characteristics, and to become *bnei-adam* (literally, "sons of Adam"—i.e., "generic human beings"); in short—to become like men. This, however, is far from simple, as Rabbi Pinkus describes:

> The *Chasam Sofer*[104] had a daughter named Gittel, who was very beautiful. Once, while walking in the street, she noticed a man following her and ogling her. This deeply saddened her, and when she reached her father's house, she wept. When her father came in and saw her weeping, he asked her why. She told him that she was sad that her beauty was a stumbling block to others, and that she was praying for her beauty to be removed from her. The *Chasam Sofer*, wondering at her great saintliness, pronounced a blessing for her, that her beauty would be taken

103. "Great Ones of This Generation"; cf. Kaplan, "Daas Torah."
104. Rabbi Moses Sofer (1762–1839).

from her, and that by virtue of her relinquishing the light of her countenance, she would be granted a son who would bring light to all of Israel through his sanctity and knowledge of Torah! And so it was.[105]

It is fascinating to see how Rabbi Pincus depicts Gittel as the perfectly modest Jewish woman, walking about innocently in the street, making no effort to attract the attention of the passing men. Even so, since she represents the female gender, this alone is inescapably the focus of the male gaze, so that she is necessarily identified as a sexual object by the men who encounter her. In other words, a Haredi woman does not have the option, as a Haredi man does, of being "genderless," nor can she ever really become "like a man"—*ben-adam*. Her simple entry into and presence in the public sphere, without any intention of being "seen" in a sexual way, are already temptations for men, because they "construct" her strictly as a sexual object. Even if, according to Jewish law, Gittel has no obligation to prevent men from experiencing temptation, still, when described here as the ideal woman, she takes it upon herself to *avoid appearing as herself* (as feminine and beautiful), thus helping men to escape sin.

Pincus (as the narrator) seems to have two choices in his description of Gittel as the image of the ideal Jewish woman. First, he could require that she avoid going out into the street altogether, but this is not viable, since the rabbi's society already requires that women support their families by working outside the home.[106] The only other option, at least for the narrator of this "constructive tale," is to somehow remove Gittel's female gender, symbolized by her beauty. In exchange for sacrificing her feminine loveliness (considered in this system as only physical), Gittel receives the reward of spiritual beauty (in this system, a male attribute), in the form of a son who will "bring light to Israel" through his study of Torah.

The Ultra-Orthodox urban environment in Israel is, for the first time, enabling the construction of a public space "in the image and likeness" of the Ultra-Orthodox yeshiva. In my opinion, we cannot understand the radical developments in attitudes to the female gender, unless

---

105. Pincus, *Nefesh Chaya*, 78. Rabbi Shimshon Dovid Pincus (1944–2001) played a unique role as a general *Musar* leader, teaching in different yeshivas and Jewish communities all over the world. He died in an automobile accident together with his wife and one of his daughters.

106. Blumen, "Crisis-crossing Boundaries."

we keep in mind this expansion of the yeshiva model, once viewed as a heterotopia, but now becoming normative in the Ultra-Orthodox public sphere. This new public space is constructed to provide a comprehensive solution to problems arising from particular Lithuanian Ultra-Orthodox conceptions of the male body. While ostensibly liberating the Lithuanian Ultra-Orthodox man from the requirement of constant self-reflection, this solution nevertheless exacts a price. Women, although full members of the Ultra-Orthodox community, are now required, when entering the public realm, to conceal and even suppress their feminine identity and nature.

After examining the attitude of *Musar* literature regarding the body and the different ways of dealing with it, I will now explore various critiques of *Musar* literature, voices expressing a different perspective on the human body, and hence also more generally on human beings and the world.

CHAPTER 5

The Teachings of Rabbi Avigdor Miller
An Encounter between Musar and Western Culture

RESISTANCE TO VALUES PERCEIVED as "secular" notwithstanding, Ultra-Orthodox Jewish thought reveals, on close examination, an ability to absorb some of these values directly into the heart of the Ultra-Orthodox discourse, where, consciously and unconsciously, they exert profound influence. This can be seen especially in one particularly pointed critique of the Lithuanian *Musar* traditions and their presuppositions, a critique rooted, in fact, within the *Musar* movement itself.

This chapter will focus on the teachings of Rabbi Avigdor Miller (1908–2001), a yeshiva director who served as spiritual mentor and community leader of American Lithuanian Judaism from the 1930s until the end of the twentieth century.[1] For Miller, the *Musar* movement's very point of departure was fundamentally flawed, in that it denies validity to essential aspects of human nature and experience, most especially those aspects that lie outside our conscious control. Miller held that *Musar* must recognize, first and foremost, the frank complexity of human nature, accepting it on its own merits, without imposing between body and soul artificial barriers that lack basis in actual human existence.

Rabbi Miller is important for my thesis precisely because he had, by the second half of his rabbinic career, incorporated into his thinking values perceived as secular. This internalization led him to take a stand against the classical form of Ultra-Orthodox life, finding there the same

---

1. On the Ultra-Orthodox community in the USA see, Finkelman, "An Ideology for American Yeshiva Students"; Sarna, *American Judaism*.

problems that had been identified by secular Jewish theorists at the beginning of the century.

The powerful transformation that occurred in Miller's thinking is felt most acutely when we compare the early period of his teaching with the later. I will not be examining here how values perceived by the Ultra-Orthodox world as secular actually entered the thinking of Rabbi Miller; for that, an independent historical study is needed. My focus is conceptual, centering on the change in Rabbi Miller's thought, and on how his new perception of the body influenced his broader teaching. Consequently, my assertion will be, that Ultra-Orthodox thought does not simply stand in contradistinction to values perceived as secular; there exists, rather, an ongoing dialogue with these same values.

The unique Jewish experience of life, of the body and of the surrounding world;[2] the endeavor to live out some meaningful connection with the realities of nature through the body, and the simultaneous determination to avoid any escape into the realm of "external life"—all these comprise the backbone of Rabbi Miller's teaching, and also of his innovative contribution to Ultra-Orthodox thought. Ultra-Orthodoxy itself, by contrast, regards any focus on corporal experience as indicating an entirely secular view of life, a fact that further emphasizes the unique nature of Miller's teachings.[3]

My considerations of Rabbi Miller's work will be set in the context of traditional Lithuanian Jewish views of the role of the human body. I will show the development of his unique hermeneutic of the body from the 1980s onward, giving new meaning to classical Jewish texts. Finally, I will take a look at different forms of criticism leveled against the thought of Rabbi Miller over the years.

---

2. The word "experience" (*havayah* in Hebrew can be problematic in a Jewish context, especially since the concept became fraught in a certain way through the writings of the early Zionist thinker, A. D. Gordon (Gordon, *Man and Nature*). *Havayah* not appear in the writings of Rabbi Miller, or of any of the Ashkenazi *Musar* thinkers in modern times. And yet, in its original connotation, *havayah* expresses exactly what Miller intended in his teachings.

3. On the Ultra-Orthodox concept of nature before the Holocaust see, Rosenstein, *Ahavat Meisharim*, 41, 51–57.

A. Biographical Prelude

The lifetime of Rabbi Miller spanned the twentieth century, and his educational activity filled almost seventy years; his life-story mirrors that of twentieth-century Orthodox Judaism in the USA.[4] He was raised in the Orthodox community of Baltimore, Maryland, a city that had no Jewish school—a simple fact of Jewish life in America at the time, although inconceivable in the context of today's Orthodox congregations. Miller, then, attended public school while receiving his Jewish education from a private tutor. At the age of fourteen, he left his hometown for New York City, to attend the yeshiva of Rabbi Isaac Elchanan; it was there that he discovered the teachings of the Lithuanian *Musar* Movement. At twenty-four, he left the USA at the direction of his moral mentor, Rabbi Yaakov Yosef Herman, and set his face toward Europe.[5] His task was to study in the Slabodka Yeshiva, directed at that time by Rabbi Isaac Sher—who became Rabbi Miller's most important teacher.

On the eve of World War II, Miller returned with his wife to the USA, where he was appointed to his first community position, in Chelsea, Massachusetts. He did not consider the spiritual level of the Orthodox Jewish community there to be satisfactory, so he refused to allow his son to study in the local school. From the 1940s until the 1970s, Miller was rabbi of the "Young Israel" Synagogue in Rugby, Brooklyn. There he entered upon his teaching path, requiring of his congregation that they uphold the standards he expected. While serving as rabbi of "Young Israel," Miller was also the spiritual director of the yeshiva of Rabbi Chaim Berlin, under the direction of the yeshiva president, Rabbi Yitzchok Hutner. In 1986, Rabbi Miller, together with his son, left both the synagogue and the yeshiva where he was working, to become both yeshiva president and spiritual director at "Beit Yisra'el" in Flatbush, NY.[6]

---

4. A book-length biography of Rabbi Miller has not yet been written, but aspects of his life are reflected in the following sources:
    http://www.jewishpress.com/pageroute.do/39200
    http://www.tzemachdovid.org/musar/ravmiller.html
    http://www.jewishpress.com/printArticle.cfm?contentid=16509
    http://www.jewishpress.com/pageroute.do/16510.

5. Shain, *All for the Boss*.

6. One account has it that Rabbi Miller left the yeshiva of Rabbi Chaim Berlin due to an argument with the yeshiva president, Rabbi Hutner; cf. http://www.statemaster.com/encyclopedia/Yitzchok-Hutner.

Throughout his life, in addition to his regular work, Rabbi Miller taught Jewish ethics and lectured at various gatherings. An important distinction must be observed between his public lectures and writings, on one hand, and his yeshiva addresses, on the other. His lectures were often recorded, and many were eventually published in book form, while he also authored books intended for a broader audience.[7] The yeshiva addresses, on the other hand, were intended for a small number of select students. A very few of these private talks were eventually published in two volumes, under the title *She'arei 'Ora*. For many years Rabbi Miller kept private notes on his speculative thinking, with the intention that these be published; it was only after his death that they appeared, in a collection called *Lev Avigdor*.

To understand the impact of Rabbi Miller's work a further distinction is needed: between works that appeared in English and other languages, on one hand, and the volumes of *She'arei 'Ora* and *Lev Avigdor*, published only in Hebrew, on the other. The works that came out in English during his lifetime were for the most part popular in style, addressing the broader American Jewish community, and adopting a typical Ultra-Orthodox educational approach. By contrast, *Lev Avigdor* and *She'arei 'Ora* are works in which Rabbi Miller develops his speculative thinking and grapples with more philosophical issues.

We can see two distinct periods in the speculative thought of Rabbi Miller:[8] (1) from the 1930s to the 1970s, and (2) from the 1970s until his death. During the first period, he continues the traditional line of Slabodka, represented primarily by his teacher, Rabbi Sher. In his teachings from 1968 onward, we see a gradual shift in the emphases in his private yeshiva addresses, but no outright contradiction of his predecessors' teachings.[9] However, from the 1980s onward, Miller's thinking

---

7. In Hebrew, there is a ten-volume series called *'Or 'Olam*, as well as the three volumes of *Torat Avigdor*. In English, scores of volumes were published for the wider Orthodox readership.

8. I am purposely stressing his speculative rather than his public teachings. In his lectures that have been published, I do not discern the transformation in thought throughout the 1980s that is visible in his speculative teachings; this is not surprising if we remember that Rabbi Miller chose to share his speculative thinking only with a small number of select students. Cf. the introductions to both volumes of *Lev Avigdor* and *She'arei 'Ora*.

9. Cf. Miller, *Torat Avigdor*, Vol. 2, 128–30, 143–46, 148–49; Miller, *Torat Avigdor*, Vol. 1, 121. The editor opted to attenuate Rabbi Miller's meaning in a marginal note, presumably due the radical nature of the argument.

shifts further, introducing theological innovation and challenging the traditional stance of his teachers.[10]

Rabbi Miller is considered one of the great opponents of the Zionist movement,[11] of branches of Judaism outside Orthodoxy, of modern psychology,[12] of secularization and of modernity.[13] He took a stand against women studying in colleges,[14] and against the reading of newspapers, literature and modern thought.[15] All of these oppositions give us the outline of a typical Lithuanian *Musar* thinker, not directly influenced by Western literature or culture or by modern Orthodoxy in the USA or Israel. This point is important in helping us to better appreciate the magnitude of Rabbi Miller's innovation in relation to the cultural milieu in which he worked.

Innovation in ideas is entirely dependent on the cultural atmosphere and climate in which the innovation occurs. Thus I can respond to the question of whether Rabbi Miller brought any innovation in relation to the teachings of Rabbi Abraham Isaac HaCohen Kook, or of some of the radical Hasidic masters (Rabbi Mordechai Yosef Leiner of Izbica, Rabbi Nahman of Bratslav, and others).[16] In my opinion, any effort to compare these thinkers, without taking into account the cultural climate in which they functioned, is misleading. Recognizing the cultural milieu of Rabbi Miller places him on a par with other American Lithuanian Rabbis (Rabbi Yitzchok Hutner, Rabbi Aharon Kotler, Rabbi Moshe Feinstein and others). Relative to this milieu, and to his predecessors and peers

---

10. The book *She'arei 'Ora* collects yeshiva addresses to small group seminars from 1983 to 2000. The book *Lev Avigdor* represents a combination of yeshiva seminar addresses of that period with his own speculative notes, edited by him but not published during his lifetime.

11. Rabbi Miller is one of the "heroes" of the Ultra-Orthodox movement against Zionism; cf. http://www.jewsagainstzionism.com/rabbi_quotes/miller.cfm.

12. Miller, *'Or 'Olam*, Vol. 10, 278–81.

13. Miller, *Torat Avigdor*, Vol. 2, 133–34; Miller, *Torat Avigdor*, Vol. 3, 109, 129–30.

14. Miller, *'Or 'Olam*, Vol. 10, 235.

15. Miller, *'Or 'Olam*, Vol. 10, 200, 283; Miller, *Torat Avigdor*, Vol. 3, 31.

16. It is important to remind the reader that the teachings of these radical Hasidic masters are not recognized in Hasidic thought after the Holocaust. Radical axioms of Rabbi Nahman, of Rabbi Mordechai Yosef Leiner of Izbica, or of Rabbi Rabbi Zadok HaKohen Rabinowitz of Lublin are not part of contemporary Ultra-Orthodox Hasidic discourse. On the other hand, the teachings of these same masters are primarily influential on the modern-religious and neo-Hasidic communities of Israel and the USA Cf. Garb, *The Chosen Will Become Herds*.

in the Lithuanian tradition from which he himself derived his authority, Rabbi Miller's thinking beginning in the 1980s constitutes not only an innovation, but a revolutionary transformation. That most of his life's work was at the heart of the American Jewish community is important, since the image of the Jewish American body differs both from the body image of the Jew in Western and Eastern Europe before the Holocaust, and from the image of the Zionist Israeli body.

Notwithstanding his opposition to the West, Rabbi Miller functioned within Western culture, and part of his thinking is a response to it. He lectured in fluent and idiomatic English, he was the rabbi of a modern Orthodox congregation, and then of the "Young Israel" synagogue, and most of his students had some sort of academic education to their credit in addition to their yeshiva studies. All this ensured that Rabbi Miller would rub shoulders on a daily basis with American culture.[17] This, it may be surmised, can explain how, with his categorical resistance to norms he considered both Western and modern, he was nonetheless deeply influenced by them. Life at the very heart of secular modernism, where the human body and the natural world are deeply meaningful categories, accounts for the significant transformation in the thought of Rabbi Miller.

B. Rabbi Miller, the Concept of the Body, and Its Ramifications

Disagreements between the *Musar* schools of Novardok and Slabodka notwithstanding, a common denominator unites them. Both methods maintain an inflexible distinction between "intellect" (deriving from God) and "feeling" (deriving from the body), with the human soul caught, as it were, in the middle. Both methods regard feeling as inferior and even in some way negative, with intellect as the higher aspect, making the human person unique among all created beings. However, the *Musar* movement denies that an exclusive focus on intellect can solve human problems. A personal space needs to be provided where an individual can acknowledge the emotional/physical aspects of life, and come to terms with them. Since the intellect represents the image of God, we

---

17. On the images of Jewish masculinities in North America from the beginning of the twentieth century to the end of World War II, see Norwood, "American Jewish Muscle."

must develop it in a positive way, for we have "a duty and a necessity to broaden and sharpen and straighten it."[18]

For the *Musar* Movement, a powerful inclination to evil is found in both the soul and the body. Rabbi Salanter sees *yetser ha-ra'* simply as the urge, imprinted in the soul from its creation and by its very nature, toward what is enjoyable and pleasurable.[19] In other words, the evil inclination is linked to the physical characteristics of every human person, and the soul's tendency is to bend in the body's direction. The goal of ethics is to know these aspects of the human soul and to successfully bring them under the control of the intellect:

> For who may bind them, who may conquer them, who may make them hasten to do what is good and profitable, if not the diligent study of ethics, to break the human heart and purify it of some of its dross, and to awaken the proper attitude for this battle: the struggle to stoutly conquer the body's limbs and preserve oneself from every harm and sickness and evil; for in this fight every urge that a person has will make the battle longer, and will increase the duty of this study of ethics.[20]

While the Grandfather from Slabodka adopts an approach different from that of the *Musar* movement, he still upholds the classical distinction between "higher" and "lower." The Grandfather's true innovation, however, is to shatter the equations of spirit=intellect/matter=body. In his view, which was influenced by the concept of the body in European honor culture, the body itself, as a creation of the divine, can be the means of discerning the spiritual—that is, the spirit within the body:

> What I am saying is that within the limbs of the human body there exists a light so great, that these very limbs now have the power to breath life into simple material things, granting them speech with highest wisdom, until they become more pleasing to the Holy One, Blessed Be He, than all of creation.[21]

The body has importance, in his view, because the spirit is also to be found therein. Still, the body is by nature material, and therefore inferior to the intellect, which is all spirit. For example, Rabbi Avraham Grodzinski, who served as *Musar* mentor in the Slabodka Yeshiva, wrote:

18. Salanter, *'Or Yisra'el*, 288.
19. Etkes, *Rabbi Israel Salanter*, 86–87.
20. Salanter, *'Or Yisra'el*, 75–76, 215–21.
21. Finkel, *'Or HaTzafun, Vol. 1*, 44.

> Everything that is related to physical pleasure is fraught with shame. Even physical nakedness itself, without any element of pleasure, is shameful, if it is not associated in some way with a divine commandment.... And if the body itself is a disgrace to a human person endowed with a soul, how much more disgraceful are bodily pleasures and desires.[22]

In his early teaching, Rabbi Miller maintained the clear distinction between the intellect, which is of God, and the body, which is of the material realm.[23] The intellect symbolizes a person's spiritual side, and each person must direct the material body to act in accordance with the dictates of the mind.[24] The correct model is to be found among the biblical patriarchs, who, even when they were required to engage in physical actions, kept their minds focused on God, unfettered by physical dimensions.[25] It is a human duty to identify the dangers of materiality in this world, and to erect a barrier between oneself and matter. In other words, matter has only one legitimacy: its own negation. This legitimate role emerges when the body is brought under control and no longer acts in its natural manner, that is, materially, but becomes a tool of the intellect and the spirit.[26]

Rabbi Miller's approach to matter and spirit influences his view of human life in this world. The world has no inherent value; it is only a place of preparation, where individuals wrestle with trials and temptations, and, if they withstand them successfully, can expect their reward in the world to come.[27] It is incumbent on us to separate ourselves from the

22. Grodzinski, *Torat Avraham*, 446.

23. "The human intellect receives its vitality from the teaching that the angel imparts to the unborn child in its mother's womb" (Miller, *Torat Avigdor*, Vol. 2, 29).

24. The greatest concern is that there will be a contradiction between a person's spiritual and physical activities; therefore a person's chief role in this world is to succeed in controlling the body with the intellect. See Miller, *Torat Avigdor*, Vol. 2, 128.

25. Miller, *Torat Avigdor*, Vol. 1, 57.

26. This is the definition Rabbi Miller gives to the difference between a "solitary" (*parush* in Hebrew) and a "saint" (*tzadik* in Hebrew). The solitary (*parush*) "desires to devote himself entirely to the service of God, and is anxious lest the pleasures of this world distract him from this path, ... while the saint (*tzadik*) has already separated himself and risen above the world and its vanities, and has no concerns about them, but to the contrary, yokes them to his own service of the divine." (Miller, *'Or 'Olam*, Vol. 7, 31).

27. Rabbi Miller describes this world as a darkness preceding the next. This description derives from the belief that this world tries to trick humankind, presenting itself as something it is not. See Miller, *Torat Avigdor*, Vol. 1, 76–82. For the reward to

world and what it offers since wealth and enjoyment can only separate humans from the divine.[28] The world is nothing but a stage upon which we obey the divine commandments. The only appropriate pleasure that is possible, then, in the material world, is the intellect's joy in knowing that God has created food and drink, for example, and other material things; there can be no delight in matter itself.[29]

During their "second stage," Rabbi Miller's teachings take an innovative turn, and we find the emergence of his most original ideas, differing from the Lithuanian *Musar* movement in which he had been so engaged. From the end of the 1960s he puts new emphasis on this world as a realm wherein pleasure is seen as permissible, if only in an appropriate fashion. The real innovation, however, comes in the 1980s, when Miller takes a stand against the very existence of a primal value-distinction between matter and spirit. Instead, he proposes to see the human person as a unified system, composed of intelligent thought that is not divorced from the person's bodily and emotional experiences, and *vice versa*: physical and emotional experiences deeply influenced by the intellect. His conviction now is that only this holistic view can accurately define the human condition.

Miller's approach forges a new relationship between the concepts spirit/matter and hence also the concepts mind/body, thus initiating transformations in thought, the most important of which I will address in this chapter. I will explain Rabbi Miller's understanding of the human person, and of human experiences of the world, the sacred text, and the evil inclination. Along the way, I will refer back to Rabbi Miller's earlier teachings on these matters, thus highlighting the transformative process in his thinking.

While his origins were in a world that maintained a strict dichotomy between intellect and body, Rabbi Miller had reached the conclusion that to identify human "good" only with the intellect, was to manufacture a split that was artificial, not evidenced in reality, and likely to impede the Jewish service of God. Careful observation shows that the intellect is not divorced from the body and its feelings. A person senses the outer world from within an inner personal world, while the sensations received from

---

come in the next world, cf. Miller, *Torat Avigdor*, Vol. 1, 183. The same direction was taken by Rabbi Aharon Kotler, one of the great Rabbis of the USA, who was active at the same time. Cf. Kotler, *Mishnat Rabbi Aharon Kotler*, Vol. 1, 39.

28. Miller, *Torat Avigdor*, Vol. 2, 40–41, 47.
29. Miller, *Torat Avigdor*, Vol. 3, 164.

without influence the formation of that inner world. Focus on an autonomous intellect, judging events without reference to bodily experiences, can lead the human person to act against nature.[30]

> No one should labor under the illusion that an ordinary study of Torah can achieve the human wholeness that is required of us. We have often seen great teachers of Torah who erred in this fashion and led others astray, and were lost.... For it is possible for a sage versed in Torah to be utterly empty of the knowledge of God and of the right way to live.[31]

> All those holy sayings, about the thoughts of the heart, teach us clearly, that abstract thoughts without the necessary feelings ... have no importance in terms of Torah. The measure of the importance of thoughts can be found only in the participation of the feelings of the heart. Thoughts that include the participation of the whole person—this is the "heart" that the Holy One, Blessed Be He, desires of us.[32]

Rabbi Miller thus defines his stand on the classic problem of *akrasia* (lack of self-control).[33] This term denotes the ethical dilemma arising when a person knows what is good, and nevertheless chooses what is evil because of the desire for immediate gratification. For Miller, intellectual

---

30. We should remember, that in the language of the *Musar* movement and the yeshiva system, the intellect is identified with the "truth," and with a reflexive way of life, appearing in the determination of halakhic norms teaching us how to live. Rabbi Miller's opposition to the hegemony of the intellect is, then, a radical step, expressing opposition to that definition of "truth." He is proposing a new understanding of "truth," one that includes appreciation for the diverse aspects of the human person. An example is found in the different interpretations given by Rabbi Miller to the Talmudic dictum (*Talmud Bavli*, Bava Kama 46b) "Why do I need a verse for this principle? It is simple logic!" (*lama li q'ra'? savra' hu'!*). In his early teaching, Miller explains that the human intellect is meant here. The intelligent function is not innate, but is given to each person by the angel who teaches Torah to the unborn child in the mother's womb (Miller, *Torat Avigdor*, Vol. 2, 30). In his later view, Rabbi Miller holds that this "logic" (*savra'*) comes not from the intellect, but from the concept of *da'at* ("knowledge"), that combines both intellectual knowing and sensory experience (Miller, *Lev Avigdor*, 47–52).

31. Miller, *Lev Avigdor*, 51–52.

32. Miller, *She'arei 'Ora. J* Vol. 1, 1. Cf. also Miller, *She'arei 'Ora. J* Vol. 2, 57–60. An even more sensitive and delicate criticism is found in a sermon from 1969; cf. Miller, *Torat Avigdor*, Vol. 1, 68.

33. For the challenge of this term in the *Musar* movement see, Ross, "Rabbi Israel Salanter's Solutions."

knowledge of "what is good" cannot be considered true knowledge without essential links to spiritual and physical realities. In fact, the overriding *Musar* principle of constant intelligent self-reflection is based on premises that are cut off from real life.[34] Rabbi Miller teaches us that human life does not derive from an autonomous intellect observing the world and analyzing how to respond; rather, life takes place *in the world*, and is composed of experiences, feelings, actions and intelligent understanding, and these together make for life's richness.[35] Any effort to create a "pure intellect" model of humanity, divorced from earthly experiences, does not reflect real humanity; teachers who hold to this model harm both their students and themselves. A person who clings to the mind and ignores the body will be defeated by temptations—that is, experiences—because both the negative and the positive events of life take place also in the body. It is incumbent on us, then, to recognize the body itself as one of the religious resources granted to the human person.

This approach clearly runs contrary to both of the "solutions" that were outlined in chapter 3. On one hand, Rabbi Miller opposes the forging of a new concept of the "self" totally divorced from the body. On the other hand, he also rejects the effort to create a "safe space" where an individual can act with uninhibited freedom, since this divorces human experience from its full educational and ethical dimensions. Rather, Miller calls for making a student more fully conscious of his experience, in order that he may translate it into moral behavior and embody it in his ethical choices.

For Miller, it does not suffice to compare the sensations of the body and the mind. He goes further, overturning accepted notions by emphasizing the importance of the body, since, in his opinion, authentic human experience is actually to be found in the body and in the feelings. As Miller

---

34. It is interesting to compare Rabbi Miller's words to those of his contemporary, Rabbi Shlomo Wolbe. For the latter, it is dependency on feelings that constitutes a flight from reality, since, in his opinion, one can never trust feelings, situated as they are in the imagination, cut off from what is real. Jews, then, should develop intelligent consciousness, which alone is linked with reality. Cf. Wolbe, *Alei Shur 2*, 290–91.

35. For this reason, according to Miller, God did not give a merely intellectual reason for taking care of the "other." On the contrary, in order to give the People of Israel an experiential knowledge of being an "other" in society, God exiled them into slavery in Egypt. This experience is imprinted in every facet of an Israelite's being, so that he or she understands fully the need to relate positively to the "other." Cf. Miller, *Lev Avigdor*, 26.

puts it: "We have seen that true knowledge is sensory knowledge";[36] "... this sensory feeling we call knowledge" (Miller here uses *de'a* in Hebrew, meaning *da'at*).[37]

It is instructive to compare Miller's use of *da'at* ("knowledge") in his earlier and later teachings. Early on, "knowledge" entails a connection between body and mind. However, the body is designated as a negative place, where the evil inclination (*yetser*) resides and leads humans to sin. One must achieve "knowledge"—that is, force the body to obey the mind:

> The human person has a realm to rule—that is, the bodily limbs—and must subject them and be responsible for them. And if there is rebellion and crime in this realm, if the eyes, or ears, or mouth refuse to obey.... then there will be need for many police officers and ministers. A special minister will be needed for the hands, to teach the *halakhot* (injunctions) that pertain to the hands, for example that it is forbidden to lift your hand [in anger] against another person.[38]

Rabbi Shlomo Wolbe explains "knowledge" differently. For him, "knowledge" links "the intellect with the virtues." However, unlike Rabbi Miller, he asserts that this link is forged when a person succeeds in making his body act in accordance with the mind.[39] Still, the words of Rabbi Wolbe are more similar to those of Rabbi Miller in the earlier stage of Miller's teaching. The same line is taken by Rabbi Yosef Leib Bloch in his work:

> A person's principle work is to develop the "I" (*ha-'ani*) so that it becomes always lively and alert, and to gather all one's forces, desires and feelings under the rule of the "I." Then, when a desire begins to ferment internally, and even before one can consider the desire valid, this power [of the "I"] will already judge it, so that whatever actions ensue will be in accordance with that judgment.[40]

Unlike traditional thinkers of *Musar*, Rabbi Miller, in his late teachings, begins by observing nature (especially human nature) in its entirety, and then follows where it leads. He rejects the systematic divorce of

---

36. Miller, *Lev Avigdor*, 26.

37. Miller, *She'arei 'Ora. J Vol.* 2, 74 Cf. also his lesson given in 1968 and appearing in Miller, *Torat Avigdor*, Vol. 1, 65–71; Miller, *Torat Avigdor*, Vol. 2, 125–30.

38. Miller, *Torat Avigdor*, Vol. 3, 147.

39. Cf. Wolbe, *Alei Shur*, Vol. 2, 32–33, 248–49.

40. Bloch, *Shi'urei Da'at*, 16.

matter from spirit, since in his view human experience simply does not validate it. In other words, Miller moves with the phenomena that present themselves to him rather than resisting or reforming them.

The duty of the human person is to receive this primary sensory experience, in itself lacking reflection, to accept it as an integral part of human existence, and to use it as a means of perceiving or "knowing" the presence of God in the world.[41] Miller identifies the starting point for learning the worship of God precisely in a human being's existence within the flow of life, an object like all other objects in this world.

A person of faith, therefore, must strive to experience as many sensory feelings as possible, to engage with the surrounding world, with nature and with animal life, to learn about biological systems, and then to reflect intelligently on the feelings arising from these encounters, understanding that these experiences are in themselves God's way of touching humans:

> As we have said, the Lord, may His name be blessed, has revealed the urgency of this matter: in this body He has fashioned a most wondrous creation, with a vast plethora of things, limitless and incalculable, whereby human beings may learn of the Creator. By this we see how greatly the Lord desired our benefit, by giving us so many of these possibilities. . . . It is only because all creation was made for the purpose of knowing the Creator, that all was made with so much diversity, and such fabulous details, each possessed of a deep wisdom. . . . The more we observe and distinguish in created beings, the more our understanding and quality of feeling will also grow.[42]

While these words show similarity to the opening of the book entitled *'Emuna VeBitahon*, by the author of *Chazon Ish* (Rabbi Karelitz), the attitudes toward nature of these two writers are diametrically opposed. For Miller, the human person turns to and experiences nature without religious preconceptions dividing nature from reality, and there encounters the imprint of the finger of God. By contrast, the experience of nature for the author of the *Chazon Ish* can only be reached after the Jew internalizes the divine injunctions of the halakha. The observant Jew undergoes

---

41. The symbolic physical locus of "knowing" (*da'at*) is the heart (*lev*). Here too there is a transition from the mind to the heart. I should point out that in his earlier writings, Miller also uses the term "heart," but there it translates as "mind" (*sechel*). Cf. Miller, *Torat Avigdor, Vol. 3*, 204; Miller, *Torat Avigdor, Vol. 2*, 28.

42. Miller, *She'arei 'Ora. J Vol.* 1, 74.

a transformation of personality, and begins to speak in the language of the sacred text. Only after this process of internalization, may the Jewish person turn to nature. The gaze that is brought to bear on nature, for the author of the *Chazon Ish*, is the external gaze of Torah.[43]

For Rabbi Miller, on the other hand, the only possible human activity is *to feel*, to receive the experience of the senses, forged from a person's attentiveness (of mind and body) toward the world and the encounter with the world:

> Look, we see spread before us a vast and wonderful creation, with myriads of details upon details, and it is not possible that all this diversity was created simply to prove the existence of God. For that, the creation of one "simple" creature would suffice, or we could reach that belief through speculative investigation. . . . Rather the intention behind all this is the role of humans to know the Creator, Blessed be He, clearly and in a sensory way, to feel with all the senses the truth of God's presence, may He be Blessed, for only then can human beings love the Creator, Blessed be He, in truth. Simple faith is not enough for this, for to know an invisible Creator, to feel the presence of the Lord who cannot be apprehended by the senses, this can only come about by "actually seeing" (*she-yireh be-'einav*). . . . In this way the physical senses participate in the knowledge of the Creator. And the more the scope of a person's experience expands through the eyes and the other senses, so also shall understanding increase, and it is for this reason that the world and all that is in it was made.[44]

Rabbi Miller's way of experiencing the world forges a direct link between human beings and nature; one expression of this is in the understanding of sacred time.[45] Lithuanian Ultra-Orthodox thought regards natural time, and the events that mark it, as opportunities for the Jew to observe the divine commandments (*ha-mitzvot*). Thus, Lithuanian thinking disconnects from natural cyclical time, and puts the focus on

---

43. For more on the formation of the human person in the teaching of the author of the *Chazon Ish*, see Kaplan, "Hazon Ish"; Brown, *The Hazon Ish*; Englander, "The Conception of the Human Being."

44. Miller, *She'arei 'Ora, Vol. 1*, 72.

45. The concept of sacred time in Ultra-Orthodox thought requires a separate study. Here I will touch on just one aspect, to shed light on Miller's unique thought. For research on sacred time, cf. Wolfson, *Alef*, 1–55; Pedaya, *Nahmanides*, 11–43; Eliade, *Myth of the Eternal Return*, 49–90.

the connection between an event in nature and its corresponding characteristic in the religious dimension, which exists—according to the Rabbis—outside nature. For example, the merit of Passover is not that it is in the spring. Rather, its merit derives from the fact that, in religious history, the people of Israel came up out of Egypt at this time; the return of this same time every year emphasizes the need for Jews to be freed from the bondage of the evil inclination. An example is found in the writings of Rabbi Yeruchom Levovitz (from Mir):

> The *mitzvot* [divine commands] pertaining to the dates of Jewish festivals do not derive their meaning from a coincidental association of this *mitzvah* with that date; rather, the "time" of the festival is precisely the cause and meaning of every such *mitzvah*. The [*mitzvah* of observing] *shabat kodesh* ["Holiness of Shabbat"], for example, is commanded on the Sabbath, and not on any other day—and this is not by chance. The words [in the Shabbat Eve service] *ki vo* ["because on this day"] indicate that all the *mitzvot* of Shabbat Holiness are precisely linked to this day, and that all the *mitzvot* of Shabbat derive from the secret of the "time" of Shabbat. We do not know which is greater—the "time" or the mitzvah; it may be, in fact, that the "time" is of more importance in fulfilling the *mitzvah* than the content of the command itself. . . . The same is true of "the time of our liberation"—for example, Passover. This festival commemorates the "time" of the revelation of the *Shekhinah* [divine Presence], and in the secret of this "time" everything is contained, and nothing lacking. It only remains for the human being to work to be spiritually attuned and ready to receive the enlightenment that flows from the secret of "time." Anyone who is thus prepared will gain everything, while anyone who is unprepared will be left with nothing.[46]

In other words, Lithuanian thought does not see the religious festivals as flowing out of the seasons of the year, but rather as expressions of sacred events that occur in (Jewish) sacred time.[47] The common denominator of this form of thought is that nature is never seen as important in its

---

46. Ha-Levi, *Ma'amarim Me-Sihotav Shel Rabbi Yeruham Ha-Levi*, 3–4.

47. The same is true of everyday events as well. When a Jew eats, the purpose of eating is to become a vehicle for the worship of God: "I eat, not for my pleasure, but only to serve the Creator." (Miller, *She'arei 'Ora. J Vol. 1*, 147). Rabbi Miller quotes this prayer only in order to argue against it. Similarly, the importance of a physical activity is seen as a function of its usefulness in the service of the divine, as we have seen above.

own right, but only as useful for some external (religious) purpose.[48] The Lithuanian tradition thus divorces a believer's experience of faith from the natural flow of the believer's life.

One result of this thinking is an unwillingness to see nature and beauty as realms that are themselves divine revelations. An example is found in Rabbi Friedman's description of his experience when visiting Switzerland:

> I walked toward the yeshiva fully aware and burning with a kind of inner fire. My heart was empty after two days around the Lucerne lakes. I felt pervaded by a dryness that evoked an awesome thirst to hear [i.e. experience] something higher than meadows, glaciers, lakes, and picturesque houses. A passion burnt in me to transcend beyond idolatrous Swiss beauty. Switzerland is a wonderful "academy" for emptiness. When the *MaHaRaL* (Rabbi Judah Loew Ben Bezalel) spoke of "matter" vs. "form"—he meant Switzerland.[49]

Rabbi Miller, by contrast, is convinced that such an attitude can only alienate one from the sacred experience of nature. He holds that natural time should never be subordinated to sacred time, but Jewish feasts must be arranged in such a way as to correspond with the cycles of nature, since a major purpose of the feasts is to allow the Jew to halt the rush of life for a bit and experience nature. It is for this reason that the Torah names the feasts according to the season of the year, rather than according to the religious values that were laid upon them:

> We see that the Torah has set names for the Feasts (*hagim*) according to the material blessing (*ha-hatzlakha*) of each period. The Feast of Weeks (*shavu'ot*) is called in the Torah the Festival of the First Fruits (*bikurim*) and there is no mention there of the giving of the Torah at this time. . . . We thus learn that the Holy One, Blessed be He, regards favorable material conditions as of great importance; the Feast of the Fruit Harvest (*ha-'asif*), the Feast of the Grain Harvest (*ha-katsir*), both have to do with the gathering in of produce, reminding us of the grace of providing food for all creatures. The meaning of this is . . . that everything brings us to knowledge of the Creator, . . . and material blessings bring people closest to this level of awareness, more than

---

48. Rabbi Miller's effort to change Lithuanian thinking on this point is very similar to the secular-Jewish rejection of tradition and their effort to revert "Jewish time" to "natural time." Cf. Bartal, "Hilon Ha-Zman Ve-Tarbut Ha-Pnai," 272–76.

49. Friedman, *Nafshi Yazaa Bedabro*, 493.

spiritual principles, since material things are more accessible to the senses, and the greatness of divine kindness is best recognized by humans in material blessings. Of course, the fundamental tenets of faith are learned at the Feasts, like the principle of "that all your generations may know, I have made you to sit in booths . . . ." Such tenets are very important; they are the very foundations of Torah. But still, from the point of view of human feeling, it is much harder to receive a sensible knowledge from a principle of faith than it is to gain a sensible knowledge from a real material grace, and for this reason the Torah names the Feasts for material blessings. This in itself explains the Festivals and makes them even more precious to us, and awakens us to embrace also the spiritual foundations of the Feasts.[50]

In summary, Rabbi Miller endeavors to restore Lithuanian ethical thinking to the real world and to nature. It is his assertion that since God created both nature and the impression of God's finger therein, it is our duty to pay attention to both. In his opinion, the highest human experience is sensory experience, and it is this that uniquely characterizes being human. It was the role of Adam and Eve—who are seen by Miller as representing the human ideal—to know God through physical experience:

> We should indeed pay attention: it is written that they [Adam and Eve] were placed in the Garden of Eden, a place of pleasure and enjoyment, while we know that this world is a world of work, a world of striving for wholeness, and not a world of sensitive pleasures, for that is reserved for the world to come. But the explanation is, that this was precisely their work, to rise to new levels of wholeness by virtue of their choices, and always through pleasure, through pleasure and sensitivity, because in the presence of material pleasures human beings can reach high levels of sensible knowledge of the goodness of God, Blessed be He, and without pleasure this is impossible. Only in this way can one reach the goal: the wholeness of nearness to the divine.[51]

---

50. Miller, She'arei 'Ora. J Vol. 1, 141.

51. Miller, She'arei 'Ora. J Vol. 1, 91. This is a sharp contrast to his earlier teaching, where he saw physical pleasure as an obstacle between the human and the divine. An interesting comparison pertains between the earlier and later teachings of Rabbi Miller on the role of Adam. In the later teachings, Miller emphasizes the physical experiences of the first human being, while in the early teachings he had described Adam as very different from people of our own time, in that the physical aspect of Adam before the Fall was negligible: "The First Adam before the sin was an entirely different creature, as if refined seven times" (Miller, *Torat Avigdor*, Vol. 3, 190–91).

He thought, then, that without physical pleasure it is impossible to reach the highest form of knowledge of God. This is because such knowledge is not merely intellectual, but includes bodily experience. The culmination of this argument is reached with the definition of the pleasure of the soul, which, for Rabbi Miller, also derives from direct sensory experience:

> And you must know that the knowledge through the senses, that we are speaking of, is also the principle desire and satisfaction of the soul. . . . [F]or thus also Moses besought the Lord and begged that he be allowed to "cross over and see," desiring to see the goodness of the land with his own material eyes, in order that he might feel [in his soul] the loving kindness of the Creator, Blessed be He.[52]

C. Rabbi Miller's Reading of Traditional Religious Concepts

Miller's innovation forced the Lithuanian *Musar* system to reconsider religious concepts that represented universally accepted theological signifiers and signified, examining them anew in the light of his ideas. I will demonstrate this by considering his interpretation of the *yetser* (the evil inclination), the image of God, and "awe/fear of Heaven" (*yir'at ha-shamayim*).

The yetser

The *Musar* movement offers several interpretations of the evil inclination. For Rabbi Salanter, the *yetser* is both the soul's innate desire for pleasure and enjoyment, and also the power of impurity (*tum'ah*).[53] The *yetser* has its locus within the person, and, with the collusion of the body, prevents the person from making an ascent in spirituality[54] For him, the battle with the *yetser* is the most important and crucial battle to be faced in human life. The Grandfather from Slabodka refused to see the *yetser* as an integral part of the human person, and referred to it rather as "a special angel sent to lead us astray."[55] All of the *Musar* thinkers have in common

---

52. Miller, *She'arei 'Ora.J Vol.* 1, 75.
53. Salanter, *Writing of Rabbi Israel Salanter,* 119.
54. Salanter, *Writing of Rabbi Israel Salanter,* 104–5.
55. Finkel, *'Or HaTzafun Vol.* 2, 218. The *yetser,* then, is a creature intentionally created by God to contain/symbolize evil. The independent existence of such a

their identification of the creative and sensual experiential aspects of the human person, deriving from a direct encounter with the world, as negative and even dangerous, and the *Musar* movement accordingly forges a reflexive spiritual system designed to oppose and control these aspects of human life.⁵⁶

Rabbi Miller's alternative approach to the *yetser* derives from the unique aspects of his teachings outlined above.⁵⁷ In his opinion, the *Musar* system has resulted in the human person struggling against creative and experiential aspects of the personality, a struggle that prevents the person from experiencing the world on its own terms, out of constant fear that the very desire for this experience is none other than the urge of the *yetser*. Miller himself sees the *yetser* very differently, not as a sort of demonic aspect of the personality, but rather as a force of habit making humans ignore the natural world and avoid experience of it, a force that cannot feel the world and is inattentive to the divine presence in nature.⁵⁸ The human struggle with the *yetser*, by Miller's account, should, then, lead a person to a deeper relationship with and experience of the world.

Rabbi Miller goes further. Knowing how the definition of the *yetser* in Lithuanian thought led to a massive preoccupation with sin, he is critical of this approach. He sees as inconsequential the understanding of the *yetser* as a sort of demon that tries to lead humans astray into trespasses and infractions of the law. The believer emphasizing the observance of strict injunctions (*halakhot*) for protection from the *yetser*, is rather like a truck driver charged with delivering a load of goods, who, instead of doing so, goes to his boss to demand a reward for not getting a traffic ticket while driving around town.⁵⁹ In another context, Miller even vents his wrath on the yeshiva world, saying outright that he believes the *yetser* is found in any yeshiva that has separated itself from the experience of nature:

> We know that the *yetser* has many tricks to wage its battle against us. And one of these is to lead people astray by the very fact that they do not ever mention [nature], so that even in the yeshiva

---

creature is an indication of the belief that human beings are essentially good.

56. Stone, *A Responsible Life*, 43–50.

57. There is some ambivalence about the *yetser* in the writings of Miller, which contain contradictory statements (Miller, *Lev Avigdor*, 129–232). I will look at this ambivalence in the fourth part of this article.

58. Miller, *She'arei 'Ora. J Vol. 1*, 92.

59. Miller, *She'arei 'Ora. J Vol. 1*, 6–7.

they speak of it only in passing, and do not emphasize or pay any real attention to it.[60]

The image of God (tselem 'elohim)

This chapter has amply shown that Lithuanian tradition ranks spirit and intellect far superior to matter. Since the term "God" in traditional Ultra-Orthodox thought signifies the culmination of wholeness, it is not surprising that in this same tradition the "image of God" is devoid of any material aspect whatsoever. Rabbi Miller, however, opposes this dichotomy; for him, matter and the senses are an integral aspect of being human, and thus an inalienable part of the way that humans must come to know God.

In a sermon entitled "A Sensible Faith," Miller outlines his thinking on a Jew's faith in God.[61] As is well known, Maimonides is perhaps the most important Jewish philosopher to reject any effort to attribute to God any material form. Not surprisingly, then, Rabbi Miller chooses to challenge Maimonides in order to give credence to his own teaching on this issue. Miller cites Maimonides' dictum, that "five kinds of people are called 'heretics' . . . [one being] whoever says there is One Lord, but that He is a body (*sic*: in Hebrew, *hu' guf*) and has form (*ba'al temunah*)."[62] And yet, as Maimonides himself noted, the image of God in the Torah is very much "incarnated" in the designation of divine names, and even in descriptions of physical attributes. In this context, Rabbi Miller writes:

> The Rambam [Maimonides] and Rabbi Abraham ben David have pointed out in their teaching that indeed many have been led astray [by physical descriptions of God] and have stumbled. . . . Why, then, does the Torah always use such language, seeing that it leads people astray? . . . The reason is, that the Torah uses material concepts in order to dispel by these very concepts an error even graver than the danger of materialization of the divine, and that is, the error of denying God's existence. . . . For we should know that to deny the real existence of the Creator, Blessed be He, is not only when there is a total refusal of the Creator's existence, Heaven forbid! No, it is also denial of the

---

60. Miller, *She'arei 'Ora. J* Vol. 1, 78.
61. Miller, *She'arei 'Ora. J* Vol. 2, 63–70.
62. Maimonides, *Mishneh Tora: The Book of Knowledge*, Laws of Repentance (*Hilchot Teshuvah*), chapter 3, halakha 7 (our translation).

Creator to even imagine that the Creator is merely some sort of spiritual force, and not to recognize that the Creator, Blessed be He, is a vital and ever-present reality.[63]

To experience God as merely a spiritual being is, for Rabbi Miller, tantamount to a denial of the existence of God. For human beings by nature have a physical and sensate aspect, and this necessitates a corresponding material dimension to human knowledge of God as well. For this reason, Miller says, "human beings must necessarily use material descriptions for the Creator."[64] Miller goes on to assert, that intellectual knowledge about the existence of God, having no anchor in physical reality, can only ever be the first step on the path of faith. The mature stage of faith must include recognition of the presence of God through the senses:

> The Torah uses so many descriptive devices, precisely so that the reader will not think that [pure] knowledge alone is sufficient. For even the clearest knowledge . . . is only a beginning, and the chief role of human beings in this life is to continue to add thereto, in order to receive a *feeling through the senses* [emphasis in the original] of the truth of the existence of [the Creator], Blessed be He.[65]

Rabbi Miller's conviction that intellectual recognition of the existence of God is only the first step in faith, is brought to bear also on his definition of the classical concept of "the decline of the generations" (*yeridat ha-dorot*). For Miller, the main difference between past generations and our own is in the depth of their connection to the senses. Former generations, who excelled in spiritual virtue, recognized the divine primarily through bodily experience. The very force of their connection to, and direct experience of God through, the senses, is in fact the

---

63. Miller, *She'arei 'Ora.J* Vol. 2, 64.

64. *She'arei 'Ora.J* Vol. 2.

65. Miller, *She'arei 'Ora.J* Vol. 2, 64. This is also how Rabbi Miller reads the words of the Rambam concerning the request of Moses to see the face (or glory) of God (Exod 33:17–23): "What was it that Moses sought to comprehend, when he said: 'Show me, I beseech thee, Thy glory?' (33:18). He sought to have so clear an apprehension of the truth of God's existence that the knowledge might be like that which one possesses of a human being, whose face one has seen and whose image is imprinted on the mind and whom, therefore, the mind distinguishes from other men." (Maimonides, *Mishneh Tora: The Book of Knowledge* (Moses Hymson trans.), *Laws Concerning the Basic Principles of the Torah*, chapter 1, halakha 10). Moses was asking for nothing else but this, to achieve a sensory faith, on the most complete level possible" (Miller, *She'arei 'Ora.J* Vol. 2, 67).

explanation for the Rambam's warnings against excessive materialization of the divine. This understanding of "the decline of the generations" leads Miller to assert that the Rambam's warnings were not addressed to our own generation, since this generation lacks the essential virtue of vital connection to sensory reality.[66]

The expression "sensory faith" (*'emunah hushit*) appears in the writings of various other rabbis of the *Musar* Movement, but there is an essential difference in the way Rabbi Miller uses it in his system of thought. An example is at hand in the teachings of Rabbi Yechezkel Levenstein, who tended to use this phrase often. For him, "sensory faith" is something to strive for, but is not essential.[67] This kind of faith is seen as less consequential precisely because it is physical. Only a person of great virtue, in his opinion, can "recognize faith in spite of matter, and have eyes of flesh that have become eyes of faith."[68] Miller, on the other hand, again rejecting the recurring dichotomy, is more worried about an intellectual faith with no connection to the body, and this is why he emphasizes the importance of experiencing faith as *essentially* a sensory revelation, with intellectual knowledge ancillary to it. Faith in God is, in short, a faith forged from and through human sensory experience, not a faith of the mind that may also be expressed in a sensory way.

Awe/"fear of heaven" (yir'at ha-shamayim)

The human person, as we have seen in the thought of Rabbi Miller, should feel comfortable in this world, as people feel when in their own home. So too, the perception of the divine is not of something outside the world (as is so often the case in Lithuanian Orthodoxy, with its emphasis on "the next world"—*ha-'olam ha-ba'*).[69] Rather, Miller sees the presence of God in and through this world, with all human sensory experience arising from some encounter of the human body with God as present in nature. So traditional Lithuanian religious expressions of "awe" (*yir'ah*) and "fear" (*pahad*) before God, derive from an "over against" perception

---

66. Miller, *She'arei 'Ora. J* Vol. 2, 66.
67. Levenstein, *'Or Yechezkel—'Emunah*, 27. See also, 46, 87.
68. Levenstein, *'Or Yechezkel—'Emunah*, 28.
69. Stone, *A Responsible Life*, 61–72.

of the place of the human person in the world, and play no role in Miller's thought.[70]

Let us not forget that Rabbi Miller grew up in a religious context that stressed the "fear of heaven" and included this idea in its theology. Miller himself refers to "all the praises and warnings that are in the sacred writings and also in the sages concerning the fear of heaven."[71] Yet in spite of this extensive tradition, Rabbi Miller refuses to submit, and insists on reading the "sacred writings" of midrash in his own unique way, moving the focus away from fear and toward real presence:

> Understand that the important thing is not the "fear" but the "heaven." In other words, what is essential is not so much what strength "awe" might bring to a person, but rather what strength comes in feeling "heaven." Anyone who increases in knowledge, that is, in feeling and in sensory depictions, as if standing in the very presence of God, and anyone recognizing the existence of God through the very works of God's hands, and through ... the actual daily events of life, to that extent such a person has seen an increase of awe.[72]

The *Musar* movement also felt the preference for "love of God" over "fear of God." Not only does Miller rank love of God above fear of God in his thought; he also expresses concern about the potential damage to those whose experience of the world is guided by fear. In his view, fear of God must not be expressed in anxiety but in a sense of gratitude to God that is perceived as part of one's actions and life events. [73]

D. Critique from Within and Without

I want to characterize two types of critique of Rabbi Miller's effort to change the traditional perception of human nature and human experience

---

70. On the use of these terms in the *Musar* movement, see, Lopian, *Lev Eliyahu Vol. 1*, 103–5; Lefkowitz, *Darkei Chaim*, Vol. 2, 249–75.

71. Miller, *Lev Avigdor*, 65.

72. Miller, *Lev Avigdor*, 65.

73. In the same vein Miller explains the physical prostrations of the faithful person at prayer during the *Shemonah Esrei* prayer, movements that in his view do not indicate fear before God, but rather express a person's deep gratitude to God for all good things (Miller, *She'arei 'Ora. J Vol. 1*, 149). The seeds of this approach are found already in his earlier thinking, in his reading of the eleventh-century Jewish ethical masterpiece, *Ba'al Hovat Ha-Levavot*. Cf. Miller, *Torat Avigdor*, Vol. 2, 146.

of the world. It is interesting to note how the criticisms themselves reveal the powerful nature of the revolution in thought that Miller's ideas evoked.

1. Self-critique

The later writings of Rabbi Miller show that he is aware how radical and how far from traditional Lithuanian thought his system is. He understands that his insistence on experiencing the world, and on human freedom at any cost, will collide with traditional values, like the need to heed "the knowledge of Torah," the need to follow the halakha even when it contradicts personal experience, and more.[74] At various points in his works, he tries to attenuate the impact of the process he has initiated. While experience is necessary, for example, he warns that experiences defined as negative in religious terms are etched on the human soul and never forgotten. Also, although the divine is indeed present in nature, it is nonetheless the case that the Western culture that distracts Jews from the worship of God, and even denies God entirely, controls the public discourse, and its influences are harmful to Jews. One must then choose very carefully which things to experience and which to avoid, and the criterion for the choice should be "the knowledge of Torah" (*da'at ha-torah*).[75]

Due to the force of temptations in the Western world, Miller is concerned about leaving the power of choice with the disciple. So, through a somewhat artificial device, Miller asks his students to understand that part of freedom is to do exactly what the rabbis tell us. In this way, he can preserve the concept of "knowledge of Torah" that requires unquestioning fidelity to Lithuanian society and its leaders.[76]

There is a significant gap between Rabbi Miller's speculative writings and his public lectures and educational directives, to the extent that the reader can barely believe that one and the same teacher authors them all. Throughout his life, in addition to his regular work, Miller taught Jewish ethics and lectured at various gatherings. An important distinction must be observed between his public lectures and writings on one hand, and his yeshiva addresses on the other. His public lectures were

---

74. Kaplan, "Hazon Ish."
75. Miller, *Torat Avigdor*, Vol. 1, 21.
76. Miller, *Torat Avigdor*, Vol. 1, 163.

often recorded, and many were eventually issued in book form, while he also authored books intended for a broad audience. On the other hand, the yeshiva addresses were intended for a small number of select students. A very few of these private addresses were eventually published in two volumes, under the title *She'arei 'Ora*.[77] In his educational/instructive books, Miller preaches a conservative life-style and a clenched attitude toward the American environment, Western culture, and women. In his public lectures, we find nothing of the ideological transformation that gains impetus in his select, small-group yeshiva assemblies in the 1980s. Similar gaps are to be found in the teachings of other Lithuanian rabbis,[78] and would benefit from a separate study.

I will only mention here one additional angle. The yeshiva world serves very much as an alternative to the world outside the "tent of Torah." The study hall provides protection from struggles that cannot enter these walls,[79] and the *beit midrash* ("house of study") is often regarded as the real "natural world," free of Western cultural influences. All this may help at least partially to explain why it is that Rabbi Miller's more controversial thought can find expression only within the walls of his *beit midrash*, and not in external forms like his public sermons and lectures.[80]

---

77. In addition, for many years Rabbi Miller kept private notes on his speculative thinking, with the intention that these be published; it was only after his death that these notes were printed in a collection called *Lev Avigdor*. I should also point out that a further distinction is needed: between works that appeared in English and other languages, on one hand, and the volumes of *She'arei 'Ora* and *Lev Avigdor*, published only in Hebrew, on the other. The works that came out in English during his lifetime were for the most part popular in style, addressing the broader American Jewish community, and endeavoring to take a typical Ultra-Orthodox educational approach. By contrast, *Lev Avigdor* and *She'arei 'Ora* are works in which Rabbi Miller tries to develop his speculative thinking and grapple with more philosophical issues.

78. An example is found in an entirely different subject addressed by Miller's teacher, Rabbi Isaac Sher. Sher asks his students in the yeshiva to read the Bible independently, without reference to the interpretations learned in childhood. And yet, in the same book, Sher goes on to assert that it is forbidden to interpret some actions of the Patriarchs as sinful, for to do so is to contradict the Jewish Sages and to lay bare the impurity of the student's own heart. To attribute sin to the patriarchs is a result of the irremediable gap that separates us in our day from the patriarchs in theirs (Sher, *Emek Ha-Havana*, 4).

79. This can also introduce confusion into the emotional lives of yeshiva students. An example is in the writings of Rabbi Shlomo Wolbe, who has to deal with students who do not understand why they should be required to marry and thus suffer exile from the world of Torah. Cf. Wolbe, *Kuntres*, third conversation.

80. There is an obvious contradiction here in Rabbi Miller's method. He taught

2. External critique

Any textual research must study what is written, but just as importantly, should note what does *not* appear in the text.[81] In this section I will point out, as a form of cultural critique, something about what does not appear in the teachings of Rabbi Avigdor Miller. I have been stressing that one of the most important differences between Miller and the classical *Musar* system is in the response to the question: What/who is the human person? Rabbi Salanter, the founder of the *Musar* movement, offered a pessimistic image of human nature, essentially and by nature under the control of the evil inclination. Miller, in his later teachings, by contrast, believes fully in human nature, not only in its intelligent aspect, but even in the sensate as well. And yet, he does not come to terms with various elements emphasized in classical *Musar* literature, including more negative views of human nature, which he seems not even to consider.

Musar teachers feared the desires of human individuals, especially sexual desire. In general, they held that humans naturally yearn for material things, and go astray in their pursuit of honor, sexual satisfaction, and riches; without effort devoted to virtue, human beings can only follow these flawed natural urges. Rabbi Miller's human individual, by contrast, is free of flawed desires, and yearns only to experience the world; there is no substantial discussion of what a person should do if prompted by a desire to experience something impermissible.[82]

Further, existentialist literature touching on the inner experiences of human beings has now made it possible to speak of complex and difficult feelings evinced by life, like illness, death, disappointment, existential pain (*angst*), grief, and depression. It must be recognized that feelings like these, ostensibly negative, are not necessarily irrelevant coincidences

---

privately that one must never create a cultural climate that forces anyone to comply, and that we all need to listen to ourselves and to nature. Publicly, however, he created exactly such a climate, requiring his listeners to comply with it.

81. Thornborrow, *Power Talk*.

82. Contrary, for example, to Hasidism in its early days, whose recognition of human physicality did not lead it to ignore its sexual aspect. See Biale, *Eros and the Jews*, 132–47. A fascinating comparison contrasts the place of the body in Rabbi Miller's teachings with various religious conservative approaches today, where the body plays different roles. Thus, for example, for Christian evangelists, the body serves as a vessel for the transfer of God's messages to humans and their surroundings. See Luheman, *When God Talks Back*, 39–71.

in experience, but may signify at times the very ontological-existential meaning of an individual's life.[83]

These feelings never appear in the purported "human experience" of Rabbi Miller. Here too, Miller's individual seems locked in a sort of perpetual, almost childish, cheerfulness and eagerness to go out and experience the world. Miller's human being cannot translate "self-knowledge" into a quest to discover aspects that require coming to terms with a broader spectrum of feelings. In fact, whenever Rabbi Miller encounters examples of existential human problems, he goes out of his way to condemn these experiences and even to belittle them.[84]

This chapter opened with the assertion that Lithuanian Jewish Ultra-Orthodox thought internalized, indirectly, secular values, translating them into the language of the Jewish believer's life of halakha. The fact that the Ultra-Orthodox Jewish community is, in the West, a tiny minority surrounded by secular majorities, made the inroads of what they consider as secular ideas into Ultra-Orthodox thought almost inevitable.[85] Having said this, we note that such value-encounters, far from being fruitless, give rise to a unique cross-pollination. They bring to the surface issues that Ultra-Orthodox thinkers do not always find it easy to grapple with, while creating uniquely acceptable translations of hitherto strange values.

I have considered in this chapter how values perceived as secular, relating to experiences of the body, are incorporated into the thinking of Rabbi Miller,as he gradually internalizes the secular affirmation of the human body and of life in this world. Further, his description of the Jewish person rejects the very dichotomy between mind and body, so basic to his own Ultra-Orthodox context, and bears more resemblance to secular Western images of the body. For Miller, the worship of God must originate in a human person's natural experience of spontaneous

83. Brenner, *Breakdown and Bereavement*; Sartre, *Nausea*.

84. One of the main expressions of his opposition to Western culture is his deep disdain for psychology, especially the psychology of depression. See, for example, Miller, *'Or 'Olam*, Vol. 10, 278, 281; Cf. also Miller, *Rabbi Avigdor Miller Speaks*, 236–39. In his instruction manuals, Miller accuses depressive personalities of bringing depression upon themselves. Cf. Miller, *Rabbi Avigdor Miller Speaks*, 154–70, 243–44 .

85. Taylor stresses this important element. While religion in the past was an integral part of the public sphere, this is not the case today. Religious life requires an active choice, since the public sphere is now secular. Secular influence on religious adherents is, then, inevitable, and a certain force must be exerted (in Foucault's sense of 'force') to prevent—at least in part—this influence. Cf. Taylor, *A Secular Age*, 1–10.

self-awareness within the world, with special attention to sensory (physical) perceptions and to feelings. Only from these beginnings can a person of faith move forward to the knowledge of the divine, and finally to the creation of religious experience.

In forging his innovative theology, Rabbi Miller was constrained to come to terms both with subliminal secular influences and with classical ideas from the Ultra-Orthodox Jewish tradition that nourished him and within which he lived out his vocation as teacher. The fertile encounter of the Lithuanian Jewish *Musar* movement with values from outside its borders, led Rabbi Miller to create a radical and personal theological translation of classical Jewish concepts, opening the way for a new form of Lithuanian traditional thought.

CHAPTER 6

The Other Voice

The Body and Sexuality According to the "Nir'eh Likh'orah"

Introduction

IN THE ACCEPTED VIEW of social criticism, critics are required to be emotionally and intellectually detached from the object of their critique. They must "stand outside the common circumstances of collective life."[1] In this perception, social critics represent the "total stranger," observing a society from the outside. Their authority as critics, and their and ability to present an objective critique, hinge on this detachment.

Michael Walzer, in his excellent profile of the social critic, contrasts the accepted view with the actions of several well-known model social critics, both in contemporary times and in the past. Prominent exemplars like Alexander Herzen, Mahatma Gandhi, George Orwell, and Ahad Ha-Am[2] were intimately connected to, not alienated from, the society they criticized. Some of these were viewed by others as "one of us." Even those who might have been perceived as strangers always viewed themselves as attached to their own society, and their critique as a reflection of their deep commitment to their societies.

These social critics are not "detached" in the accepted sense. While they do critique their own societies in the light of ideas from other contexts and cultures, these critics always aim inwards, striving to connect

1. Walzer, *Interpretation*, 36.
2. Walzer, *Interpretation*, 39.

foreign ideas to their own cultures;[3] they do not set up new values and new criteria entirely foreign to their own societies. Their unique perspective enables them to point out that the society in which they live and act is failing to live up to its own standards. In this approach, the critic repeatedly points out a society's latent potential to re-examine itself, in order to truly abide by its own values.

In this chapter I will introduce an example of such an engaged critique: a unique and new *Musar* method, requiring a dramatically different approach to the human body. This method is referred to by the pseudonym of its originator: the "*Nir'eh Likh'orah*"—meaning, literally, "It seems that perhaps . . . ." This pseudonym (shortened here for convenience to "NL") was carefully chosen. "It would appear, perhaps . . ." is used frequently in the halakhic tradition by rabbis who are interested in offering their personal interpretation of Jewish law, often against the traditional interpretation. The expression symbolizes humility ("perhaps...") and recognition of the splendid historical interpretation of the halakhic past, while at the same time attempting to offer a new interpretative reading of the halakhic texts ("It would appear . . ."). As I will show in this chapter, the NL's *Musar* method contains the essentials of Rabbi Miller's, but is bolder when it comes to the relationship with the body, viewed in the NL's method as the defining aspect of human beings.[4]

The real identity of the *Nir'eh Likh'orah* was unknown until 2012, when he chose to change his way of life, leaving the Ultra-Orthodox community and the yeshiva in Israel where he worked. Today, he continues to post blogs concerning *Musar*, now under his real name—Nir Stern—while simultaneously devoting himself to his new vocation as a kindergarten teacher, still in Israel.

Nir Stern was relatively young when he began to study in Ultra-Orthodox yeshivas, and later he was ordained as a yeshiva rabbi with the more traditional Jewish name of Yitzhak (his middle name).[5] Rabbi

---

3. Walzer, *Interpretation*.

4. On the relationship between the religious culture and the virtual sphere see, Brasher, *Give Me That Online Religion*; Englander and Sagi, *Sexuality and the Body in the New Religious Zionist Discourse*.

5. "Nir" is a modern Zionist Israeli name, meaning "a plowed field." It is not surprising that the NL decided to use his second, more traditional Jewish name—"Yitzhak"—as an Ultra-Orthodox rabbi.

Yitzhak Stern continued to study and teach in Lithuanian yeshivas, and was a student of Rabbi Shlomo Wolbe.[6]

The NL's eventual decision to leave the Ultra-Orthodox community is significant, teaching us that his unique *Musar* opinion, although created within and loyal to the *Musar* movement, has no place in today's Ultra-Orthodox world. His *Musar* teaching has been identified as the "totally other," with no possibility of a bridge toward, mediation with, or tolerance for his view in the hegemonic *Musar* approach. This is how Rabbi Stern explains his decision to leave the Ultra-Orthodox community:

> For many years, I have searched for a way that will allow me to be an Ultra-Orthodox [Jew], and not simultaneously feel that I am spiritually suffocating. I did not find a way. I am currently in a very complicated, hard, and painful process, trying to psychologically absorb the possibility that I must live with the inner feeling that I am no longer Ultra-Orthodox. On the one hand, I am at peace with this; I know within myself that this is right and necessary for me. And yet, of course, I also have a strong internal voice that is very afraid, crying out against my decision.... I definitely do not want to influence anyone from the Ultra-Orthodox community, causing them to entertain doubts [about their faith]. The fact that I personally did not succeed [to live as an Ultra-Orthodox] does not mean that in my opinion it is impossible to live authentically as a real, live, and healthy Ultra-Orthodox [Jewish person].[7]

In his writings in the virtual sphere as the NL, Rabbi Stern has chosen to deal with those sensitive subjects that Rabbi Miller decided to ignore in his *Musar* works. As mentioned in the previous chapter, although Miller presents a pioneering position, seeing the body as an important and significant part of human life, he imagines an ideal human figure. In so doing, he ignores many features of real people, and of the real body, such as desires and passions in general and sexuality in particular. In addition, Miller gives no thought to the conflict between the desire of individuals for self-fulfillment and the halakhic literature, that requires the individual to act according to its orders and laws. The NL will attempt

---

6. Quotes from posts of the NL after he left the Ultra-Orthodox community appear in the blog: https://nirstern.wordpress.com/. For his blog as an Ultra-Orthodox rabbi, see *http://gmarabavakama.wordpress.com/*. All citations of the NL in this chapter for which I do not provide specific online links are from his article on male masturbation.

7. https://gmara.wordpress.com/

to give an appropriate response to these failures in the teachings of Rabbi Miller.

A. The Virtual Halakhic Discourse

The *Nir'eh Likh'orah* is not the only 'incognito' *halakhic* teacher; works of *Musar* dealing especially with sensitive subjects have often been published anonymously. However, even writers who choose anonymity always preface their books with a *haskamah* (literally: "agreement"), composed by the leaders of the Ultra-Orthodox Lithuanian community, indicating religious approval of both the book and its writer. Such an *imprimatur* affirms the writer's good standing and confirms that the book is "kosher."

The NL refuses to accept any *haskamah* from community leaders for his blog compositions. He argues that including a *haskamah* would identify him with one or another specific stream of *Musar*, and that his readers might accept or ignore his writings depending on how they regard the rabbinical grantors of the *haskamah*, rather than evaluating his own *halakha* on its merits. In one of his blogs, he writes:

> I prefer to leave readers with question marks, . . . leading to reflection and a search for truth, attitudes that I believe, in general, are better for a believer and a person who lives with the Torah. Today's [Ultra-Orthodox] education [system] tends to foster the sense that whoever has decided to believe in the Torah, and has chosen a rabbi as teacher, has ceased from the constant struggle of the quest for truth. In [the Ultra-Orthodox way of life] according to Torah, there is a tendency to lean on tradition, on the ancient rabbis, and on the way the great teachers have taught the community. But every individual also needs a personal way of life: to stand alone, by an absolutely free act of the will, with the Creator—and this intimate way must be discovered by each individual. In my humble opinion, this mode of being is the main and innermost source of the life of faith, . . . and this is a mode that the [Ultra-Orthodox] educational system tends to stifle.[8]

Yet another unique aspect of the NL's *Musar* writings lies in his choice to disseminate his teachings on the Internet, rather than in traditional Ultra-Orthodox publications. This is the first time that Lithuanian rabbinic discussion has turned to this unique channel in the online

---

8. From his article on male masturbation.

sphere, so different from both the oral tradition (*Torah she-b'al-peh*) and the written (printed) Torah (*Torah she-bikhtav*). For the first time in Ultra-Orthodox history, space is created for public reaction, as readers post their comments and share their thoughts about these rabbinic discussions.[9] Suddenly, readers who have been in essence passive throughout Ultra-Orthodox history are for the first time able to become active participants in the conversation following the publication of a new text.

The work of the NL in the blogosphere contributes to the shattering of cultural barriers separating rabbis from their students, eroding the hegemony the hierarchical relationship historically evident in the *Responsa* and *Musar* genres. In this new virtual arena, the student becomes, to a certain extent, an active partner in the enacting of religious law and *Musar*. In the blogosphere, a new community is being formed, one in which authority is shared (although not entirely equally) among all its members, and power is no longer held solely by the rabbinical hegemony.

Furthermore, access to this virtual arena, combined with the ability to maintain anonymity, allows students to turn directly to rabbis of *Musar* and *halakha*, describing the difficulties they are experiencing in their lives, without the fear or shame they might experience absent anonymity.[10] In the writings of the NL, one can find a repeated critique of the power dynamic between the hegemonic Ultra-Orthodox rabbis and the Ultra-Orthodox public. The virtual sphere, for the NL, is clear proof that a different religious dialogue is not only needed, but actually possible.[11]

B. The Attitude of the *Nir'eh Lich'orah* to the Body and Sexuality

In his essay "On the Definitions of 'Expelling Seed in Vain,'" which focuses on the subject of male masturbation, the NL invites his readers to

---

9. It is important to mention that the NL's decision to publish his writings as a blog is a political act, since in recent years Ultra-Orthodox rabbis are engaged in a struggle against the use of the Internet by members of the community. While he may not state this explicitly, the virtual writings of the NL are an act of defiance *vis á vis* the rabbis' stance.

10. For a further discussion on this subject see, Englander and Sagi, *Sexuality and the Body in the New Religious Zionist Discourse*.

11. The NL is not the only halakhic writer to shift to the virtual sphere. Another, using the pseudonym '*Or HaYosher* (*Light of Honesty*), has begun posting blogs and engaging in a profound dialogue with the NL. '*Or HaYosher* contributes for the most part his interpretation of the Talmud, but also some articles on *Musar* subjects.

join him in reading the Jewish sources, creating a shared learning experience (*havrutah*) that will lay the foundation for new Jewish law on this sensitive subject in the future. The virtual reader is invited to question, and to agree or disagree with, the interpretation the NL offers.

The *halakhic* question of male masturbation signals one of the most existential and sensitive struggles in the lives of Ultra-Orthodox yeshiva students. While earlier discussions typically open straightaway with citing the Jewish sources, the NL departs from the norm, opening his essay with a description of the frustrated emotions of male yeshiva students. In so doing, he puts the focus on understanding the shift in the meaning of sexuality in the twenty-first century, an understanding he views as an essential precondition for any response to this halakhic question.

The NL then goes on to cite the traditional Jewish sources on the subject, making his case that according to these sources male masturbation is not a sin. Now the NL goes a step further. He understands that many yeshiva students will continue to suffer from feelings of guilt, even after reading his claims that Jewish law does not forbid masturbation—for the simple reason that students will continue to think of it in a negative ethical light, closer to a sin than to virtue.

Taking this into account, the NL asks his readers to review the sources of the Jewish *Responsa* on the subject of male masturbation "just as they are," that is, without allowing their negative feelings into the discourse. He points out, that if the reader sticks to the classical sources, reading them "just as they are," it will be evident that the prevailing attitude of Lithuanian yeshivas (i.e., Jewish law forbids masturbation outright) is nothing but a myth, not consistent with the texts themselves.

The very title of his essay indicates that the NL will focus on the claim that the act of "expelling seed" is prohibited only if it is "in vain." Readers are encouraged, therefore, to clarify what is meant by "in vain." Traditional Ultra-Orthodox teachings apply the term to bachelors and married men alike. In this understanding, any sexual acts that are not part of procreation, or the fulfillment of a husband's duties to his wife in giving her sexual satisfaction, are prohibited. As the NL spells out:

> For us, whenever we hear of the prohibition of "expelling seed in vain," we immediately interpret this as relating in its content and essence to how we should rightly worship the Lord, by resisting our own appetites, or limiting them in one way or another. . . .
> In fact, there is no connection at all between the content of this

halakhic prohibition, on one hand, and virtuous divine worship on the other.

According to the NL, a study of the Jewish sources produces a very different understanding. The term "in vain" is relevant only in the case of a married person who rejects altogether the notion of creating descendants. In other words, according to the NL, Jewish law here uses "in vain" in a very specific sense, referring to marital relations, and does not discuss the life of a bachelor.

It might be asked, then, whether there is justification for forbidding masturbation for other moral reasons, if not on the basis of Jewish law. Traditional *Responsa* and *Musar* sources make a distinction, in cases of sexual arousal, between someone who is "forced" (*'anoos*—meaning sexually aroused unintentionally, or even against one's will) and someone who has chosen to make himself sexually aroused. In this conventional understanding, it is much more acceptable to allow masturbation for the yeshiva student in the first situation (unintentionally aroused) than for the student in the second situation (intentionally aroused).

This distinction, according to the NL, is unfounded in reality. Because of the sheer volume of sexual stimuli surrounding human beings in contemporary reality, it is impossible to distinguish unambiguously between those who have chosen to become sexually aroused and those who wish to concentrate on their studies, but find themselves aroused in spite of themselves. Therefore, the NL argues, masturbation should be allowed in both cases.

The NL goes on to claim, that since in Jewish law (as he has already shown) masturbation is in fact not prohibited for bachelors, it follows that this is a sexual act the enjoyment of which is not shameful, but entirely permitted. The conclusion that the NL draws is that masturbation is *not* in itself an act that is—morally speaking—closer to sin than to virtue.

The discourse of the NL on masturbation is a fascinating example of an author of *halakha* who is aware of being radical and even of setting a precedent by promoting a new discourse on sexuality. It is true that the NL devotes many pages to a formal reading of the traditional Jewish halakhic sources. However, already from the opening of his response, one senses his unique and surprising effect on his readers.

The NL opens with an "act of contrition," a confession of his own personal mistake. He cites his answer to a question he was asked by a yeshiva student, who wrote that for all his efforts, he does not succeed in refraining from masturbation. Responding, the NL writes:

> When I started writing my response it seemed clear to me that the law according to the *Shulchan Aruch* [one of the chief classical Jewish halakhic works] prohibits [masturbation]. I have written, therefore, that it is only *not* a sin in cases when the student feels "forced" (*'anoos*). However, after I started writing, God gave light to my eyes, to see that it is clear, [even] according to the *Shulchan Aruch,* that the prohibition applies only to the case of a married man . . .and that for a bachelor . . . there is no prohibition at all. . . . Therefore, [the bachelor] can do it [masturbate] without any discomfort or anxiety, observing the essence of the Jewish law, and we have no need to seek special permission because he is "forced."

The NL acknowledges here that he previously held incorrect assumptions as a *halakhic* and *Musar* rabbi. He confesses that in the past, when asked about the *halakha* on masturbation, he held that it was forbidden for bachelor and married man alike, and permitted *only* for a student who is "forced" to arousal by external stimuli. What changed, then, to make him reconsider his assumptions? Why, after many years of reading the classical Jewish texts, did he come to an entirely different reading, so at odds with the interpretations not only of other Ultra-Orthodox, but even of Zionist or Modern Orthodox rabbis?[12]

The NL himself thinks about this question and even poses it in his blog. His answer is that his position is not, in fact, an innovation. Many other *Musar* rabbis read the classical Jewish texts in the same way, and have felt that the traditional reading on the subject of male masturbation was wrong, but did not share these thoughts in public, afraid of the effect this would have on the traditional Ultra-Orthodox way of life.

In this way, I suggest, the NL highlights a fascinating example of the rabbinical hegemony willingly allowing their Jewish community to remain in ignorance of the correct *halakha*, in order to preserve a particular way of life. The rabbis have taken this decision even when, or perhaps even because, it creates frustration among yeshiva students, helping to extend the rabbinical hegemonic control over these students precisely through the feelings of guilt thus engendered.

---

12. See Englander and Sagi, *Sexuality and the Body in the New Religious Zionist Discourse,* chapter 2.

In addition to his willingness to voice thoughts that other rabbis kept concealed, the NL shows a unique sensitivity and attentiveness to descriptions of the physical experiences of yeshiva students. Unlike other rabbis, he never denies the experiences of the human body:

> I know personally, many gentle, noble and intelligent young men who decided with all their strength and with all their heart never under any circumstance to fail [by masturbating]. Yet they could not persevere in this. They wonder, then: "How can it be, that my behavior is not at all under my control? Even though I made a decision with all my strength, it is as if there is another being inside me who does not obey me. In all other areas of my life, whatever I decide to do, I am able to follow through; why then is this so different, as if my body will not obey me at all?"

As we can learn from this quote, many yeshiva students internalize the idea that "there is another being inside me, who does not obey me." They perceive a gap between what they identify as their "self," on one hand, and their body's urges on the other. We have already seen (in chapters 2–3) that many of the *Musar* teachers encourage yeshiva students not to see their physical body as natural part of their "true" self, but rather as external to the self. For them, Western culture's identification of the body as part of one holistic self is an illusion, created by the evil inclination (*yetzer hara'*), which students are obliged to resist.

By contrast, the NL gives attention to the physical and emotional plight of the students as the basis for his *halakhic* question. The students have felt that the *halakha* banning masturbation artificially creates a division in their self, forcing them to disengage from their embodied experience. According to the NL, if these students experience their sexual desires as an integral part of their self, not capable of being silenced, then the rabbis must accept this experience, recognizing it as a healthy social norm, not an illusion created by the evil inclination.

Moreover, the NL does not allow us to conclude from the fact that this sexual experience occurs frequently in our time to yeshiva students, and is not recognized at all in the Jewish historical tradition, that it is nothing but a result of "modernism," a problem to be eradicated by the rabbis. On the contrary, the NL teaches that the modern era requires a realignment of *halakha*, finding new solutions that will allow yeshiva students to live with their natural feelings and not fight against them.

Before modern times, says the NL, a man's sexual desire and its physical manifestations were considered to be subject to free will and self-control. He could choose whether to give internal or external expression to his desire, or to completely suppress the libido and go on with his life. By contrast, today's yeshiva student, like most modern men, truly defines his identity based on his sexuality, which is something he does not choose. Therefore, he does not believe, as people did in the past, that he can choose at different moments whether he wishes to be sexual or not.[13] Moreover, sexuality takes place mostly in unconscious areas of his mind not subject to his control:

> These days, there is an external stimulus, acting on the inclination and the nature of a person, forcing him or her toward desire.... Thus, the person who desires [to freely choose active sexual expression] is really no different from the person who does not desire this.

A human being is always the product of a culture and environment influencing the individual self in different ways, direct or indirect—through identification and involvement, or through rejection, alienation and isolation. Ultra-Orthodox rabbinic hegemony recognizes the influence of culture and environment, but only partially, as the rabbis try to establish an alternative sphere to the secular-Western one: the world of the yeshiva as a sacred island in an ocean of secular contamination. The NL, by contrast, claims that the Ultra-Orthodox aspiration to total isolation from Western society is not possible. For him, proof of this impossibility is to be found in the anguished depictions students share concerning their efforts to combat their sexual desires, and their "failure:"

> Trying to stay away from stimuli will not help. Even if someone travels by *mehadrin* bus [i.e., the Ultra-Orthodox bus lines in Israel that maintain separation between genders] [it will not help, since] he will have already seen what happens on non-*mehadrin* buses, or [he will have been standing next to girls] at the station, waiting for his bus. The more he tries to distance himself from his imagination [of the other gender], the more he will think about that other bus [the mixed-gender one].... Even if he tries to raise a partition between himself and whatever stimulates him, this will only make him crave all the more what he knows is behind the partition.

Modern life, in other words, requires a deep conceptual change in the attitude of Jewish law toward human sexuality, since the *halakha*, as the

---

13. Foucault, *The History of Sexuality*.

NL reminds us, was not written for modern human existence. In modern times, desire and self are intertwined:

> After the stimulus arises, the need to find relief is a necessity as natural as eating and drinking. The attempt to fight this need gives rise to an attempt to stifle and kill and brutalize the self. ... In the longer term, this will kill part of the soul's essential vitality, and this in the case of a person who is in good mental health. For anyone with some mental health vulnerabilities, such attempts [to stifle needs] could occasion much more serious danger.

The above quote reveals the NL's explicit purpose to speak out against writers of halakha and *Musar* who call for the suppression of certain aspects of sexual desire. This new model goes further, however, and contradicts the image of the ideal figures in the Lithuanian Ultra-Orthodox community. Chief among these is the *godol,* the Lithuanian Jewish cultural hero described in hagiography as a man who dedicates his life to struggling against his body's impulses and needs.

The NL aims to replace this idealized and Sisyphean hero with a role model familiar with the concrete reality of human life, including biological and cultural desires and constraints:

> The reason no one abides by the letter of these ideal restrictions is that [the Lithuanian leaders] understand that whoever does so will suffer spiritual harm. In the Lithuanian community, it is said that you can tell when someone has moved on from being a new convert to being "really Ultra-Orthodox" when they start chatting in the synagogue during the prayer.[14] This is not just a joke. Anyone who has devoted a lifetime to observing halakha knows, that it is not possible to strictly observe halakhic restrictions like this one, and still have a long, happy and mentally healthy life.

The NL relies on an "emergency" halakhic stipulation referring to an individual who is "forced" (*'anoos*) to experience arousal, in order to suspend the general Jewish law concerning the sin of masturbation.

---

14. According to the Jewish law, one should not speak with other worshippers during prayer. There is a constant struggle between rabbis who want people to keep this law, and lay leaders who feel at home in the synagogue and see it also as a cultural meeting place for members of the community. According to the NL, it is only people who are new to the community, and still have this desire to observe each and every detail of Jewish law, who don't speak during the prayer.

Importantly, however, while '*anoos* is an indication in halakhic language of a real emergency situation, the NL refuses to confine its meaning to actual specific emergencies. Rather, he interprets '*anoos* as applying generally and existentially to the contemporary human condition. The NL points out that there is a chasm between the divine desire for human beings to reach their full spiritual potential, on one hand, and the realities that prevent them from doing so, on the other.

According to the NL, human beings are "forced" or compelled by their very nature. Regarding the term '*anoos*', he writes:

> There is a gap [in human experience] between expectation and reality. For example, if a child behaves badly, and steals, one father might say, "I cannot accept that my son is a thief; I am angry with him!" Another father, however, might look carefully at why this happened. Perhaps the son was suffering from loneliness or some other spiritual anguish, or was simply immature, and made a bad choice for that reason, rather than from evil intention. Perhaps the child was short-sighted, not taking into consideration the harm done to the person who was robbed. This father thinks, "I will try to understand, lovingly and intimately, what my son is really going through." . . . [Similarly], it is my understanding that the halakhic term "*anoos*" means simply that an action is not subject to conscious choice. It is written that "[t]he Holy One, Blessed be He, does not deal imperiously with His creatures." It is reasonable to interpret this as meaning that He will not command you to choose what is not in your power to choose. He will not, for example, command that you fly like a bird. . . . It is therefore clear to me that the Holy One Blessed be He does not require this of me, and I am exempt from such a command. If you ask, then, why this command is written [in Jewish halakha], I would have to say that apparently, in an ideal world, people would be able to fly. . . . But far be it from me to think that the Holy One Blessed be He is the least bit angry with me, or dissatisfied that I do not have wings, or [for that matter] that my sexuality is not organized in a particular way.

The last sentence in this citation emphasizes the disagreement of the NL with many of the *Musar* systems we examined in chapter 3, systems that urge yeshiva students to create a new understanding of the self, devoid of sexual desire and its physical expressions. Going further, the NL now offers an enhanced teaching of *Musar* on this issue. It cannot be, he says, that we, as *Musar* rabbis, should consider the need to respond to sexual stimuli as reprehensible. On the contrary, *Musar* teachers must now purge the Ultra-Orthodox term *'anoos* of its negative moral connotations.

Responsible *Musar* rabbis will admit, says the NL, that a substantial time elapses after the average yeshiva student becomes a sexual being and before Ultra-Orthodox society regards him as mature enough to fulfill his sexual needs within a marital relationship. Since this hiatus cannot be ignored, the NL suggests that *Musar* rabbis rule that, during these years, masturbation is a positive act without any negative connotations.

The NL goes further, and argues that even marriage, which allows the yeshiva student a heterosexual relationship, does not constitute an adequate solution for all the sexual needs of both spouses. In the NL's opinion, it would be unrealistic to demand of husband and wife to bear the heavy responsibility of providing all of each other's sexual needs. Due to the restrictions of Jewish purity laws, for example, there will be numerous occasions when the couple will not be permitted to have intimate sexual contact.[15] The NL argues, therefore, that even after marriage, husbands (and wives) should not feel guilty when they masturbate. These acts, says the NL, should not only be understood by the *Musar* movement as "emergency" responses permitted by the *'anoos* principle; they should be regarded as positive acts of blessing:

> There is no religious or scriptural link between the desire [*ta'avah* in Hebrew] for marital concourse on one hand, and the prohibition of wasting one's seed, on the other. Nowhere in the Torah do we read of any ugliness or disadvantage to the sexual urge [*ta'avah*], and neither is there any ugliness or disadvantage to the satisfaction of that natural need, already awakened, even if this involves masturbation.

I want to focus on the NL's fascinating use of the Hebrew word *ta'avah*—which means both "desire" and "lust."[16] In Lithuanian Ultra-Orthodox usage, *ta'avah* always means "lust," classifying any sexual desire as

---

15. According to Orthodox Jewish law, a couple cannot have sexual intimacy for almost two weeks each month.

16. According to Lithuanian mythology, in 1953 there was a meeting between the main leader of the community in Israel, Rabbi Karelitz, and the first Israeli Prime Minister, David Ben-Gurion, to discuss the question of drafting Ultra-Orthodox yeshiva students into the military, and other subjects as well. During the conversation, Rabbi Karelitz said to Ben Gurion, "What you as a secular person identify as 'love,' we [as observant Orthodox] identify as *karet* [i.e., a grievous sin punishable by death]." In other words, what is "love" for the secular world is "lust" in Ultra-Orthodox theology. About this meeting see, Ravitzky, *Freedom Inscribed*, 225–29.

negative. The word "lust" is what the philosopher of language John Austin calls a "performative utterance."[17] Its role is to induce a person to feel shame, and, in the Lithuanian Ultra-Orthodox context, to encourage the yeshiva student to distinguish sexual passions (always identified with the evil inclination) from the "real" and "appropriate" self.

If, as Austin claims, linguistic practice plays an important role in the establishing of the subject, then a shift of language, away from the conventional and toward a different and even contradictory meaning, has the potential to cause substantial change in the subject. Thus, the NL's repeated choice of the word *ta'avah* in its positive meaning of "desire," rather than "lust" is a calculated political strategy, intended to challenge negative connotations and replace them with positive ones. In the NL's teachings, *ta'avah* becomes a "performative utterance," taking on a new meaning, with the power to establish a new *Musar* subject. He writes:

> The perfection of the divine work in this world is found in the way that the most physical aspects of human life are lived to the fullest. Many tales in the Talmud tell us that the holy Sages had an unequivocal lust for life and desire for this world. Rabbi Yeruham HaLevi has said that atonement does not mean the uprooting of desires. In some of his discourses, he makes it extremely clear that the essence [of divine work in this world] is the body and only the body. According to HaLevi, the entire purpose of creation is to reveal [God's] glory to all creatures, and this is possible only when divine glory is physically embodied. If we do not see the beauty [of God] in the flesh, then that beauty has not been truly revealed. To look into the eyes of an infant, to enjoy her smile and caress his hair, to see a woman who awakens our desire, to observe the sunset, or a forest or the sea.... Even if we can conceptualize these things on an abstract spiritual level ... this is not a living comprehension, not a vital discovery.... After all, the purpose and essence of human life is found in physical existence; the soul serves the attainment of this end.

The NL takes issue with the majority consensus among Lithuanian *Musar* teachers, who might encourage their students to recognize the beauty of nature, but not to put this appreciation into practice. Rabbis lecture about the beauty and importance of nature when they feel that the Ultra-Orthodox community is being criticized for not appreciating the natural world. But, like Rabbi Miller's "positive" description of the body,

17. Austin, *How to Do Things with Word*.

for these Rabbis "nature" is abstract and conceptualized, thought up within the walls of their yeshivas rather than encountered by venturing out into nature itself. Thus their views are far from the reality of nature, which is not idyllic but contains both beauty and horror.

The NL critiques these *Musar* rabbis, for example, in the passage quoted above, rejecting the "conceptualized" and "abstract" in favor of "living comprehension" and "vital discovery." Physical feelings as described in typical *Musar* are "sterilized" of any sexual aspect or physical desire. The NL, on the contrary, emphasizes the realism of desire and physicality, using descriptions like "the beauty of God in the flesh," and "a woman who arouses desire."

The NL believes that, in Lithuanian *Musar*, the negative judgment of the body as inferior to the mind can be traced back to an assumption discussed in the first chapters of this book. Ultra-Orthodox Judaism, as we have seen, posits an identification of physicality with the *unreflective* aspect of human existence, an aspect to be despised.[18] For the NL, this is fundamentally wrong. It is undeniable that in the natural human condition there are unreflective elements, but these too were created by God and, therefore, must not be despised as inferior to the spiritual. Moreover, even if a person has succeeded, through great effort, to expand self-reflection, or to minimize unreflective actions as the *Musar* teaches, consciousness is still only the tip of the iceberg. In the terms of *Musar* itself, "the major decisions of a person come from the 'animal soul' [a *Musar* term for the unconscious]."[19] Indeed, as the NL reminds us, *Musar* references to

> "the dark forces," or "the ugly inclinations," considered negatively as "bestial" aspects of human beings, are thought of thus only because of the arrogance of the "logical" side of our human nature, the same side that also feels shame about the "bestial" sides, denying them and treating them with a cruel alienation.

The revolution in halakha and *Musar* that Rabbi Isaac Stern (the *Nir'eh Likh'orah*) endeavored to bring about, ended in an existential crisis with his decision to leave the Ultra-Orthodox community. For the

---

18. The development of this theory is described at length in chapter 2. In the NL description of this attitude: "when we mention the part of the mind which is "*nefesh behemit*" (animal soul) we understand it as a part of our humanity which insult us. To call a human being an animal is not a praise in our understanding."

19. From his article *Kohot HaNefesh 'Ikar Ha'Adam* ("The Powers of the Soul are the Essence of the Human Person") http://gmara.wordpress.com

present, the leading *Musar* rabbis have abstained from responding to his essays. Indeed, the only response to the NL's teaching on masturbation comes from the only other significant contemporary *Musar* blogger—known as the '*Or Ha-Yosher*—who writes:

> First of all, it is my understanding that [the NL] is a wise person. Anyone who has been touched by true piety, and who has tasted the sweetness of the labor of Torah, may rightly see [the NL] as one of the unique fellowship of wise scholars from the generation of wisdom before our confused and lost generation.[20] It is my strongest desire to humble myself before a man so great. Only after I have stated this important proviso,[21] may I dare to present my own thoughts on this most urgent subject.

The '*Or-HaYosher* goes on to support the NL's stand on the issue of masturbation. He also points out that this stand has precedent in the oral tradition of Ultra-Orthodoxy:

> Indeed, in times past, when there were still Great Sages of the Torah (*gedolei torah*) among us, their homes were open to anyone in need and their hearts were devoted to any Jew, whomever he [*sic*] might be. Yeshiva students could turn to these sages for counsel, and receive personal and private halakhic guidance [i.e. orally, not in writing]. In our own day, however, it has become almost impossible to receive true answers from hearts both loving and understanding. The NL, then, has done well to make known his opinion on the permission [of masturbation]. As he wrote, he knew from experience that many yeshiva students were crushed [by shame] simply because they were unaware that the essence of the halakhic prohibition of masturbation is *de-rabbanan* [i.e. not from the Torah, but a lesser rabbinic interpretation]. If the need arises, the act of masturbation is permitted by the halakha, as the NL explains. . . . And it seems to me that only good can come from publishing his words.

One might think that in addressing the problem of masturbation, the NL was dealing with a fairly minor halakhic subject, rarely in fact discussed at all by his predecessors, and one that some might call petty. However, we learn from the experience of the NL that there are critical

---

20. An Ultra-Orthodox moniker for the generation before the Holocaust. According to the Ultra-Orthodox narrative, most Jews were at a much higher spiritual level before the *Sho'ah*, as compared to after.

21. This whole passage employs language intended to honor the NL.

and fundamental ethical issues hidden within this "insignificant" halakhic question. Once he had clarified his halakhic reading, he went further, and found himself beyond the boundaries of the official Lithuanian discourse on the human body. Time will tell whether the insightful writings of Rabbi Isaac Stern, known as the *Nir'eh Lich'orah*, will inspire the shedding of more light on the accepted boundaries of the Ultra-Orthodox discourse, challenging and redefining, or, on the contrary, supporting and validating them.

PART II

*The Image of the "Ideal" Body:
Wounded and Holy*

CHAPTER 7

Ultra-Orthodox Lithuanian Hagiography

A. Hagiographies of the *Gedolim* as a *Musar* Genre

HAGIOGRAPHIES OF ULTRA-ORTHODOX LITHUANIAN saints (called *gedolim*—"Great Ones")[1] describe the lives of this community's spiritual heroes. Scholarly research on Ultra-Orthodox theology has not yet addressed these narratives, which constitute the clearest and most reliable reflection of the *Musar* image of the "ideal" body. In my treatment, I will first outline the characteristics of this genre, and discuss its stated and hidden goals. In subsequent chapters, I will turn to an in-depth analysis of the stories, in order to distill their image of the "ideal" male body.

Compared to its Hasidic counterpart, Lithuanian hagiography is a young phenomenon. From the beginning of the eighteenth century, Hasidic tales served as a powerful tool for oral transmission of the Hasidic heritage from generation to generation. In the early twentieth century, with increased access to the printing industry and a growing need to preserve the heritage, these tales began to be published and disseminated more widely. New technologies like audio and video recordings, cell phones, and websites further enhanced the Hasidic testimonies of the *tzadikim*, or "righteous ones." All of these innovations were utilized to preserve the image of the *tzadik* as the (male) Hasidic hero, with a

---

1. The term *tzadik* is used in Hasidism for the community leader, spiritual mentor and saint. In the Lithuanian community *tzadik* is also used, but the more characteristic title is *godol*. The leader's public role in the community is also referred to with titles such as: *maran rosh hayeshiva* ("Our Master, Head of the Yeshiva"), *posek hador* ("Leading Judge of this Generation"), *hamashgiach* ("*Musar* Leader"), etc. I have chosen to favor the general honorific term *godol*.

unique background story, way of life, mode of worship and community bond.[2] For its part, the Lithuanian community has only in the past few decades begun recording the life stories of its *gedolim* (singular: *godol*), usually immediately after their passing. While these teachers and leaders are mostly men, there is a striking new, though limited, phenomenon of books on the lives of saintly Lithuanian women as well.[3]

In the study of hagiography, three dimensions intersect: historiography, moral literature, and the question of recognition.[4] The historiographical dimension revolves around the depiction of the saints in the context of the period in which they lived, while the moral literature dimension focuses on textual representations of the saints and their moral values. The third aspect is the analysis of the saint's cultural recognition or disappearance, and the extent of the influence of works about the saint, both at the time of publication and in future generations.[5]

The point of departure for my present study, is that hagiographical essays do not accurately reflect historical events. Rather, a hagiography adopts a particular viewpoint: "the lives of saints were sacred stories designed to teach the faithful to imitate actions which the community had decided were paradigmatic."[6] A recurring question in the research literature concerns the extent to which scholars must insist on the historicity of events described in the literature.[7] In my own work, rather than emphasizing, historicity, I am more interested in the literary-moral depiction, in the acceptance and influence of these stories within the

2. Ba-Gad, "Min HaAvar Harachok Vea'ad HaHoveh"; Dan, *Ha Sippur ha Hasidi*.

3. There are several books, for example, on Sarah Schenirer, the initiator of Ultra-Orthodox education for women in Eastern Europe before the Holocaust. Another example is Batsheva Esther Kanievsky, the wife of Rabbi Chaim Kanievsky, who is the subject of a book published in English. See Wienberger, *Rebbetzin Kanievsky*. Although the entire book is dedicated to her life, it is fascinating that there are no photographs of Batsheva Esther after her school days until she is fifty years old. While male rabbis appear in numerous illustrations, the book has no visual depiction of any other woman.

4. On the relationships between the holy hero and the social environment where they were born and raised, see, Gay, "Winnicott's Contribution to Religious Studies," 387–91.

5. Chen, "Merovingian Hagiography," 60.

6. Heffernan, *Sacred Biography*, 5.

7. Already by 1942, for example, Doble had dedicated a lecture to the question of the right tools for exploring hagiographies, in order to find in them knowledge of the actual lives of the holy people described. See Doble, "Hagiography and Folklore." See also, Rapoport-Albert, "Hagiography with Footnotes," 119–20.

community, and in their use for social and cultural ends. Although my study is not primarily historical, I will examine the gaps between historical and literary representations in significant cases where the editors of the hagiographies—consciously or unconsciously—shed light on the subjects at the center of this book.

The distinction between a historical personality and a literary figure is, of course, an essential characteristic of hagiography, just as a sharp distinction between the saint (during his lifetime) and the present-day reader is a fundamental condition for this literature's functionality. Research indicates that the literary image of a personality usually achieves the status of a saint only after the person's death, with sanctity increasing as the years go by.[8] In other words, hagiographies depend on the public's historical forgetfulness, with distance in time and the loss of personal connection enhancing the influence and credibility of the sacred figure. However, in the case of Lithuanian saints active in the second half of the twentieth century in Israel and the US, literature on their lives is often presented to readers who knew them in person, although usually only toward the end of their lives. The editors of Lithuanian hagiographies must face this difficulty in their task, as well as the equally challenging cultural disconnect between the generation that preceded the Holocaust and the one following it. To establish some of the requisite historical distance, these editors dedicate most of their texts to describing the lives of the *gedolim* prior to the Holocaust. Although this literature describes figures whose lives often bridged the gap between pre- and post-Holocaust generations, it avoids detailing the devastation of the Lithuanian Ultra-Orthodox community during the war. Simultaneously, a certain distance is created between the hero and the readers, even if they were privileged to know the saint in his life after the Holocaust.

The Lithuanian community has a strict ban on reading any history not written by Ultra-Orthodox educators or disseminated by the rabbinic hegemony,[9] which makes it easier for these editors to shape conceptions of the past, especially the years preceding the Holocaust, and instill "sacred" values through the accounts of the *gedolim*.[10] However, unlike the

---

8. Chen, "Merovingian Hagiography."

9. Yerushalmi, *Zakhor*, 77–104; Hakak, "'Blessed be the Sage's Memory?" 390.

10. Caplan, "Sifrey Limud LeHistoria Bahevra HaHaredit." We should mention that even historical books written by leaders of the Ultra-Orthodox community are studied almost exclusively by women of high-school age. Men devote their days only to Torah and Talmud studies and not to histories, even Ultra-Orthodox ones.

unchallenged legitimacy of *tzakik* hagiographies in Hasidic communities, the literature of the *gedolim* in Lithuanian circles must struggle for its reputation. I have already described the need for post-Holocaust *Musar* literature to establish respect for its voice in the yeshivas; this need is even more pronounced for hagiography. Since the Lithuanian community greatly favors profound immersion in the Talmud as the only proper vocation for the Jewish man, editors of hagiography must provide an apology showing how it supports Talmudic study; they must also justify the creation of a new religious genre (the *gedolim* literature), which did not exist before the Holocaust. These tensions can be found within the stories themselves, as in the following tale of the saintly Rabbi Yechiel Michel Feinstein:

> The grandson of Rabbi Simcha Sheps . . . once asked to visit our Rabbi [Rabbi Feinstein] in order to hear stories about his grandfather, Rabbi Simcha. When he arrived at the house, he was referred to the room where our Rabbi sat studying. However, since the grandson had not come to ask about the Talmud, and did not want to disturb our Rabbi in the middle of his studies, he stood quietly next to our Rabbi's desk for about half an hour. During that time, our Rabbi was able to study exhaustively three full pages of Talmud, as well as the relevant *Rashi* and *Tosafot* [commentaries]. At the end of the half hour, our Rabbi became aware that someone was standing next to his desk, and asked him, "How I can help you?" The young man replied that he had come to hear stories about his grandfather. . . . "Well," replied our Rabbi, "if you wish to speak with me about the study of Torah, I will be happy to do so! *But stories—no!! That would be a desecration of Torah!!*" . . . Now there is an essential difference between the tales our Rabbi was able to tell and the stories the grandson wanted to hear. . . . This is because our Rabbi's tales were never "just stories"; rather they were distilled *musar* and pure *hashkafa* [literally: "outlook"—meaning correct ideology and worldview] !! . . . That was our Rabbi: *all of his personality was entirely composed of Torah and Musar!!*[11]

The critique of Lithuanian hagiography is similar to that which *Musar* literature encountered in its early years, when the traditional yeshiva system claimed that Talmud was sufficient for students, and that they should not devote even a fraction of their time to other religious

---

11. Anonymous, *Sar HaTorah*, 5. Rabbi Yechiel Michel Feinstein (1906–2003) served as a *Musar* leader in *Heichal Rabbeinu Chayim Halevi* Yeshiva in Boston and later in NY together with his uncle, Rabbi Moshe Feinstein.

endeavors.[12] In addition, hagiographers must explain why this genre emerged so recently, rather than in previous generations. In a quick review of the literature, it is immediately apparent that the editors take an apologetic tone in their introductions, and attempt to answer these critiques. They offer compelling reasons for the necessity of hagiographical literature, characterizing it as a natural continuation of, and companion to,*Musar* literature. The argument for a natural link between *Musar* and hagiography is well illustrated in the literature. Note the words of Rabbi Chaim Kanievsky, for example, in his *haskamah*[13] to a hagiography devoted to his father—Rabbi Yaakov Yisrael Kanievsky:

> Many esteemed authors have already written the tales of the *gedolim* of Israel, in order to learn from their deeds. [These stories] also inspire piety [literally: "the fear of Heaven"] by showing how earnestly [these saints] tried, with all their might, to do the will of our Father in Heaven, and how much heavenly assistance they received in this endeavor. You will never find a book of *Musar* better than this.[14]

Rabbi Kanievsky does not hesitate to argue for the importance of the *gedolim* narratives, whose moral significance lies in capturing the tremendous effort these heroes devoted to the service of God.[15] For this reason, he claims, we should see these texts not as a separate genre, but as the epitome of *Musar* literature. A new "historical" narrative emerges here, according to which the Lithuanian society has always written hagiography, as an integral part of *Musar* tradition.

12. See chapter 1.

13. The *haskamah* is the Lithuanian Ultra-Orthodox Jewish equivalent of an *imprimatur*. In books published in this community, one or more *haskamot* may appear in a preface, in the form of letters composed by a leader of the community, vouching for the book's religious acceptability, or *kashrut*. Rabbi Shmaryahu Yosef Chaim Kanievsky (b. 1928) is the son of Rabbi Yaakov Yisrael Kanievsky and is married to Batsheva Esther, the daughter of Rabbi Elyashiv. He studied at the Lomze Yeshiva in Israel, and served in the Israel Defense Forces during the 1948 War of Independence. After the deaths of his father and of Rabbi Elyashiv, he took up the torch as leader of the community. Rabbi Kanievsky is known for his rulings on social issues, as for example his forbidding of smartphones, in order to avoid the internet. On the other hand, he is among the Haredi leaders who encourage the involvement of secular Israeli law enforcement in cases of sexual abuse of children in the Haredi community.

14. Kanievsky, *Toldot Yaakov*, preface.

15. On the common practice of religious communities studying the bodily movements of their holy persons in order to better emulate them in virtue, see Taylor, *Archive*, 19.

The hagiography of Rabbi Yaakov Yisrael Kanievsky was edited by that luminary's grandson, Rabbi Avraham Yeshayahu, the son of Rabbi Chaim Kanievsky. Rabbi Yeshayahu explained in greater detail the importance of the genre:

> It has been said that it is very difficult to write any account of [the lives of] the righteous (*hatzadikim*). For what can one say about them? That all their lives they strove and yearned to engage in the work of Torah and good deeds, to reach spiritual perfection, and to do the will of their Creator? On the other hand, the *Chazon-Ish* [Rabbi Karelitz] has been quoted as saying, that reading tales about the righteous leads to piety ["the fear of Heaven"], to good progress in the learning of Torah, and to the fostering of virtue. This is how I understand it: you must know that it is impossible to tell or describe life of a [spiritually] great person (*'adam gadol*) since each day and every moment of that life is a book in itself, unimaginable and indescribable. ... But it is possible to write this: that every single moment of a holy life is devoted to a single purpose—and that is to please the Creator. In fact, I prefer not to refer to any account [of a saint's life] as a "story." Rather, our purpose it to gather together a few pearls from the treasure-trove of a holy life, collecting them in the pages of a book, so that whoever reads may experience a strong desire and aspiration of the soul, to emulate him [the *godol*], and discover strength in Torah and the fear of Heaven.[16]

Here, Rabbi Yeshayahu obliquely shares—and resolves—the doubts about hagiography that plagued him during the editorial process. In his opinion, the reader should not see his book as a neutral biography based on rational narrative and chronological sequence. That would do injustice to the image of the Lithuanian *godol*, whose life was an uninterrupted service of God, with no particular moment more important than any other. For Rabbi Yeshayahu, hagiography is an educational genre with a literary flavor, its anecdotes about the *godol* selected intentionally to influence the reader's behavior. Rabbi Yeshayahu thus affirms the ideological and moral purpose of this genre. It is this purpose that inspired my decision to trace the image of the *godol*'s body through hagiography, in order to understand how the editors use ideal representations of the body as an educational tool to shape the perceptions and experiences of the reader's own physicality.

---

16. Kanievsky, *Toldot Yaakov*, 13.

In my interpretation, then, the rabbinic hegemony insists that these books be accepted as exemplars of *Musar*, rather than as historical narratives, and the aim of this insistence is to protect the status of these saints from readers' criticisms. As I will demonstrate in the next chapter, designating a human figure as a spiritual "superhero" requires positing a gap between his way of life and the reader's. Transcribing the sanctity of the Lithuanian *godol*, however, entails an essential tension, since his character as it emerges in the texts often too closely resembles that of the reader. The editors' solution is to declare that the hagiography, rather than exactly describing the life of the *godol*, is intended to help readers sharpen their moral virtues in light of the *godol*'s excellence. A certain pallor in the radiant image of the saint is intended, not to diminish his superiority, but rather to make it easier for the common person to identify with and emulate him. In this way, rabbinic leaders can maintain the idealized status of the saint, while creating texts that are relevant to the ordinary lives of their students.

In the Lithuanian Ultra-Orthodox community, the exigencies of daily life are in constant tension with the yeshiva requirements of constant study. On one hand, students are expected to devote their lives to a religious focus on Talmudic theory, with no regard for personal practical application. On the other hand, the *Musar* genre was created by Rabbi Salanter precisely to encourage self-reflection and reconnect the yeshiva student with life's inherent complexity.

Following the Holocaust, especially in the Ultra-Orthodox community in Israel, the *Musar* movement lost its prestige and influence in the yeshiva sphere.[17] As *Musar* leaders struggled to establish fixed times in the yeshiva schedule for the study of *Musar*, they had to shape that study to mimic that of Talmud. Consequently, consciously or unconsciously, students disconnected *Musar* texts from the existential concerns of their life. The appearance in the yeshiva of hagiographies extolling the daily lives of *gedolim* may be interpreted as another implicit attempt to restore *Musar* to the concrete life of the students.[18] Hence the emphasis placed by the editors on viewing the stories as living testimony, rather than as abstract biographical descriptions.

Apart from restoring the spirit of the *Musar* literature, the hagiographies serve another purpose: they establish a bridge from past to

17. See chapter 1.
18. In this way, the *gedolim* genre imitates Hasidic hagiography. See Englander, "Halakha as Praxis."

present—while preserving the qualitative difference between the two.[19] As is well known, the Lithuanian Ultra-Orthodox Jewish community was nearly wiped out by the mortal blow of the Holocaust (the *Shoah*). No one knew if it could ever recover and rebuild the "World of Torah." Survivors in the community recognized the possibility of creating a meaningful future by reawakening the ethos of the past and revivifying the Lithuanian yeshivas. The rabbinical hegemony of the survivors saw community members born into the post-war institutionalized yeshiva system as spiritual orphans, cut off from the more vibrant pre-Holocaust, Eastern European Torah tradition. As James Young has argued, "by creating the myth of a common past, . . . like Yom Hashoah creates the conditions for recognizing a common future, as well."[20] The editors of the "*gedolim* tales" believed that this destruction of entire Jewish communities signaled the end of an intimate, living ethical tradition, once passed lovingly from father to son. Though not necessarily "historical" from an academic point of view, this tradition helped establish constitutive identity.[21]

Thus these tales of "Lithuanian heroes," whose origins were in a Jewish world that no longer exists, and who went on to lead their faithful after the *Shoah*, become all the more important, exerting a powerful influence on Ultra-Orthodox consciousness of the past. Given that history books *per se* are, as we have seen, generally forbidden, the "*gedolim* tales" are the primary sanctioned source for knowledge of pre-Holocaust Jewish life.[22] Their editors, in fact, exercise practically unlimited control of Ultra-Orthodox perception of the events of the period, and in the absence of any independent criticism of the hegemony, there is no need to silence anyone who might claim these stories are not objective.

The ideological aims of the rabbinic hegemony are further supported by a perceived existential rift between pre- and post-*Shoah* generations. This rift is an unchallenged assumption in the Ultra-Orthodox dogma known as "*yeridat ha-dorot*" (literally: "the decline of the generations"), which asserts the inferiority of post-Holocaust scholarship and spirituality. Accordingly, the accounts praising the *gedolim* focus mostly on their early years, when they studied in Europe at the beginning of

19. Shaul, "Shikum." This is also true of the Hasidic genre. See Rapoport-Albert, "Hagiography with Footnotes," 154–55.

20. Young, *Texture of Memory*, 281; Shaul, "Shikum," 370.

21. As described by Yerushalmi, *Zakhor*.

22. Bartal, "True Knowledge and Wisdom"; Caplan, *The Internal Popular Discourse in Israeli Haredi Society*; Rapoport-Albert, "Hagiography with Footnotes."

the twentieth century. These pre-Holocaust times are cast in a markedly romantic light, to highlight the chasm separating the lost glory of the Jewish past from its pale reflection in the present:

> With all my heart, I thank God that for most of my life, for more than seventy years, I was privileged to be close to the saints [*gedolim*] and leaders of Israel, and to bask in the warmth of their light. More, I had the privilege to serve them, and to hear from their holy mouths the knowledge of Torah.[23] ... That was a turbulent time, such as Israel [i.e. the Jewish people] has not known since they became a nation. It was a time when slaughter came upon European Jewry, and six million Jews were martyred [literally: "killed for the sanctification of the (God's) Name"]— May God avenge their blood! And among them were the vast majority of the Torah sages [*gedolei torah*] of that period.[24]
>
> Since I was privileged to be counted among those who served many of the Torah sages [*gedolei ha-torah*] of the previous generation, so the Torah sages [*gedolei ha-torah*] of our own generation, who sustain us with their teachings [literally: "from their mouths"], have entrusted to me the task of transmitting, to ours and future generations, an account of the great deeds of "our teachers" [*rabbeinu*—i.e., those rabbis from before the Holocaust].[25]

B. The Idealized Image of the *Godol*

Who, then, was the Lithuanian *godol*? Beyond the narrow definition of his role in a prominent public position as director of a yeshiva, *Musar* supervisor or halachic expert, the *godol* was often perceived as a community's eminent spiritual leader. While, in Hasidism, the Rebbe inherited his leadership position by virtue of his family status,[26] in the Lithuanian context that distinction depended rather on prior demonstration of his remarkable knowledge of the Torah—or, more accurately, Talmud. Unlike the Hasidim, with their principle of *yichus* ["family ties"], whereby a

---

23. He uses the term "Da'at Torah" which goes beyond the literal translation of "knowledge of Torah." In the Ultra-Orthodox context, the assumption is that any declaration made by the *godol* is like the word of God and should be accepted as it is, without debate. See Kaplan, "Daas Torah"; Brown, *The Hazon Ish*.

24. Lorincz, *Bemechitzatam Shel Gdolei HaTorah*, 1.

25. Lorincz, *Bemechitzatam Shel Gdolei HaTorah*, 5.

26. Asaf, "Leadership."

son inherits outright the revered status of his father, the Lithuanian community takes a more democratic approach: any male seriously invested in learning Torah may merit the "crown of Torah," and later be accepted as community leader. The public aspect of this recognition plays an important role in the *gedolim* narratives.

The relative "democratization" of leadership in the Lithuanian system also has implications for the above-mentioned existential distinction between the saint and the ordinary reader. In the Hasidic genre, *yihus* provides the element of distance through the exalted paternal lineage of each Hasidic leader. For the Lithuanian *godol*, on the other hand, the hagiographies must emphasize other elements in order to highlight the distinctions. Many texts focus on the unique personality of the rabbi. The remarkable spiritual presence of the saint is expressed in a variety of ways, like a unique piety that is evident even at a very young age, an unusually vigorous commitment to Talmud, a rare acuity of intellect, and—especially—a dismissive attitude toward the world and the body, both of which might hinder the *godol*'s total devotion to sacred study.

We have pointed out that the explicit purpose of hagiography as a *Musar* genre is to inspire today's yeshiva students to identify with and model themselves on the saints of the past. The ascetic elements we have just cited, however, are certainly not intended for emulation by readers. The editors of the accounts know that descriptions of a *godol*'s extreme asceticism may alienate yeshiva students, and may even cause emotional or physical harm to anyone who tries to imitate them. To prevent undesirable consequences, these editors often warn readers that such self-castigations are appropriate only for great spiritual masters, not for ordinary members of the community. The texts themselves thus reveal an ambivalence on the part of the genre's editors. On one hand, they seek to exalt the *godol* so that he will not appear inferior to the ascetic heroes of Hasidism, and yet this very act undermines the intended educational impact of these tales.

C. "The Making of a *Godol*": A Test Case in Historicity versus Ideology

Not all accounts adhere to the strict formulae for distilling the ideal qualities of the *godol*. In 2002, Rabbi Nathan Kamenetsky published *The Making of a Godol*, devoted to the life of his father, Rabbi Yaakov

Kamenetsky.²⁷ This book has many historical descriptions of the cultural and social landscapes of the elder Kamenetsky's formative years, including a striking reference to an interest in Russian poetry that he shared with a contemporary—Rabbi Aharon Kotler.²⁸ Here, the typical unidimensional, idealized and symbolic representations of a *godol* give way to more nuanced descriptions of a personality developing over time as a very human, often indecisive, and sometimes even amusing character.²⁹

In the genre of *godol* hagiographies, Kamenetsky's *The Making of a Godol* is also exceptional in another respect: an intentional focus—unique in Lithuanian hagiographies—on accurate historical descriptions of the subject's lifetime. The author, explains his quest for historicity as an expression of respect for, and commitment to, the great history of the Jewish people. He even goes so far as to directly critique other editors of the genre for taking the liberty to rewrite history to enhance piety. In one telling example, he cites Faygili Sacks, the youngest daughter of Rabbi Israel Meir Kagan (better known as "The *Chafetz Chaim*") to the effect that the common lore concerning her father is nothing but fiction.³⁰ He also quotes Rabbi Joel Teitelbaum, the leader of the Hasidic Satmar community, who refused to write stock hagiographies of righteous Hasidim because "one cannot educate through lies."³¹ It is true that Kamenetsky also quotes Rabbi Shimon Schwab—who represents the dominant ideology of the *gedolim* genre—as saying that only God can know history perfectly, while any human attempt to write "real" history can only fail. Schwab further claims, as Kamenetsky is aware, that in trying to write "realistic" history, authors will necessarily succumb to passing on "gossip," and this can only send the wrong message to yeshiva students.³²

In this way, Rabbi Nathan Kamenetsky carefully illustrates the opposing perspectives on the role of historicity in the *gedolim* genre. Finally, however, he affirms his fidelity to the quest for historical truth, or at least

---

27. Kamenetsky, *Making of a Godol*. See also, Hakak, "'Blessed be the Sage's Memory?'" 387–88. Rabbi Yaakov Kamenetsky (1891–1986) served as a community rabbi in different cities in North America, and was one of the prominent leaders of the community in the U.S.A. in the second part of the twentieth century. He was head of the *Torah Vodaath* Yeshiva in New York.

28. Kamenetsky, *Making of a Godol*, 305.

29. Compare to Hakak, "'Blessed be the Sage's Memory?'" 408.

30. Kamenetsky, *Making of a Godol*, xx.

31. Kamenetsky, *Making of a Godol*, xxv.

32. Kamenetsky, *Making of a Godol*, xxiv–xxv; Schwab, *Selected Writings*, 234.

to an effort not to intentionally distort history. Accordingly, he provides references to the sources he uses, and even shares with readers his skepticism about some of these sources, even if their provenance is eminent rabbis of the community.[33]

The *Making of a Godol*—in its pioneering English language edition—quickly garnered popularity due to its unique approach and to the deep respect for the author's father among Lithuanian Jews, especially in the United States. However, the Lithuanian rabbinical hegemony boycotted the work, and copies were even burned at the Lakewood Yeshiva in New Jersey. Kamenetzky eventually bowed to the pressure of the boycott, and published a revised second edition in 2005. Despite his efforts, a second boycott, of the revised version, was sponsored by Rabbi Yosef Shalom Eliashiv.

The struggle over *The Making of a Godol* illustrates both the potential danger that the dominant hegemony sees in the hagiographical genre, and their determination to keep it in line with Lithuanian ideology. Further, the controversy over this book highlights a gap between the Lithuanian Ultra-Orthodox community in the State of Israel, and its counterpart in America. Writing from Israel, in a letter to Rabbi Kamenetzky, Rabbi Shlomo Welbe voices this opinion of the book's revised second edition:

> It was my intention to select the twenty passages or so in your book about which I had questions, and to sit with you and discuss whether they should be included or not. To my great regret, I have actually found hundreds of places where you write in a way that is harmful to [the honor of] the Torah sages [*gedolei ha-torah*]. This means that your entire approach in this book is contrary to the way we have honored our Torah sages for generations. Furthermore, in our educational work with our students, we are always most careful to describe our *gedolim* as paragons of perfection; this is in fact required of us by our own sages in this generation [*gedolei doreinu*]. I am very sorry, my friend, that you have reached such a pass that I must write this to you, but I have no other opinion or advice to give.[34] After you worked for years on this book, you now find yourself being

---

33. To support his decision, Rabbi Kamenetzky quotes from letters of the last rabbi of Habad and from Rabbi Sarna, who both also critique the Ultra-Orthodox community on this subject.

34. In this passage, Rabbi Wolbe refers to Rabbi Kamenetzky in the third person, either to express respect or a certain critical distance.

informed that in the opinion of our highest rabbinic authorities [*ha-g'eonim*] your book must not be published. I understand how difficult it is for you, as "one who carries the honor of his Torah" [an Ultra-Orthodox compliment] to accept and abide by the ruling of the sages [*hagedolim*]. This only I can assure you: that you will be rewarded for doing so, both here [in this life] and in the world to come.[35]

In short, not even a respected author like Rabbi Nathan Kamenetzky, with his impeccable Torah credentials and unquestionable personal knowledge of his subject, is free to write an honest account of his saintly father's life and times, without being subjected to condescending censorship by the dominant strain of the Lithuanian hegemony, with its uncompromising commitment to the perfect image of the *godol*.

The obvious conclusion that we must draw from our study so far, is that all the descriptions of the *gedolim* that we will examine in the next two chapters, have been meticulously edited and censored in accordance with strict hegemonic formulae. These narratives, then, more than anything else, depict the *image* of the ideal rabbi and of his ideal body, images that the Lithuanian leadership attempts to "engineer" and then impart to its followers as perfect models of Jewish piety.

---

35. Wolbe, *Igraot*, 109–10.

CHAPTER 8

The Body of the *Godol* in Childhood and Youth

A: Creating the Image of the Lithuanian Saint

IN THIS CHAPTER, WE will examine texts containing crucial descriptions of the earliest years of the life of the Lithuanian *godol*, from infancy until marriage, and explore the role of these descriptions in the design of the ideal male body in the hagiographies of the Jewish Lithuanian culture. The unique attitude of the adolescent *godol* toward his own body is a central motif of this genre, with important implications for the way the saint will shape his life as he matures into a holy figure.

The study of folklore identifies a recurring theme in the genre of legends of the saints: these are figures chosen for extraordinary sanctity from childhood—and sometimes even from before their birth. In this they differ from ordinary community members, who are the audience of these tales.[1] Jewish hagiographical tradition, likewise, has included depictions of the childhood and youth of saintly personalities since biblical times. The holy figure has by definition an unusual character, distinct in virtue from that of the readers. The more extreme the description of the figure, the easier it will be for the editors to explain his selection as holy.

This sanctity may be distinguished by either quantitative or qualitative criteria. Most of the Hasidic masters, for instance, are described as having a supernatural essence that defies the laws of nature, something qualitatively inaccessible to others.[2] The editors of Hasidic hagiogra-

---

1. See the many sources mentioned in Benarroch, *Saba ve-Yanuka*, 'Treyn de-inun hada'. See also, Campbell, *A Hero with A Thousand Faces*, 318–34.

2. Englander, "Halakha as Praxis." On images of the Hasidic leaders as children

phies who posit an essential qualitative difference between their masters and their readers simplify their task; they need not multiply proofs of the rabbi's unique personality traits in order to demonstrate his holy distance from ordinary folk.

Lithuanian Ultra-Orthodox ideology, by contrast, opposes attributing extraordinary mystical qualities to a saint. In this tradition, every (male) Jew has the potential to become a *godol*, since "[the crown of Torah] is still at rest. Anyone who wishes to take it, may come and take it."[3] Holiness, in this model, awaits acquisition by anyone who strives for it, and is not determined *a priori* by an ontological distance between the saint the community. Lithuanian hagiographies, then, emphasize a quantitative distinction: the saint has the same good attributes as ordinary people, but in greater depth. For example, a *godol* might be honored for unceasing works of charity toward the poor; the reader may then decide to dedicate his or her life to charity, and thus also become a saint.

If, as Lithuanian editors insist, there is no qualitative or ontological gap between the *godol* and the community of ordinary readers, the difference must lie in the saint's acquired virtues and spiritual development.[4] The *godol*'s own physical body is, as we shall see, one of the primary arenas where Lithuanian editors describe and illustrate this development from the saint's youth to adulthood.

The editorial temptation to create an ontological gap between the *godol* and the reader remains, however, so strong, that even Lithuanian hagiography sometimes presents a more complex picture. The saint may be born, for instance, into a family devoted for many generations to Torah study, a dedication rewarded with the gift of a child-*godol*.[5] Similarly, the *godol*'s mother may have devoted herself, or more accurately, her body, to the Torah, as did the mother of Rabbi Avrohom Yeshaya Karelitz. This account opens with a common tree-planting metaphor for parenting Jewish children:

> Nine cedars did Rabbi Shmaryahu-Yosef and his wife [Rasha-Leah] plant in Israel. In fact, they had fifteen children, but lost

---

see, Sagiv, "The Rectification of the Covenant."

3. *Talmud Bavli*, Yoma 72 b.
4. Hakak, "'Blessed be the Sage's Memory?'" 404–6.
5. Cohen, *Pe'er Hador, Vol. 1*, 62; Schwartz, *Achar Mitato*, 7; Yivrov, *Ma'ase Ish*, 13. On Rabbi Yechezkel Levenstein see, Lorincz, *Bemechitzatam Shel Gdolei HaTorah*, 10; Sorotzki, *Marbitzey Torah Umusar 4*, 208. On Rabbi Aharon Kotler see, Sorotzki, *Marbitzey Torah Umusar 3*, 216.

six of them very soon after their birth. Rasha-Leah's doctors strictly advised her from the outset against pregnancy and childbirth; they warned her that her life could be at risk. Her father, Rabbi Shaul Katzenellenbogen, even suggested that his son in law, Rabbi Shmaryahu-Yosef, divorce his daughter [in order that he might marry another wife and father children with her instead]. She [Rasha-Leah], however, in her great righteousness, and as if her heart foretold her that she would give birth to saints and sages, refused the counsel of her doctors, declaring, "For this purpose was I created,[6] and may Heaven show me mercy!"[7]

Here the mother is described as willing to sacrifice her body, possibly even her life, for the Jewish traditional female ideal: to bear sons and raise them as *gedolim*. The (male) editor of this story has her proclaim "for this I was created," indicating that apart from this role her life has no purpose.

Strikingly, the editors of this tale, in describing the mother and her self-sacrifice, quote the words of Rabbi Yehuda HaNassi originally addressed to a doomed animal.[8] In the classic Talmudic story, Rabbi Yehuda leads a calf to the slaughter house; when the calf begs for mercy, the Rabbi replies, "For this you were created." Later, the rabbi is punished for his callousness with chronic pain.[9] In our hagiography, however, the mother embraces her role uncomplainingly, believing that giving birth to a saint is more important than preserving her own life.

It is the potential mother of the saint, not the father, who is expected to sacrifice her body to merit a righteous son. In my opinion, the ideology behind this expectation far outweighs the simple biological fact that the woman gives birth and not the man. In general, in many cultures, a woman's life is defined in relation to her children and her husband. In Lithuanian Jewish culture specifically, the woman is identified with

---

6. *Talmud Bavli*, Baba Metziah 85a.

7. Cohen, *Pe'er Hador*, 63–64.

8. Cohen, *Pe'er Hador*, 63–64. Later in Cohen's book there are descriptions of the brothers and sisters of Rabbi Karelitz. When the editor describes the sisters, he does not mention their names, only the names of their husbands; nor does he provide any details about their lives (Cohen, *Pe'er Hador*, 64). Another example of the expectation that women will sacrifice themselves appears in a work dedicated to the life of Rabbi Eliyahu Lopian. The editor of this book relates that when the rabbi was mortally ill, his wife prayed to God that she might die in his stead; God heard her prayer, and she expired. (Lopian, *Lev Eliyahu Vol. 1*, 17).

9. *Talmud Bavli*, Baba Metzia 85a

materiality and the man with the spirit, exemplified by the study of Torah.[10] A woman's essence is acquired by virtue of her supporting role in a social performance in which males play the lead. It is unsurprising, then, that it is precisely the woman who sacrifices her physicality to be rewarded with a saintly son, in fulfillment of the role assigned to her gender.[11] Thanks to her sacrifice, her redemption is achieved through material means (physical birth), and this redemption is embodied in a *man* identified from birth as endowed with the spirit.[12]

We have noted above how Lithuanian authors emphasize the quantitative differences between various aspects of the child-*godol*'s personality and those of the typical reader, with the chief difference being that the young saint has only one essential desire in life: the study of Talmud. The Talmudic passion overrides every other desire; it is so intense in these child-saints that they refuse any other engagement, even the study of biblical texts, or, ironically, hagiographies of other *gedolim*,[13] to say nothing of giving attention to anything material, especially one's own body.

The Talmudic Aramaic term *yanuka'* (literally "the infant") appears in Jewish hagiographies with much the same connotations as the *Wunderkind* ("wonder child") of other cultures, and with the same highlighting of childish features such as simplicity and sexual innocence.[14] In addition, in the Jewish context, the child-*godol* or *yanuka'* differs from his peers in two other important aspects. First, he is not ever a true "child" in the modern sense since as a toddler he already possesses a mature and cohesive personality. While other children devote time to games, to exploring nature, and to other experiences of the world, the child-*godol* is described as concealing himself within the house of study, avoiding all external stimuli, as this description of the young Rabbi Feinstein illustrates:

> He attracted the attention of all the townspeople, causing amazement. Distancing himself from other children, separate

---

10. Gross, *Netzah Yisrael*, 62–80.

11. Yalom, *A History of a Wife*.

12. The expected sacrifice of the woman (representing "matter") for the man (representing "spirit") is even more emphatic in stories focused on the personality of the *godol*'s wife, who devotes her life to providing for all the material needs of her saintly husband, so that he may dedicate himself to his calling, which is by nature spiritual: learning Talmud. See for example, Anonymous, *Kol Chozev*, 12–14.

13. See for example, Kanievsky, *Toldot Yaakov*, 20.

14. Benarroch, "God and His Son," 64.

from all of them, his thoughts were not their thoughts, nor his deeds their deeds. He himself never sought the familiar company of other youngsters, with their love of naughty pastimes and frivolity. For him, nothing could be good in this world but Torah alone.[15]

The preternatural maturity of the *yanuka'* is fully focused, of course, on Talmud, as in the case of Elinka Ha-Matmid:

When he withdrew into a corner to study, it was impossible to distract him from his learning.[16] In fact, prankster children no younger than he would compete with each other in their vain efforts to distract Elinka Ha-Matmid.[17]

In a similar vein, Rabbi Pesach Frank recalls his friend Rabbi Menachem Levinson—at the tender age of three—chiding himself for his meager achievements in Talmudic studies: "Three years of my life have already passed me by," he lamented, "and what have I achieved in them?"[18]

The second and related aspect characterizing the Lithuanian *yanuka'* hagiographies is their stress on the intellectual talent that graces the "child-saint." Impressive analytical skills, sharp intelligence, and—in fact—sheer genius are all common to these narratives, and all serve the editors' intention of establishing a decisive quantitative distinction between the young *gedolim* and the readers of these tales.[19]

Recently, some members of the rabbinic hierarchy have recognized the damage this idealized image of the *gedolim* may cause their readers.[20] The author of a work entitled *She'ifot* ("*Ambitions*")—for example—dares to raise this taboo subject, citing a *haskamah* ("letter of consent" or *imprimatur*) he received from Rabbi Wolbe, and then adding:

15. Cohen, *Pe'er Hador*, Vol. 1, 163.

16. "His learning" here renders the Hebrew *girsato*—from the root *g.r.s.* meaning "to grind" or "crush." This is a strong term used in classical Jewish sources to describe a sacred study so intense and thorough that it is as if the scholar is "grinding" the text. The cognate Aramaic noun *girsa'* denotes a "version" or "interpretation" of a sacred text.

17. Sorotzki, *Marbitzey Torah Umusar*, Vol. 3, 54. Ha-Matmid (literally: "the constant one") is a common nickname for a yeshiva student who devotes himself to constant study of the Talmud.

18. Anonymous, *Hi Sichati*, Vol. 1, 37.

19. Shmuelevitz, *Sefer HaZikaron*, 20; Sorotzki, *Marbitzey Torah Umusar*, Vol. 3, 80–81; Abramski, *Melech Be-yofio*, 11.

20. Hershkovitz, *Sheifot*.

[I tell here] tales of *gedolim* . . . many of whom were far from being geniuses (Hebrew *'iluyiim*) in their talents! [But] these far-fetched accounts that we read in a book like this, serve to prompt us to think about our own ethics (*musar*) and to ask ourselves why it is that we have not grown in [our understanding of] Torah?[21]

Later in the same book, this author remarks that "most of the *gedolim* were not gifted [as children]." He even claims that neither Rabbi Israel Meir Kagan (the most famous Lithuanian rabbi in the early twentieth century),[22] nor Rabbi Shimon Shkop (widely considered to be uniquely intelligent) had any special talents as children or adolescents, but achieved their status only by dint of a lifetime of "powerful investment and efforts in learning Torah."[23] This writer knows that his rejection of childhood wonder tales is a radical departure from the norm. In order to soften the blow, he mentions only rabbis who passed away before the Holocaust, not leaders who may be known personally by the readers. He also is quite apologetic, and justifies his decision by citing the precedent set by Rabbi Karelitz, who also spoke of *deceased* rabbis who were unremarkable in their youth, but did not use the names of sages from his own generation.[24]

The difference between the child-*godol* and the rest of the children in the Lithuanian *Haredi* community is rooted in the proportionate relationship between matter and spirit. Readers understand, of course, that the other children, too, are interested in studying Torah. They, however, experience tension between this desire and other wishes, including the desires and natural urges of the body, and other material aspects of life. Their struggle is not only with their bodies, but also within their souls, which are split by conflicting desires and not entirely devoted to Talmud study—certainly not with the intensity of the child-*godol*. By contrast, the child-saint is described as possessing a soul entirely invested in Talmud; it is *only* his body that may become a hindrance, if seduced by material urges.

21. Hershkovitz, *Sheifot*.
22. Known as *Chofetz Chaim*, after the title of his book.
23. Hershkovitz, *Sheifot*.
24. Hershkovitz, *Sheifot*, 194. Compare to Hakak, "'Blessed Be the Sage's Memory?" 408.

B. The Design of the Body in Childhood

As a child and adolescent, then, the *godol* identifies his true "self" entirely with his aspiration to study Talmud, and anything that does not contribute to this desire and its realization is viewed as negative, even threatening. The boy's body, and his physical needs, are assigned an instrumental status, and hence the ambivalence toward the body in these tales. On one hand, it is through the body that the desire to learn is actualized, since the more healthily the body functions, the more possibilities the boy will have to devote most of his time to study. On the other hand, the *yetser* (evil inclination) is perceived as rooted in the body as a force that may continually tempt him to neglect the study of Torah.[25]

These hagiographies do not condone ascetic practices that might directly harm the body of the child-*godol*, although this caution dissipates when the youth reaches yeshiva age, as we shall see later in this chapter. In early childhood years, *gedolim* identify themselves completely with the "spirit" while they perceive the body as a tool, which—if properly managed—will function to help them achieve their desire to study. This is how the younger Rabbi Yaakov Yisrael Kanievsky is described during lunch break in the *cheder* (religious school) in his childhood town:

> After a few hours of effort, the teacher closed the Talmud volume and sent the boys to get some recreation and work off their youthful energy. . . . But while the other children were running to and fro and horsing around, the young Yaakov Yisrael stood still, leaning against a wall behind the schoolhouse, resting and gathering strength for further study. . . . When the other boys cheerfully shouted to him as he stood there resting, "Here—catch the stick!"—he, for his part, calmly replied, "I do not wish to run around and get tired; I just want to rest so I will be able to study later."[26]

Sometimes, totally immersed in learning, the young *gedolim* forget to eat and drink. When pressed, they finally acquiesce and take some nourishment, recognizing that if they harm their bodies, their capacity to learn will be diminished.[27] The adults in their lives try to mitigate the effects of their devotion by encouraging them to act like other children. In a text about the life of Rabbi Yaakov Moshe Kulefsky we read:

25. Anonymous, *Kol Chozev*, 23.
26. Kanievsky, *Toldot Yaakov*, 19–20.
27. Anonymous, *Hi Sichati*, Vol. 1, 249.

Once, when he fell ill, he was taken by his parents to a doctor, who told them that their son needed physical activity and outdoor recreation in the sun. His mother asked him to go and play with the other children, and even sent him out to play in the yard, locking the door and windows, with the intention of forcing him to engage in games with his friends. About half an hour later, the boy Rabbi Yaakov Moshe found his way back into the house by crawling down the chimney entrance, emerging covered with soot and charcoal. He sat down at the table and continued his study and his laboring at Torah.[28]

This story, like many similar tales, pits the child's (spiritual) will against his bodily (material) needs. It opens by assessing the needs of the body, when the parents realize that the insatiable desire to learn comes at the expense of their son's physical health. The narrative goes on to describe parental efforts to contain or re-direct the child's devotion, and closes with the triumph of the young saint's will over all obstacles. The figure of the child-*godol* who climbs the roof to enter the house (or study hall) through the chimney is prevalent in stories of the righteous. It is told of Hillel the Elder (110 B.C.E. – 10 C.E.), one of the most well-known Talmudic figures, that since he was too poor to pay the guard at the entrance to the house of study, he climbed the roof, quenching his burning thirst for Torah by listening to the lessons through the chimney flue, until he fainted from weariness.[29] The sooty, exhausted body of the young saint always pays the price for his soul's relentless dedication to learning.

Alongside such descriptions are others that present the body, not as the victim of the child's devotion, but as a hindrance to and distraction from the child's commitment to spiritual matters. In a book devoted to the life of Rabbi Schwadron, the editors note that children's voices coming from the playground next to his parents' home would "tempt" him to join their games.[30] Rabbi Schwadron himself connects playing games, as a physical act, with the evil inclination: "Thank God, I managed to escape

---

28. Anonymous, *Hi Sichati*, Vol. 1, 249, 365. He was head of the "Ner Yisroel" yeshiva in Baltimore.

29. *Talmud Bavli*, Yoma 35b.

30. Here it is important to remember the gap already discussed between presentations of Jewish lives in hagiographies and real biographical data in historical descriptions. For academic scholarship on the differences, see, Assaf and Etkes, eds., *Heder*. A study of historical accounts makes it clear that the editors of spiritual biographies create an ideal picture, far from the historical reality.

them [i.e. children's games]. God saved me; I also had a good teacher [*melamed*] who helped me fight off this inclination [*ha-yetser ha-zeh*] as well."[31]

The child-*godol* has difficulty distinguishing between normal and healthy physical needs, and expressions of his innate sinful tendencies. He perceives the boundary between these realms as subtle, and feels he must be very careful not to confuse the two. Accordingly, the child-saint often adopts a strict physical regimen, an ascetic lifestyle that can take many forms. It is said Rabbi Yechiel Michel Feinstein refrained from eating any tasty or pleasing foods[32]; Rabbi Eliezer Sach slept without a blanket in the European winter to minimize his hours of slumber;[33] from a young age, Rabbi Shimshon David Pincus walked down the street with his eyes closed (to avoid distractions), while his mother held his hand.[34] Many rabbis, in their younger years, were very rigid in observing laws of impurity and purity.[35] Their stubborn struggle with the body, especially in neglecting the normal needs of early childhood, often caused irreparable physical harm. It is said of many *gedolim* that they suffered severe pain later in life as a result of the harsh limitations they imposed on their bodies during childhood. This is how one text describes Rabbi Eliyahu Rogler:

> His intense devotion to Torah study during his adolescence and young manhood caused him severe headaches, and eventually led to an illness that he suffered from all his life, often having to wrap his aching temples with healing compresses. Once he told his friends about his troubles, saying: "A less serious scholar, suffering from such pains, would surely take his own life." And yet, our teacher never abandoned for even one moment the study of Torah, his life-spring and his soul's delight. He never paused, never giving his own sickness and physical weaknesses the slightest attention. Even when his physicians warned him urgently not to fatigue his mind or nerves with perusal of books, he did not heed their advice, but continued to be a living example of the scripture, which reads: "This is the divine law, that a man may die while in the tent [of Torah. See *Numbers* 19:14]."[36]

31. Anonymous, *Kol Chozev*, 23.
32. Anonymous, *Sar HaTorah*, 58.
33. Kanievsky, *Toldot Yaakov*, 124.
34. Sofer, *Raboteinu Shebedarom*, 17.
35. Yivrov, *Ma'ase Ish*, 14.
36. Yivrov, *Ma'ase Ish*, 954.

In the examples we have been citing, the young *godol* is described as virtuous from the beginning of his life, knowing only one desire: the study of Torah. In other accounts, however, a darker picture emerges, of an unwitting and obedient child who is given no choice but to accept the harsh yoke of righteousness:

> "Torah and only Torah," his father had always told him, and Rabbi Moshe Shmuel, who "would not stray either to the right hand or to the left" from the injunction of the great sage [ha-*ga'on*] his father,[37] treasured these words in his heart.... On the day that Moshe Shmuel began to put on the *tefillin* [phylacteries] for himself, his mother [*ha-rabbanit*][38] put her hand on her son's arm.... But the marks [of the phylactery straps] on Moshe Shmuel's arm were very red, deep and hot; and his mother noticed that her son Moshe Shmuel was in considerable pain.... [And all this because, in the past], when his father had wrapped the *tefillin* on Moshe Shmuel's arm [for him], he had unintentionally tied them too tightly.... "Why did you not tell your father (*Abba*) to loosen the straps?" his mother asked.... "One should never criticize *Abba*!" he replied, as if he considered this obvious.... "And why did you not then loosen them yourself?" ... "It would never even occur to me," [he replied], "to change what *Abba* had done."[39]

Another example appears in a story about Rabbi Shalom Schwadron, known in his childhood as "Sholemke."[40] The tale opens with young Sholemke playing in the village streets with other children, during the Hebrew month of *Elul*, a time devoted to repentance.[41]

> At quite an early hour, his mother would go out to the village square, by the well. She stood some distance [from her son, who was playing outside], and she was deeply worried. Her voice echoed far and wide: "*Elul* ! Sholemke, in these days even the

---

37. This line is based on a Deuteronomy 17:11.

38. Rabbi Moshe Shmuel's mother is referred to throughout this passage as *ha-rabbanit*—"The Rabbi's Wife"—without using her own name.

39. Israel, *Rabbi Moshe Shmuel*, 67–69.

40. *Sholemke* is a gentle, childhood Yiddish nickname from Rabbi Schwadron's first name—Shalom.

41. In the Jewish calendar, *Elul* is the twelfth month of the year, usually coinciding with parts of August and September. In the Jewish tradition, this month is a time of repentance in preparation for the High Holy Days of Rosh Hashanah (the Jewish New Year) and Yom Kippur (the Day of Atonement).

fish of the sea are trembling [with fear of divine retribution], and you are out playing around?!" ... Years later, at the age of seventy, [Rabbi Schwardon] still remembered his mother's cry of *Elul!* Addressing a great gathering of listeners, he would tell the story of his mother's tears in the days of *Elul*—and he would weep too, tears meeting tears.[42]

Through the tightly bound straps of the *tefillin*, the father unconsciously engraves his expectations on his son's flesh: "Torah and only Torah." The mother's pious weeping for her son's lack of piety inspires in him a guilt that drives him toward sanctity. Michel Foucault pointed out that society "engraves" its ideologies, both visible and hidden, upon the physical body. Judith Butler explains:

> In the context of prisoners, Foucault writes, the strategy has been not to enforce a repression of their desires, but to compel their bodies to signify the prohibitive law as their very essence, style, and necessity. The law is not literally internalized, but incorporated, with the consequence that bodies are produced which signify that law on and through the body; there the law is manifest as the essence of their selves, the meaning of their soul, their conscience, the law of their desire.[43]

Examining how the Lithuanian community makes its mark on its children's bodies can reveal the community's values, including those pertaining to the body itself. Mirroring the effect on prisoners in Foucault's writing or Kafka's Penal Colony, Lithuanian ideology is engraved on the child-*godol*'s body through the use of force.[44] Tying the *tefillin* tightly marks the father's law on the child's flesh, and the child does not dare to protest. The father's will merges with the body of his child, and becomes,

---

42. Anonymous, *Kol Chozev*, 11–12. Later in his life, Rabbi Schwadron ("Reb Shalom") himself mirrored this behavior with his daughter: "One of Reb Shalom's daughters, seven years old, behaved in a way that Reb Shalom thought inappropriate. One morning Reb Shalom returned from his morning prayer, took the child on his shoulder, went into his room, and placed her on the table facing him. Then he burst into tears, ... with heartrending sobs, but without directing a single word to his daughter. ... From that moment on, the girl's negative attitude disappeared, and she was unable to repeat her previous [reprehensible] behavior" (Anonymous, *Kol Chozev*, 87).

43. Butler, *Gender Trouble*, 183.

44. Foucault emphasizes the process of "engraving" the ideology of society on the bodies of prisoners. Foucault's choice to study the bodies of the "other" is significant, since by understanding the role of the "other" in a society, one can learn how "normality" is defined in the same society. See Foucault, *Discipline and Punish*.

in fact, the child's own will. A more subtle "engraving"—but still with physical manifestation—is the mother's coercive weeping reflected in the guilty tears of the grown Rabbi.

C. Perception of Space and Time in the Yeshiva

Young *gedolim* identify with their desire for learning but are suspicious of their bodies because of their inability to correctly distinguish between basic physical needs and the urges of the evil inclination. Yeshiva life promises precisely this kind of discernment, so the child-*gedolim* are usually sent to the yeshiva at a younger age than other boys.[45] The yeshiva is a space where they may devote most of their time to the highest level of Talmudic study, together with their peers, under the supervision of the best teachers. But the yeshiva is not merely a study center; the *gedolim* narratives portray it as similar to a heterotopia, an exceptional space outside of normative spheres. This haven provides a safe environment for Jewish youths to experience critical passages in the development of their personality, both in relation to their own bodies and to the surrounding society.[46] The goal of the yeshiva is to completely transform a boy, uprooting him from both outside society and Nature, enabling him to be reborn, not as a son of his parents but as a "son of the yeshiva [*ben yeshiva*]."

Descriptions of the boys' new lifestyle in the yeshiva often emphasize differences in perceptions of time and space compared to the outside world. First, an ordinary sense of time is lost; a boy may forget his age and when he last met people from outside the yeshiva. Rabbi Shach thus describes his own experience:[47]

---

45. A significant reason for the *gedolim* entering yeshiva at such a young age is their precocious talent in Talmudic study, and the inability of their parents and rabbis to provide them with Talmud teachers at their advanced level. According to the *gedolim* tales, the "child-saint" entered the yeshiva between the ages of ten and thirteen, much earlier than his contemporaries. On Rabbi Shach see, Bergman, *Maran Harav Shach*, Vol. 1, 11. On Rabbi Sarna see, Sorotzki, *Marbitzey Torah Umusar*, Vol. 4, 81. On Rabbi Kotler, see p. 218.

46. To understand the complexity of yeshiva life and the relationships between younger and elder students, see Stampfer, *Lithuanian Yeshivas*.

47. The relationship between the yeshiva and the surrounding Jewish community is interesting, since the yeshivas bear the name of their city or village, but may be in many ways cut off from ordinary community life.

> Continuous and monotonous study caused us to . . . all but totally forget ourselves. Without sitting myself down to concentrate on the question of how old I was, I could never have even remembered my own age! I recall that when I was thirteen, I used to take my daily meals (*achalti yamim*) with a [Jewish] householder in the town of Ponevezh [near the yeshiva]. After some time had passed, I found that I could not remember when I had last had a meal at this person's home. Once when I was walking in the town, I met the householder on the street. I asked him: "Please, sir, can you tell me how long it has been since I had a meal with you?"—and he replied immediately, "That was two years ago!" Suddenly, I realized that I was now fifteen years old.[48]

In the yeshiva, the boys' maturation is measured by the number of Talmudic topics and tractates they study, rather than by age. They do not intentionally go to bed at night, but doze off when fatigue overwhelms them; as a result, days and nights become intertwined until they are almost indistinguishable:[49]

> [The student] did not eat or sleep on any regular schedule. He used to study continuously for more than ten hours, and when his study ended, at any hour, even in the middle of the day, he would go and eat something, and then sleep. Even at noontime, you can close the shutters and go to sleep.[50]

This is how one story describes Rabbi Aharon Kotler, as a thirteen-year-old student at the Slabodka Yeshiva:

> One night Rabbi Aharon was so tired that he fell asleep on the desk [*shtender*][51] in the yeshiva hall. The *Saba* ["Grandfather" i.e., Rabbi Finkel] passed him, leaned over softly, kissed his

---

48. Bergman, *Maran Harav Shach*, Vol. 1, 47–48. Rabbi Elazar Menachem Man Shach (1899–2001) served as head of the Ponevezh Yeshiva in Bnei-Brak, and was the main Lithuanian Ultra-Orthodox leader in the second part of the twentieth century. Rabbi Shach was deeply involved with religious politics in Israel. He is known for his harsh words against Israeli secular society, for his conflict with the Habad Hasidic dynasty, for helping to create the first Sephardic political party (Shas), and later for his confrontations with Sephardic community leader Rabbi Ovadia Yosef. Rabbi Shach's funeral occasioned a remarkable mass gathering of approximately 200,000 mourners.

49. Israel, *Rabbi Moshe Shmuel*, 116.

50. Anonymous, *Mepihem Shel Rabotynu*, 290.

51. A typical yeshiva study-table.

forehead tenderly, and whispered: "A living Torah scroll! . . . A living Torah scroll!"⁵²

In classical Jewish hagiography there is a famous midrash about the legendary Rabbi Akiva who returned home after twelve continuous years at the yeshiva.⁵³ He stood at the front door of his house, listening to a conversation between his wife and a neighbor. His wife said, that if Akiva came home, she would implore him to return to the yeshiva for another twelve years. Without even knocking on the door, Rabbi Akiva immediately returned to the yeshiva for another twelve years. Rabbi Chaim Shmuelevitz is known for saying of this midrash: "This is why Rabbi Akiva decided not to enter his house after twelve years, but returned immediately [to study] for another twelve years: the interruption would have troubled him deeply; twelve plus twelve is not twenty four."⁵⁴ Time in the yeshiva is measured according to continual duration of study, and nothing more. Whoever is not learning is cut off from his spiritual roots; his time becomes sterile, worthless and devoid of meaning.

Transforming the perception of time and especially the standard division of time is intended to influence the learning experience. With this principle in mind, Rabbi Chaim Ephraim Zeichik presents the difference between physical pleasure and spiritual pleasure:

> People who are immersed in the vanities of this world . . . cannot experience the years of their lives as a continuous and uninterrupted reality. . . . The pleasure [they feel] in the first hour of the day has no connection or relevance with the pleasure of the second hour, because as long as the second hour has not yet arrived, the person enjoys, for now, only the first hour. . . . The pious person [literally: "the man who fears the Name (of God)"] is blessed with such eternal tools that he is able to fold together into one the pleasure of all twenty four hours of a day, and thus to get a taste of heaven. He can also, in the evening of his days, sink into his thoughts, reviewing in his mind's eye the pleasures of all his many years, feeling them again as if he were within the very moment he is imagining, as if that moment were alive in this. . . . In this he resembles his Creator, for whom everything is eternally present.⁵⁵

52. Sorotzki, *Marbitzey Torah Umusar*, Vol. 3, 219.
53. *Talmud Bavli*, Nedarim 51a.
54. Shmuelevitz, *Sichot Musar*, 52–53, 101; Stern, *Bait u-Menucha*, 22.
55. Zeichik, *Or Chadash*, 247–48.

Toward the end of his life, Rabbi Elazar Shach was asked by his students whether they should practice *mishmer*—a vigil of Talmud study for the whole night between Thursday and Friday, imitating the old yeshiva tradition in Lithuania. Rabbi Shach rejected the idea and explained that the way the question was posed attests to a lack of understanding. The students assumed a conscious decision to *study at night* in addition to *studying by day*. The Rabbi pointed out that during his yeshiva days, there was really no difference between night and day: "We did not [set out to] '*do mishmer*.' It is just that we would sit down to study as night fell, and when we raised our heads from the Talmud we saw that the day was dawning!"[56] In other words, in the extreme context of the yeshiva lifestyle, ordinary time is nullified. Yeshiva time is not regulated by arbitrary or artificial measures like clocks or hours, but is subordinated to the spiritual logic of continuous educational activity.

Rabbi Yaakov Yitzchok Ruderman describes how sometimes these opposing conceptions of time came into direct conflict:

> When I was fourteen years old, studying in Slabodka Yeshiva, on the eve of Rosh Hashanah, I took upon myself the task of reading the entire Talmud during "winter time"[57]—before Passover. But, before "winter time" began, on the 29th of the month of *Tishrei*, a message reached the yeshiva that my late father had passed away. The "Grandfather" [Rabbi Finkel], who knew about the vow I had taken on the eve of Rosh Hashanah, kept the news of my father's death from me until I completed reading the Talmud, about six months after I had already become an orphan. . . . Only then, the "Grandfather" approached me with the "old rumor" [of my father's death]. Then, as if apologizing for the delay, he added: "Your Talmud is worth more than saying Kaddish."[58]

This story demonstrates how distinct systems of time compete, and how the yeshiva's system of time, represented in the story about studying Talmud, takes precedence. Rabbi Finkel decided for his student that his vow

---

56. Anonymous, *Hi Sichati*, Vol. 1, 82. See also, Sorotzki, *Harav MePonivez*, 23.

57. The yeshiva winter semester begins with Rosh Hashanah around October and ends around late March with Passover.

58. Bergman, *Orchot Chasideha*, 388. Kaddish is the traditional Jewish prayer recited to commemorate a death. An orphan recites the Kaddish every day while praying with the community during the first year after the death of the loved one. A similar story is told about Rabbi Sarna, who refrains from telling his student, Rabbi Meir Chadash, that his father passed away (Bergman, *Shimush Talmidei Chahamim*, 162).

to learn the entire Talmud was more important than knowledge about his father's death, even though it had religious implications according to mainstream Jewish law. Outside of the yeshiva, the *halakha* sets a time for the orphan to recite the Kaddish. In the "yeshiva time zone" this requirement is delayed for six months, in accordance with yeshiva priorities.[59]

The perception of space as well as time changes in the world of yeshiva students. In the yeshiva, living space is virtually reduced to the study hall. Although there is a dormitory, as often as not students never enter it, but simply catch a few hours sleep on a bench in the study hall.[60] The boys refrain from visiting their families' homes and sometimes sever relationships with them for many years:[61]

> Rabbi Aharon [Weinstein] was a great sage, and completely immersed himself in the study of Torah. They say that during the week he did not change his clothes at all. He was completely immersed in the Torah from morning to evening, hidden in the yeshiva hall and "killing himself in the tent of Torah."[62] Although he could not make time to leave the study hall to change his clothes, they were always clean. For long hours he would lean over the Talmud, and only when he felt his strength ebbing away and his body breaking down, would he fall exhausted to the bench and take a short nap.[63]

Similarly, when Rabbi Shach was told that his mother and brother, whom he had not seen for many years, were only a few miles away from the yeshiva, he did not rush to meet them:

> A "slice of life" reached [Rabbi Shach] when he was told by one of his yeshiva companions: "Your family is just across the border. This is a wonderful opportunity to meet with them!" This message stunned Rabbi Shach and unleashed in him a flood of emotions. To meet is mother! And how she would delight in seeing him! And how dearly he would love to see his younger siblings! How he yearned to meet them all, and to embrace his mother and even weep a bit for the death of his father. . . . But

---

59. It should be noted that, from a halakhic point of view, this choice does not run counter to Jewish law, since the student himself was not aware of his father's death, and therefore was not obligated to recite the Kaddish.

60. Anonymous, *Mepihem Shel Rabotynu*, 231; Kanievsky, *Toldot Yaakov*, 21.

61. Schwartz, *Achar Mitato*, 47–48; Kanievsky, *Toldot Yaakov*, 21–22.

62. This is an Ultra-Orthodox expression used to describe a person who completely dedicates himself to the learning of Torah.

63. Israel, *Rabbi Moshe Shmuel*, 116–17.

then, he took a fateful decision. In his heart, he knew his mother's innermost desire, and what would most "truly" bring her joy. "Who says of his father and mother, 'I do not see them,' and of his brothers and sisters, 'I know them not'" (Deuteronomy 33:9). Those Levites who served the Name [*ha-shem*—i.e., God] in the Holy Temple [in Jerusalem], for twenty whole years they did not see their own father or mother, and would not even recognize their own siblings. Rather, they were hidden away in God's House [*bayit ha-shem*], observing the sacred service.[64]

The radical conception of space and time in the yeshiva contributes to the redefinition of good and evil, based on the fundamental distinction between the service of the body (symbol of materialism) and the worship of God (the apex of spirituality). Here, the definition of "good" is Talmud study, and *nothing more*. The yeshiva structure even includes under the categories of "body" and "materiality" any Jewish religious expressions not in the Talmud. As the understanding of "materiality" broadens, the original distinction between spirit and matter, which the editors of the stories strive to retain, is gradually undermined. The texts describe the efforts required by the boys to calm their passion for learning, at hours designated for prayer or observance of the Jewish law.

The testimony of Rabbi Avraham Yitzchak Gershonowitch, head of the *Tiferet Tzion* ("Zion's Glory") Yeshiva in the city of *Bnei Brak*, in Israel, makes clear the ambivalence of the *gedolim* toward any religious activity that deviates from the study of Talmud: "One does not find life in observing the commands [mitzvoth] of Jewish law; rather, vitality of the spirit comes only through study of Torah [i.e. Talmud]."[65] Similarly, Rabbi Shmuel Auerbach affirms that one of his most challenging tasks is "his efforts to avoid thinking about Torah [i.e. Talmud] at the hour of daily devotions."[66] . . . His concentration during prayer costs him great

---

64. Bergman, *Orchot Chasideha*, 135–36. The yeshiva's alternative organization of time and space can explain why the yeshiva hegemony opposed the historical work of Rabbi Nathan Kamenetsky, who positions the *gedolim* in the mainstream time-frame of history, not only within Jewish contexts, but also within the broader context of Europe (Kamenetsky, *Making of a Godol*, 305).

65. Anonymous, *Hi Sichati, Vol. 2*, 922. When these writers say "Torah" they often mean "Talmud." The challenges of observing Jewish halakha also appear in stories about *gedolim* from earlier generations, prior to the Holocaust. For example, it is said that Rabbi Igra Sofer used to bite his arm in order to focus at prayer times, since his mind was constantly wanting to study Talmud, rather than engaging in prayer. See Anonymous, *Hi Sichati, Vol. 1*, 38.

66. Anonymous, *Hi Sichati, Vol. 2*, 133.

effort, since is mind is constantly at work, probing, analyzing, comparing and refuting."[67]

The body becomes a means toward quieting the desire for learning, when the young *gedolim* must let go of their Talmud studies in order to observe Jewish law. For example, Rabbi Shach writes about his teacher:

> His utter absorption in study made it difficult for Rabbi Itchele to focus even on listening to readings from the sacred scriptures [*kri'at ha-torah*]. Accordingly, he would adopt all sorts of artificial means to distract his attention from the deep thoughts that enveloped his mind, in order to better attend to the reader's voice. He would utter, for example, strange syllables in a booming voice, in order to shake himself awake from the depths of his cogitations. Or, he would pace about the room, rocking his body to and fro, in a desperate effort to still the roaring waves of his own thoughts.[68]

The hagiographies reveal yeshiva culture's ambivalence toward the body, the commitment to learning and the worship of God. The radical severing of "spirit" from "body" creates a new challenge: the aspiring saint must now struggle, not just against the body, as is typical, but also against the incessant urgings of the mind. The man of *Musar* seeks ways to subdue the relentless mind that ignores the reflective self, employing the body to quell his Talmudic thoughts, so that he may practice other forms of Jewish spirituality, such as prayer. The accounts illustrate the complex attitudes of "ideal" rabbis, not only toward their bodies, but also toward the Jewish community its traditional religious practices, and even its fundamental relationship with the divine. Rabbi Shlomo Wolbe, for example, shares the following words in the name of Rabbi Yechezkel Levenstein:

> Rabbi Hazekel [i.e. Yechezkel] once told the yeshiva's *mashgiah* [mentor of Musar]: "Go, tell your students that the Creator of the World exists!" For a long time this *mashgiah* wondered what this might mean. What kind of yeshiva student would be ignorant of the existence of the Creator? Then he finally understood the rabbi's meaning. It is true that we learn; but are we even aware that we are learning the sacred teachings of God Himself [*torat ha-shem*]? . . . This same *mashgiah* would ironically tell the tale of the yeshiva student who is telling his companion

---

67. Shmuelevitz, *Sefer HaZikaron*, 31.
68. Bergman, *Maran Harav Shach*, Vol. 1, 39.

about a wonderful dream he had. In this dream, he says, he saw the Lord of the Universe [Himself]. To which the other decisively replies: "That is impossible!" The first student is hurt, and retorts, "How can you be so sure?" To which his companion replies, "It is simple! You can only dream about what occupies your mind during your waking hours. When did you ever have time to think about the Lord of the Universe?"[69]

D. The Design of the Body in the Yeshiva

The unique perception of space and time in the yeshiva is the platform upon which the *godol's* body is shaped, as he enacts a series of daily ascetic practices to ensure that his spirit can control and dominate his body.[70] The manipulations the *gedolim* bring to bear on their bodies are common features of their hagiographies, regardless of where they studied. The boys' bodies are not necessarily punished directly, but rather through neglect. With all their time and energy devoted solely to long hours of Talmud studies and spiritual pursuits, their bodies are abandoned, gradually devolving into asceticism.

There are, however, in stories of the *gedolim*, two distinct forms of explicit manipulation of the body through outright ascetic practices, corresponding to the two main traditions of Lithuanian religious life: the Slabodka method and the alternative yeshiva perspective.

As we have already seen, Rabbi Finkel, the founder of the Slabodka method, forged a new perception of the Jewish man.[71] Yeshivas directly influenced by his philosophy developed quite distinct concepts of the ideal image of the *Musar* man and his body. According to this model, each man is composed of body and soul, both having important roles in his socialization; only after he has equally mastered both body and soul can he attain complete self-realization. In this philosophy, the body, like the soul, begins in a raw state, and gradually matures through an

---

69. Wolbe, *Avnei Shlomo*, 103–4. This story is not a criticism of the students, but rather a proof of their devotion to Talmud study, which is so total that it leaves them no time to reflect on the divine. See Friedman, *Shtaygen*, 282.

70. Scholars define asceticism differently. Some, such as Ware, see it as mental and physical training to achieve specific goals. See Ware, "The Way of the Ascetics," 3. Others, such as Kaelber, emphasize the element of renunciation of immediate pleasure in order to reach a higher stage of spiritual attainment. See Kaelber, "Asceticism," 441. See also, Sobosan, "Self-Fulfillment."

71. See chapter 5.

extended educational process. Asceticism, as we shall see later in the chapter, has no meaning in itself, but functions only as a complementary tool for individual development. On the other had, in alternatives to the Slabodka method in other *Musar* lineages, self-disciplinary acts directed against the body have a purpose in themselves. Their goal is to liberate the soul by shattering the bonds of the body, which is perceived as attempting to seduce the soul into sin.

I will open this section with the design of the body and asceticism in *Musar* methods in general, and then will proceed to focus on the unique method of Slabodka.

All of the *gedolim* hagiographies include descriptions of at least passive injury to the body, as a result of the intense desire to study Talmud. Rabbi Yaakov Yisrael Kanievsky, as the following description indicates, did not intentionally practice asceticism; he simply did not notice, that instead of his morning bread he had eaten a piece of plaster that fell from the ceiling. The description opens with a biblical citation, to set the tone of fasting as a context for holy behavior, and then goes on to describe Rabbi Kanievsky's sublime indifference to food:

> "When famine was upon the land . . ." [1 Kings 8:37]. All [the yeshiva students] were standing in line to receive their portion of bread, but Our Teacher [*rabbeinu*—i.e., Rabbi Kanievsky] had a different idea in mind. "In the time I would be spending waiting in line for my bread," he thought, "I could instead be learning another few pages of Talmud." So he sat in the yeshiva, bent over his tractate, immersing himself in his Talmud and forgetting all about the world around him.
>
> Rabbi Yaffen used to tell that he once saw Rabbi Kanievsky [as a young student in the yeshiva] sitting on his bench [toward evening], reflecting on the Torah, and beside him was the meal someone had brought him that morning. When Rabbi [Yaffen] asked Our Teacher [Kanievsky] why he had not eaten all day, the latter replied that he had indeed eaten, and having had his fill had recited the blessing after a meal. Rabbi Yaffen was astonished. "How can this be," he asked, "when your meal is still here, untouched, on the bench beside you?" Later, he found out that a lump of plaster had fallen from the ceiling of the House of Study [onto the bench], and our Teacher had eaten that, immersed all the while in his studies. Then, he had recited the blessing, under

the impression that he had just eaten his breakfast, and not noticing anything amiss.[72]

The description of Rabbi Yaakov Dovid Gordon is very similar:

> When he was an eleven, he went to study in another city.... Since he was penniless, the helpless youngster walked fifteen miles to the city of Telšiai.... Without any mode of support except the modest yeshiva scholarship, he lived a life of great distress and penury, far beyond [what is required by] the Torah, and without even a lump of salt to his name. Only the love of the Torah that had made an abode in the boy's heart gave him strength to overcome all his difficulties.[73]

In order to understand the phenomenon of asceticism or voluntary deprivation of the body, we must take into account the surrounding cultural, environmental, and economic factors.[74] Indeed, there is a close connection between the cultivation of myths about asceticism and the unstable economic situation of yeshivas and other Jewish communities in Lithuania at that time. The lack of basic means of subsistence left young people no choice but to forget their bodies and satisfy their hunger through nourishing sublimations—notably the study of the Talmud. The conditions of poverty and poor nutrition in Lithuanian yeshivas are described as follows:[75]

> In the yeshivas of that time, young children could not expect good physical conditions.... They were not served satisfying or nourishing fare. The only food offered to these young spiritual heroes—who had left their warm homes and loving families in order to be raised up in the Torah and in divine worship—was spiritual sustenance, and of that there was never short supply. Precisely thus, overcoming difficulties and trials, constantly coping with both physical and spiritual torments, standing firm daily through the hardest tests, these tender youngsters matured [*hithashlu*] and built up their personalities. When they felt hungry, they satisfied themselves with another page of Talmud, with another aspect of interpretation (*tosaphot*). And when they could find nowhere to lay their weary limbs to rest after a long

---

72. Anonymous, *Hi Sichati*, Vol. 1, 326.
73. Anonymous, *Hi Sichati*, Vol. 2, 925.
74. Deal, "Toward a Politics of Asceticism."
75. Anonymous, *Mepihem Shel Rabotynu*, 238, 290.

and busy day [of learning], they would simply go on studying, until their last strength was gone.[76]

In some cases, the editors of these stories present the poverty of the yeshivas in a more positive light, not as an external condition of the general economy, but as an intentional choice to withdraw from the life of this world. For example, it is said that the head of the Novardok Yeshiva did not have a second chair to offer the young Rabbi Yechezkel Abramsky when he arrived for his entrance interview. Favorably impressed by Abramsky, the Novardok rabbi sent his grandson to buy a single sugar cube for the promising new student. Ostensibly, this is another description of the state of poverty in the Jewish community, but the editor presents the story as an example of an intentional "minimization of pleasure" (*mi'yut ta'anug*)—one of the forty-eight necessary paths to gain the "crown of Torah" (*Mishna Avot* 6:6). In other words, even if, in fact, the yeshiva did not have enough furniture or food due to poverty, the editor used this story to illustrate how a proper *godol* should live.[77]

This strategy also highlights the gap between the "old days" of the *gedolim* in Lithuania, on one hand, and the lives of present-day readers in the State of Israel and the USA, on the other. The editors establish a connection between the pre- and post-Holocaust generations, while simultaneously emphasizing the unbridgeable qualitative difference between the two eras, through highlighting the difficult economic conditions in pre-Holocaust yeshivas. Readers are thus encouraged to draw inspiration from these stories and their heroes, without trying to wholly imitate their potentially unhealthy living conditions. Contemporary yeshiva students who wish to devote themselves to the study of Talmud with "all their soul and all their might" have no reason to damage their bodies in this pursuit.

The *Musar* sources continually remind the readers that knowledge attained through suffering is deeper than that achieved at leisure, or through the enjoyment of learning.[78] However, the boundary between overt self-deprivation and training the body for the spiritual life is not always easily discerned, as illustrated by the following examples:

---

76. Anonymous, *Sar HaTorah*, 18–19.

77. Gold, *Bnei Chail Vol. 1*, 203. See also p. 197. The story appeared also in Levi, *Mashal HaAvot al 48 Kinyanei HaTorah Vol. 2*, 12 under the category of *mi'yut ta'anug* ("minimization of pleasure").

78. See, for example: Gold, *Bnei Chail Vol. 1*, 288.

Once, when there was a community fast day, and the next day food was hard to find because of the famine, our Rabbi [*rabbeinu*—refers to Rabbi Kanievsky] fasted for two days. On the eve of the third day,[79] our Rabbi decided, since there is [spiritual] merit in fasting for three consecutive days, that he should fast another day, and so he did. Later he said that he barely felt that he was fasting on the first day, a bit more on the second, and on the third day he was hungry.[80]

When they wanted to install a fan in [Rabbi Kanievsky's] room, he refused, and had it removed. His reason was simple: that [without a fan] there would be less of "this world" [in the room]. For the same reason, he prevented the installation of air conditioning in his room, despite the breathing difficulties he often suffered from. . . . When they brought him tasty food, he refused to eat it.[81]

It is told of the *Chafetz Chaim*[82] that sometimes he would pour himself a glass of water, and instead of drinking he would set the glass in front of him, with the intention of subduing his "lust."[83]

The stories' stated purpose, and the concrete expressions of asceticism, are not always clear and unequivocal. The young men in the yeshiva set out to transform and remake their physicality. They bring pressure to bear on the body, to force it back to a primal, formless material, rendered broken and mute. Then, they endeavor to reshape the body in such a way as to submit it to their will. Self-imposed starvation, consuming tasteless food,[84] speaking rarely, sleeping little, rolling in the snow[85] and wearing

---

79. In Judaism, a day begins at sundown on the previous day; this is called "the eve" of the approaching day. For example, "the eve" of Saturday (Shabbat) is sundown on Friday. In our passage, the rabbi fasted for two days, and as the second day ended ("on the eve of the third day") he decided to fast for another twenty-four hours.

80. This story comes from the description of the life of Rabbi Yaakov Yisrael Kanievsky. See Kanievsky, *Toldot Yaakov*, 178.

81. Kanievsky, *Toldot Yaakov*, 178. See also, p. 92; Lopian, *Lev Eliyahu: Musar*, 166.

82. This is the honorific title of Rabbi Israel Meir Kagan.

83. *Chizuk* 6 (2006), 297.

84. It is said that Rabbi Dessler intentionally ate bland or tasteless food. See Sorotzki, *Marbitzey Torah Umusar, Vol. 3*, 55. See also, Anonymous, *Sar HaTorah*, 58. About Rabbi David Povarsky and Rabbi Yechiel Michel Feinstein who decided not to eat butter, only dry bread, during their years in the yeshiva.

85. See Anonymous, *Kol Chozev*, 43.

sackcloth that scratches the skin[86]—are all examples of the kinds of self-discipline students employ to eliminate natural behavior from their bodies. It is reported of Rabbi Shvadaron that, while engaged in nightly Talmud study, he would attach his side-locks by a rope to the ceiling; whenever he would doze off, the rope would jerk him painfully awake.[87] The greater the reputation of the *godol*, the more extreme and severe are the descriptions of the ways he inflicts harm on his body.[88] Thus, for example, it is said of Rabbi Avraham David of Buchach (1771–1840):

> So persistent was he in Torah study [i.e. Talmud], that he would not lie down to rest. When his body became very weak and he felt unable to go on without sleep, he would cling with his holy hands to a strong rope suspended from the center of the room's ceiling, supporting himself thus so that he would not doze off while he continued his studies, until all his strength was gone, when he would fall helplessly to the floor, sound asleep. And as soon as he awoke, he returned to his Talmud with great enthusiasm. And always, when he perceived that he was weary, with slumber creeping upon him, he would begin shouting, "The murderer sleep comes and wants to kill me!" This is how he would "slay himself in the tent of Torah" because of his love for her [the Torah].[89]

Rabbi Moshe Meidner, head of the *Torat Chessed* Yeshiva in Baranowitz, would "mix into the plates of food that were served to him, all kinds of fiery spices, and grains of tobacco as bitter as rue, to reduce the pleasure his body derived from eating."[90] In a book about the life of Rabbi Karelitz, he is quoted as saying that "you should starve yourself so that the pure spirit may come upon you,"[91] and "you should take great heed against pleasurable eating."[92] Rabbi Shmuel David Munk, the rabbi of Haifa, is

---

86. Anonymous, *Kol Chozev*, 44.

87. Anonymous, *Hi Sichati*, Vol. 1, 151.

88. According to the Ultra-Orthodox narrative, former generations were superior to the current one. In stories about asceticism, for example, when editors focus on figures from past generations, the intensity of self-discipline increases. Rabbi Chaim from Volozhin (1749–1821), for instance, is said to have refused bathing for long periods. Also, he was so focused on his studies, that he didn't notice, on one occasion, that his clothing had caught fire, and he was almost burned alive.

89. Anonymous, *Hi Sichati*, Vol. 1, 271.

90. Anonymous, *Hi Sichati*, Vol. 2, 1012.

91. Yivrov, *Ma'ase Ish*, 95.

92. Yivrov, *Ma'ase Ish*, 162.

said to have stabbed his body with pins "to hurt his body lest it succumb to sleep."⁹³ In the same vein, Rabbi Dov Cohen is credited with practices of bodily mortification for the purposes of "celibacy and asceticism":

> Reduction of pleasure, sleeping without a pillow, sitting on a hard chair without leaning back, not lingering over meals, refraining from friendly conversation, . . . fasting, avoiding pleasurable foods. . . . In one of his notes, he even hints about bathing in ice-water as a form of self-discipline. At home, his wife would regularly prepare for him—plain porridge. When her son asked why she had chosen this dish, she replied, "It was your father (*Abba*) who asked me always to make him porridge—*precisely because he did not like it!*"⁹⁴

The disciplined body changes in response to the harsh treatment of the young *godol*, and one significant aspect of this transformation is the fact that the body stops demanding its most basic needs:

> Just as the burning bush withstood the devouring flame, so too the emaciated body of this delicate youth withstood the most unbearable and painful trials. With his hair uncut and frightfully unkempt, clothed only in patched rags, the skin of his face shriveled and his eyes smoldering in their sockets, the young man sat and studied. Over and over, he plunged his mind's attentive gaze unremittingly into the deepest passages of the sacred texts.⁹⁵

> For me there is no distinction between before I eat and after I eat . . . I do not feel any difference. . . . Only when members of my family place food before me, then I trust that they are letting me know that I have apparently not yet eaten.⁹⁶

The tales of the *gedolim* present an image of bodies severely limited in healthy activity, neglected, emaciated, and filthy. A story about Rabbi Salanter recounts:

93. Anonymous, *Hi Sichati*, Vol. 1, 292.

94. Cohen, *Vayelchi Shneihem Yachdaiv*, 421–22. Descriptions of intense self-harm are so common, that sometimes the *gedolim*, in their older years, claim that the accounts are fabricated, and they did not treat their bodies in these extreme ways. Similarly, Rabbi Milikovsky said, of Rabbi Naftali Yehuda Zvi Berlin (1816–93) that he did not, in fact, burn his fingers with a candle in order to avoid falling asleep. See Anonymous, *Hi Sichati*, Vol. 1, 315.

95. Bergman, *Maran Harav Shach*, Vol. 1, 107.

96. Cohen, *Pe'er Hador*, 12.

> Some residents of the community once came to him, complaining that a terrible and choking stench was coming from the synagogue's house of study. But Rabbi Israel [Salanter] answered them brusquely, saying: "You should know, in fact, that the odors of those who sit here engaged in Torah study are, to the Holy One Blessed Be He, more precious even than your own prayers!"[97]

The "new body" of this ascetical method is, by virtue of the pain inflicted upon it, totally obedient to the devout mind, unable to function on its own without receiving an explicit command. This is a body devoid of id, an implement entirely at the service of the student's devotion to sacred study.[98]

The stories do not conceal the fact that a large number of *gedolim* suffer later in their lives as a result of the harsh treatment of their bodies in their boyhood. They develop chronic illnesses, and at a relatively early age their bodies fail to keep up with the pace and quality of learning that they seek.[99] Most of the *gedolim* narratives describe these physical ailments and frailties as glorious testaments to the strength of their character and eventual mastery over their bodies. In the words of Kanievsky, for example:

> "Happy the man whose afflictions are from the Torah." This means that if his afflictions come to him due to his striving for the Torah and the *mitzvoth* (divine commands), then these afflictions bring great and awesome merit. This is because such a man suffers for the sake of the Holy One Blessed Be He, and for the sake of His holy Torah.[100]

Devotion to the holy Torah justifies all the pain and suffering of the *gedolim*. Very few, upon reaching old age, regret their extreme asceticism, or realize that the ruthless battle against their bodies ultimately led to the victory of the body and of the evil inclination. In my reading, the ultimate triumph of the saint's physicality resulted, ironically, from the very

---

97. Meler, *Nasich Mamlehet Ha-Torah*, 309. On asceticism as a way to gain control over the body, see, Corrington, "Anorexia, Asceticism, and Autonomy," 52.

98. In the stories of the *gedolim* after the Holocaust, one can find more complex narratives; for some examples, see chapter 9. This kind of asceticism also appears in the academic work of Nadler. See Nadler, *The Faith of the Mithnagdim*, 78–102.

99. There are many examples of this bodily struggle. See for example, Cohen, *Pe'er Hador*, 163; Anonymous, *Hi Sichati*, Vol. 2, 954, 961, 976, 1022–23, 1059.

100. Bergman, *Maran Harav Shach*, Vol. 1, 33–34.

bodily afflictions he worked so hard to achieve, which inevitably required so much attention that the quality of the *godol*'s sacred studies suffered. The very *gedolim* perceived as physically strong in their youth, dedicating their early lives to Talmud study, are those later described as paying a heavy price and enduring tremendous suffering. In other words, constant self-mortification, far from effacing the body, makes it ever more present in one's awareness.[101]

E. The Slabodka Method and European Honor Culture

The stories of the *gedolim* give a special place to the Slabodka way of life, and to its influence on the personality and body of students who studied in yeshivas following the unique ethical method of the founder, Rabbi Nosson Tzvi Finkel, known as "*Der Alter fun Slabodka*" ("The Grandfather of Slabodka").[102] Rabbi Finkel forged a particular interpretation of the *Musar* genre, deeply influenced by the founder of the *Musar* movement, Rabbi Israel Salanter, and his student, the "Grandfather of Kelm," Rabbi Simcha Zissel Ziv Broida.[103] The vital elements Rabbi Finkel's method developed as a response to his rival, the "Grandfather of Novardok," Rabbi Yosef Yozel Horowitz, who also drew from the mainstream *Musar* doctrine.[104]

It is surprising to find that the Novardok method, far from having a noteworthy place in the *gedolim* genre, is almost totally ignored. The hagiographers omit any descriptions of the "strange" behavior of Novardok students in urban spaces, an omission most striking in stories of *gedolim* who lived their lives in a Novardok context. The editors do not hide the fact that these *gedolim* studied at the Novardok Yeshiva; they even refer

---

101. Two significant examples are Rabbi Chaim Shmuelevitz and Rabbi Yaakov Yisrael Kanievsky. See Anonymous, *Hi Sichati*, Vol. 1, 203. On their physical suffering see, Anonymous, *Hi Sichati*, Vol. 2, 1022–23; Anonymous, *Darka Shel Torah*, 110–11.

102. Katz, *Tenu'at HaMusar*, Vol. 3; Brown, "Human Greatness and Human Diminution"; Tikochinski, *Musar Yeshivot*. The first Slabodka Yeshiva was in the Lithuanian town of Slabodka. Other yeshivas in the same spirit were opened; they all kept the name Slabodka, and thus the term came to be associated with a whole system of Jewish thought.

103. On Rabbi Simcha and his unique *Musar* method see, Katz, *Tenu'at HaMusar*, Vol. 5, 25–278. On the differences between Slabodka and Kelm see, Tikochinski, "Land of Israel," 137–58.

104. See Orlansky, *Lapid Esh Novhardki*; Zaritzk, *Gesher Tzar*; Ben-Artzi, *Novardok*; Tikochinski, "Zaichik."

to the "Grandfather of Novardok" as a great Talmud scholar who established his own *Musar* following. However, the content of the Novardok method, and its influence on the behavior of yeshiva students and on their body image are almost totally absent from the texts.[105]

As other research has already described in detail, the chief innovation in the philosophy of Slabodka was an emphasis on human greatness, as opposed to the pessimistic picture of human nature painted by both Rabbi Salanter and the "Grandfather of Novardok."[106] According to Rabbi Salanter, in order for men to find release from themselves, from their evil inclination, they must break the bonds of both their personalities and their bodies. The Novardok method believed that, only after this break, is there a possibility to rebuild personalities free of the evil inclination.[107]

---

105. In the two-volume rabbinic work describing the essential elements of the system of the *Musar* movement's leaders, there is not even a single chapter devoted to the "Grandfather of Novardok" or his philosophy. One of Ultra-Orthodox literature's editorial methods for concealing unwanted information is for the editors to lavish praise on an individual or system, without ever revealing the actual guidelines of the system itself. In this way, the editors avoid imparting the content of the theological method in question, while at the same time communicating the sense that this system has been given due consideration. Cf. for example: "Novardok [Yeshiva], under the leadership of Rabbi Yozel, [Rabbi Yosef Yozel Horwitz—known as the *Alter* of Novardok] encouraged all who entered its gates to swim against the current. This was the famous Novardok, a unique school of thought in the *Musar* movement, that kindled in the hearts of its thousands of students a burning flame of *Musar* and heavenly awe. This was Novardok, where untrammeled paths were opened to anyone seeking perfection, and where, in his time, Rabbi Yosel shook the lintels and thresholds of the yeshiva world. This same Rabbi Yosel, vibrant and brave, subtle and devout, one of the most wonderful of Rabbi Israel Salanter's pupils, strove constantly to exalt the spiritual status of the human being, with storm and whirlwind, with holy audacity, devoting himself utterly to the cause, turning his back on the world and all its temptations, and all in order to bring the heights of spirituality to earth, and to draw to himself and raise up together with him, anyone whom he might touch." (Sorotzki, *Harav MePonivez*, 37). Information on Novardok (sometimes spelled Novhardok) is mostly found in non-Ultra-Orthodox literature (Ben-Artzi, *Novardok*; Goldberg, *The Fire Within*, 129–53; Zaritzky, *Gesher Tzar*; Tikochinski, "Land of Israel").

106. Brown, "Human Greatness and Human Diminution."

107. There are some deep connections between Novardok's pessimistic view of human nature and the method of the *Chazon-Ish*—Rabbi Karelitz. The main difference, however, as I have shown elsewhere, is that the Novardok method believes that we are capable of "deconstructing" and transforming the old self, whereas Rabbi Karelitz believes that any desire to change ourselves is part of the evil inclination. The only way to find redemption from ourselves is by immersing our entire lives in the Jewish law, and in this way finding liberation through Torah. See Englander, "The Conception of the Human Being."

In contrast, according to Rabbi Finkel, "the Grandfather of Slabodka," it is an immutable fact that each human person is created in God's image.[108] Hence, *Musar* teachings should emphasize not the baseness but rather the exalted status of humanity. Only when we recognize our inherent spiritual potential, can we combat the darker sides of the personality, renouncing sin and desire, as the following passage suggests:

> Regarding *gadlut ha-adam* ("human greatness"), it should be noted that the *Musar* sages approached this subject in various ways; most emphasized and stressed man's lowliness, as evidenced by the impure matter of which he is made, as well as his physical weakness and moral shortcomings. The only remedy for man, they say, is to always remember: "Know whence you came, and whither you are going."[109] Thus he may purify his behavior and attain spiritual wholeness. The method [taught by] "The Grandfather [of Slabodka]" was completely different. He always emphasized human greatness and the possibility of ascending to immeasurable [spiritual] heights by merit of worthy deeds.[110]

The Slabodka method also rejected the popular Ultra-Orthodox concept of *yeridat ha-dorot* ("the decline of the generations"), which asserts that each generation of teachers and students is inferior in their talents and morals to its predecessor. This concept fosters sentiments of gratitude and loyalty toward the past, leaving no choice but to accept traditional norms without question and without demur. In this spirit, many *Musar* works declare that "What is new is forbidden by Torah."[111] Midrashic tradition supports this idea, noting that the Israelites survived their exile in Egypt because "they did not change their names, their language or their attire."[112]

The "Grandfather of Slabodka"—by contrast—demands respect for the present generation, citing the Talmudic dictum: "Jerubaal in his generation [is no less to be honored] than Moses in his generation."[113]

---

108. However, according to "the Grandfather of Slabodka," every human person is also flawed due to the original sin of Adam and Eve (Finkel, *'Or HaTzafun Vol. 1*, 12–13, 22–23).

109. Mishna Avot 3.1. Translation from Tropper, *Wisdom*, 260.

110. Laasin, *Sichot Musar*.

111. This is a famous quotation cited in the name of Rabbi Sofer.

112. *Shir ha-Shirim Rabbah* (Vilnah), Parasha 4.

113. *Talmud Bavli*, Rosh-Hashanah 25b.

This perspective highlights the great responsibility human beings have, since they cannot complain that their generation is essentially inferior. The Slabodka method thus ascribes to individuals more free will, echoing changes in the social moral code of Europe at the time.[114] Every Jew is called to see himself, not as inferior, but rather as equal to yet different from his ancestors. Like them, he must assume full responsibility for his choices and actions.

> Once, in the Slabodka Yeshiva, there was a young man, a student in the intimate circle of "The Grandfather." . . . He left the yeshiva. . . . Not only that, but rumor had it that this young man had become an outright "opponent" [*mitnaged*] of the Slabodka method. . . . After a while, a letter arrived from this student, explaining everything that he was doing. . . . When Rabbi Isaac Shaar read this letter to "The Grandfather," [Rabbi Finkel] he noted on his face, as he listened, nothing but signs of pleasure at what he heard. Rabbi Isaac . . . was amazed, and asked, . . . "Why are you smiling?" Replied "The Grandfather": "It was here, [at Slabodka], that this student learned the courage to resist. *This is* Slabodka: *Critique!*"[115]

The radical moral contribution of Rabbi Finkel goes far beyond emphasizing the place of the image of God in each individual. In my opinion, it is impossible to understand the uniqueness of the Slabodka method if we divorce it from the European concept of honor that was at its zenith in this period. In order to illustrate this point, I will first describe the European honor culture and its harsh critique of the Jewish body. Then, I will return to the discussion of Slabodka, situating its method in the context of the expansion of the European honor system.

Since both anthropology and cultural studies offer lengthy descriptions of the relevant differences between dignity and honor cultures,[116] there is no need for me to go into theoretical detail. I will simply summarize the issues, focusing on the characteristics most relevant to this chapter.[117]

114. Katz, *HaSaba MiSlabodka*, 111.

115. Bergman, *Shimush Talmidei Chahamim*, 165.

116. For two of the many important academic works on the subject, see: Peristiany and Pitt-Rivers, *Honor and Grace in Anthropology*; Campbell, *Honor, Family and Patronage*.

117. There are many distinctions between types of societies and cultures, and here I focus on one such distinction: honor/dignity. I am aware that there are different uses of these words in English, and that many scholars do not distinguish between

In *honor societies*, honor correlates with an individual's social status and is perceived as represented by possessions, like property and other assets. Honor (and its attendant social status) may be acquired during an individual's lifetime through compliance with social norms, i.e., by appropriate normative behavior. An individual may gain honor in a community through behavior perceived as honorable. One person may also seize the honor of another, since living in an honor society is a zero-sum game: when one person or community gains honor, another must lose it.

Notably, as Peter Berger wrote, "honor only applies among those who share the same status in the hierarchy."[118] Groups within an honor society often preserve their honor through the exclusion of certain "dishonorable" individuals, groups, and nations. However, there are also typically certain groups who are not considered to be part of the "honor game" at all: they neither gain honor, nor lose it. In Europe, for example, in some periods and locations, Jews were not considered an honorable community, and were entirely excluded from the honor system. Or, if they were considered part of an honorable community, they were assigned a low honor ranking. None of this means that European Jews were not deeply influenced by honor culture. In fact, although they were excluded from the honor of the general society, they created their own Jewish culture and theology of honor.[119]

On the other hand, *dignity*, as opposed to honor, is understood as the universal value and worth of any and every human person, regardless of gender, race, age, class or group affiliation.[120] As Orit Kamir defines it:

> Human dignity is the inherent value ascribed to the category "human." It is, therefore, inherent in the human nature of every human being.... We can think of it as a stamp of human quality that is imprinted in each of us. It is important to stress that as a value, dignity is an ethical *ought* and not an empirical, factual *is*; it is normative and not descriptive. Human dignity does not depict people's empirical value; it constitutes them as normatively

honor and dignity. However, I am consciously using these terms as they are currently understood in cultural studies, as formal concepts representing distinctive views with distinctive ways of behaving. In this chapter, honor and dignity are cultural concepts, and their specific definitions are important for the understanding of my argument.

118. Berger, "On the Obsolescence of the Concept of Honor," 340.
119. Englander, "The 'Jewish Knight' of Slobodka."
120. Bourdieu, "The Sentiment of Honor in Kabyle Society"; Kamir, *Israeli Honor and Dignity*, 27–43. Although this complicates the discussion, we should note that in Hebrew, "honor" and "dignity" are both represented by the Hebrew word *kavod*.

worthy merely because they are human.... Because we believe that all humans are identical in their human nature and partake equally in the human category, they also partake equally in the inherent human value, i.e., human dignity.[121]

One of the main differences between honor and dignity cultures is that "the concept of honor implies that identity is essentially, or at least importantly, linked to institutional roles. The modern concept of dignity, by contrast, implies that identity is essentially independent of institutional roles."[122] After the French Revolution, and into the twentieth century, European civilization oscillated between these two poles: on one hand, *honor culture* with its emphasis on earned (or assigned) exclusive rights and achievements for some, and, on the other hand, *dignity culture*, with its focus on unconditional and universal rights for all, especially as a counterpoint to and critique of the mechanical and existential alienation of post-industrial Europe. It can be assumed that all modern societies contain values of both dignity and honor cultures.[123]

Given the description of the *yeshiva* student's body that we have seen above, it is not surprising that in non-Jewish European eyes, the Jew appeared to be a despicable creature, entirely devoid of honor.[124] Moreover, Jewish men were often perceived by non-Jews as somehow "feminine," and hence associated with the "shadow side" of the honor coin, i.e.—shame. Just as a woman was seen as essentially devoid of honor, struggling all her life to avoid being "shamed," so Jewish men were perceived as lacking the honor of masculinity, as if shame were engraved in their very flesh.[125]

In addition, from the eighteenth century on, the European Enlightenment expanded notions of citizenship, bringing more Jewish communities into the general European society. As a result, the European perceptions of dignity and honor sparked some Jewish reactions: first the *Haskalah*, and then Zionism. The *Haskalah* (the "Jewish Enlightenment"), was a movement in the eighteenth and nineteenth centuries advocating liberation for Jews and better integration into European society

121. Kamir, *Betraying Dignity*, xvii.
122. Berger, "On the Obsolescence of the Concept of Honor," 343.
123. On the nuances of Europe's transformation from being an honor culture to gaining more elements of a dignity culture, see, Peled, *The New Man' of the Zionist Revolution*, 20–21.
124. Neumann, *Nazi Weltanschauung*, 224–25.
125. Biale, *Eros and the Jews*, 196–267; Gluzman, *The Zionist Body*.

and culture. The Zionist movement, for its part, aspired to abolish the prototypical "Diaspora Jew" entirely, and to create a "New Jew"—one connected both to the land and to the body. Both movements envisioned Jews with more dignity as well as more honor.[126] In the tales of the *gedolim*, however, both the Jewish Enlightenment and Zionism are described as insidious forces tempting young Ultra-Orthodox Jewish men and women to abandon Orthodoxy.[127] The success of both the *Haskalah* and Zionism eroded the status of the yeshiva; even those who didn't abandon their studies were influenced by the new spirit awakened by these movements.

The decline of the yeshiva is described in the *gedolim* tales, not only in terms of large numbers of students abandoning their benches of study, but also in the growing number of young Jewish women refusing to marry yeshiva students. All these changes are described as blows to the *kavod* (honor/dignity) of Torah. In the same vein, the struggle of the yeshiva rabbis against both the *Haskalah* and Zionism is seen as a defense of the *kavod* of Torah. As Rabbi Birnbaum puts it:

> Those were days of extremely difficult trials. The Zionists had taken over [the minds of the yeshiva students]. In place after place, they took control [of students' minds], dragging the honor [*kavod*—my emphasis] of the Torah in the dust. A student who remained studying at the yeshiva did so only through great personal sacrifice. There was simply no chance of finding him a wife—for who would want to marry a yeshiva student?[128]

These narratives attest to the importance of honor during this period, and Rabbi Birnbaum's description of the "dishonoring" of Torah reveals links between the values of honor societies and the way yeshiva students experienced their status. In a society built on human dignity, on the other hand, neither the Torah nor the yeshiva student could be humiliated in this fashion, since dignity is an intrinsic part of being human. Birnbaum, by stressing that Zionists defiled the honor of the Torah, and even managed to convince some students to join Zionism, shifts the

---

126. Presner, *Muscular Judaism*.

127. Rabbi Abramsky confesses that there was a time when he read the poetry of Rabbi Yehuda Halevi, in order that he too—like the *maskilim* ["intelligentsia"] of the Jewish Enlightenment—might be considered an expert on literature and poetry (Abramski, *Melech Be-yofio*, 14).

128. Interview with Rabbi Birnbaum; Anonymous, *Mepihem Shel Rabotynu*, 271–72.

discussion of Torah ideals away from dignity and squarely into a classic honor-shame matrix.

After this brief overview of the role of honor in Jewish society in the nineteenth and twentieth centuries, I now return to Rabbi Nosson Tzvi Finkel, "the Grandfather of Slabodka" and suggest a new reading of his thought. Here I will highlight the concept of honor in Slabodka philosophy through the founder's writings on the status of the human being and the human body.

Rabbi Finkel understood the power of the *Haskalah* and Zionism, in that they allowed Jews to enter the realm of European honor; he offered an alternative to his yeshiva students by adopting the symbolic language of honor. As we have indicated, he took a stand that contradicted the views of conventional yeshivas, stressing the intrinsic greatness of the human person, on the understanding that humanity is created *betselem 'elohim*—in the divine image. Yeshivas must stop stressing human insignificance, and begin proclaiming human greatness. Only when we recognize the full spiritual potential hidden within us can we struggle with the darker sides of personality, and rid ourselves of sin and the *yetser*—the evil inclination.

Deriving the status of the human individual from the principle of *betselem 'elohim* is critical, considering the implication that all human beings—whether Jew or gentile, woman or man, adult or child—are equally created in the image of God. But if Rabbi Finkel had been satisfied with that definition, he would have established humanity on the principles of *dignity*, according to which every human being is *ipso facto* endowed with intrinsic worth, and thus must be treated equally. However, he does not embrace this interpretation. He distinguishes clearly between Jews—who are members of the covenant revealed at Sinai—and gentiles, who are not, and are therefore inferior and have less *honor*.[129]

We must remember that in "honor societies," individuals and groups never exist in their own right, but always in contradistinction to others, with whom they engage in a struggle for control and distribution of "honor" as a limited resource. In fact, it is precisely this agonistic confrontation over the concept of "honor" that indicates how each competing group in this struggle understands that the rival group is likewise included in the "honor category." Groups outside this category are not "in the game" at all, and so it is not possible to be in competition with them. For example, until the Jewish Enlightenment, no Jew in Europe would

---

129. Finkel, *'Or HaTzafun Vol. 1*, 89–90.

ever be challenged to a duel, since such a challenge is also a recognition that the person challenged has a place in the honor discourse.

The unique ethos of the Slabodka Yeshiva introduced its members into the honor system. However, as the stories make clear, bids to attain honor in the yeshiva were by no means undertaken in the same context as non-Jewish European society, or in the manner of the *Haskalah* and Zionism. Rabbi Finkel ["The Grandfather"] thus chose not to adopt all the rules of European honor, but only the principle of honor itself, translated into the yeshiva idiom. His intent was to create in his yeshiva students the feeling, that the same sacred study that seemed despicable in the eyes of the Jewish Enlightenment and of Zionism, had in fact the quality of honor. In addition, Rabbi Finkel forged an intra-yeshiva honor culture that distinguished Slabodka Yeshiva from all others. The students of Slabodka, for example, were identified *as Europeans* by other yeshiva Jews, and thus became the object simultaneously of jealousy and revulsion.

Rabbi Finkel was aware that to introduce the yeshiva into the honor system was a departure from the norm. In his book he defends his course of action, making reference to the Talmudic concept of *'inyanei derech 'eretz*—i.e., "desirable modes of human behavior":

> "Desirable modes of behavior" span a broad spectrum, from simple manners to the highest possible level. . . . Each nation has its own code of civility, and anyone visiting that country has a duty to conduct himself accordingly. For example, in the land of *Ashkenaz* [Germany], people are scrupulous about external politeness: in the fashion of dress, in the manner of speech and gestures, and in all the daily protocols and norms. To someone from another country, it may seem sometimes ridiculous to put so much stock in such trivia. But Germans see such things as matters of principle. . . . I was told that one German professor fainted when he saw a man whose coat had a button missing. So it is imperative for anyone who comes into their jurisdiction to observe their customs. And this is not merely the duty of human politeness, but derives also from the words of the Torah. We conclude that every simple norm, even something as small as a button, may have great value, and no one is permitted to neglect it for any reason, even in the pursuit of the highest matters on earth.[130]

These words were directed to a readership composed of yeshiva students and rabbis. Rabbi Finkel clearly realizes that, by advocating respect

---

130. Finkel, *'Or HaTzafun Vol. 1*, 166, 172.

for the rules of honor, he is likely to draw criticism from influential Jewish leaders, whose primary goal is to distance yeshiva students from the Jewish Enlightenment. It is an axiom of Jewish tradition that the children of Israel succeeded in preserving their identity, and resisting assimilation, through carefully maintaining their traditional Jewish garb. And now, "the Grandfather" is instructing his students to adopt the secular honor code, including Western European norms of dress.[131] Rabbi Simcha Zissel Broida, who was a disciple of Rabbi Finkel and headed the Slabodka Yeshiva in Israel, put it this way: "To be worthy of becoming a 'son of the Torah [ben torah],' one must first be a 'son of culture'; only then may one earn 'the Crown of Torah.'"[132]

It is not surprising to find that many of the images in the Slabodka method are taken from the discourse of military service, perceived by the rabbis as the ultimate honorable sphere. The heads of yeshivas, the *Musar* rabbis, and the students are all compared to generals and soldiers. The military follows the highest standard of honor rules, and so do the members of the yeshiva.[133] The *gedolim* tales relate that strict discipline was observed in the yeshiva, with an almost military distinction drawn between honorable mature students and youngsters who had not yet earned honor. This finds expression, *inter alia*, in the seating of elite students on the eastern side of the yeshiva—the more important side, since this is the direction of prayer:[134]

> Distinctions of status and different seating arrangements for mature and younger students were greatly emphasized in the Mir Yeshiva. The youngest men sat in the front rows, while the mature elite of the yeshiva student body gathered in the back. Each row of seats had its own inherent importance, and passage from one row to the next was no small matter . . . while a thoughtless move from one bench to another was downright dangerous.[135]

131. Stampfer, *Lithuanian Yeshivas*, 286.

132. Meler, *Nasich Mamlehet Ha-Torah*, 297.

133. The rabbis of the Slabodka Yeshiva are compared to army generals. See Gelis et al., *Heiiru Pnei Kol Ha-Mizrach Ad She-Berhebron*, 267. This comparison was inspired, in my opinion, by the prohibition excluding generations of European Jews from actual military service, a prohibition dictated by—among other reasons—the exclusion of Jews from the European honor culture.

134. Stampfer, *Lithuanian Yeshivas*, 288.

135. Shmuelevitz, *Sefer HaZikaron*, 36.

In addition, a careful record was kept of who exactly would have the honor of being summoned to stand forth to read the Torah portion during prayer services.[136] Younger students were required to give deference to the yeshiva rabbis and older students, rising to acknowledge them in recognition of their superior status. Similarly, during the festival of *Simchat Torah*,[137] when the entire yeshiva danced in concentric circles, only the rabbis and most honored students were allowed to dance in the inner circles.[138] The leader of the original Slabodka Yeshiva, "the Grandfather of Slabodka" himself, possessed the greatest honor; it was absolutely forbidden to enter into his presence without permission.[139] Anyone to whom he granted public attention, gained honor:

> Once, when Rabbi Leib Hasman visited "the Grandfather"'s residence in Slabodka, he [Rabbi Finkel] honored his important guest with the customary cup of tea. When "the Grandfather" saw that Rabbi Leib was not drinking the tea, he asked him: "Why do you not drink; has the tea not cooled enough?" To which Rabbi Leib replied, with a smile: "As long as this tea remains in the cup, I can continue to enjoy the honor of receiving it. Once the tea is gone, however, the honor too will have disappeared."[140]

Just as "the Grandfather" had the power to bestow honor, he could also shame students as an act of punishment. He would express rejection of a student, for example, through the form of his speech:

> When he thought that a certain student was not learning properly, he would distance himself from him. Suddenly a student would become aware that "the Grandfather" was addressing him with the formal plural "*Ihr*" ("you," plural), instead of the informal and cordial address "*Du*" ("you," singular). The student, upon hearing that formal "*Ihr*," was liable to faint [from shame].[141]

---

136. Meler, *Nasich Mamlehet Ha-Torah*, 297; Tikochinski, *Musar Yeshivot*, 115–19.

137. *Simchat Torah* is the Jewish festival marking the closing of one annual cycle of Torah readings in the synagogue, and celebrating the opening of a new cycle.

138. Anonymous, *Mepihem Shel Rabotynu*, 289.

139. Wolbe, *Avnei Shlomo*, 107.

140. Bergman, *Shimush Talmidei Chahamim*, 216.

141. Gold, *Hachzek BaMusar*, 48. The language of the Slabodka Yeshiva was Yiddish.

It is fascinating to see how, according to these stories, every attempt to undermine the hierarchy of honor is perceived as a breach of *Musar*. A student who had the temerity to ask one of the rabbis to lend him his *tallit* (prayer-shawl) received a severe reprimand,[142] as did a "young" student who dared to sit at the dining table designated for "older" students ("young" and "old" refer here to honor-status rather than chronological age).[143]

The difference between Slabodka and other yeshivas is not only in the relationships of the young students to other yeshiva members, but also in their attitude to study. We have already noted that in these tales, the adolescent student is generally characterized as making Talmud his life's primary ambition. By contrast, in the Slabodka Yeshiva, Talmudic study is not seen *only* as an end in itself, but rather as a means of achieving honor. The young man desiring to attain honor is challenged, as it were, to an intra-yeshiva "duel" with the rest of the students and rabbis, almost as d'Artagnan was challenged in the opening passages of *The Three Musketeers*. Knowledge of Talmud, rhetorical skills, and an ability to pose hard questions and offer insightful solutions, while locked in prolonged debate on a Talmudic passage,—all these are "weapons" ready to hand for a daring Slabodka student engaged in such a yeshiva "duel":[144]

> In those days it was by no means easy to receive the "highest crown" (of Torah) or to reach a place of honor among the yeshiva elite (*bekhirei ha-yeshiva*). "The Grandfather" [Rabbi Finkel] watched over and closely guarded these distinctions, as if they were "officers' citations" in his yeshiva, only allowing a truly worthy student to wear such a crown, as a reward for his extraordinary talent and knowledge. Before that, each aspirant had to pass an examination by the luminaries of the [preceding] generation [*gedolei ha-dor*]! Then, he must survive the rod of a critical review of his work by the best of his yeshiva peers. He was required to present them with his most original insights into the Talmud, and they, for their part, would blast him with questions as if he were in a smelter's furnace! And if he emerged unscathed from under their critical pummeling, then it was "the Grandfather" himself who would place the victory wreath upon his brow. And once a student had earned such honor, many other benefits would follow quickly on. When "the Grandfather"

---

142. Meler, *Nasich Mamlehet Ha-Torah*, 297.
143. Anonymous, *Mepihem Shel Rabotynu*, 270.
144. Sorotzki, *Harav MePonivez*, 29.

> held forth in conversation in his chamber, for example, this student might now sit with him at his table. He could now listen to special discourses meant only for the ears of selected students. He might, even, be called up to chant the "sixth portion" of the Sabbath or Festival Torah reading—an invitation that the Grandfather had carefully reserved to himself alone the right to extend.[145]

It appears from this story that honor was valued highly in this yeshiva sphere, with every student's honor status determined by his success in abiding by norms of behavior that were clear and familiar to all. To gain the status of a Jewish "teenage saint," one had first to pass a series of trials in order to gain the supreme social capital of this group—"Torah honor."

The attribution of honor—as we have seen above—is always relative to the societal context; to acquire it one needs to be engaged in both familiarity and struggle with other members of the community. Hence, while a student elsewhere was not required to prove himself in relation to his yeshiva companions, and could focus on his desire to learn Talmud, things were different at Slabodka. As in all known honor cultures, here too we read of the supreme investment these "holy teens" made to prove their Talmudic strength, relative to other students. A student's "rank" as a young *godol*—a yeshiva prodigy—was strictly defined by an orderly system of clear rules, and by difficult examinations conducted, not only by the heads of the yeshiva, but also by other prodigies, who had already achieved "rank" and could now test the younger students.

Sometimes, according to the tales, the competitive study of Talmud did shift from intellectual prowess to actual physical engagement. In a story about the relationship between Rabbi Yosef Kahanman and his teacher, Rabbi Eliezer Gordon, we read:

> He [Rabbi Yosef] used to tell, that once he confronted Rabbi Eliezer with a serious Talmudic dilemma. While they were immersed in "uprooting mountains and grinding them to bits" in the fervor [of their study] of Torah, the teacher [Rabbi Eliezer]] was unaware of how enthusiastically he had grasped his pupil's thumb, twisting it hard. Even [the student] himself, Rabbi Yosef, his attention fully focused on the debate, did not even feel it when his thumb was thrown out of joint and its bone fractured.[146]

---

145. Meler, *Nasich Mamlehet Ha-Torah*, 54.

146. Sorotzki, *Harav MePonivez*, 29. There are echoes here of a famous Talmudic tale about Rava, who smashed the finger of his friend, Rabi Yosef, during their studies

The religious "dueling" adopted by the Slabodka yeshivas was alien to the spirit of the normative yeshivas at the time, which rejected competition over Talmudic subjects, since it is not knowledge that God requires, but devoted effort in Torah. Even today, in most yeshivas, there are no mandatory examinations.

European Christian discourse in this period was—for its part—also ambivalent about confrontational competition. For example, although the duel was widely accepted as a condition for admittance into the students' unions, and as a means for deciding which was the most honorable students' union, devout Christian students often refused to duel. According to them, true manly courage should not be expressed with swords and pistols, but with pious words and religious devotion.[147] These Christian students were therefore perceived as androgynous figures whose (honorable) masculinity was admixed with (dishonorable) femininity. The Jewish Slabodka method's not dissimilar response to the duel is adapted to the spiritual challenger: it becomes a "duel of Torah devotion" for religious students. Although its purpose is identical to a physical duel in terms of acquiring honor, the material weapon is replaced by the word and the sharpened mind.

Having described the Slabodka Yeshiva as a structured space designed to produce *gedolim* with honor, I will now discuss the role of the body within this "Jewish honor culture," before going on to a reading of the image of the body that emerges from the *gedolim* tales.

F. The Concept of the Body in the Slabodka Yeshiva

In any honor society, the body plays a unique role. What is termed the "living body" is a sort of mystification of the body itself, and reflects the normally invisible personality of the individual.[148] This reflection will include, among other things, clothing, posture and the precise control of bodily gestures. If, in ordinary yeshiva communities, the neglect of both the body and the "living body" served the purposes of the student's aspirations to study, in the Slabodka Yeshiva the opposite was true. Rabbi

---

(*Talmud Bavli*, Shabbat 88a). See also the story about Rabbi Kotler, who yanked the hair of Rabbi Moshe Finkel during their studies (Gelis et al., *Heiiru Pnei Kol Ha-Mizrach Ad She-Berhebron*, 171).

147. Fetheringill-Zwicker, "Performing Masculinity."

148. Neuman, *Nazi Weltanschauung*, 153–84. See also, Willing, *Gadlut Ha-Adam*, 140–41, 352–55.

Finkel is described in the tales as insisting that his students take good care of their bodies, and dress respectably, emulating the surrounding European society. He traced the imperative to care for the body to the biblical concept of *tselem 'elohim*, the divine image inherent in the body itself. He rebuked students who neglected their physical appearance, or who moved in a heavy and gangling manner. He claimed that to see a body lacking grace arouses a sense of contempt in the beholder, harming the honor of the yeshiva student and the yeshiva itself. Of all extant stories of the *gedolim*, only in those identified with the Slabodka method is there such sympathetic reference to the body as the mirror of the soul, and such descriptions of the beautiful bodies of handsome young *gedolim*:[149] "Once, Rabbi Eliyahu was required by the doctor to remove his shirt; I noted that his skin was as smooth and radiant as the skin of a baby."[150]

The asceticism employed in other yeshivas was designed to liberate the soul from the chains of the body, to create an independent mind and self. However, in Slabodka yeshivas, the value of a person derives from his honor, which the body plays a central role in achieving, through a respectable outward appearance. Unlike the behavioral dictates of asceticism or celibacy, but more in harmony with a military mindset, Slabodka cultivated a meticulous pride not only in outward public appearance, but also in the strict personal discipline necessary to achieve this honorable image.

Note that the Slabodka method does not contest the body-mind dichotomy; indeed, this is exactly what enables the transfer of focus to the body. Also, the measure of force brought to bear on the body to reshape it is often no less intense in Slabodka than in other yeshivas. However, the image of the body arising from Slabodka tales is different in both form and function. If, in other yeshivas, neglect and even harm are visited on the body in the name of learning, not so in Slabodka. Here, the body is required to function according to the order of the mind, in a way that will provide an appropriate reflection of the human person in the world. In an honor society, control of the body and its movements is a gauge of honor. The whole purpose of ascetical practices in the Slabodka context is to lift the body to a level of perfection, as that term is understood in such

149. In his *Musar* writings, Rabbi Finkel emphasized the need to cherish the body, especially on Friday (the eve of the sacred Sabbath), and insists that this is not tantamount to wasting study time, as all of the contemporary *Musar* teachers held. See Finkel, *'Or HaTzafun Vol. 1*, 221.

150. Anonymous, *Rabbi Hirsch*, 424–25. Rabbi Hirsch Pali writes about Rabbi Eliyahu Lopian.

a society. As imperfect human beings, we inherit both body and soul in an immature and flawed natural state; if we seek spiritual honor, we must elevate both to their optimal level.[151]

At Slabodka, the physical self is enrolled in a rigorous ascetical regimen aimed at re-designing an "honorable body," as is richly reflected in the Slabodka narratives. In one, Rabbi Finkel scolds a student who peeled an apple for him but dared to touch the flesh of the fruit with his fingers; according to "the Grandfather," a soldier would never make such a mistake when peeling fruit for his army commander.[152] Another story has a student placing his hat on the dining table, and being scolded for lack of manners.[153] The food ethos at Slabodka is in general quite different from that of other yeshivas. Rabbi Kanievsky, for example, while studying in the Novardok yeshiva, once ate some plaster that had fallen from the ceiling onto the table in front of him; he was oblivious to the taste or aesthetics of such "food" since his whole focus was on the true nourishment of learning.[154]

Perception of the body also influences perception of sacred space. In the Lithuanian Jewish culture in general, and normative Lithuanian yeshivas in particular, prayer is seen as a context in which the person may allow his body to move in an uncontrolled manner, as a spontaneous expression of *dvekut* (devotion), a spiritual surfeit that mere words could never capture.[155] However, unintentional movement of the body is out of accord with "honor culture," which demands total control and continuous reflection.

At Slabodka, the *gedolim* tales describe various strategies used by the yeshiva members to control their bodies, like entering the presence of "the Grandfather" with hands held behind the back to prevent them from swinging freely. Indeed, Rabbi Finkel was explicitly opposed to bodily movement during prayer, and routinely rebuked any of his charges who rocked or swayed in *dvekut*.[156] Slabodka students were challenged to a Jewish version of knightly gallantry; their comportment was required to

---

151. On the use of asceticism as a means of perfecting the body, see: Newbold, "Personality Structure."

152. Katz, *Tenu'at HaMusar*, Vol. 3, 185.

153. Katz, *Tenu'at HaMusar*, Vol. 3, 198.

154. Anonymous, *Tiferet Bachurim*, 326.

155. Anonymous, *Mepihem Shel Rabotynu*, 289. On Shamanism in the Hasidic movement, see, Garb, *Shamanic Trance in Modern Kaballah*, 75–118.

156. Katz, *Tenu'at HaMusar*, Vol. 3, 195.

be highly intentional and reflective. Rabbi Wolbe, for example, was proud of the yeshiva where he had learned, because not one of its students would raise his head from the Talmud page before he did, even when visitors came to the yeshiva hall.[157] A radical expression of the aspiration to absolute bodily control is found in this description of Rabbi Lupian, for whom—even in his old age—the slightest movement not ordered by the intellect is perceived as an attack on *Musar* values:

> So disciplined was he from his youth, that when he walked in the street his head would turn neither to the right nor to the left; rather he gazed directly forward, seeing only the way ahead. One day, he waited an embarrassingly long time at a bus stop. The bus was late. All the other people waiting there were losing their patience; every other second they strained their necks up the road, trying to see if it was arriving. Only Rabbi Eliyahu Lupian stood, motionless, as was his wont. Finally, even he had reached the end of his patience, and so he turned his head to look in the direction from which the bus should appear. Instantly, however, he started, and turned his gaze abruptly forward again, in great fear. A deep sigh escaped his heart. "In the yeshiva," he said, "I certainly would have earned a reprimand for that unnecessary sideward glance."[158]

Similarly, the clothing worn by members of the Slabodka movement reflected the conscious elegance of their physical comportment. Rabbi Zeitchik describes his first encounter with a student of the Slabodka Yeshiva:

> One day a young man arrived in our town. He was mature, handsome and meticulously dressed in a frock coat and a rigid top hat. This was the Slabodka style of dress, for they—unlike at the Novardok yeshiva—are careful what they wear. They have been educated in the eminence and exaltedness of the human person. The young men wear dark frock coats during the winter, and white suits and white straw hats in the summer, like noblemen.... [The newcomer] spoke graciously, and in fact made a very good impression, well dressed and confident as he was.[159]

---

157. Bergman, *Orchot Chasideha*, 11–12.
158. Sorotzki, *Marbitzey Torah Umusar, Vol. 4*, 160.
159. Anonymous, *Mepihem Shel Rabotynu*, 235–36.

By way of contrast, note the description of Rabbi Shach, as an example of the physical comportment and dress of a yeshiva student who is *not* from the Slabodka system:

> My shoes were too small for my feet, and my toes protruded from them; I had no towels for washing; my hair, uncut for a whole year and a half, stuck together in long strands, absent any norm of human hygiene. My trousers were torn, and the scrapes on my legs were exposed, so that I was obliged to reverse the trousers, to make the rip less obvious, and to wear them like that.[160]

The Slabodka student, on the other hand, is described as attired in the latest fashion—exactly following the strictest dictates of style in the "honor society." There is a story of Rabbi Finkel himself pointing out to one young man that the loop on his coat was not aligned perfectly with its corresponding button.[161] In the Mir Yeshiva, the cloakroom had an appointed custodian, whose job was to impose fines on students whose coats had, say, a rip in their lapel.[162] Rabbi Broida is credited with the gesture of closely investigating the quality of a gold watch that was traditionally given by the father-in-law to a yeshiva student at his wedding. The rabbi would conduct a scrutiny to see if the watch was "worthy," and this became a yeshiva custom, intended to honor a newly wed student.[163]

An extreme expression of Slabodka honor culture appears in the description of the funeral of Rabbi Broida, when all the yeshiva students were instructed to wear their festive Sabbath attire—something considered quite taboo by contemporary Jews. The explanation given, was that this contributed to an honorable funeral, a funeral expressing "the Grandfather's" principle—"human greatness."[164]

G. Tensions within the Lithuanian Ultra-Orthodox Community

I opened by describing how the authors of the *gedolim* tales present them as "living parables" and models of devout behavior. In this, the Slabodka

160. Bergman, *Maran Harav Shach*, Vol. 1, 104.
161. Anonymous, *Sar HaTorah*, 68.
162. Wolbe, *Avnei Shlomo*, 103.
163. Anonymous, *Sar HaTorah*, 431.
164. Anonymous, *Sar HaTorah*, 431.

method poses a stark challenge to contemporary Jewish norms. While Slabodka was endeavoring to emulate European honor culture, the general Lithuanian Ultra-Orthodox community was distancing itself from it. Moreover, there is a significant discrepancy between past and present images of Slabodka Yeshiva members—i.e., *gedolim* as they appear before the Holocaust, and after, as heads of yeshivas in Israel. The pre-*Shoah* "young saints" of Slabodka were clean-shaven, and dressed in the best fashion of Berlin or Vienna. There is no trace of this look among today's Slabodka leaders, and no "reasonable" contemporary yeshiva student can even imagine adopting such style and comportment—simply because they are so similar to the society of the "other" (i.e. the non-Ultra-Orthodox) in the surrounding world. Although photographs of the Slabodka *gedolim* from before the Holocaust are constantly seen by the current Lithuanian Ultra-Orthodox community, and certainly evidence a "Westernization" of part of the rabbinic hegemony, the editors of the *gedolim* tales avoid addressing this issue directly. They do not even mention the familiar critique of the Slabodka system by the rabbis of the "Old *Yishuv*"—i.e., the local Jewish community before the State of Israel—exemplified by the Kabbalistic Rabbi Yeshaya Zelig Margaliot:

> And not as we see now so often—for all our transgressions! Like the so-called "sages" who, to cause offence, refuse to wear the garments of the Land of Israel, but insist on offending further by donning the immodest garb of foreign parts, with upper garments far too short and underwear far too long, and also cutting off their *pe'ot* [side-curls] or concealing them behind their ears, and even wearing on their heads indented top-hats![165]

By my reading, if the editors of *gedolim* tales do not mention such criticisms, it is due to the taboo against questioning the status of the *gedolim* as luminaries of Israel and models of Torah—which could violate the requirement to respect the "Torah knowledge" of the rabbinic hegemony.[166]

There is an additional consideration: the Lithuanian Ultra-Orthodox principle of *yeridat ha-dorot* ("the decline of the generations"). According to this principle, "modern" is always "worse" and Jewish life of today is understood as in every way inferior to life in the "glorious past" of Ultra-Orthodoxy. In the pre-Shoah photographs, however, the Jewish

---

165. Margaliot, *Ashrei HaIsh*, 71. See also, Tikochinski, *Musar Yeshivot*, 189. In a note, Margaliot points out that the European hats referred to here had indentations thought to resemble a cross.

166. Kaplan, "Daas Torah."

saints of that "glorious past" wear modern and westernized garb, considered debased and uncouth by the rabbis of today. This, disturbingly, turns *yeridat ha-dorot* upside down. A recent Ultra-Orthodox website puts the problem as follows:

> As the process of secularization and *haskalah* [enlightenment] gained force in Eastern Europe, and with the parallel decline of the status of yeshiva students (who were tagged by their detractors in *haskala* literature and contemporary media with all sorts of negative and insulting epithets, like "benighted," "parasites," "bench-sitters," and the like), the heads of the large Lithuanian yeshivas saw the need to strengthen the status and the self-confidence of the yeshiva students. For this reason, the rabbis dressed the student in the "last word" in male fashion [of the beginning of the twentieth century]: classy short light-colored suits, matching ties, wide-brimmed hats, modern spectacles and walking sticks.[167]

In a dialogue between Rabbi Friedman and Rabbi Rothenberg, head of the *Beit Meir* Yeshiva [in Bnei-Brak, Israel], when Rabbi Friedman expresses similar criticisms, Rabbi Rothenberg answers, with a deep sigh:

> We really should have a separate interview for this whole subject. It touches my very soul, and I am happy you have raised it. The Lithuanian Jewish community of those days, when it was poor, gave precedence to all those who labored at the Torah, and thus granted humility some honor. Today, honor derives from entirely other sources, with the tendency to bring some influences from the street into the yeshiva's house of study.[168]

The Ultra-Orthodox reaction just cited is an example of a *post facto* strategy of apologetics known in Jewish sources as *be-di'avad*. This strategy insists on justifying the behavior of the *gedolim* in regard to dress and behavior in terms of special contingencies at the time, and in line with the Jewish dictum: "Sometimes, to serve God, you must violate your Torah" (see Psalm 119:126). In this view, such "aberrant" behavior (like wearing "modern" clothing) cannot be considered a conscious choice reflecting careful theological considerations, but is rather an inevitable result of circumstance. The cloistered nature of Ultra-Orthodox-Lithuanian society

---

167. http://www.peopleil.org/Details.aspx?ItemID=7547&searchMode=2&itemPath=%5B0%5D%5B10%5D%5B365%5D%5B7547%5D&index=1

168. Friedman, *Nafshi Yazaa Bedabro*, 386.

enables the suppression of phenomena that are incompatible with what one group sees as "normative" for Jews.

I believe that, in today's Israel, the rabbinic hegemony's current representation of the body in the Slabodka method—i.e., images of the "golden age" of well-groomed young men of Slabodka—is primarily a foil against the Israeli image of the "Zionist body." Yeshiva students in Israel, who do not serve in the army and are not athletically active, often perceive the "Zionist body" as a forbidden desire.[169] Stories from the pre-Holocaust Slabodka Yeshiva context constitute a kind of "proof" that they too may achieve an honorable body, in defiance of secular Zionism, if they wish to do so.

The way the Holocaust narrative is constructed in Ultra-Orthodox consciousness supports the current ambivalent stance of the Lithuanian rabbinic hegemony in its simultaneous rejection and affirmation of the "honorable body" of Slabodka. The perception of honor underwent a change in Europe after World War II, and Lithuanian Ultra-Orthodox Jews increasingly saw German culture—the "pinnacle" of honor societies—as responsible for the annihilation of the Jewish world of Torah.[170] This made it easier for rabbinic authorities to rationalize the "contradictions" implied by photographs and stories of the *gedolim*. On one hand, the image of the body of the "honorable Jew" of Slabodka is rejected, as too evocative of the anti-Semitic West; on the other hand, it is also preserved as a counterpoint to the image of the "Zionist body."

For today's Ultra-Orthodox rabbinic hegemony, the rejection of the "honorable body" as a viable mode of Jewish ethics seems definitive. Yet, in the daily discourse of Jewish communities nourished by memories, Slabodka remains, paradoxically, a complex symbol of both admiration and denial. The *Musar* system still offers *gedolim* tales as models of ethical Jewish living, and yet, in the daily realities of Jewish practice, the positive physical ideals modeled there are now categorically forbidden.

My claim is that in recent years there has been a radicalization of rabbinical direction, and that the current *Musar* rabbis do not allow yeshiva students to emulate eminent teachers who studied in the mainstream yeshiva system. An examination of the accounts of the *gedolim* shows, that the elements of their psyche, the experiences of their youth, and the problems they faced are all presented as *radically different* from

---

169. Aran, "Denial Does Not Make the Haredi Body Go Away"; Hakak, "Haredi Male Bodies"; Aran, "Fundamentalism and the Masculine Body."

170. Adler, *BeGei Tzalmavet*, 131–32.

those of the contemporary reader. The saints of the past acted as they did, as a result of, among other factors, a particular socioeconomic situation: the dire poverty of Lithuanian Jewry between the World Wars. The *gedolim*'s context was so utterly removed from ours, that their way of virtue, as important as may be for our instruction, is absolutely inimitable. In fact, in the edited accounts, these same *gedolim* themselves, in their adulthood, forbid their students from trying to imitate their way of life. At the same time, they speak of the "golden age" of their youth with longing, and claim that their "old-time" sanctity demonstrates their excellence as scholars.

Thus, the critical quantitative divide between the *gedolim* of the tales, and the readers of today, is widened. Prohibitions against imitating the *gedolim* abound in *Musar* literature, especially from the last decade. Among other concerns, these texts are intent on preventing yeshiva students from imitating the *gedolim* in disrupting familiar normative models of yeshiva space and time. For example, Rabbi Gold writes:

> I remember that when I was studying in the holy yeshiva there was one young man there who was amazingly diligent, and never stopped learning Talmud [Aramaic: *lo' pasik pumieh migirsa'*]—it was astonishing! But he was isolated from the social life of the yeshiva; he was so studious that he even continued learning all day on Friday (the eve of the Sabbath), only pausing to wash his hands in honor of the Holy Shabbat—but even then he washed hurriedly in a couple of moments and then returned to his Talmud. Many of the other students were envious of his diligence, but on one occasion the mentor (*mashgiah*) of that yeshiva said to them: "You have no reason to envy him. His method and manner of learning will not last long, and when he ceases being so relentless in his study, his downfall will really be a hard one." [Unlike this young man,] the wonderful and truly diligent students who brought so much glory to the world of Torah through the great constancy [of their devotion] were men whose minds were also always engaged with their fellow human beings, and who were dearly loved by all.[171]

According to Gold, the devotion and diligence of the *gedolim* did not exclude them from the community. This conciliatory account contrasts with the many extreme descriptions discussed during this chapter, a shift in direction that may indicate a growing concern in recent years, that the

---

171. Gold, *Hachzek BaMusar*, 176.

traditional image of the *godol* may actually be harmful to boys who seek to resemble their mentors.[172]

The stories about the childhood and adolescence of the *gedolim* fail the declared purpose of the genre of Lithuanian hagiographies: to inspire emulation. How, then, can these tales bridge the gap between the ideals found in the texts and the average individual Jewish life? In spite of all its efforts, Lithuanian piety has not prevented its Haredi saints from receding—like the Hasidic Rebbe—to the far side of an essential gap between saint and reader. The recipient of *Musar* teachings is required to study *Musar* writings and apply their principles to his own life through personal reflection. The *godol* described in the hagiographies, on the other hand, devotes all his energy to Talmudic study and none to *Musar*.[173] It can be assumed, then, that the actual purpose of the stories is to serve the hegemony's effort to discourage *Musar* study and unite the community around Talmud as the central value in their lives.

These tensions, which arise initially from disagreement about what constitutes a young saint's ideal body image, reveal how a religious culture, ostensibly subject to a rigid and comprehensive system of control, is in fact a fabric of diverse and at times contradictory trends. The contradictions of diversity will deepen as, in the next chapter, having explored the various images of the young saint's body and behavior, I go on to examine the functions and boundaries of the ideal body image of the adult *godol*.

---

172. Gold, *Bnei Chail*, Vol. 1, 165. Caution about ascetical practices applies to sleep as well. Rabbi Gold did not approve of the idea that sleeplessness is especially virtuous. "It is our opinion that those great [sages] of Israel [*gedolei Yisra'el*] who slept less than the number of hours recommended by Maimonides, did so either because their physical constitution naturally did not require a full eight hours of slumber, or, conversely, that they slowly habituated their bodies to need less sleep. This they would do by very gradually over a period of time reducing their sleep by ten minutes, and then some time later by a few more minutes, and so on, until their bodies became accustomed to less sleep without their health being damaged in any way."

173. It is said that, already at a young age, Rabbi Yaakov Yisrael Kanievsky had decided not to read any hagiographies, considering them a waste of his ability to study Talmud (Kanievsky, *Toldot Yaakov*, 20). In another book, it is written that even "the Grandfather of Slabodka" said that Rabbi Kanievsky did not need to study any *Musar*, since he was going to become one of the main leaders of the community, and could learn proper behavior and theology from the Talmud (Anonymous, *Besufa Ubesaara*. 31).

CHAPTER 9

The Image of the Body of the Adult *Godol*

A. The *Godol* in Adulthood

IN THIS CHAPTER, I will examine how the *gedolim* narratives depict these holy men's bodies in the years following marriage. I will explore how their younger years in the yeshiva, isolated from both Ultra-Orthodox and general society, influenced the behavior of adult *gedolim* in the world for the rest of their lives, and whether their efforts to spiritually "re-create" their bodies were successful. Finally, I will focus on the boundaries between the immutable "given nature" of the body, on one hand, and the body's newly acquired "re-created nature" on the other.

As we have seen, the saint's yeshiva life was wholly devoted to Talmud. All other aspects of life were treated as obstacles, to be surmounted as the young *godol* struggled against his body and its desires, striving to subject them to his reflective mind. However, in Lithuanian thought in general and in these hagiographies in particular, the "problem of the body" extends far beyond physicality, to encompass broader dilemmas of human existence in the world. For example, the average yeshiva student accepts that marriage is a rite of passage into the Ultra-Orthodox "street," with all of its insecurities, including sexuality, governed by the evil inclination; he therefore does his best to embrace both married life and Talmudic studies. The *godol*, on the other hand, rejects both this transition and the price it exacts. He will only marry a woman who recognizes his total dedication to Torah and devotes her life to supporting his mission of sacred study. The *godol*'s wife is the "ideal Jewish woman," taking entirely upon herself the support of the household, making it a haven from influences and temptations of the outside world, so that her saintly husband may pursue his Talmudic studies without distraction. In rare cases, a *godol* may even continue to reside in the yeshiva after his marriage, rejoining his wife and family only on weekends.[1]

It is therefore not surprising that the Lithuanian *godol* shuns leadership positions, refusing to be appointed rabbi of a community or city, since this would entail interaction (and friction) with the life of the community. Rather, he seeks to maintain a role within the yeshiva, where he is in touch only with Torah scholars. Rabbi Yechezkel Levenstein, for example, reportedly asked a halakhic court judge, Rabbi Shlomo Shimshon Karelitz, how the latter could preserve the purity of his soul while constantly exposed to the evil influences of his judicial role:

> "How, Sir, can you fulfill your duties as judge, without harm to your spirituality? Are not the cases brought before the court for your consideration an admixture of filthy and disgusting elements, products of the secular way of life, which is rebellious, licentious, corrupt and lustful, and debases the soul? How can a rabbinical judge listen and attend to all these sorts of stories—as his role requires of him!—and still preserve without harm his holiness and nobility of soul?"

Rabbi Shlomo Shimshon's response was instructive. "It all depends," [he said] "on the actual focus of your gaze and thought! Some rabbinical judges, when they rule on a particular case, 'visualize' the occasion that gave rise to the claim, in all its impure circumstances. These judges, indeed, are liable to suffer spiritual harm, since it is difficult to handle muck without being soiled. On the other hand, there are judges who adjudicate without 'seeing' in their mind's eye the acts in question. Rather, as they hear a case presented, they translate it in their minds into [terms of] halakha. What stands out in their minds and occupies them is the correct determination of halakha in this case, and on this they focus all their thoughts. For these judges, the narrative of each case reflects, not the filth of wanton circumstances but rather divine eternal law [*halakha nitzkhit*] and the word of a living God, whose holiness is thus clothed in the garb of worldly occurrences."[2]

---

1. This arrangement persists today, as well, but is unusual. Rabbi Shlomo Fisher, one of the rabbis in 'Itri Yeshiva, in Jerusalem, resides in the yeshiva during the week, visiting his family on Shabbat.

2. Levi, *Mashal HaAvot al 48 Kinyanei HaTorah*, Vol. 1, 296. The image of the *godol*

In other words, any real-life circumstances that the *godol* may encounter in his Jewish community will be immediately "distanced" and translated into the language of Jewish law. For an adult rabbinical judge, just as for an adolescent yeshiva student grappling with an overly explicit *sugiyah* (Talmud portion), the ability to transpose a live case into a theoretical object of traditional Torah study has the effect of defusing any potential ethical dilemmas, or any threats to a saint's purity.

The *gedolim* are typically described as pious souls, whose minds and bodies mirror only the fervor of their devotion, without paying the slightest attention to external realities. Rabbi Chaim Kamil, for example, is described as ignoring a mouse scrambling up his clothing while he studied.[3] It was said of Rabbi Elazar Menachem Shach that he collided with electric poles when walking in the street, and forgot to open his umbrella during a heavy rain. He was once found by his students wandering in the street carrying a torn and empty grocery bag, so inwardly focused on his Talmud study that he failed to notice that the provisions he had purchased earlier had all tumbled out.[4] His mind could be so occupied with the sacred text that he might even fail to recognize a clear sign of danger, as one of his students recounts:

> I innocently assumed that the head of the yeshiva [Rabbi Shach] had just left [the study hall] for a moment, and would be back in a little while. I waited by [the door to] his residence, and after a minute or two a strong odor of burning reached my nostrils, coming from within, and specifically from the kitchen. I hurried there, and saw Rabbi Shach standing by the stove. In one hand he held a volume of Talmud, and in the other a spoon with which he was stirring an empty pot that was at the point of burning. What had happened? The [rabbi's] righteous wife had asked him

---

arising in this description differs greatly from the image of the Hasidic master (*rebbe*). In Hasidism, it is clear to every *rebbe*, from a young age, that he will lead his community later in life, primarily addressing the mundane lives and material challenges of his people. See Cohen, *Pe'er Hador*, Vol. 2, 186; Bergman, *Maran Harav Shach*, Vol. 1, 10.

3. Sofer, *Raboteinu Shebedarom*, 347. Similar descriptions can be found in the Talmud, with focus on unwavering devotion during sessions of prayer. See *Talmud Bavli*, Brachot 33a.

4. Schwartz, *Achar Mitato*, 56. See also, Bergman, *Orchot Chasideha*, 292. Clearly, in these tales Rabbi Shach is seen as the ultimate model scholar, immersed in his studies and oblivious to the external world. He had already earned this reputation as a teenager in the yeshiva, when, it is told, he never washed his dishes between meals and was puzzled by the bad smell they imparted to his food. Bergman, *Maran Harav Shach*, Vol. 1, 138.

to make her some porridge, and of course he had rushed to the kitchen to fulfill her request. Holding his Talmud in one hand [to continue his studies], he put the ingredients into the porridge pot, and began to stir them with a spoon. Focusing all his effort on the Talmud, he went on stirring around and around, unaware that the liquid ingredients had long since evaporated and the whole pot of porridge had all but turned to charcoal.... "This [very] fire," Rabbi Zilberman later declared, "burns [in the afterlife] all those who defame the nation of Israel."[5]

It is not only physical objects that merit the sublime inattention of the *gedolim*, but family members as well. Rabbi Shach would leave his house for a walk, holding his grandchildren's hands, and when the youngsters let go and wandered off he would amble on, oblivious, with his arms still outstretched to both sides.[6] Rabbi Yosef Shlomo Kahaneman, on the instruction of his teacher Rabbi Kagan, remained in the yeshiva with his Talmud while his wife was giving birth to their son, and, eight days later, was still at his studies and so not present at the circumcision ceremony.[7] It is said of one of the greatest rabbis that, after an intense bout of Talmud study, he brought his mind back to the present moment and began searching for his wife, only to remember that she had died more than a month earlier.[8]

During the Holocaust, devout rabbis placed their devotion to the text as a buffer against suffering, to maintain their sanity while coping with the loss of dear ones. One bereft father cried: "O my child! My only child! The Nazi tore him from my arms and shot him before my eyes. [As for me,] I controlled my emotions with an iron fist, and had the privilege of ending that day with [study of] one of the chapters of the Talmudic debate on *migo* . . . ."[9] The same source describes Rabbi Yisrael Ze'ev hiding from Nazi pursuers with his wife, in a pit next to a pigsty:

> From morning to night, for half a year, the depths of the pit echoed with the subjects of [the Talmudic tractate of] *Zevahim*. This time of terror forced [the rabbi] to seek ever new perspectives [on the text]. He needed something else, something

---

5. *Chizuk* 4, 173–74.
6. Schwartz, *Sefer Kdushat Israel*, 89.
7. Lefkowitz, *Darkei Chaim*, Vol. 2, 170.
8. Friedman, *Shtaygen*, 328.
9. Friedman, *Shtaygen*, 40–41. *Migo* refers to a complex and popular Talmudic subject within the yeshiva world.

different, in order to keep his sanity. He told me that the months he had spent in the pit were measured for him, not by days and nights, but rather by the thirty cycles of his recitation and study of *Zevahim* from memory.[10]

Despite this discipline of total focus on the sacred text, pious men did experience some intrusions from the outside world into their life of devoted study. Such distractions are described in the narratives as marks of the *godol*'s spiritual inferiority, or as functions of the generational gap between pre- and post-Holocaust *gedolim*. Saints prior to the Holocaust, it is suggested, surpassed post-Holocaust *gedolim* in self-control and the ability to close themselves off from outside reality. Rabbi Eliezer Gordon (1841–1910) is said to have continued learning Talmud while his daughter lay dying. From time to time he would ask whether she had passed away yet, since her death would—according to Jewish law—prohibit him from studying.[11] Later, as the moment of his own demise approached, Rabbi Gordon ensured that his disciple, Rabbi Yosef Shlomo Kahaneman, had left the room, so that the latter, who was of priestly lineage, would not contract ritual impurity through exposure to death.[12] Similarly, it was reported that Rabbi Elchonon Wasserman (1887–1941), when his wife's life was in danger during pregnancy, rather than leaving the yeshiva to return home and support her, received an exemption from making the journey, in order not to forfeit any time from his Talmud study.[13] When, subsequently, news arrived that his wife had given birth to a son, Rabbi Wasserman did not interrupt his studies to respond.

After the war, such absolute discipline became more rare. When, for example, Rabbi Shach, who represents the post-Holocaust period, was informed of the death of his fourteen-year-old daughter, he tried to console himself with intensive Torah study; later, however, he shared that he had been distracted by his grief and had failed to focus on his studies.[14]

---

10. Friedman, *Shtaygen*, 41.

11. According to Jewish law, when there is a death in the family, one is not allowed to study, or to observe certain other aspects of normative Jewish life, until the funeral, or—in some cases—until a week after the funeral.

12. Sorotzki, *Harav MePonivez*, 27.

13. Sorotzki, *Harav MePonivez*, 63.

14. Schwartz, *Sefer Kdushat Israel*, 53–54. See also, Bergman, *Maran Harav Shach*, Vol. 1, 365–66.

B. The Reflective Being and Its Boundaries

Two models emerge from the tales of Ultra-Orthodox *gedolim*, giving rise to two contradictory *Musar* ideals of the body. One mode, exemplified by the stories about Rabbi Shach, is to maintain such a profound concentration on the Talmud as to forget the body and ignore its existence, while any change in one's physical surroundings, like your grandchildren letting go of your hands, goes unnoticed. This model is the most familiar to readers of these hagiographies.

There is, I suggest, a second and less obvious model for the daily life of these saints. In this mode, the body is subordinate to the order of constant contemplation, and so must obey—at least in every visible movement and action—the dictates of the reflective mind. Far from being ignored, the body and its most minute movements are included in the realm of reflection, every moment of every day. An example is found in a disciple's description of Rabbi Michel Feinstein:

> I observed how Rabbi Michel sat, then got up and went to another room, where he stayed for a few moments, and then returned. On that occasion, one of his students who was present turned to me and said, "Do you see what is happening here?! . . . One can see that at this very moment [we are reading in] the *Shulchan Aruch* [an important book of halakha] where it says that one should sit—and so our Rabbi sits. . . . And now, the *Shulchan Aruch* says that one should stand up—and so our Rabbi gets up. . . . In our Rabbi, one could [thus] observe the embodiment of Torah. . . . When our Rabbi stands up, the meaning is that the Torah stands up, and when our Rabbi sits down, this means that the Torah sits down. His [spiritual] work on himself has, over years of practice, reached such a high level of self-emptying and deference to the holy Torah, that a perfect unity has formed between him and Torah. He and the Torah have become, essentially, one."[15]

A very similar observation of "absolute self-control" appears in Rabbi Shlomo Wolbe's eulogy for Rabbi Yechezkel Levenstein:

> Imagine someone for whom the "work of *Musar*" is to sit on a chair and then get up. Do we have any idea what "*Musar* work" simply sitting at table entails? For almost forty years I have known Rabbi Hatzke'el [a familiar reference to Rabbi

---

15. Israel, *Rabbi Moshe Shmuel*, 1–2.

Levenstein], and I never once saw him leaning against the back of the chair, whether during prayers or while reciting the *Shema*. Now *that* is work! . . . I could not bear to watch how he ate, the way he tortured his body. . . . One of his doctors said, that even when [the rabbi's health] was at its worst, with his blood pressure almost at zero, one could observe his absolute control over each and every movement he made. Do we have any understanding of how a man [*'adam*] is able to work on all his movements, controlling them even in such circumstances? There is no doubt that his whole day was composed of thousands of decisions, thousands of choices, from the moment he awoke until he retired at night. . . . Nothing occurred without [his conscious] supervision.[16]

Rabbi Wolbe here sets the late Rabbi Levenstein up as the model of an ideal *godol*, by focusing especially on his conscious bodily actions—nearly the antithesis of the laudatory descriptions of Rabbi Shach already cited. For Shach, the role of the *Musar* person is ideally to *transcend* the body and to focus on the mind, exemplifying the "protected body" model we outlined earlier (see chapter 3). For Levenstein, on the other hand, significant portions of the day—and of one's energy—are devoted exclusively and intentionally to the body, ideally *transformed* into a reliable reflection of the disciplined mind, illustrating the alternative model we have termed the "new self."

By subdividing time into countless discrete and conscious instants, Levenstein interrupts the "flow of life" in order to determine how his body acts in the course of behavior that would otherwise be automatic, precisely because it does not "naturally" require observation. Wolbe sees Levenstein as a model of *Musar*, because even simple movements like sitting and standing, are understood as moral acts, in the sense that they should not merely *happen*, but rather be intentional. The "thousands of decisions" comprising Levenstein's day are marks of a *Musar* ideal diametrically opposite to the ideal of an ongoing and uninterrupted "flow of Talmud study."

Moment by moment intentionality also figures prominently in descriptions of Rabbi Dovid Povarsky. Once, having broken his arm, he was advised that the injured limb should be immobilized in a plaster cast. This would have interfered with the halakhic requirement of "laying

---

16. Wolbe, *Avnei Shlomo*, 99–100.

tefillin" (wrapping the phylacteries around the forearm during prayer). Rabbi Povarsky had a simple solution:

> [H]e asked the doctor why the plaster was necessary. "So the rabbi will not move his arm," says the doctor. "Why would I move my arm if it is not necessary to do so?" Rabbi Dovid asked. And so, for three months, Rabbi Dovid walked about with a broken arm, without a cast, and did not move it even a hair's breadth. His outstanding disciple, Rabbi Yosef Zvi Reinhold, testifies that months later, when an x-ray was taken, it became clear that the fracture had been fully integrated. This in turn made it clear that the rabbi's arm had not remained immobile independently [of his will], that in fact it could not have turned even a fraction of an inch without it's master's knowledge. At that moment, a great light shone on Rabbi Dovid's face. It was the supreme triumph of a *Musar* soul who for months had succeeded in exercising sovereignty over the instincts of the arm, and excising from his bodily movements any inclination not compatible with the reign of [conscious] knowledge.

In the tales concerning Feinstein, Levenstein, and Povarsky, for the first time in Lithuanian culture, the body of the *godol* becomes a *Musar* "text"—a lesson and object of contemplation for the *Musar* student.

In Hasidic contexts, observing the righteous and holy man engaged in an "event" of real life is regarded as one of the central ways of approaching the divine. A clear example of such an "event" comes each week, after the Friday night (*Erev Shabat*) meal. At that time, while yeshiva students in the Lithuanian tradition simply eat the *Erev Shabat* meal and return to their Talmud studies, the Hasidim hurry to the home of their Rebbe, to participate in the *Tish* (the Shabbat meal at the Hasidic rabbi's home). Beyond being a community gathering for the purpose of hearing a Torah commentary by the Rebbe, the Hasidic *Tish* gives disciples a festive opportunity to closely observe their teacher's physical comportment for the entire evening. The holy man's partaking of his meal, with all his attendant devotions, songs and conversations, amount to an essentially religious event, witness ideal expressions of eating.[17]

> It is not for nothing that the Hasidim urged their steps, . . . braving every difficulty and danger along the way, to gather in the company [*betsel*: literally—"in the shadow"] of our holy teachers [*rabboteinu ha-kedoshim*] on every Sabbath of the year. As they

17. Englander, "Halakha as Praxis."

took their places around that pure table [i.e. the Hasidic *Tish*], they would stand as if rooted to the spot, transfixed and motionless, intent only on their Rebbe [*ha-rabbi*], his instruction, his manner of eating, and his [devotional] singing—[understanding these] all together as a single [sacred] teaching. It is told, for example, of that marvelous Hasid, Rabbi [Zalman] Sandrovitch that his devotion to our master [*maran*—literally "our lord"] the "Holy Grandfather" [*ha-saba' kadisha'*] was boundless. This was most especially true when he was in the company of [*betsel*] the "Holy Grandfather" on Sabbaths and Holy Days, when [Rabbi Zalman] would lose all touch with his surroundings, as every fiber of his soul was bonded solely to the Rebbe [*ha-rabbi*] and his ways. On one occasion, when he spent a sacred Sabbath [Eve] with the "Holy Grandfather," [Rabbi Zalman] was standing on a bench near the pure table [i.e., the *Tish*], with his eyes fixed firmly on the face of the Rebbe. One of his sons needed to get his attention, and was unable to approach him in the press [of disciples]. So the lad pulled at the hem of his father's coat, crying, "Father! Father!" Rabbi Zalman remained totally oblivious to what was happening. His son looked at him more closely, to make sure that this was in fact his father that he was addressing. It was then that he observed that the floor over which his father was standing was drenched and wet from the many tears that were streaming continuously from his father's eyes.[18]

One of the primary purposes of Hasidic hagiography is to teach an intense observation of each and every one of the Hasidic leader's movements, not only during the Sabbath meal but at any time and in any situation. Motion or stillness, speech or silence—all contain lessons for the disciple.[19] Powerful Hasidic influences, including this emphasis on observation, permeate Lithuanian Ultra-Orthodox society.

However, there is a significant difference between the Hasidic Rebbe and the Lithuanian *godol*. The Hasidic tales are greatly engaged with and fascinated by the Hasidic saint's enjoyment of food,[20] cigarette smoking,[21] chess and checkers, and even slumber.[22] The remarkable intensity of these sensible delights is predicated, however, on a perception of Hasidic saints

18. Brecher and Gafni, *Netivot Melucha*, 109–10.
19. Brecher and Gafni, *Netivot Melucha*.
20. *Tzeirey Viznitz* 17 (1994), 8. Rott, *Kdosh Yisrael*.
21. On the meaning of smoking in the Hasidic tradition see, Rott, *Kdosh Yisrael*, 308.
22. Rott, *Kdosh Yisrael*, 165.

as superhuman beings, fundamentally different, by their very nature, from ordinary people. Their enjoyment of life is *emphatically not* to be imitated by the Rebbe's disciples. Since there is this deep, ontological gap between the saint and his followers, Hasidic students quickly learn that the concepts of body and physicality that are familiar to them from their own experiences are not to be compared to those of their saintly leaders. In hagiographies of the Lithuanian *godol*, on the other hand, the image of the saint is indeed fully human, and intended to serve as a *Musar* exemplar and object of imitation. Pleasure and enjoyment, then, must be completely absent from the visible and physical "performances" of the *godol*, to avoid encouraging hedonistic behavior on the part of students.

Spiritual training of the body for the reflective life does not guarantee an ultimate material transformation of the body; the process is an unceasing striving toward an unreachable goal. The *Musar* effort to achieve a highly reflective life demands a continuous critical gaze, a constant examination of choices and actions, an acute observation that never wavers into unconscious experience of the flow of life. One might say, even, that the Musar man maintains a distance between himself and life, never fully accepting human existence as part of nature. Reflection in itself never becomes a "new nature"; even after decades of practice, the righteous continue to closely observe every movement, sensation or emotion that arises:

> In the last days of his life, [Rabbi Levenstein] said that one must be strengthened and determined not to cry when he prays, because an old and weak man tends to cry easily.... The tears do not stem from a real feeling in the heart but from the weakness of the physical forces.[23]

Even Levenstein, seen as the model of a man in constant spiritual control, fails to fully subdue his body as he grows old. He has no choice but to feel certain emotions, forced by his physicality to become human, in the most basic and natural way.

In another example of extreme striving against human nature, we read of Rabbi Shalom Schwadron, when one of his children contracted a contagious illness, hurrying to transfer all his other children to his mother's house, lest they also become sick. His mentor, Rabbi Isaac Sher, questioned Schwadron about his motives in moving the children in this way, to which Schwadron replied: "The child is ill, and [so] I am taking

23. Sorotzki, *Marbitzey Torah Umusar*, Vol. 1, 236.

the [other] children to my mother's house." Rabbi Isaac did not miss this opportunity to obliquely reprimand his student, as Rabbi Schwardon relates:

> Then Rabbi Isaac fixed his gaze on me, and declared: "In other words, the adult beast takes and leads the young beast.... [For] even animals will care for their young very well in such a fashion." Then Rabbi Isaac went on to explain, adding, "*Ner Was*? What, then, should we say [in a situation like this]? [Say,] rather, this: that you are about to [observe the Jewish halakha and] do an act of lovingkindness, for [the benefit of] a Jewish child, who, incidentally, happens to be your own child as well."[24]

Rabbi Isaac Sher's point here is that a man of *Musar* should resist, not only human physical needs but also human *instinctive* needs—even if these lead us to positive and caring action. A father's natural desire to protect his children is understood here as nothing better than animal impulse ("even animals will care for their young"), unworthy of the *Musar* ideal of perfect contemplation. We have seen that *Musar* literature aims to establish human beings—and especially Jewish religious men—in a unique position in the world, different from animals in that they do not act from their baser instincts. A moral act expressing natural will is not complete, unless it also interrupts these instincts and introduces intentional reflection and choice. It remains true that a man of *Musar* must protect his children from disease. This is not, however, because they are his children, or even because natural compassion motivates him to defend the vulnerable; rather, he must always act from moral observation, and in accordance with Jewish law.

***

What does the *Musar* regulation of the body and its boundaries ultimately look like? Lithuanian leaders like Rabbi Levenstein and Rabbi Feinstein who exercise exemplary physical control are depicted with their limbs essentially immobile, their heads erect, and their faces never tilted to one side. They eat only with great awareness, and speak only when their intellect gives an explicit command. They are, in short, models of self-restraint and spiritual dignity.

---

24. Anonymous, *Kol Chozev*, 67–77.

Except in unusual cases, Lithuanian *Musar* stories apply such conscious control only to the external, visible body. It does not extend—as in some Eastern ascetical systems—to internal organs and functions like the heart and circulation, the stomach and digestion, or the bowels and secretions. The distinction between external and internal physicality is not unique to the Ultra-Orthodox Lithuanian culture; it appears in the early Jewish literature of the Mishna and Talmud.[25] However, while Mishnaic and Talmudic sages care deeply about questions concerning the inner body, the Lithuanian thinkers ignore these queries almost completely.

Finally, in his struggle for acute awareness of each and every physical event, the Lithuanian *godol* fosters an experience of time distinct from that familiar to most Western individuals. As we have seen above in the "thousands of decisions" of Rabbi Levenstein, the recurring call to self-reflection and external observation of all behaviors uproots one from the continuum of life. The natural flow of time is repeatedly interrupted, and experienced by the *Musar* man as disjointed bundles of observable time-fragments.

C. The Disabled Body

The Lithuanian hagiographies encourage ascetical practices, but not the intentional crippling or disabling of the body. However, an acceptance—or even affirmation—of physical disability resulting from a life of virtue is certainly present in the literature of the *gedolim*, and provides a special case in studying these Jewish holy men.

The neuropsychological studies of the French philosopher Maurice Merleau-Ponty point to a direct link between the body and an individual's world-view. Since the body plays such a central role in the forging of human identity and of each individual's grasp of reality, then it follows that radical changes experienced by the body—not only congenital defects but especially disabilities acquired later in life—will entail profound conceptual changes as well. Physical disabilities or defects—as, for example, the loss of a limb—are not conceptualized simply as misfortunes that negatively impact an individual's ability to function; rather, they occasion a restructuring of the person's understanding of reality and mode of relating to the surrounding environment. In other words, while a whole and healthy body will perceive reality in one way, the disabled body's

---

25. Englander and Kamir, "Body and Shame."

experience is utterly different.[26] According to Merleau-Ponty, disability requires individuals to recognize that their perceptions and experiences of the world have changed.[27]

Similarly, the *Musar* thinkers closely observe the movements of the body, recognizing that these reveal a particular category of knowledge, imprinted deep within the physical self. This knowledge is understood as a certain natural orientation, recognizable in almost every physical agency, without the mediation of the intellect. Often, as human beings, we can only be wonder-struck by an unconscious act or behavior of our own body. Retrospection here is the key: as we look back upon our experiences, we can become aware of what the body "knows" how to do without any explicit conscious direction. Sitting in my room, I may realize that a thought has been sparked by the sound of music from the adjoining flat. Or, I may be driving along the street, and become aware that I have already seen a particular advertisement poster that now engages my gaze. It makes no difference whether I wish to look at it or not: I know that I have already seen it. Even if I now avert my eyes, this can never alter the original "seeing" that occurred before I decided "not to see." Put another way, I would not have known that I wanted to avert my gaze, had that first "seeing" not already occurred without my conscious consent.

For *Musar* teachers, this all constitutes a moral problem: we seem forced to live "in the world," constantly bound to it by a body that instinctively receives and reacts to sensory information before the intellect can intervene. Physical disability, however, gradually or suddenly opens a "gap" between the body and the world, offering an occasion to suspend the immediacy of the physical relationship with reality, and to give precedence to reflective activity.

Indeed, the stories show that exemplary *Musar* teachers embrace their disabilities, seeing them as opportunities to deepen their commitment to a *Musar* life. They often refuse to accept medical advice or seek the aid of auxiliary devices that could mitigate their disability. The choice or necessity of living with a disability both require adjustments, not only by the disabled person, but also, and especially, by those around him. For example, when Rabbi Yaakov Israel Kanievsky lost much of his capacity for hearing, he refused to use a hearing aid, which would strengthen his communication with his environment. As a result of his deafness, Rabbi

---

26. Merleau-Ponty, *The Phenomenology of Perception*, 95–99.
27. Merleau-Ponty, *The Phenomenology of Perception*, 95–99.

Kanievsky's students and family could no longer speak to him, and instead had to write him notes. The rabbi saw this as a gift from heaven:

> Blessed be the One [literally, "the Name"] who has [thus] shown me loving kindness! For [now] I cannot hear [them], so they cannot interrupt my Torah study too much; for, after all, how much can one write in a note?[28]

Similarly, Rabbi Chaim Kamil refused to wear eyeglasses when his vision began to fail him as he aged. He explained that from now on his conscious reflection would not always come after "what he had already seen." Rather, he would exercise deliberate choice each time he observed the world, by asking, for example, that certain individuals draw closer so that he might see them. In this way, Rabbi Kamil asserted, images from the world could not force themselves upon him without his consent.[29]

D. Sexuality, Laughter, and the Paradox of the Dancing Rabbis

Even when he is married, the Lithuanian *godol* continues to be deeply concerned about sexual stimuli. This is true not only in relation to women in general, but even in regards to the *godol*'s wife, with whom Jewish halakha clearly permits him to enjoy sexual experience. Many of the *gedolim* are said to have persisted in their celibacy even after marriage.[30] It is important to note that sexual abstinence is never discussed or described until after the *godol* has entered married life. Presumably, since sexual experience of any kind is forbidden during adolescence and before marriage, our sources avoid this "sensitive" subject entirely, portraying the young *godol* as essentially asexual. An exception that proves the rule is found in Rabbi Shach, who said of himself that he had never in his life masturbated, a testimony that includes his adolescence.[31]

Many narrators warn their (male) readers against any interaction with foreign women—a biblical phrase meaning here any woman who is not your wife. Even teaching Torah or lecturing to a gathering that

---

28. Kanievsky, *Toldot Yaakov*, 99. See also p. 178.

29. Sofer, *Raboteinu Shebedarom*, 434–35.

30. Pincus, *Nefesh Shimshon*, 69. On Rabbi Kamil see, Kamil, *Raboteynu SheBadarom*, 500.

31. Schwartz, *Achar Mitato*, 44.

includes women is discouraged.[32] Rabbi Shach described with approval the sanctity of the city of *Slotsk* in Lithuania, where women were not allowed to attend synagogue, except once a year to hear the sounding of the shofar on Rosh Hashanah. This was an exemplary preservation of the role of the Jewish woman as guardian of sexual purity, a view given biblical authority with the oft-quoted biblical verse (Ps 45:14): "all the honor of the king's daughter is within"—understood to mean "within the home," i.e., not in public.

Many rabbis in this tradition have remarked that the sex drive does not abate with age, but rather only increases. Therefore, despite all their struggles to spiritually train the body and subject it to the authority of reflective awareness, the rabbis cannot finally exercise conscious control over sexuality. To compensate for this failure, they impose as many external social restrictions as they can.

Laughter plays a fascinating role in the world of the Lithuanian *gedolim*. Like sexuality, it is considered a physical phenomenon not amenable to conscious direction. Laughter, and even smiling, are both interpreted as displays of excessive pleasure. In spite of every effort to suppress these "unnecessary" physical expressions, and to banish them from the realm of what is considered necessary for the body, still the laugh and the smile persist in marking moments when a person loses control, succumbing to external stimuli.[33]

Indeed, the smile and the laugh were great concerns for the righteous, so much so that, in the hagiographies, some of the *gedolim* are described as never once smiling.[34] Rabbi Schwadron spoke out against any displays of levity like jokes or puns, and asserted that if a *godol* presented his face with a smile, it was only out of politeness toward his guests.[35]

Laughter may be seen as an essential physical and emotional aspect of "ludic release" in human consciousness. Ostensibly outside the conscious control of even the most righteous, laughter presents the editors of the *gedolim* hagiographies with the challenging observation that these

---

32. Kamil, *Raboteynu SheBadarom*, 439; Anonymous, *Kol Chozev*, 132.

33. The Hebrew linguistic root for laughter is *ts.h.k.* (*tsahak*). In Jewish tradition, not surprisingly, this root is interpreted to represent a place where the physical aspect gains the upper hand over humanity, and erupts in violence and sexuality. See *Rashi* on Genesis 21:9.

34. This is how the text described Rabbi Elchanan Waserman. See Anonymous, *Mepihem Shel Rabotynu*, 265; Gold, *Bnei Chail Vol. 1*, 207.

35. Gold, *Bnei Chail Vol. 1*, 208.

saints are bound to their bodies just as is every other person. In this context, a relevant story about Rabbi Schwadron in discussion with some of his yeshiva students has a strange and unexpected ending. The tale opens with Schwardon (known to his students as "Rabbi Shalom") relating in his own words the content of the conversation, which relates to one of the students expressing interest in the physical pleasures of other (non-Jewish) cultures:

> One of our yeshiva students began to seek out other cultures [*lifzol litzdadim*—literally, "to go looking around"] . . . I asked him this brief question: "Which do you think lives better in this world, and which is happier, a man or a beast?" . . . "Understand this," I explained to him: "A cow enjoys her straw and hay no less than what you enjoy eating. She has no need to travel any distance, nor does she experience troubles, headaches, or any soulful distress." . . . Suddenly, the young man blurted out this anguished utterance: "Truly, how sorry I am that I was not born an animal!" . . . The moment I heard this sentence come out of his mouth, I retorted, raising my voice: "You poor fool, you should not be sorry—you are already a beast!"

The tale is here picked up by one of the students who observed this conversation. Rabbi Shalom addresses his disciples with deep emotion:

> "Dear brothers," [he said . . .] with tears in his wise eyes. "Does man come into the world to eat and drink? Is it only 'Eat and drink, for tomorrow we die!' (Isaiah 22:13)? When it comes to that sort of thing, any animal is, after all, better at it than we are!"[36]

There is a pause in the discussion, as Rabbi Schwadron's ethical "victory" over the wayward student sinks in. Conventionally, this might have been the end of the *Musar* narrative, but it has an astonishing zen-like coda:

> Rabbi Shalom kept silent for a long moment. Suddenly, he began to smile. The smile widened, spreading across his face. Those who were gathered there watching him began to smile too. Everyone was smiling, and they did not even know why! "Ah, ha!" said Rabbi Shalom. "We laugh! Sure! Of course! There is [certainly] something to laugh about!"[37]

36. Anonymous, *Kol Chozev*, 353–59.

37. Anonymous, *Kol Chozev*, 353–59. Rabbi Sholom Schwadron (1912–1997) studied in the Hebron Yeshiva. He imparted *Musar* teachings throughout the Jewish world, and his stylistic references to the city of Jerusalem earned him the honorific

This is perhaps one of the most ironic and revealing passages in our *gedolim* sources. Why did they laugh? After supposedly landing a crushing dialogic blow in a debate about the *Musar* duty to deny the body, Rabbi Shalom defuses the ethical tension with one mysterious smile. Are we to imagine his students, not only smiling with him, but overcome by an inexplicable and uncontrollable bout of hilarity? Was this simply contagious laughter—a physical impulse without logical cause—or was Rabbi Shalom alluding to something (who knows what?) truly humorous? The questions remain unanswered and open. Whatever the underlying message, this remarkable tale of a serious teacher sharing smiles and laughter with his protégés could be permissible only in the context of the protected space of the yeshiva.

The work of Mikhail Bakhtin, the renowned Russian literary critic, may shed some light on the enigmatic episode of Rabbi Shalom's laughter. Bakhtin introduced to critical discourse the concept of "carnival"—denoting a time and space in which rigid social boundaries and expectations are subverted.[38] In carnival's temporary context, participants are allowed—even invited!—to violate the social rules typically governing their behavior. While carnival is usually temporally and spatially defined, the distinction between it and normative way of life is not absolute; the two modes permeate each other. Society not only defines its laws and the consequences for those who violate them, but also dictates prescriptions or guidelines for a sanctioned breaking of its rules, thus setting the boundaries of carnival space in advance. There, some conventions may be discarded, while others must continue to be strictly observed.

In this sense, carnival is the exception that defines the general rule; the upending of social norms is not arbitrary, but rather answers to the hierarchy in power. The intentional relaxation of select strictures is only possible when its purpose, in the final analysis, is to preserve the dominant social order essentially unchallenged.[39]

In the Jewish tradition, the holiday of *Simchat Torah* ("The Joy of Torah")[40] provides an opportunity for carnivalesque orthodoxy and riot-

---

pseudonym *HaMagid HaYerushalmi* ("The Jerusalemite Teacher").

38. Bakhtin, *Rabelais and His World*.

39. Cohen Shabot, *On the Grotesque Body*, 84–86.

40. *Simchat Torah* occurs on the last day of the week-long Jewish holiday of Sukkot, and has its own distinct meaning. On *Simchat Torah* Jews read the last portion of the five books of Moses (the Torah) and return to Genesis to commence reading again, from the beginning. The holiday's theme is fervent joy and gratitude for the gift

ous order. In an anonymously authored hagiography of Rabbi Schwadron, readers are told that the customary dancing on *Simchat Torah* does not essentially belong to the body, but to the spirit:

> The legs: they must never dance of their own volition, but always as emissaries of the mind and the heart! And that mind, that heart, must not make the legs dance simply in response to some "mood" or other. Rather, [one dances] because the deepest roots [of the soul] have been shaken by the intense excitement of *Simchat Torah*—the Joy of Torah![41]

In order to emphasize this idea, during the first of the seven cycles of prescribed holiday dancing (known as the *hakafot*), the younger yeshiva students are not invited to dance alongside the head of the yeshiva and his group. Instead, they stand outside the "inner circle" to observe how "ideal Jews" dance, and they are warned not to be swept up into any inappropriate dancing of their own. Nonetheless, consider the following description of the *Simchat Torah* gathering in Rabbi Schwardon's yeshiva:

> During the first cycle of dancing (*ha-hakafah ha-rishonah*), the students [*ha-bachurim*] did not dare to enter into [the inner circle]. These students danced with fervor in a large circle all around the hall, watching as the yeshiva leaders and luminaries danced in the middle, clasping the Torah scrolls in an intimate embrace. . . . The first [young student] to burst into the very heart of that inner circle was the *tzadik* ("righteous one") Rabbi Shmuel Hillel Shinker. He could no longer stand outside, while the melody burned within him as fire burns among thorns. . . . He danced with his eyes closed, and his face hotly flushed [with exertion]. . . . Then, he was joined by the *tzadik* Rabbi Shlomo Bloch, who was swept up [in the dance], leaping with great devotion and clapping his hands, [crying out] "Blessed be our G-d! Blessed be our G-d! [*baruch elokeinu!*]" Over on the other side of the hall, Rabbi Moshe Menkevich started dancing too. Both [Rabbi Bloch and Rabbi Menkevich] were spinning ecstatically [*cholelu berikud*] from one end [of the hall] to the other. . . . The hall was now the scene of much winey indulgence, of fervent prostrations, and of joyful weeping.[42]

---

of Torah.

41. Anonymous, *Kol Chozev,* 436.
42. Anonymous, *Kol Chozev,* 436–39.

For ten pages, the editor of this account goes on about the carnivalesque celebration of *Simchat Torah*, describing usually sober rabbis imbibing alcohol, elderly sages cavorting with all of their strength, and worried wives running around trying to prevent their husbands from hurting themselves.[43] Later that evening, we are told, Rabbi Schwardon, together with the other rabbis and their disciples, caroused through the streets of Jerusalem. Encountering an Orthodox elder out for a walk, the inebriated *gedolim* demanded that he bless them. At first he refused, but when the insistent saints grabbed him and lifted him up into the air, he promptly gave them his benediction.

The body of the saint celebrates the intoxication of freedom. When his wife begs him to stop dancing, solicitous of his health, one of the older rabbis replies: "Wherever I would weep on Rosh Hashanah and Yom Kippur, there I will be joyful on *Simchat Torah*."[44] The yeshiva, which is in essence a refuge from bodily desires and a sacred space for prayer (especially on the High Holy Days) now, on *Simchat Torah*, becomes the very place where the passions burn, in chaotic excitement, the moment they are freed. If *Yom Kippur*—the Day of Atonement—is the pinnacle of reflective spirituality and soul-searching, then *Simchat Torah*—the Joy of Torah—is a street carnival of the senses, entirely devoted to the body.

The anonymous account we are quoting is set near Jerusalem, in the context of the Hebron Yeshiva, the flagship institute of the Slabodka *Musar* method in the Land of Israel. The Slabodka yeshiva system, as we have already described, emphasizes the importance of "honor," expressed through a dignified physical comportment, impeccable manners, and a spiritual sort of "Jewish nobility." Now, on *Simchat Torah*, the staid social hierarchy of Slabodka is suspended for a limited time. Rabbis and their select disciples dance shoulder to shoulder with ordinary students, their honorable inhibitions forgotten.

The bodies of the *gedolim*, it must be remembered, are accustomed only to constant learning, never to any physical activity or exercise. When these scholarly saints suddenly jump to their feet to dance, according to the accounts, their physical frame often simply fails them, and

---

43. Naturally, Jewish holy men of this tradition are not capable of "drinking like men." All their lives, they have been distanced from the world of matter, represented in this story by alcohol. It is small wonder that now, when they experience the effects of wine, they must be prevented from harming themselves by their wives, since women in this culture are identified with matter.

44. Anonymous, *Kol Chozev*, 442.

they collapse helplessly to the floor. In other cases, the tales describe their clumsy limbs bathed in sweat in their efforts to dance, or their tendency to slump to the ground as a result of their lack of fitness—and intoxication. All in all, these quasi-grotesque descriptions portray the exact opposite of the venerable Torah sage, vaunted by the *Musar* tradition for his self-restraint and uncompromising reflective sanctity.

The word "Torah" is often understood in religious tradition as "Divine Law," and throughout our study of the Lithuanian *gedolim*, we have seen their Torah study embodied in daily observance of Jewish law in *halakha*. It is fitting, then, that our remarkable tale of the most carnivalesque of Jewish holy days opens with the "Joy of Torah" and closes with a return to sober contemplation, the "fear of heaven" and fidelity to *halakha*.

As the carnival night of *Simchat Torah* in Jerusalem wears on, Rabbi Shalom (Schwardon) and the perambulating yeshiva rabbis pay an impromptu visit to the home of a revered Torah sage known as the *Brisker Rov*.[45] One of the students continues the story, telling how they gain entrance to his living room, presumably in a somewhat raucous manner, and then:

> Suddenly, the *Brisker Rov* came [into the room] to honor [us] with his presence. . . . Rabbi Shalom raised his eyes, saw [the *Brisker Rov*], grasped himself tightly and abruptly came to his senses. Overwhelmed by consternation, he shouted, "Oh, oh! *Ich hab mora*'! I am terrified!" This [the student continues] is a sight that I will never forget: at the same instant [that Rabbi Shalom shouted], the [*Brisker Rov*, startled], leapt backward and immediately returned to his chamber.[46]

Rabbi Schwadron, with the carnival parade, arrives drunkenly at the home of the "Rabbi from Brisk," who symbolizes, perhaps more than anyone else in Lithuanian culture, the strict authority of the Jewish law. Tales of the *Brisker Rov* focus on his totally reflective comportment, his every act governed by conscious awareness of *halakha*. On this night, however, the "unforgettable sight" for the visiting student—more stunning even than the inebriated sages in the carnival parade—is the spectacle of the startled *Brisker Rov*. Shocked by the uncontrolled behavior of his riotous rabbinic guests, and abandoning his usually reflective and measured

---

45. Rabbi Yitzchok Zev Halevi Soloveitchik (1886–1959), also known as the *Brisker Rov* ("Rabbi of/from Brisk") spent the final years of his life in Jerusalem.

46. Anonymous, *Kol Chozev*, 444–45.

manner, he leaps instinctively back into his private room, as if to hide himself within the bounds of the law.

When Rabbi Schwardon and his fellow rabbis realize that their raucous display of physicality has breached the equanimity of the Brisker Rov, they know they have gone too far. Rabbi Shalom's cry in Yiddish—*Ich hab mora'!*—echoes the biblical word *yira'h* (sacred fear, awe) which denotes the "fear of heaven." It is this emotion, finally, that inspires the wayward holy revelers to return to the rules of their spiritual *Musar* society, to return to *halakha*.

***

The carnival is over. And yet, in spite of the descriptions of the dancing rabbis, with their clumsy and ridiculous limbs and their irrepressible excitement—or, actually, precisely *because of those descriptions*—the full radiance of the bodies of these *gedolim* shines on still, with all the wonder and splendor of their sanctity. Now, the moment of "holy madness" past, that holiness re-enters the daily round, lived in each moment of devotion to Torah and *halakha*. *Simchat Torah* is only a moment of disorder, intended to restore everything to order, more surely and more irrefutably than before. The carnival interlude is described in such a way that the reader must understand, that the life of *Musar* has meaning only when it is fundamentally reflective.

Summary

As I write these lines to summarize this book on Jewish ideas of the human body, the world is in the throes of an historic global coronavirus pandemic. Past pandemics have, of course, affected millions of people worldwide. Still, in this present crisis, diverse human societies have become one in a paradoxical and unprecedented way. Never before have so many human beings been forced to distance themselves from each other, in order to protect the most essential of human values: the health and survival of the human body.

Traditional Ultra-Orthodox (Haredi) Jewish life worldwide has been severely impacted by the coronavirus crisis. For the first time since the catastrophe of the Holocaust, synagogues and houses of study everywhere have finally emptied, and closed their doors. It is a terrible truth, supported by medical evidence, that members of Ultra-Orthodox groups have suffered more illness and death from the coronavirus than many of the surrounding populations. One of the salient reasons for this difference has been the reluctance of influential rabbis and community leaders to announce unequivocally that it is more important to safeguard the life of the human body than to continue the traditional group study of the sacred Jewish texts. While other people everywhere isolated themselves for safety, in the gathering places of the Ultra-Orthodox Jewish world the bodies of zealous and devoted Jews continued to touch, and to destroy, each other.

This situation has now been, of necessity, changed. In the Ultra-Orthodox Jewish community, for the first time in history, the perceived spiritual value of Torah study has been overruled by the value of physical survival. It soon became evident to Haredi society at large, that the urgent warnings of medical authorities, mandating the closure of public spaces and the imposition of preventative isolation, were heeded too late. Further, this delay cannot be blamed on any negligence on the part of the authorities. It was, manifestly, the intentional self-imposed isolation of Ultra-Orthodox Jews from the outside ("Western") world that prevented the Haredi community from taking essential prophylactic measures until it was too late. By then, scores had already been infected by the virus, and—tragically—many perished.

The coronavirus pandemic has radically changed Ultra-Orthodox Jewish life. Within the space of a single month, for instance, the virtual reality of social media has—of necessity—penetrated Haredi society, and it is unlikely that this process can ever be reversed.

The role of rabbinical leaders in this community has also been permanently altered. These leaders made fateful decisions for their faithful in the early days of the pandemic, based on the guidance of their own respected assistants. In retrospect, many of them now understand that this same hegemony censored crucial information concerning the nature of the viral epidemic. As a result, their leadership decisions were gravely wrong, with results that were all too often fatal to those in their charge. The sheen of rabbinical integrity has been seriously tarnished.

Myriads of pious yeshiva students, for their part, now find themselves confined, day and night, at home with their families, as they shelter in place to avoid the spread of the virus. These students have been accustomed, for centuries, to seeking spiritual refuge in the intentionally all-male sacred space of the yeshiva. Now, they live surrounded, hour after hour, by their wives, mothers, daughters, and sisters, without even a single hour's respite from feminine company. Such changes in physical circumstance have occurred with dramatic and immediate force; only time will tell how deeply they will influence concepts of the body and its role in Ultra-Orthodox Jewish culture. As one yeshiva director has put it, in a single month Haredi life has undergone cultural upheavals, that in the normal context of history might have taken several decades, at least.

My intention in writing this book is, first and foremost, to create a dialogue with the Ultra-Orthodox society of my origins. My labors in the academic world have equipped me with theoretical tools and research sensitivities that enable me to identify, in the Haredi community, characteristics that may escape the attention of those who still live entirely within that world. In this book, I endeavor to offer an "external" view—albeit a reflective and loving one—to aid members of this community as they decide how to shape their way of life. To this end, I intentionally distance myself from anything that smacks of gossip or hearsay, and from any dimension of defamation or voyeurism. My intention is to observe honestly, and to communicate compassionately, what I have learned about the reality of the human body within Haredi society.

It is my sincere hope, that Ultra-Orthodox readers will choose to receive and ponder the words I offer here, remembering that "what comes forth from the heart—enters the heart."

Bibliography

Abramski, Menachem Ezra. *Melech Be-yofio, Vol. 1*. Jerusalem: Private, 2004. [Hebrew]
Achituv, Yoske. *Mashavei Ruach*. Jerusalem: Israel. Hartman Institute Press, 2013.
Adler, Sinai. *BeGei Tzalmavet*. Jerusalem: Private, 2003. [Hebrew]
Anonymous. *Besufa Ubesaara*. Jerusalem: Private, 2010. [Hebrew]
———. *Darka Shel Torah*. Jerusalem, Private, 2002. [Hebrew]
———. *Hi Sichati, Vol. 1*. Jerusalem, Private, 2001. [Hebrew]
———. *Hi Sichati, Vol. 2*. Jerusalem, Private, 2002. [Hebrew]
———. *Kedoshim Tihiu*. Jerusalem: Private, 1981. [Hebrew]
———. *Kol Chozev*. Jerusalem: Private, 1999. [Hebrew]
———. *Mepihem Shel Rabotynu*. Bnei-Brak: Private, 2008. [Hebrew]
———. *Rabbi Hirsch*. Jerusalem: Private, 2008. [Hebrew]
———. *Sar HaTorah*. Jerusalem: Private, 2004. [Hebrew]
———. *Tiferet Bachurim*. Jerusalem: Private, 2001. [Hebrew]
Afterman, Adan. *Devequt: Mystical Intimacy in Medieval Jewish Thought*. Los Angeles: Cherub Press, 2011. [Hebrew]
Aran, Gidon. "Denial Does Not Make the Haredi Body Go Away: Ethnography of a Disappearing (?)." *Contemporary Jewry* 26.1 (2006) 75–113.
Aran, Gidon, et al. "Fundamentalism and the Masculine Body: The Case of Jewish Ultra-Orthodox Men in Israel." *Religion* 38 (2008) 25–53.
Asad, Talal. *Formations of the Secular: Christianity, Islam, Modernity*. Stanford, CA: Stanford University Press, 2003.
Assaf, David. "Leadership and Inheritance of Leadership in Nineteenth Century Hasidism." In *On Leadership and Leaders*, edited by Hana Amit, 59–72. Tel Aviv: Ministry of Defense, 2000. [Hebrew]
Assaf, David, and Immanuel Etkes, eds. *Heder: Studies, Documents, Literature and Memoirs*. Tel-Aviv: Israel. Tel-Aviv University Press. 2010.
Auerbach, Shmuel. *Ohel Rachel: Elul*. Jerusalem: Private, 2002. [Hebrew]
Barnard, Malcolm. *Fashion as Communication*. London and New-York: Routledge, 1996
Austin, J. L. *How to Do Things with Word*. Cambridge: Harvard University Press, 1962.
Ba-Gad, Vered. "Min HaAvar Harachok Vea'ad HaHoveh." In *Leadership and Authority in Israeli Haredi Society: Challenges and Alternatives*, edited by Kimmy Caplan and Nurit Stadler, 99–126. Tel Aviv: Hakibbutz Hameuchad and Van Leer Jerusalem Institute, 2009. [Hebrew]
Bakhtin, Mikhail. *Rabelais and His World*. Cambridge: M.I.T. Press, 1965.

Bartal, Israel. "Hilon Ha-Zman Ve-Tarbut Ha-Pnai." In *New Jewish Time: Jewish Culture in a Secular Age—An Encyclopedic View, Vol. 1.*, edited by Israel Bartal, 272–76. Tel Aviv: Keter, 2007. [Hebrew]

———. "True Knowledge and Wisdom: On Orthodox Historiography." *Studies in Contemporary Jewry* 10 (1994) 178–92.

Ben-Artzi, Shmuel. *Novardok*. Tel Aviv: Yediot Ahronoth, 2007. [Hebrew]

Benarroch, Jonatan. "God and His Son: Christian Affinities in the Shaping of the Sava and Yanuka Figures in the Zohar." *Jewish Quarterly Review* 107.1 (2017) 38–65.

———. *S"aba ve-Yanuka, 'Treyn de-inun hada': 'alegoriah, semel u-mitos ba-sifrut ha-zoharit*." PhD diss., Hebrew University, 2011. [Hebrew]

Berdyczweski, Micha Josef. *Collected Works Vol. 1*. Tel Aviv: Hakibbutz Hameuchad, 1966. [Hebrew]

———. *Collected Works Vol. 6*. Tel Aviv: Hakibbutz Hameuchad, 2004. [Hebrew]

———. *Collected Works Vol 7*. Tel Aviv: Hakibbutz Hameuchad, 2006. [Hebrew]

Berger, Peter. "On the Obsolescence of the Concept of Honor." *European Journal of Sociology* 11.2 (1970) 338–47.

Bergman, Asher. *Maran Harav Shach, Vol. 1*. Bnei-Brak: Private, 2006. [Hebrew]

———. *Orchot Chasideha*. Bnei-Brak: Private, 1999. [Hebrew]

———. *Shimush Talmidei Chahamim*. Bnei-Brak: Private, 2001. [Hebrew]

Biale, David. *Eros and the Jews: From Biblical Israel to Contemporary America*. Berkley, CA: University of California, 1997.

Bloch, Yosef Leib. *Shi'urei Da'at*. Tel Aviv: Nezah, 1989. [Hebrew]

Blumen, Orna. "Crisis-crossing Boundaries: Ultraorthodox Women Go to Work." *Gender, Place and Society* 9 (2002) 131–52.

The Book of Common Prayer: The Episcopal Church. New York: Church Publishing, 1979.

Bourdieu, Pierre. *In Other Words: Essays toward a Reflexive Sociology*. Translated by Matthew Adamson. Cambridge: Cambridge University Press, 1990.

Bourdieu, Pierre. "The Sentiment of Honor in Kabyle Society." In *Honor and Shame: The Values of Mediterranean Society*, edited by J. G. Peristiany, 191–214. Chicago: Chicago University Press, 1966.

Boyarin, Daniel. *Carnal Israel: Reading Sex in Talmudic Culture*. Berkeley: University of California Press, 1993.

———. *Intertextuality and the Reading of Midrash*. Bloomington, IN: Indiana University Press, 1990.

Brasher, Brenda. *Give Me That Online Religion*. San Francisco: Jossey-Bas, 2001.

Brecher, Israel, and Baruch Gafni. *Netivot Melucha*. Bnei-Brak, Israel: Private, 2020. [Hebrew]

Brenner, Yosef Haim. *Breakdown and Bereavement*. Translated by Hillel Halkin. New Milford, CT: The Toby Press, 2004.

Brod, Harry. "A Case for Men's Studies." In *Changing Men: New Directions in Research on Men and Masculinity*, edited by Michael S. Kimmel, 263–77, London: SAGE, 1987.

Brown, Benjamin. *The Hazon Ish: Halakhis, Believer and Leader of the Haredi Revolution*. Jerusalem: Magnes, 2011. [Hebrew]

———. "Human Greatness and Human Diminution: Changes in the Mussar Methods in the Slabodka Yeshiva." In *Yeshivot and Battei Midrash*, edited by Immanuel Etkas, 244–72. Jerusalem: Zalman Shazar Center, 2007. [Hebrew]

———. "Kedusha: The Sexual Abstinence of Married Men in Gur, Slonim and Toledot Aharon." *Jewish History* 27.2 (2013) 472–522.
———. *The Lithuanian Musar Movement—Personalities and Ideas.* Moshv Ben-Shemen: Modan, 2014. [Hebrew]
Brown, Benjamin, and Nissim Leon, eds. *The Gdolim: Leaders Who Shaped the Israeli Haredi Jewry.* Jerusalem: Magnes, 2017. [Hebrew]
Butler, Judith. *Gender Trouble: Feminism and the Subversion of Identity.* London: Routledge, 1999.
———. *Honor, Family and Patronage: A Study of Institutions and Moral Values in a Greek Mountain Community.* Oxford: Clarendon, 1970.
Caplan, Kimmy R. *The Internal Popular Discourse in Israeli Haredi Society.* Jerusalem: Zalman Shazar Center, 2007. [Hebrew]
———. "Sifrey Limud LeHistoria Bahevra HaHaredit: Hador HaRishon." *Iyunim Bitkumat Israel* 17 (2007) 1–42. [Hebrew]
Chadash, Meir. Meir. *Netivot, Vol. 3.* Jerusalem: Private, 2005. [Hebrew]
Chasman, Yehuda. *Or Yahel, Vol. 1.* Tel Aviv: Nezach, 1937. [Hebrew]
———. *Or Yahel, Vol. 3.* Tel Aviv: Nezach, 1938. [Hebrew]
Chen, Yitzchak. "Merovingian Hagiography and Carolingian Propaganda." *Historia* 8 (2001) 53–71. [Hebrew]
Cohen, David. "Keter Torah." *Chizuk* 5 (2004) 74–79. [Hebrew]
Cohen, Dov. *Vayelchi Shneihem Yachdaiv.* Jerusalem: Private, 2009. [Hebrew]
Cohen, Shlomo. *Pe'er Hador.* Bnei-Brak: Netzach, 1970. [Hebrew]
———. *Pe'er Hador, Vol. 2.* Bnei-Brak: Netzach, 1974. [Hebrew]
Cohen Shabot, Sara. *On the Grotesque Body: A Philosophical Inquiry on Bakhtin, Merleau-Ponty and Other Thinkers.* Tel Aviv: Resling, 2008. [Hebrew]
Constitution and Canons of the Episcopal Church (Title III). New York: Church Publishing, 2006.
Coontz, Stephanie. *Marriage, A History: From Obedience to Intimacy or How Love Conquered Marriage.* London: Viking, 2005.
Corrington, Gail. "Anorexia, Asceticism, and Autonomy: Self-Control as Liberation and Transcendence." *Journal of Feminist Studies in Religion* 2.2 (1986) 51–61.
Dan, Joseph. *Ha Sippur ha Hasidi.* Jerusalem: Keter, 1975. [Hebrew]
Deal, William E. "Toward a Politics of Asceticism: Response to the Three Preceding Papers." *Asceticism,* edited by Vincent L. Wimbush and Richard Valantasis, 424–42. Oxford: Oxford University Press, 1995.
Delumeav, Jean. *Sin and Fear: The Emergence of a Western Guilt Culture 13th–18th.* Translated by Eric Nicholson. New York: St. Martin's Press, 1990.
Dessler, Eliyahu Eliezer. *Michtav me-Eliyahu Vol. 1.* Jerusalem: Private, 1956. [Hebrew]
———. *Michtav me-Eliyahu Vol. 5.* Jerusalem: Private, 1997. [Hebrew]
———. "Minut Shelo Lishma." *Chizuk* 5 (2004) 4–8. [Hebrew]
Doble, G. H. "Hagiography and Folklore." *Folklore* 54.3 (1943) 321–33.
Dobbins, Richard. *Teaching Your Children the Truth about Sex.* Florida: Siloam, 2006.
Douglas, Mary. *Purity and Danger: An Analysis of Concepts of Pollution and Taboo.* London: Routledge, 1966.
Efros, Israel, ed. *Complete Poetic Works of Hayyim Nahman Bialik Vol. 1.* New York: The Histadruth Ivrit of America, 1948.
El-Or, Tamar. "Are They Like Their Grandmothers?" *Anthropology and Education Quarterly* 24 (1993) 61–83.

———. "The Length of the Slits and the Spread of Luxury: Reconstructing the Subordination of Ultra-Orthodox Jewish Women through the Patriarchy of Men Scholars." *Sex Roles* 29.9–10 (1993) 585–98.

———. "Visibility and Possibilities: Ultra-Orthodox Jewish Women between the Domestics and Public Spheres." *Women's Studies International* Forum 20 (1997) 665–74.

Eliade, Mirce. *Myth of the Eternal Return*. Translated by W. R. Trask. Princeton: Princeton University Press, 1955.

Elliott, John H. "Disgraced Yet Graced. The Gospel according to 1 Peter in the Key of Honor and Shame." *Biblical Theology Bulletin: A Journal of Bible and Theology* 25.4 (1995) 166–77.

Englander, Yakir. "The Conception of the Human Being and its Halakhic Function in the Writing of the Hazon Ish." *Hadarin: Hartman Institute Academic Journal* 2 (2010) 183–214. [Hebrew]

———. "Design of the Body in 'The Light Burn', a Novel by Aharon Appelfeld." In *24 Readings in Appelfeld's Writings*, edited by Avi Lipsker and Avi Sagi, 57–84. Ramat-Gan: Bar-Ilan University Press, 2012. [Hebrew]

———. "Halakha as Praxis: The Body of the Zaddik in 20th Hasidic Stories." *Mechkarei Yerusalim be-Safrut Ivrit* 27 (2014) 103–32. [Hebrew]

———. "The Halakhic Body: A Phenomenological Perspective on the Halakhic Body." In *The Halakhah as Event*, edited by Avinoam Rosenak, 68–95. Jerusalem: Magnes and Van Leer, 2016. [Hebrew]

———. "The 'Jewish Knight' of Slobodka: Honor Culture and the Image of the Body in an Ultra-Orthodox Jewish Context." *Religion* 46.2 (2016) 186–208.

Englander, Yakir, and Kamir, Orit. "Body and Shame in the World of Tanaim and Amoraim (Ancient Jewish Sages)." *Jewish Studies* 49 (2013) 57–101. [Hebrew]

Englander, Yakir, and Avi Sagi. *Sexuality and the Body in the New Religious Zionist Discourse*. Translated by Batya Stein. Boston: Academy Press, 2015.

Etkes, Immanuel. *Rabbi Israel Salanter and the Beginning of the 'Musar' Movement*. Jerusalem: Magnes, 1982. [Hebrew]

Feder, Ayala. *Mizvah Girls': Bringing up the Next Generation of Hasidic Jews in Brooklyn*. Princeton: Princeton University Press, 2009.

Fetheringill-Zwicker, Lisa. "Performing Masculinity: Jewish Students and the Honort Code at German Universities." In *Jewish Masculinities German Jews, Gender, and History*, edited by Benjamin Maria Baader, et al., 114–37. Bloomington, IN: Indiana University Press, 2012.

Finkel, Nosson Tzvi. *'Or HaTzafun Vol. 1*. Jerusalem: Private, 1990. [Hebrew]

———. *'Or HaTzafun Vol. 2*. Jerusalem: Private, 1990. [Hebrew]

Finkelman, Yoel. "An Ideology for American Yeshiva Students: The Sermons of R. Aharon 1942–1962." *Journal of Jewish Studies* 58.2 (2007) 314–32.

Finkelman, Shimon, and Nathan Sherman. *Reb Moshe: The Life and Ideals of HaGaon Rabbi Moshe Feinstein*. Jerusalem: Artscroll, 1986.

Foucault, Michel. *Discipline and Punish: The Birth of the Prison*. Translated by Alan Sheridan. New York: Pantheon, 1979.

———. *The History of Sexuality Vol. 1*. Translated by Robert Hurley. New York: Vintage, 1990.

Friedlander, Chaim. *Darkei HaChaim Vol. 1*. Bnei-Brak: Private, 2006. [Hebrew]

———. *Kuntres LeChatanim Bnei-Torah*. Private, Bnei-Brak: Private, 1986. [Hebrew]

———. *Siftey Chaim*, Vol. 1. Bnei-Brak: Private, 2003. (Hebrew)
———. *Siftey Chaim*, Vol. 2. Bnei-Brak: Private, 2005. [Hebrew]
Friedman, Yaacov. *Nafshi Yazaa Bedabro*. Jerusalem: Private, 2011. [Hebrew]
———. *Shtaygen*. Jerusalem: Machon Hagut, 2006. [Hebrew]
Garb, Jonathan. *The Chosen Will Become Herds: Studies in Twentieth-Century Kabbalah*. Translated by Yaffah Berkovits-Murcian. New Heaven, CT: Yale University Press, 2009.
———. *Shamanic Trance in Modern Kaballah*. Chicago: University of Chicago Press, 2011.
———. "Towards the Study of the Spiritual-Mystical Renaissance in the Contemporary Ashkenazi Haredi World in Israel." In *Kabbalah and Contemporary Spiritual Revival*, edited by Boaz Huss, 117–40. Beer Sheva: Ben Gurion University of the Negev Press, 2011.
Gay, Volney P. "Winnicott's Contribution to Religious Studies: The Resurrection of the Culture Hero." *Journal of the American Academy of Religion* 51.3 (1983) 371–95.
Geertz, Clifford. *The Interpretation of Cultures*. New-York: Basic, 1973.
Gelis, Abraham, et al. *Heiiru Pnei Kol Ha-Mizrach Ad She-Berhebron*. Jerusalem: Hebron Yeshiva, 2009. [Hebrew]
Gifter, Mordechai. *Pirkey Torah*. Jerusalem: Private, 1993. [Hebrew]
Gilman, Sander L. *The Jew's Body*. London: Routledge, 1991.
Gluzman, Michael. *The Zionist Body: Nationalism, Gender and Sexuality in Modern Hebrew Literature*. Tel Aviv: Hakibbutz Hameuchad, 2007. [Hebrew]
Goffman, Erving. *Asylums: Essays on the Social Situation of Mental Patients and Other Inmates*. New York: Doubleday Anchor, 1961.
Gold, David Doron. *Bnei Chail Vol. 1*. Bnei-Brak: Private, 2007. [Hebrew]
———. *Hachzek BaMusar*. Bnei-Brak: Private, 2011. [Hebrew]
Goldberg, Hillel. *Israel Salanter: Text, Structure, Idea*. New York: KTAV, 1987.
———. *The Fire within: The Living Heritage of the Musar Movement*. New York: KTAV, 1987.
Goldschmidt, Baruch. *Kuntres Sehel Tov*. Lakewood, NJ: Private, 1992. [Hebrew]
Gordon, A. D. *Man and Nature*. Jerusalem: Ha-Sifria Ha-Zionit, 1957. [Hebrew]
Greenberg, Jerrold S., and Francis X. Archambault. "Masturbation, Self-Esteem, and Other Variables." *Journal of Sex Research* 9 (1973) 41–51.
Grodzinski, Avraham. *Torat Avraham*. Bnei-Brak: Private, 1978. [Hebrew]
Grosbord, Shraga. "Shilton HaSehel." *HaNe'eman* 36.10 (1951) 20–31. [Hebrew]
Gross, Benjamin. *Netzah Yisrael*. Tel Aviv: Devir, 1974. [Hebrew]
Ha-Levi, Yeruham. *Ma'amarim Me-Sihotav Shel Rabbi Yeruham Ha-Levi*. Bernowitz, Lithuania: Mir Yeshiva, 1939. [Hebrew]
Hakak, Yohai. "'Blessed be the Sage's Memory? Haredi Reflections and Challenges to the Portrayal of Torah Sages from Past Generations." *Israeli Sociology* 9.2 (2008) 387–412. [Hebrew]
———. "Haredi Male Bodies in the Public Sphere: Negotiating with the Religious Text and Secular Israeli Men." *Journal of Men, Masculinities and Spirituality* 3.2 (2009) 100–122.
———. *Spirituality and Worldliness in Lithuanian Yeshivas*. Jerusalem: The Floersheimer Institute for Policy Studies, 2005. [Hebrew]
Halperin, David M. *One Hundred Years of Homosexuality*. London: Routledge, 1990.

Hansen, Thomas Blom. "In Search of God's Hand: On Masculinity and Religion." *International Studies in Religion and Society* 9 (2009) 123–42.
Hecht, Benjamin. *Shut Libnei Ha-Neurim*. Safed: Private, 2008. [Hebrew]
Heffernan, T. J. *Sacred Biography: Saints and Their Biographers in the Middle Ages.* Oxford: Oxford University Press, 1988.
Henkin, Yehuda. "Contemporary Tseni'ut." *Tradition* 37.3 (2003) 1–48.
Hershkovitz, Ithak. *Sheifot*. Jerusalem: Private, 2003. [Hebrew]
Hundert, Gershon David. *Jews in Poland and Lithuania in the Eighteenth Century: A Genealogy of Modernity.* Berkeley: University of California Press, 2004.
Hutner, Yitzchok. *Pachad Itzchak: Sukkot*. New York: Private, 2003. [Hebrew]
———. *Pachad Itzchak: Igrot*. New York: Private, 2007. [Hebrew]
Israel, Yaakov. *Rabbi Moshe Shmuel*. Jerusalem: Private, 2008. [Hebrew]
Iserlish, Moshe. *Mechir Iiain—Perush Al Megilat Ester*. Jerusalem: Private, 1926. [Hebrew]
Kaelber, Walter O. "Asceticism." In *The Encyclopedia of Religion*, edited by Lindsay Jones et al., 526–30. Detroit: Macmillan Reference USA, 2005.
Kamenetsky, Nathan. *Making of a Godol: A Study of Episodes in the Lives of Great Torah Personalities.* Jerusalem: PP, 2002.
Kamil, Chaim. *Raboteynu SheBadarom*. Jerusalem: Private, 2000. [Hebrew]
Kamir, Orit. *Betraying Dignity: The Toxic Seduction of Social Media, Shaming, and Radicalization.* Berlin: Fairleigh Dickson, 2019
———. *Israeli Honor and Dignity: Social Norms, Gender Politics and the Law.* Jerusalem: Carmel, 2004. [Hebrew]
Kanievsky, Yaakov Yisrael. *Chayey Olam*. Bnei-Brak: Private, 1957. [Hebrew]
———. *Kovetz Igrot*. Bnei-Brak: Private, 1986. [Hebrew]
Kanievsky, Avraham Yeshayahu. *Toldot Yaakov*. Bnei-Brak: Private, 1995. [Hebrew]
Kaplan, Lawrence. "Daas Torah: A Modern Conception of Rabbinic Authority." In *Rabbinic Authority and Personal Autonomy*, edited by Moshe Sokol, 1–60. Northvale, NJ: Jason Aronson, 1992.
———. "Hazon Ish: Haredi Critic of Traditional Orthodoxy." *The Uses of Tradition: Jewish Continuity in the Modern Era*, edited by Jack Wertheimer, 145–73. New York: JTS, 1992.
Katz, Dov. *HaSaba MiSlabodka*. Jerusalem: Feldheim, 1996. [Hebrew]
———. "Orthodoxy as a Response to Emancipation and the Reform Movement." In *Kehal Israel: Jewish Self-Rule through the Ages, Vol. 3*, edited by Israel Bartel, 135–46. Jerusalem: Zalman Shazar Center, 2004. [Hebrew]
———. *Out of the Ghetto*. Tel Aviv: Am Oved, 1985. [Hebrew]
———. *Pulmus HaMusar*. Jerusalem : Feldheim, 1972. [Hebrew]
———. *Tenu'at HaMusar, Vol. 3*. Jerusalem: Feldheim, 1975. [Hebrew]
———. *Tenu'at HaMusar, Vol. 5*. Jerusalem: Feldheim, 1975. [Hebrew]
Kaufman, Tsippi. *In All Ways Know Him: The Concept of God and Avodah Be-Gashmiyut in the Early Stages of Hasidim.* Ramat Gan: Bar-Ilan University Press, 2009. [Hebrew]
Kirkley, Evelyn A. "Is It Manly to Be Christian? The Debate in Victorian and Modern America." In *Redeeming Men: Religion and Masculinities*, edited by Stephen B. Boyd et al., 80–88. Louisville, KY: Westminster John Knox, 1996.
Kook, Abraham Yitzhak HaCohen. *'Orot*. Jerusalem: Mosad Harav Kook, 1963. [Hebrew]

Kotler, Aharon. *Mishnat Rabbi Aharon Kotler, Vol. 1.* Lakewood, FL: Yeshiva, 2005. [Hebrew]
Kotler, Aharon. *Kuntres Keter-HaTorah.* Bnei-Brak: Private, 1972. [Hebrew]
Kristeva, Julia. *Kristeva Reader.* Edited by Troil Moi. New York: Columbia University Press, 1986.
———. *Powers of Horror: An Essay on Abjection.* Translated by Leon S. Roudiez. New York: Columbia University Press, 1982.
Kukis, Mordechai. *Siach Mordechai, Vol. 1.* Jerusalem: Private, 1991. [Hebrew]
———. *Siach Mordechai, Vol. 2.* Jerusalem, Private, 1993. [Hebrew]
Laasin, Yaakov Moshe. *Sichot Musar.* New York: Private, 1952. [Hebrew]
Lefkowitz, Yizhak Dov. *Marbe Yeshiva Marbe Chohma.* New York: Private, 1950.
Lefkowitz, Michel Yehuda. *Darkei Chaim, Vol. 2.* Bnei Brak: Private, 2007. [Hebrew]
———. *Darkei Chaim, Vol. 1.* Bnei Brak: Private, 2006. [Hebrew]
———. *Imrei Da'at.* Bnei-Brak: Private, 1999. [Hebrew]
———. *Ol-Torah.* Jerusalem: Private, Jerusalem, 1994. [Hebrew]
Levenstein, Yechezkel. *Kovetz Inyanim.* Private, Bnei-Brak, 1967. [Hebrew]
———. *MeMizrach Shemesh: Bamidbar.* Bnei-Brak: Private, 1998. [Hebrew]
———. *'Or Yechezkel, Vol. 1.* Bnei-Brak: Private, 1976. [Hebrew]
———. *'Or Yechezkel—'Emunah, Vol. 7.* Private: Bnei Brak, 1983. [Hebrew]
———. *'Or Yechezkel—Irah UMusar.* Bnei-Brak: Private, 1996. [Hebrew]
Levi, Moshe. *Mashal HaAvot al 48 Kinyanei HaTorah, Vol. 1.* Bnei-Brak: Private, 2002. [Hebrew]
———. *Mashal HaAvot al 48 Kinyanei HaTorah, Vol. 2.* Bnei-Brak: Private, 2002. [Hebrew]
Lopian, Eliyahu. *Lev Eliyahu: Musar.* Jerusalem: Private, Jerusalem, 1971. [Hebrew]
———. *Lev Eliyahu Vol. 1.* Jerusalem: Private, Jerusalem, 1978. [Hebrew]
———. *Lev Eliyahu Vol. 2.* Jerusalem: Private, Jerusalem, 1979. [Hebrew]
———. *Lev Eliyahu Vol. 3.* Jerusalem: Private, Jerusalem, 1983. [Hebrew]
Lorincz, Shlomo. *Bemechitzatam Shel Gdolei HaTorah,* Vol. 1. Jerusalem: Binat Halev, 1997. [Hebrew]
Lorincz, Shlomo. *Binat HaMidot.* Jerusalem: Binat Halev, 1997. [Hebrew]
Luheman, T. M. *When God Talks Back: Understanding the American Evangelical Relationship with God.* New York: Knopf, 2012.
Margaliot, Yeshaya Z. *Ashrei HaIsh.* Jerusalem: Private, 1934. [Hebrew]
Meler, Shimon J. *Nasich Mamlehet Ha-Torah.* Jerusalem: Private, 2001. [Hebrew]
Merleau-Ponty, Maurice. *The Phenomenology of Perception.* Translated by Colin Smith. London: Routledge, 1962.
Miller, Avigdor. *Lev Avigdor.* Brooklyn: Private, 2002. [Hebrew]
———. *'Or 'Olam, Vol. 7.* Arad: Simon, 2007. [Hebrew]
———. *'Or 'Olam, Vol. 10.* Arad: Simon, 2010. [Hebrew]
———. *Rabbi Avigdor Miller Speaks,* Vol. 1. Brooklyn, Private, 2004.
———. *She'arei 'Ora, Vol. 1.* Brooklyn, Private, 2006. [Hebrew]
———. *She'arei 'Ora, Vol. 2.* Brooklyn: Private, 2006. [Hebrew]
———. *Torat Avigdor, Vol. 1.* Bnei-Brak: Private, 2002. [Hebrew]
———. *Torat Avigdor, Vol. 2.* Bnei-Brak: Private, 2003. [Hebrew]
———. *Torat Avigdor, Vol. 3.* Bnei-Brak: Private, 2004. [Hebrew]
Milles, Sara. *Discourse.* London: Routledge, 1997.

Nadler, Allan. *The Faith of the Mithnagdim: Rabbinic Responses to Hasidic Rapture.* Baltimore: Johns Hopkins University Press, 1997.

Naker, Eldad. *Kol Atzmotai Tomarna: Sfat Ha-Guf KaHalakha.* Jerusalem: Private, 2005. [Hebrew]

Neuman, Boaz. *Nazi Weltanschauung—Space, Body, Language.* Tel Aviv: Haifa University Publishing House and Sifriat Ma'ariv, 2002. [Hebrew]

Neuman, Robert P. "Masturbation, Madness, and the Modern Concepts of Childhood and Adolescence." *Journal of Social History* 8 (1975) 1–27.

Newbold, R. F. "Personality Structure and Response to Adversity in Early Christian Hagiography." *Numen* XXXI (1984) 199–209.

Norwood, Stephan H. "'American Jewish Muscle': Forging a New Masculinity in the Streets and in the Ring, 1890–1940." *Modern Judaism* 29.2 (2009) 167–93.

Ochana, Abraham. *Kocha Shel Torah Lishmah.* Jerusalem: Private, 2005. [Hebrew]

Orlansky, Israel. *Lapid Esh Novhardki.* Jerusalem: Private, 1993. [Hebrew]

Pachter, Shiloh. "*Shemirat ha-Brit*: The History of the Prohibition of Wasting Seed." PhD diss., Hebrew University of Jerusalem, 2006. [Hebrew]

Pedaya, Haviva. *Nahmanides: Cyclical Time and Holy Text.* Tel Aviv: Am Oved, 2003. [Hebrew]

Peled, Rina. *The New Man' of the Zionist Revolution: Hashomer Hatzair and Its European Jews.* Tel Aviv: Am Oved, 2002. [Hebrew]

Peristiany, J. G., and Julian Pitt-Rivers, eds. *Honor and Grace in Anthropology.* Cambridge: Cambridge University Press, 1992.

Pincus, Shimshon. *Nefesh Shimshon.* Jerusalem: private, 2004. [Hebrew]

———. *Nefesh Chaya.* Jerusalem: private, 2006. [Hebrew]

Povarsky, David. *Musar Ve-Daat*, Vol. 1. Bnei-Brak: Private, 1986. [Hebrew]

———. *Musar Ve-Daat: Yemei HaRachmim VeHadin.* Bnei-Brak: Private, 1987. [Hebrew]

Presner, Todd. *Muscular Judaism: The Jewish Body and the Politics of Regeneration.* London: Routledge, 2007

Rapoport-Albert, Ada. "Hagiography with Footnotes: Edifying Tales and the Writing of History in Hasidism." *History and Theory* 27.4 (1998) 119–59.

Ratzabi, Yitzchak. *Kdushat Bnei-Israel.* Jerusalem: Private, 2008. [Hebrew]

Ravitzky, Aviezer. *Freedom Inscribed: Diverse Voices of Jewish Religious Thought.* Tel Aviv: Am Oved, 1999. [Hebrew]

Regnerus, Mark D. *Forbidden Fruit: Sex and Religion in the Lives of American Teenagers.* New York: Oxford University Press, 2007.

Robbins, Derek. *The Work of Pierre Bourdieu: Recognizing Society.* Buckingham, UK: Open University Press, 1991.

Rosenblum, Yonason. *Rav Dessler: The Life and Impact of Rabbi Eliyahu Eliezer Dessler the Michtav M'Eliyahu.* New York: Mesorah, 2000.

Rosenstein, Moshe Chaim. *Ahavat Meisharim.* Łomża, Poland: Private 1930. [Hebrew]

Rosenstein, Shlomo. "Mihtav LeBein Hazmanim." *Chizuk* 1 (2001) 73–74. [Hebrew]

Ross, Tamar. "Moral Philosophy in the Writings of Rabbi Salanter's Disciples in the Musar Movement." PhD diss., Hebrew University, 1987. [Hebrew]

———. "Rabbi Israel Salanter's Solutions to the Problems of Weakness of the Will." *Mechkarei Yerushalaim Bemachshevet Yisrael* 11 (1993) 139–87. [Hebrew]

Rott, Nathan Eli. *Kdosh Yisrael.* Bnei-Brak: Private, 1985. [Hebrew]

Sagi, Avi. *Albert Camus and the Philosophy of the Absurd*. Translated by Batya Stein. Amsterdam: Rodopi, 2002.

———. *'Elu va-Elu': A Study on the Meaning of Halakhic Discourse*. Tel Aviv: Hakibutz Hameuchad, 1996. [Hebrew]

Sagiv, Gadi. "The Rectification of the Covenant and the Element of Asceticism in Chernobyl Hasidism." *Jerusalem Studies in Jewish Thought* 23 (2011) 355–406. [Hebrew]

Salanter, Isreal. *'Or Yisra'el*. Jerusalem: Private, 2006. [Hebrew]

———. *Writing of Rabbi Israel Salanter*. Jerusalem: Bialik, 1973. [Hebrew]

Sarna, Jonathan D. *American Judaism: A History*. New Haven, CT: Yale University Press, 2004.

Sarna, Yehezkel. *Daliyot Yehezkel*, Vol. 2. Jerusalem: Mosad Haskel–Yeshivat Hebron, 1976. [Hebrew]

———. *Daliyot Yehezkel*, Vol. 1. Jerusalem: Mosad Haskel–Yeshivat Hebron, 1989. [Hebrew]

Sartre, Jean-Paul. *Nausea*. Translated by L. Alexander. Cambridge: Cambridge University Press, 1979.

Schwab, Shimon. *Selected Writings: A Collection of Addresses and Essays on Hashkafah, Jewish History and Contemporary Issues*. Lakewood: C.I.S., 1988.

Scholem, Gershom. *Explications and Implications: Writings on Jewish Heritage and Renaissance*, Vol. 1. Tel Aviv: Am Oved, 1976. [Hebrew]

Schwartz, Yoel. *Achar Mitato Shel Harav Sach*. Jerusalem: Davar, 2002. [Hebrew]

———. *Binyan Adei-Ad*. Jerusalem: Private, 1980. [Hebrew]

———. *Gadlut HaAdam*. Jerusalem: Private, 1995. [Hebrew]

———. *Sefer Kdushat Israel*. Jerusalem: Private, 2004. [Hebrew]

Schweid, Eliezer. "Mutual Responsibility of the Jewish People and Self-Realization." *Iyyun* 33.1-2 (1984) 327–37. [Hebrew]

Schweid, Eliezer. *From Ruin to Salvation*. Tel Aviv: Hakibbutz Hameuchad, 1994. [Hebrew]

Segal, Lynne. "Changing Men: Masculinities in Context." *Theory and Society* 22 (1993) 625–41.

Shain, Ruchoma. *All for the Boss: The Life and Impact of Rabbi Yaakov Herman, a Torah Pioneer in America*. Jerusalem: Feldheim, 2001.

Shapira, Abraham. *The Kabbalistic and Hasidic Sources of A.D. Gordon's Thought*. Tel Aviv: Am Oved, 1996. [Hebrew]

Shapira, Moshe. *Afikey Maim: Hanukah ve Purim*. Jerusalem: private, 2002. [Hebrew]

Shaul, Michal. "Shikum HaChvarh HaCharedit BeIsael Betzel HaShoah." *Iyunim Bitkumat Israel* 20 (2010) 360–95. [Hebrew]

Sher, Isaac. *Emek Ha-Havana be-Torah ve-Hazal*. Jerusalem: Private, 1941. [Hebrew]

Shmuelevitz, Chaim. *Sichot Musar 1971–1973*. Jerusalem: Private, 1980. [Hebrew]

———. *Sefer HaZikaron*. Private, Jerusalem: Private, 1986. [Hebrew]

———. "ShTihiyu Amelim BaTorah." *Chizuk* 4 (2004) 13–14. [Hebrew]

Simon, William. *Postmodern Sexualities*. London: Routledge, 1996

Sobosan, Jeffrey G. "Self-Fulfillment, Asceticism, and the Function of Authority." *Journal of Religion and Health* 16.4 (1977) 333–340

Sofer, Abraham Eliezer. *Raboteinu Shebedarom*. Jerusalem: Private, 2009 [Hebrew]

Soloveitchik, Joseph Dov. *The Halakhic Man*. New York: Jewish Publication Society of America, 1983.

Sorotzki, Aharon. *Harav MePonivez*, Vol. 1. Bnei-Brak: Private, 2009. [Hebrew]
———. *Marbitzey Torah Umusar*, Vol. 1. New York: Private 1974. [Hebrew]
———. *Marbitzey Torah Umusar*, Vol. 3. New York: Private, 1977. [Hebrew]
———. *Marbitzey Torah Umusar*, Vol. 4. New York: Private, 1977. [Hebrew]
Stadler, Nurit. *Yeshiva Fundamentalism: Piety, Gender, and Resistance in the Ultra-Orthodox World*. New York: New York University Press, 2009.
Stampfer, Shaul. *Lithuanian Yeshivas of the Nineteenth Century: Creating a Tradition of Learning*. Oxford: Littman Library of Jewish Civilization, 2012.
Strandberg, Victor. *Greek Mind, Jewish Soul: The Conflicted Art of Cynthia Ozick*. Madison, WI: University of Wisconsin Press, 1994.
Stern, Yechiel. *Bait u-Menucha*. Jerusalem: Private, 1999. [Hebrew]
Stone, Ira F. *A Responsible Life: The Spiritual Path of Musar*. New York: Aviv, 2006.
Taylor, Charles. *A Secular Age*. Stanford: Stanford University Press, 2007.
Taylor, Diana. *The Archive and the Repertoire: Performing Cultural Memory in the Americas*. Durham, NC: Duke University Press, 2003.
Tennen, Hanoch. *The Conception of an Existential Ethics in Karl Jaspers' Philosophy*. Ramat Gan: Massada, 1977. [Hebrew]
Thornborrow, Joana. *Power Talk: Language and Interaction in Institutional Discourse*. Toronto: Longman, 2002.
Tikochinski, Shlomo. "'Forget the Life and Remember the Death: Rabbi Chaim Zaichik Lessons of the Holocaust." In *Zikaron Basefer*, edited by Assaf Yedidia, Nathan Cohen, Esther Farbsten, 116–39. Jerusalem: Rubin Mass, 2008. [Hebrew]
———. "Musar Yeshivot from Lithuania to Israel: Slabodka Yeshiva, Its Emigration and Establishment in Mandate Palestine." PhD diss., Hebrew University, 2009. [Hebrew]
———. "The 'Musar Yeshivot' and Their Move to the Land of Israel, 1925–1035." In *Education and Religion: Authority and Autonomy*, edited by Immanuel Etkes, Michael Heyd, Tamar Elor, and Baruch Schwarz, 220–68. Jerusalem: Magnes, 2011. [Hebrew]
———. *Torah Scholarship, Musar and Elitism: The Slabodka Yeshiva from Lithuania to Mandate Palestine*. Jerusalem: Zalman Shazar Center, 2016. [Hebrew]
Tropper, Amram. *Wisdom, Politics and Historiography: Tractate Avot in the Context of the Graeco-Roman Near East*. Oxford: Oxford University Press, 2004.
Turner, Terence S. "Social Body and Embodied Subject: Bodylines, Subjectivity, and Sociality among the Kayapo." *Cultural Anthropology* 10.2 (1995) 143–70.
Ury, Zalman F. *The Musar Movement: A Quest for Excellence in Character Education*. New York: Private, 1970.
Vaanunu, Shimon. *Torah Me-shulchan Rabotenu*. Jerusalem: Private, 1998. [Hebrew]
Van der Kolk, Bessel A. *The Body Keeps the Score*. New York: Penguin, 2014.
Volozhin, Chaim. *Nefesh Ha-Hayim*. Jerusalem: Private, 1995. [Hebrew]
Walzer, Michael. *Interpretation and Social Criticism*. Cambridge: Harvard University Press, 1987.
Ware, Kallistos. "The Way of the Ascetics: Negative or Affirmative?" In *Asceticism*, edited by Vincent L. Wimbush and Richard Valantasis, 3–15. Oxford: Oxford University Press, 1995.
Weinberg, Yisrael Noah. *The 48 Ways to Wisdom*. Jerusalem: Private, 2010. [Hebrew]
Weintraub, Yisroel Elya. *HaChodesh HaShvii*. Jerusalem: Private, 2010. [Hebrew]

Wienberger, Naftali, and Naomi Wienberger. *Rebbetzin Kanievsky: A Legendary Mother to All.* Brooklyn: Mesorah, 2012.
Wilber, Ken. *No Boundaries: Eastern and Western Approaches to Personal Growth.* Boston: Shambhala, 2001.
Willing, Simcha. "Gadlut Ha-Adam and the Greatness of Humanity: A Textual Analysis of Rabbi Nathan Tzvi Finkel's Psycho-Religious Educational Philosophy." PhD diss., New York University, 2016.
Wolbe, Shlomo. *Alei Shur,* Vol. 1. Jerusalem: Feldheim, 1948. [Hebrew]
———. *Alei Shur,* Vol. 2. Jerusalem: Feldheim, 1986. [Hebrew]
———. *Avnei Shlomo.* Jerusalem: Private, 2006. [Hebrew]
———. *BeTzel HaChohma.* Jerusalem: Private 1987. [Hebrew]
———. *Igraot UKtavim,* Vol. 1. Jerusalem: Private 1996. [Hebrew]
———. *Kuntres Ma'amrei Hadracha Le-Hatanim.* Jerusalem: Private, 1999. [Hebrew]
———. *Sichot.* Jerusalem: Private, 2005. [Hebrew]
Wolfson, Elliot. *Alef, Mem, Tau: Kabbalistic Musings on Time, Truth and Death.* Berkeley: University of California Press, 2006.
Wozner, Shai. *Legal Thinking in the Lithuanian Yeshivoth: The Heritage and Works of Rabbi Shimon Shkop.* Jerusalem: Magnes, 2016. [Hebrew]
Weitz, Yechiam. *Aware but Helpless.* Jerusalem: Yad Ben-Zvi, 1994. [Hebrew]
Yalom, Marilyn Yalom. *A History of a Wife.* New York: Pandora, 2001.
Yaffe, Dov. *LeOvdeh BeEmet: Sichot.* Jerusalem: Private, 2007. [Hebrew]
Yerushalmi, Yosef Hayim. *Zakhor: Jewish History and Jewish Memory.* New York: Schocken, 1989. [Hebrew]
Yivrov, Zvi. *Ma'ase Ish,* Vol. 1. Bnei-Brak: Private, 1999. [Hebrew]
Young, James E. *The Texture of Memory: Holocaust Memorials and Meaning.* New Haven, CT: Yale University Press, 1993.
Zaritzky, David. *Gesher Tzar.* Bnei-Brak: Netzach, 1969. [Hebrew]
Zeichik, Chaim Ephraim. *Or Chadash.* Jerusalem: Private, 2009. [Hebrew]
Zochowski, Dov. "Gadlut HaAdam." *HaNeeman* 73 (1956) 43–44. [Hebrew]

Index

angel, 42, 45, 58–62 76, 122, 135n23, 137n30, 145
animal, 42–43, 45, 145, 170, 190, 247, 252
   bird, 167
   rat, 64
   pig, 58
   horse, 74, 77
   cow, 64, 252
   parasites, 233
ascetic/ascetism, 19, 83, 85, 89, 184, 194, 196, 206–8, 210, 211–13, 272, 228–29, 268, 271, 285
awe, 84, 145, 149–50, 215n105, 257

battle/struggle, 10, 64, 82, 105, 108, 111, 134, 145–46, 159, 213
body
   ideal body, vii, 6, 21, 40, 72, 75, 173, 175, 187, 236
   imaginary body, 40, 75
   body image, 13, 40, 133, 215, 236
   beard, ix
   side-locks (body), ix, 211
   crippling, 248
   disability, 248–49
   healthy, 63, 86, 100, 108, 158, 166, 196, 212, 248
   womb, 135n23, 137n30
Bourdieu, Pierre, 34n27, 78, 116n76, 218n120, 264, 270
boundary(ies), ix, 5, 20, 50, 57, 64–66, 70–72, 77, 97, 114, 126n106, 172, 196, 209, 236–37, 242, 247, 253, 264, 273
Butler, Judith, 80–81, 198, 265

censored, 36, 187, 260
Chasman (Rabbi: Yehuda), 49n32, 58–59, 66–68, 82n26, 86–88, 265
childhood, vii, 100n6, 152n78, 188, 193–97, 236, 270
Christian (Christianity), 13n18, 78, 79n17, 82n25, 153n82, 227, 264, 268, 270
clothing, ix, 68, 75, 90n52, 109–10, 112n58, 123, 211n88, 227, 230, 233, 239

dance, 224, 254–56
death, 1n1, 9, 29, 30n20, 67–68, 87, 101, 131, 152–53, 168n16
desire, 29, 98, 105–6, 139, 145–46, 180, 191, 193–99, 204–5, 207, 215n107, 216, 226, 247
   physical, 49, 56–57, 59–61, 67–71, 85
   forbidden, 47, 60, 82, 90, 94, 96, 234
   sexual, 37, 47, 58, 66, 107–9, 112, 153, 164–71
   ta'avah, 168–69
temptation, 26, 33, 46, 61, 64, 87, 95, 102, 110n50, 112, 124–26, 138, 151, 189, 215n105, 238

276 INDEX

Dessler (Rabbi: Eliyahu Eliezer), 32, 51, 70n100, 103, 265, 270
devotion, 2–4, 14, 26, 45, 47, 60, 87–88, 92, 103, 119, 184, 194–96, 206n69, 213, 227, 229, 235, 239–40, 245, 254, 257
dignity, 217–21, 247, 268
disgust, 21, 64–67, 72, 238
dream, 16, 49, 51, 206

elder, 199n46, 255
Enlightenment
    European, x, 119
    Jewish, 9, 14–15, 142, 220–23, 233
eros/erotic, 63n72, 75
evil inclination, ix, 14, 26–29, 45n13, 46, 48–53, 56–64, 66, 70–73, 79, 82–83, 93, 103, 107–11, 134, 136, 139, 145, 164, 169, 194–95, 215, 221

Failure, 83, 85, 104, 159, 165
Feinstein (Rabbi: Moshe), 86n39, 132, 266
Feinstein (Rabbi: Yechiel Michel), 178, 191, 196, 210n84, 242, 244, 247
feminine/femininity, 12–14, 82, 88, 115, 125–27, 219, 227, 260
food, 2–4, 66–68, 72, 86–87, 136, 143, 196, 207–12, 229, 239n4, 245
Foucault (Michel), ix, 47, 87, 98–99, 110, 154n85, 198, 266
Friedlander (Rabbi: Chaim), 33, 43, 45, 48–49, 54–55, 57, 67–68, 75–76, 78–79, 84, 97, 104, 118, 124, 266
Friedman (Rabbi: Yaacov), 64n77, 74, 77, 86, 233, 267

guilt, 60, 76–77, 83–85, 100–101, 265

Hasidim (Hasidism), 4n4, 19n40, 26n5, 92, 100, 101n16,
153n82, 175n1, 183, 185, 244, 268
hegemony, 6, 9, 29, 34–37, 77, 81, 90, 95–96, 103, 108–9, 112, 114, 117, 121, 123, 125, 137n30, 160, 163, 165, 177, 181–82, 186–87, 232, 234
Holocaust, x, 3–5, 10, 19–20, 25, 29–34, 41, 95, 105n34, 120, 132–33, 171n20, 176–78, 181–83, 193, 204n65, 209, 213n98, 232–34, 240–41, 259, 272–73
homosexuality, 10, 99, 112, 267
Hutner (Rabbi: Yitzchok), 75n2, 104–5, 130, 132, 190n8, 195, 246, 268

illness, 41, 77, 153, 196, 246, 259
    compress, 63
    disease, 247
    hearing aid, 249
    hospital, 110
    plaster cast, 243
    sick/sickness, 134, 196, 246
internet, 11, 37, 159–60, 179n13
instinct, 28, 44, 57–58, 98, 107, 118, 244, 247

Kanievsky (Rabbi: Chayim), 176n3, 179
Kanievsky (Rabbi: Yaakov Yisrael), 1–4, 96, 106, 118, 121, 179–80, 194, 207, 210, 213–14, 229, 236n173, 249, 268
Karelitz (Rabbi: Avrohom Yeshaya), 1n1, 7, 30, 51–52, 94, 102, 108, 140, 168n16, 180, 189–90, 193, 211, 215n107
Kotler (Rabbi: Aharon), 113–14, 132, 185, 200, 227n146, 269

laugh/laughter, 250–53
Lefkowitz (Rabbi: Michel Yehuda), 30n21, 71, 89, 93, 103, 109, 112, 119, 269
Levenstein (Rabbi: Yechezkel), 30, 32, 56–57, 70–71, 85, 112,

120, 149, 189n13, 205, 238,
    242–48, 269
loneliness, 45–46, 77, 167

marriage, 21, 80, 87, 99–100, 107–8,
    114–20, 123, 168, 188, 237–
    38, 250, 265,
Merleau-Ponty, Maurice, 7, 53–56,
    248–49, 265, 269,
masculinities, 12–15, 82, 133n17,
    219, 227, 264, 266, 268, 270
masturbation, 99–109, 158–71, 267,
    270
military:
    officers, 139, 225
    generals, 223
    soldiers, 82, 111–12, 223,
    army, 1–2, 104, 111–12,
        223n133, 229, 234,
    commander, 111, 229,
    weapons, 112, 225, 227
    uniforms, 110–12
    IDF, 82
    duel, 222, 225, 227
mind, 7, 13, 15–16, 20, 36, 41, 50,
    52–58, 65–67, 80, 82, 87,
    135–41, 148n65, 149, 154,
    165, 170, 196, 204–7, 228,
    237, 239–43, 254, 272
miracle, 70–71, 111
modesty, 109, 112, 121–24
monastic, 19, 99, 116

next world, 14, 136, 149
"new self," 75, 79, 81–82, 87, 97, 107

pastor, 77–78, 81, 89–90
Pincus (Rabbi: Shimshon Dovid),
    126, 196, 250n30, 270
pleasure, 46, 68–72, 76, 86–88,
    96, 100, 107, 118, 135–36,
    142n47, 144–45, 201, 206,
    209, 211–12, 217, 246, 251

Povarsky (Rabbi: David), 45n14,
    59–62, 81–82, 87n41, 89n48,
    94n63, 210n84, 243–44, 270

poverty, 208–9, 235
prayer, 19, 31, 50, 92, 120, 142n47,
    150n73, 166, 190n8, 198,
    202n58, 204–5, 223–25, 229,
    239n3, 244, 255, 264
"protected body", 88–91, 94–97,
    107, 243

Radin (Rabbi: Israel Meir, "Hafetz
    Chaim"), 28n12, 86n36,
responsa, 29, 35, 101n13, 160–62

Salanter (Rabbi: Israel), 27–28, 41,
    59–60, 91, 134, 145, 153,
    181, 212–15, 266–67, 271
satisfaction, 67–68, 145, 153, 161,
    168
self-flagellation, 106, 108
Shach (Rabbi Elazar Menachem
    Man), 199–205, 231, 239–
    43, 250–51, 264
shame, 17–18, 67, 79n17, 62, 79,
    83–85, 135, 160–62, 169–71,
    219, 221, 224, 248n25, 264,
    266
Shmuelevitz (Rabbi: Chaim), 34n28,
    46n19, 69, 192n19, 201,
    205n67, 214n101, 223n135,
    271
sin, 28, 59–61, 81, 152n78, 196
sleep, 15, 36, 49–53, 89, 95, 102, 115,
    200, 203, 210–12, 236n172
    dream, 16, 49, 51, 206
space
    private, 25, 37, 46n18, 56,
        59–61, 75–77, 81, 83–85, 89,
        92, 100–107, 117, 124, 126,
        139, 144n51, 146, 152n78,
        161–63, 166, 168n16, 207,
        216, 221, 257, 265
    Public, 10, 14, 25, 77, 83–84,
        90, 95, 99–100, 115, 117,
        120–27, 154n85, 251, 259,
        266–67
    the street, 96, 99, 112, 115, 117,
        120–26, 196, 200, 230, 233,
        239, 249, 255, 270
stimulus, 47, 68, 102, 165–66

Tefillin, 197–98, 244

Wolbe (Rabbi: Shlomo), 33–35,
    45n12, 48n27, 57–58, 86–89,
    93–94, 98, 107–8, 112n56,
    118–20, 138–39, 152n79,
    158, 186–87, 192, 205–6,
    224n139, 230–31, 242–43,
    273
woman/women, 11–12, 14, 21,
    25n2, 37n41, 38, 59–61, 65,
    72, 80–81, 90, 93, 99–100,
    107, 109, 112–16, 119–26,
    132, 152, 169–70, 176–77,
    190–91, 219–21, 237, 250–
    51, 255n43, 264, 266
  ideal woman, 126
  femininity, 12–13, 82, 227

Yeshiva
  Hebron, 33, 52, 90n51, 111,
    252n37, 255, 267, 271
  Novardok, 1n1, 27–30, 79n16,
    133, 209, 214–15, 229–30,
    264
  Slabodka, 21, 27–31, 90n51,
    105n34, 130–34, 145, 200,
    202, 206–7, 214–17, 221–34,
    236n173, 255, 264, 268, 272
  Telshe, 27
Youth, vii, 2, 9, 71, 102, 104, 112,
    188–89, 193–94, 199, 212,
    214, 230, 234–35

Zionism, 2n2, 9, 15, 18, 132n11,
    219–23, 234

www.ingramcontent.com/pod-product-compliance
Lightning Source LLC
Chambersburg PA
CBHW071239230426
43668CB00011B/1510